THE CONTINUING PROBLEM
OF
INTERNATIONAL POLITICS

THE CONTINUING PROBLEM OF INTERNATIONAL POLITICS

GEORGE H. QUESTER

CENTER FOR INTERNATIONAL STUDIES
CORNELL UNIVERSITY

√

TO RUDOLPH AND ETHEL OLSON

PREFACE

Teaching a course in international politics has always been a stimulating experience. If the topic can be depressing, because no real and permanent solutions to the problem of peace come into sight, it is nonetheless heartening to watch students sort out their priorities when a need for choice becomes obvious, internally making the hard decisions in a way that does not terminate simply in gloom or escape. The international arena may indeed be a place where problems never really get "solved," but only postponed or contained at best; but the world that serves as this arena nonetheless moves along.

My deepest debt thus rests with the students at Harvard University, Cornell University, and the University of Rochester who sat through the lectures on which this book is based, and whose responses have made it a better and easier piece of work. I would not be flattering these students in the slightest by stipulating that I have drawn a great number of insights from their questions, their class comments, and their course papers. Another set of ideas has been garnered, of course, from the many colleagues with whom I have had a chance to interact over the past years. Some of their work is cited in the text, and in the bibliographical suggestions appended with each section. Much more has been absorbed than can be cited, however; too many of such colleagues transmit ideas without demanding recognition or acknowledgment at the moment or later. Let this serve therefore as a general "thank you."

This book may convey an excessively "traditional" or "pessimistic" tone for a book on international relations in the 1970's, in that it stresses the structural factors that keep a threat of war hanging over us all. If extensive international commercial interaction has eliminated this threat by the year 2000, a very different book may have to be written, or courses on international politics may not even need to be taught anymore. If the proliferation of nuclear weapons conversely escapes all control and check, we may have an international problem on our hands far worse than any we have ever confronted. Very possibly neither will happen, and the worrisome world of international dealings will continue along, following many of the lines described here.

As always, my greatest personal debt in the writing of this book is to my wife, Aline Olson Quester, who was the first to be convinced that it could be done.

Ithaca, New York   George H. Quester
October 1973

TABLE OF CONTENTS

CHAPTER ONE

*Definition
and
Concepts*

Why study international politics as a separate subject? Political scientists have repeatedly reviewed the discipline in terms of such a question. Is there something unique about the international system, so that different patterns and rules apply? Why not treat the international arena as one more area of regularized government, much as we treat federal authority as compared with that of states and localities?

A common answer is that the international arena is defined by an absence of commitment to higher authority, majority or otherwise. If Belgium and the Netherlands were to differ on the procedures to be followed along their borders, there would be no higher tribunal to which they would be bound to refer their dispute.

Yet many commentators today would reject any definition based on such a legal or verbal aspect of behavior. Aren't we simply noting that Belgium and the Netherlands have never promised to obey the directives of any higher authority in such cases, while provinces within the Netherlands have indeed made such a promise for disputes among themselves? Men often violate their promises; almost as often, they cooperate and deliver goods even when they are not bound by promise to do so. Perhaps any political distinctions based on such nondetermining verbal relationships should thus be avoided.

The distinction between the national and international environments is nonetheless important, and real. If we seek something more tangible, we can find it in something closely related to the above-cited absence of higher coordinating authority, the possibility of war.

War is much more than simple violence, the violence which occurs in many cities, in many societies. War is violence coordinated and organized to a colossal degree, harnessing "economies of scale" to make possible destruction which would be unimaginable otherwise. War can not occur in this form today between Pennsylvania and New York; primarily because it seems impossible between these entities, we regard them as part of the same "nation." War is distinctly possible between Israel and Egypt, and here we all concur that an international environment exists. War may be quite improbable between Canada and the United States, or between Norway and Sweden, but would we perceive it as impossible? Probably not, and an "international" relationship is thus perceived and defined to persist. International politics might thus be defined, not by the occurrence of war, but by the absence of any institutional structures effectively making war inconceivable. This "possibility of war" benchmark is an arbitrary and artificial construct, to be sure, as applied by the observing political scientist, but it is a benchmark also widely used by statesmen in the "nations" themselves.

Peace is, of course, highly likely between the United States and Britain, or Norway and Sweden. Yet the surest barrier to war here is as yet not institutional, but rather the existence of other nations with which each of these states has far worse relations. The Soviet Union today could be expected to exploit any war between the U.S. and Britain enormously; therefore, such war recedes in likelihood. Cases where wars in the end are only definitively prevented by the threat of war from a third state are fully within the international system. The threat of Canadian intervention is not what keeps Kentucky and West Virginia at peace; therefore these states are not international entities, but part of a single nation.

FURTHER READINGS

Aron, Raymond. *Peace and War: A Theory of International Relations.* New York: Praeger, 1967.

Wolfers, Arnold. *Discord and Collaboration: Essays on International Politics.* Baltimore: Johns Hopkins University Press, 1962.

Wright, Quincy. *The Study of International Relations.* New York: Appleton-Century-Crofts, 1955.

Why War?

As a means of coming to grips with the phenomenon of war, one might ask whether wars ever serve any rational purpose, or whether all wars necessarily illustrate some basic error or foolishness on the part of those who begin them.

A certain number of wars could indeed be blamed directly on foolish or mistaken expectations, for example, on "who will win." If each side expects that its army can defeat the other, one must be in error, and a good outside systems analyst should indeed be able to tell who is wrong. The Italian attack on Greece in 1940 seems to have been based on such miscalculations. The systems analyst might, of course, find it more difficult to convince the generals or politicians on either side that their position was hopeless; perhaps this might reflect foolish national passions which become aroused in the heat of battle. Perhaps it shows instead that even the best systems analyst can be wrong in his predictions.

Error may thus be silly, but it may not be easy to eliminate, and wars may begin or continue as a result. Yet not every war is based on such error. To turn to perhaps the most depressing cause imaginable for war, symbiotic conflict, one side might actually prefer war rather than offering the minimum required for the other to surrender. Perhaps the opposite population would severely cramp one's life-style by mere existence in the same region, so that one cannot easily offer them life and peace, even in exchange for their surrender. For illustrative cases, we might go to the treatment of American Indians by white pioneers, or even the Israeli attitude toward Arab Palestinians. People usually have an option for surrendering and agreeing to submit to the governance of new rulers in the territory they have populated. As POW's or as a captive nation, they could earn their keep, perhaps hoping for rebellion and political victory far into the future. If the conqueror has absolutely no desire or need for their labor, however, he may not even feel able to offer them the option of staying. In such horrible instances, both sides will prefer war to peace even if they are fully aware of all the consequences. For at least one side, the war has become one of extermination or eviction; for the resisting side, armed struggle is no more horrible than peace, for the latter entails being murdered or driven from one's home.

Happily for mankind, such symbiotic incompatability between cultures is rare. Normally the losers in a war are able to offer the winners enough to purchase the right to remain in the area at peace. Yet even a lesser amount of hostility concerning the political and cultural future of a region can provide a cause for war, if there is only a little bit of error or uncertainty on who would win the war if it were continued.

Yet hostility does not have to be either symbiotic or mistaken to cause fighting. A third cause of war may involve no direct ignorance at all, as each side would prefer peace to war, but would even more prefer to launch a surprise attack if the other were to relax his vigilance. Weapons which favor taking the offense may set up this kind of war situation.

This is in essence the "prisoners' dilemma," where the gains for a double-cross are always greater than for cooperation, (and the costs of a mutual double-cross are severe, but less than the costs of foolish unilateral cooperation, when the other side has decided on a double-cross). In effect each side knows that the other must betray the peace by shooting; because we know that he will shoot, we are also better off shooting. Indeed, we would be better off shooting even if he were to stop.

If weapons which favor the offensive cannot be eliminated, preventing war would require a mutual monitoring system such that each side would be immediately warned if the other was commencing a betrayal. Then we would not need to fear a sneak attack, and we could not profitably contemplate a sneak attack on the other army. But without such a system, peace is continually impossible.

Each side would indeed prefer peace to the wasteful war which results, a war in which both armies are actively defending themselves and attacking the other. Yet each side will still more prefer the war in which it alone had attacked, as the other had laid down its arms. When peace is preferred to bilateral war, but unilateral war is generally preferred to peace, the result is almost inevitably bilateral war.

The original "prisoners' dilemma" scenario depicts two vagrants—"Column" and "Row"—taken into custody by a somewhat unscrupulous sheriff on untrue charges of burglary, and then held in adjoining separate prison cells as the sheriff attempts to extract confessions from them. Each prisoner is informed that he will go free if he turns state's evidence against the other, if the other has still not confessed, and that the other would then get ten years in prison. If both plead innocent, both will receive shorter sentences (one year); but if both confess to turn state's evidence, both will get six years in prison.

Since the wall between the two prison cells is soundproof and the prisoners are not able to communicate, neither can be sure that the other is not betraying him to the sheriff, or that his own betrayal would be detected

	"Column"	
	Plead Innocent	Plead Guilty
Plead Guilty	−10 0	−6 −6
Plead Innocent	−1 −1	0 −10

"Row"

by the other in time for counteraction. Each prisoner is thus better off confessing no matter what the other does, and each therefore "confesses" to receive six years in prison, although honest cooperation would have gotten both men off with a much lighter sentence. A matrix showing penalties as minus scores could thus be completed as follows; "Column's" losses appear in the upper right corner of each box, while "Row's" losses appear in the lower left.

The absence of reliable and reassuring communications and monitoring mechanisms is always crucial here. If there had been a window between the cells, so that the two men could have heard each other's interrogation, then it would have been appropriate and easy for each to hold out against the sheriff's pressure. The outcome of the "prisoners' dilemma" situation thus is not directly accountable to the wisdom or stupidity of the "prisoners," but rather to the presence or absence of devices which assure each side that it will know in time if the other is about to cheat (and that the other side will know in time if we are about to cheat), all of which would make cooperation generally both safe and advisable.

The physical environment will provide this in some cases, whereby the dilemma (perhaps by definition) does not exist. The intervention of "honest broker" third parties might suffice otherwise, and the state (as for example in Hobbes' analysis) has often played this role in domestic conflicts. It will thus be important in the analysis of international events to recognize the kinds of payoffs that could structure a "prisoners' dilemma" situation, and the kinds of communication facilities which would be required to prevent the dilemma from generating so counterproductive an outcome as war. Perhaps an international inspectorate could have kept both sides from rushing to mobilize armies and attack in 1914, perhaps not.

A fourth cause of war is not quite a prisoners' dilemma, but has much of the same instability. In this case, shown in the matrix which follows, each side would actually prefer peace to double-crossing the other side, but is deeply afraid of the consequences should the other side want to commit

	"Column" Wait	"Column" Attack
"Row" Attack	-10 / -2 (or 0?)	-6 / -6
"Row" Wait	-1 / -1	-2 (or 0?) / -10

a double-cross. One can not be sure here that the other side prefers peace to attacking. One moreover cannot be sure that the other side knows we prefer peace to unilaterally attacking him. For either reason, we must prepare to defend ourselves, which will seem to be preparations also for attacking him. Whenever he similarly seems to be preparing to attack us, moreover, we must accelerate our preparations. Hence any slight increase in the perceived probability of war becomes self-confirming.

Unlike the previous case, peace here does not simply require that both sides know that they *could* not get away with a sneak attack. In truth, neither side would want to get away with it even if it could. Peace rather depends on convincing each other that neither side would *want* to get away with a sneak attack. Yet this may be every bit as difficult to achieve as the remedy for the prisoners' dilemma above. If the Cold War has been a misunderstanding, who can convince each side that the other never was aggressive? Wars can thus continue because each side is ignorant of what the other would do in a peaceful situation, or of what his preconditions for peace would be. There are theorists who assume that almost all conflict arises from such paranoid misperceptions of hostility, where each party is indeed ready to settle on much better terms than the other has supposed.

It may indeed be true that many wars have been launched or prolonged on precisely such a "mirror-image" basis. Yet we must avoid the excessive optimism attributing all armed conflict to situations so easily remedied by better communication. To give just a simple example of a diametrically opposite phenomenon, a fifth cause of war sees each side overrating the opposite's desire for peace, that is betting that the other side will soon surrender if the war can only be prolonged a few more months.

This is again a case of war prolonged by error. Uncertainty here arises not on determined military effectiveness, but on the comparative resolution of each side, so that it would be even more difficult for our outside analyst to establish which side was correct on this predictive problem. If each side expects the other to give up first, one at least is obviously wrong, but which one? Would the Nixon regime or the regime in Hanoi give up first in Vietnam? The analogy here is quite close to the game of "chicken," where one must only be the last to swerve off the road to win the game and to escape all further penalties.

This pattern shows up in much of politics besides war. From any position which is less than ideal, a spectrum of moves is possible which should be an improvement for both sides. Since each side knows this, each may be tempted to hold out at the position least favorable to both in an attempt to win the bulk of the improvement for itself. The failure to reach the "optimality frontier" thus becomes an endurance contest where each side is betting that the other will give up first. One side, of course, is wrong in its bet by definition, but it is hardly pathologically stupid in this error, especially when the gains of winning the contest of wills may be great and long-lived, especially when we ourselves cannot tell, as dispassionate observers, who will give up first. Contests of wills of this kind go on all the time in politics, albeit normally free of violence.

FURTHER READINGS

Boulding, Kenneth E. *Conflict and Defense.* New York: Harper Torchbrooks, 1963.
Kecskemeti, Paul. *Strategic Surrender.* Stanford, Cal.: Stanford University Press, 1958.
Rapoport, Anatol. *Fights, Games and Debates.* Ann Arbor: University of Michigan Press, 1960.
Richardson, Lewis F. *Arms and Insecurity.* Chicago: Quadrangle Books, 1960.

Why No World Government?

Why indeed are there no governmental institutions sufficient to prevent such wars? Why is there no world government to make the promises and deploy the forces to guarantee that disputes can never be escalated to organized violence? The answer in the end requires us to list all the considerations which peoples and nations historically have placed ahead of peace.

We could begin with sociological barriers to international government, barriers based on the ethnic differences which separate men by language, religion, race, and culture. Languages are different, and to combine speakers of different languages into a single decision-making unit can severely threaten the minority group. Whoever must learn a second language in addition to the one he is born with will be under a considerable handicap in seeking jobs either in government or private industry. Each ethnic group may thus favor a single national language, for the efficiency it offers, but each will try to force the other to convert. Faced with such a threat, the linguistic minority, not surprisingly, might try to use armed force to escape such a policy, to seek independence in what thus becomes an international relationship.

Similar considerations apply to religious questions, at least whenever the religions have an internal requirement that effort be made to convert all other human beings to the one true faith. Accident may have made one area Roman Catholic and another Protestant; if this accident of history has persisted into this century, however, it may be difficult to get either group to place the peace of a national unity ahead of the moral independence afforded by international anarchy. Even political traditions of a seemingly superficial variety can be sufficiently important to preclude national union. If pressed on why Canada should not become unified with the United States, some Canadians will refer to the British parliamentary and judiciary tradition as it superficially contrasts with the forms of the United States. All such relationships of minority to majority are bound by relatively insuperable rules of scale, whereby the larger faction almost certainly gets to call the tune, and the smaller, often with great difficulty, must adjust. For example, the "international" aspect of North Atlantic relations might be relieved if Iceland were to join the United States, but how much of Icelandic style, language, and so on could survive in such a union?

A second set of obstacles to political union can emerge simply from economic issues. If the units to be merged began with unequal fractions of the world's wealth, the union would tend to foster a fairer redistribution of this wealth. With even a little greed in the system, however, it will not be so surprising if the wealthier unit resists the merger, despite the fact that this resistance makes war possible between the units, when it could have been made impossible. Aside from inequities in original distribution, there may be substantial differences of economic system. People can become accustomed to either a market or a demand economy; nations which have become accustomed to differing economic systems may thus be resistant to any union which would force standardization on a single system.

One does not have to be a doctrinaire believer in the market, or in laissez-faire economics, to concede that the best economic decisions are not always made by some highly centralized source. If individual entrepreneurs or local political entities can often respond better to economic need, the retention of political independence can thus produce a more efficient economy than might result with world government. Local economic independence can also allow a nation to impose a certain austerity on itself, as it uses tariffs and import restrictions to avoid the temptations of buying from more advanced regions. By "going without" in the short run, a less developed area can achieve a richer future.

Apart from sociological and economic barriers, there are persistent political obstacles to establishing the kind of unified political institutions which would make war impossible. To begin, we must note the vested interest of the political job holders who might lose employment if countries were to merge. Two countries merging into one can have only one president and one prime minister. If national sovereignty poses continual threats of world anarchy, it also creates more slots to which ambitious men may aspire.

As noted earlier, political systems may be mutually incompatible, through historical accident if not through differences in the temperament of the people ruled. Legal and governmental systems depend heavily on tradition, and traditions are not so easily combined and merged with real viability. The world's national political systems, moreover, differ greatly in their degrees of check or restraint. If a relatively total system were thus blended with a much more restrained process, the persons and practices of the more total system might easily come to dominate the entire entity.

One only has to consider the case of the two Germanies to illustrate many of the problems listed here. On the basis of political and economic systems there are real differences to be overcome after 25 years of separation. On the basis of numbers, West Germany might be predicted to have most of its way after any union were resumed. On the basis of power in the political system, East Germany with its secret police, party and paramilitary organizations might be able to reverse this outcome.

All the arguments above can help to explain national "wills to resist" international government. Yet one must go a little further to explain the ability of nations to resist such a world order, when many people indeed might still welcome such government simply for its greater guarantees of peace.

Why does international politics not simply terminate itself as the stronger state conquers the weaker by military force? It seems entirely plausible that in every confrontation of two states, one will be stronger than the other. Complicating this military model considerably are the defensive advantages of terrain, advantages which traditionally have given mountain-dwellers an advantage even against greater numbers, as long as these mountaineers stand in their own redoubts to defend them. It would thus be possible that either army could defeat the other, if the other were only foolish enough to venture out of its own fortresses to go over to the attack. Defending one's own home, or terrain one knows intimately, has always suggested some advantages even when the terrain was flat. The advantage of the defense may thus explain why the international system has at least two members.

A slightly different mechanism then explains why these two members will typically involve a third and more members of the system. We refer here to a balance of power mechanism, whereby states are induced to intervene in other states' quarrels always on the side of the weaker, merely with the intent of preserving its independence and viability. This intervention need not reflect any love for the faction being rescued, or even any guilt finding as to who launched the war in the first place. Nations that mistakenly launch wars sometimes are so badly beaten that their independence as a state is immediately threatened. Rather, this "balance of power" approach derives from our calculation that third powers should be preserved simply because the same conclusion will inspire them someday to preserve us as a third power. The maxim would be: if you cherish independence, act so as to preserve it for others. Support those that would lose, not those you love, or those who were morally right. Support a state only until it is out of danger, and never so far that another state would be put into danger.

The balance of power mechanism can be an explanation simultaneously for division and unity. A state cherishing its independence seeks to keep the outside world divided. It seeks to keep itself united. Factions which would declare independence on their own may stay loyal to the nation, as long as division would make it so much easier for a menacing outside power to move in and impose its authority.

The obstacles to any military monopoly assuring world peace might be discussed in another context—whether the difficulty lies in getting there, or in staying there. The mechanisms described above may explain why it will always be close to impossible to establish world government by military means. The Roman Empire and its Pax Romana may have been one exception; the American monopoly of the atomic bomb might have been another, if only the United States had established a Pax Americana by forcing the Soviet Union to forgo producing its own bomb.

Yet if the threat of outside military forces is an important element in holding armies and nations together, would this not disappear once world government had eliminated all such outside confrontations? What indeed would preclude mutinies by battalions of the one-world army in such cases, battalions which would demand independence for some fragment of the globe, and perhaps be able to enforce their demands. Combinations which today are bizarre might become very potent in the world government situation. If South Carolina plus the Icelandic battalion garrisoning it, plus some disenchanted nuclear physicists, were to attempt to secede from the world in 1995, would they not be able to succeed? Even today, the record of subordination in international military forces under United Nations authority has not been flawless, as for example during the Katanga secession attempt.

One might thus almost conclude that world government is impossible by a crazily tautological definition: world government involves the absence of the currently most feared form of violence, but this situation would encourage the next most feared form. If war thus became impossible through the existence of the world-state, mutiny, with all the unpleasantness of war, would become more possible.

Yet our definition probably exaggerates the hopelessness of the international situation. The plausibility of mutiny is not really as oppressive as the plausibility of war, and mutiny also does not have to be as likely. Rome was built on a combination of military superiority and military subordination. Such subordination was sociologically achieved and might be achieved again in the future.

When international suspicion has slowly abated and a permanent governmental superstructure has evolved, the theory of functionalism might explain how it happened. When certain processes or techniques affect several countries simultaneously, such nations may decide to establish a larger governmental framework to achieve the economies of scale thereby suggested, and incidentally to make war much more difficult or impossible in the process. It is not that the various nations have decided that peace by itself is worth forgoing national sovereignty; rather, something else was worth this sacrifice of sovereignty, and peace becomes an incidental by-product.

There are definite limits, however, to the extent of substantial international organization required by such functions. Peace and international organization could emerge as an incidental by-product of the need to move the mails, but only if the movement of mails really demands this much superstructure. Karl Wittfogel has presented an argument that the requirements of irrigation in some parts of the world have necessitated centralized governments, where fragmentation and international conflict would otherwise have occurred. Mail delivery and weather forecasting and various other international functions do not require nearly as much coordination as irrigation, for men have indeed been ingenious in cooperating in these areas even during wars. American weather forecasters received weather information from Siberian stations of the USSR even during the Korean War, when such forecasts were used to brief bombing missions over North Korea. Mails have been delivered between the United States and Communist China even while the two are involved on opposite sides of the Vietnam War. The tireless Swiss bureaucrats of the Universal Postal Union perhaps deserve praise for their "common-sense" success in keeping the mails moving; yet perhaps they deserve blame instead, for letting the world escape the need for choice, the choice between giving up mail service and giving up the war option.

The "functionalist" road to peace might, of course, have been better illustrated by the European Economic Community (EEC) and its sister organizations, the European Coal and Steel Community (ECSC) and Euratom. Many motives have driven Europeans and outsiders to support these organizations, ranging from a straightforward desire for the economic benefits produced, to a metaphysical belief in the rightness of union, to the conscious hope that peace within Europe could be inadvertently guaranteed by the logic we have just discussed. France and Germany might thus never have renounced the war option just for the sake of peace, in this view, but would give up the option as a means to coordinating their economic well-being.

Yet it was precisely this inadvertent sacrifice of sovereignty that led Britain at earlier stages and France under President DeGaulle to resist the integrative processes of European economic union. In the delays and battles of this resistance, the functionalist impetus toward full political union may have been thwarted, so that the expanded European Community of nine members (with Britain, Ireland, and Denmark in 1972 deciding to join the original "six," France, West Germany, Italy, Belgium, The Netherlands, and Luxembourg) will be incapable of becoming a political unit. This is ironically illustrated by the shots occasionally fired across the boundary between the Republic of Ireland and Northern Ireland, even as London and Dublin were completing the process of "joining Europe."

There might be other ways to achieve peace—perhaps by de-internationalizing the style of the international system; that is, by transferring over characteristics of what we regard as the more desirable domestic political atmosphere. The domestic sphere is, of course, characterized by an absence of warlike violence, an assurance to all of us. It is also characterized by a sense of limits to goals, power, and influence, coupled with a certain deferral to authority, to the "rules of the game," which serves as a constraint rather than assurance. The absence of war threat may allow genuinely closer identifications among fellow citizens, while the constraints, plus fears of attack from outside the country, induce some artificial identifications as reinforcement.

This kind of domestic togetherness, therefore, is at least partially an artifact responding to outside military threats; one must thus again be cautious about any optimism on duplicating the process for the world as a whole. A more truly objective closeness among nations has paradoxically not been so highly correlated with peace. We are all too well acquainted with wars fought among European nations sharing remarkably similar cultures. It is clear that tension between Japan and the United States rose steadily as Japan came more and more to resemble the United States. It would be premature and perverse to argue that cultural closeness normally causes tensions instead of preventing them. Rather, the closing of cultural gaps is typically accompanied by a closing of geographic gaps; a geographic closeness often sets the stage for real conflicts of interest, where previously there would have been few, if any, interactions at all.

Similarly, we must be wary of assuming that political closeness will necessarily foster peace. Perhaps it is really true that democratic governments will have good relations with each other, but one should not be taken in by the historical propaganda which painted Austria or Germany in 1914 as unrepresentative regimes fighting democratic Britain and France. Perhaps Communist regimes would be unlikely to engage other Communist regimes in warfare, but what of the recent military confrontations between Moscow and Peking? It is thus simply a little too early to tell whether any convergence of the world's nations toward greater homogeneity and uniformity will really make war so much less likely. Some more pessimistic conclusions must still at least be considered; that trouble is always likely when it is possible, that the disappearance of the common enemy will often plunge former allies into hostility and confrontation with each other, even if they be similar in national style. If all the countries of the world except the U.S. and Switzerland were to disappear, would not tension be likely between these two? One should remember the attitudes of the United States and Britain on naval matters after the German fleet had been scuttled. From 1919 to 1923, an arms race emerged in which commentators could seriously discuss a naval war between the English-speaking powers.

FURTHER READINGS

Gallois, Pierre. *The Balance of Terror.* Boston: Houghton Mifflin, 1961.
Haas, Ernst B. *Beyond the Nation State.* Stanford, California: Stanford University Press, 1968.

Herz, John H. *International Politics in the Atomic Age*. New York: Columbia University Press, 1962.

Waltz, Kenneth. *Man, The State, and War*. New York: Columbia University Press, 1959.

Wittfogel, Karl. *Oriental Despotism*. New Haven: Yale University Press, 1957.

"Realism" or "Idealism"?

Since the warlike and ungoverned international arena persists, how do states behave within it, and how should they behave? The discussion of these two questions was for a long time phrased in terms of "realist" versus "idealist" positions, the former sometimes also being labeled by the German term of Realpolitik.

The Realpolitik analysis focuses on power-maximization as the explanation of much or all of foreign policy behavior. If the analysis were even only approximately correct, it could indeed enormously simplify the prediction of such policy decisions. In economics, for example, it is a very useful approximation to assume that most decisions of the firm are determined by pursuit of profit. If it increases our net returns, we will hire an extra man; if it does not, we will fire him. So in international relations, the power-maximizing model might save us the trouble of poring over enormous quantities of data. Religion, ideology, irredentism, and so on all would cease to be important factors in their own right; we would only need to know whether they affected the power position of the states involved, and we could go directly to predicting policy on such issues.

Yet there may be serious doubts about whether power is indeed such a universal goal in world politics. Perhaps we can convince ourselves that the USSR or Communist China are relentlessly trying to expand their control over human affairs in the world, and perhaps this charge might even be plausibly advanced against the United States, but is it really plausible against Switzerland or Iceland? The United States does indeed devote enormous resources to tools of power, but it also allows its citizens to squander other enormous sums on luxury automobiles. Surely we are, therefore, not maximizing power, choosing it over the alternatives at every opportunity. Surely Iceland and Switzerland are nations, but they devote almost no effort to influencing the outside world politically, and thus are barely interested in power, much less deterministically dominated by it.

Perhaps an alternative formulation might be more plausible, that nations do not seek to maximize power, but that individual political figures do. Most human beings, in this view, may pursue other goals, but the peculiar type of individual who enters politics is drawn to this by a special craving, that for "power." If we wish to predict decisions, therefore, we might have to focus on individuals such as Stalin, Mao, Gomulka, or De Gaulle. Their quest for power would hardly induce a reaching for power abroad at all times, however, for at times the solidifying of a position at home might require a quiet interim on the external fronts.

If the quest for power is not a true description of how states act in their foreign policies, perhaps it is rather intended as a prescription of how states should act, if they are to be at all successful as states. One could indeed claim that this is necessary almost by definition. We can not accomplish anything in human affairs without the power to accomplish it; therefore to be in favor of any particular accomplishment is to be in pursuit of the corresponding power. This argument is already well stated in the writings of Thomas Hobbes, who indeed argued that individuals as well as states would have to live by such rules.

This argument is either tautological, however, or quite incorrect. Men, and states, must continually choose between accumulating power and expending it, just as a capitalist must choose between increasing his capital stock or his personal economic consumption. There are many examples of the exercise of power in the international arena that hardly seem to have been an accumulation or harboring of power. When we decide to encourage one form of government in some states and to discourage another, we may well be satisfying some moral feeling, but in the process we are probably becoming tied down, freeing several other states to defy our will.

The Realpolitik theorists indeed confront a logical problem in that they never quite make it clear whether states do maximize power, or must do so, or should do so. One can not easily argue all these points at the same time. If all states already pursue power, it is a little redundant to lecture them that they should do so. As in other aspects of life, to say "should" may be to contradict "do."

If there are deficiencies in the "realist" position, the counter-arguments of those labeled "idealists" also can be subjected to criticism. For this style of analysis offers a contrary series of maxims for the proper conduct of foreign policy, maxims whose logical ground may be just as unclear as that criticized above.

The "idealist" or "liberal" advice for the nation entering an international arena would run as follows: One should seek open international agreements, openly arrived at. One must never begin wars. Furthering international understanding will increase the chances for peace. Democracies can be counted upon not to begin wars. Similarly, economic justice and economic progress will fortify the prospects of peace. Persons and nations in international affairs should be treated only as ends in themselves, and never simply as a means. In general, morally good developments reinforce each other. God, or some other higher force, would have been very perverse not to make all right things compatible.

The difficulty, of course, comes with judging whether these statements purport to describes values or facts. It is not easy to quarrel with clergymen or others who will tell us that our moral goals should not be power, but peace; not power, but equity or democracy; not power, but an opening of all of world society. There might be moralists to argue flatly the reverse, but these are rare in American society.

More typically, the rebuttal might come from upholders of the dichotomy between facts and values, who deny the possibility of proving or meaningfully discussing such propositions. Only means can be analyzed or proven in this view, not ends. Means are a matter of physical fact, ends are an expression of personal feeling or preference. The question "Does democracy really lead to peace?" can be debated and answered in this view. The question "Is democracy good?" cannot.

There is indeed no consensus on whether values should be screened out of analyses of international relations. Theorists of religion or of natural law will respond that right and wrong are just as much matters of provable fact as the impact of democracy on peace. Others will argue that abstention from moral judgement in political analysis biases the writer toward certain moral positions, perhaps leaving him powerless to criticize or resist the most obnoxious or totalitarian regimes. A compromise might yet be suggested whereby persons seeing moral truth as it relates to foreign policy are encouraged to describe it as they see it, while others remain free to ignore such messages if they can find no way to test or prove them.

Laying aside the issues of fact/value dichotomies, we still must test the factual assumptions implicitly or explicitly made in the liberal-idealist argument. Do "good things" in international politics tend to advance together, or is it possible that we will have to choose between moral advances? For example, does an advance in democracy always support the prospects of peace? The realist counterattack could quickly point to cases where just the opposite relationship has held true. Of Arab states confronting Israel, for example, the states with the more traditional or oligarchic structure have been generally more ready for accommodation, while those with greater mass political mobilization and representation have been more fanatically opposed to Israel.

And what of the relationship of economic development and advancement as it relates to peace? Here again one can find examples where the two go together, but also cases where a conflict seems apparent. Indian attitudes on foreign policy have clearly hardened toward toughness and nationalism, away from Gandhian internationalism, in the same years that India's industrialization program has shown real progress. Economic progress in nuclear power indeed now offers temptations of nuclear weaponry, which may see India become more power-oriented than it ever has been.

Is there similarly any good linkage between economic development and the likelihood of democracy? Most liberals would assert that there is; yet closer analyses of political development suggest that economic growth often deranges the social and political arrangements of the past so that governments will be extremely unstable, so that democracy may be very precarious.

Similarly with regard to the relationships between international understanding and peace, both these may be extremely desirable developments from a liberal-moral point of view, but it is far from certain that war becomes less likely between nations getting to know each other. Honest and open negotiations may seem conducive to trust and to peaceful settlement of disputes, but history records many disputes which could be settled only behind the backs of the peoples or oligarchic elites involved. Negotiations between Israel and Jordan have always seemed extremely vulnerable to publicity. If they could be kept secret long enough, there was some chance of accommodation and success, but the first leak to the public could doom a ruler to assassination. Wandering outside the field of international politics, one can even voice doubts on whether full and open disclosure of all political processes is so compatible with democracy. A certain degree of myth or pluralistic ignorance may indeed be required to maintain the rules of the game and the political moderation characterizing the American and British political processes.

Hence, one part of the realist's political message may hold a great deal of validity, not that nations must always exclusively pursue power, but that they can not pursue morality in all its forms, since nature so often does impose cruel choices. The statesman who finds a way for us to have our cake and eat it too will be entitled to as many rewards as we can give him; but it is foolish to await such accomplishments regularly, for they often will be impossible. Faced with such impossibilities, it will not be surprising if even the most moral or liberal nation devotes some attention to its power position.

FURTHER READINGS

Carr, Edward H. *Twenty Years Crisis. 1919–1939.* New York: St. Martin, 1946.
Morgenthau, Hans J. *Politics Among Nations; the Struggle for Power and Peace.* New York: Knopf, 1967.

The National Interest

As part of any discussion of how nations do or should behave, one is inevitably drawn to definitions of the "national interest." We may definitely encounter semantic confusions here, for some political analysts use the term to refer to what all the citizens of the nation will want, while others are referring simply to the desires of those who make the decisions. The difference in emphasis relates again to the differing perspectives of domestic and international analysis. Commentators on domestic affairs typically are identifying a goal in "the public interest" or "national interest," while international analysts are affixing the phrase "national interest" to a policy already in effect. Hence by the latter usage, German "national interest" in 1938 is not what all Germans (counted somehow equally) would have preferred, but rather what Hitler and his entourage did prefer.

Perhaps the difference stems from a certain callousness and indifference when discussing someone else's country rather than our own. More likely, it reflects a general sense of powerlessness for influencing international politics through foreign domestic processes. If we are desperately trying to guess whether concessions at Munich will make German military moves more or less likely thereafter, the desires and perceptions of Hitler and his group may really be all that matters.

One could turn here to the question of group rationalities, and whether they are really as meaningless as they are sometimes made out to be. We are accustomed to reading and writing that "Germany wanted," "Germany decided," "Germany acted and Germany got," and so on, and we are then confronted by evidence that no nation is as coordinated or monolithic as these words seem to imply. The authors of such phrases obviously have not made this mistake of assuming that such a single-person actor "Germany" exists. Rather the phrase is a shorthand for "whoever makes the decisions" that determine German army movements or German trade policy. Years later, we will discover that it was Hitler who decided this, Goering that. For the moment one may yet guess the decisions correctly without being sure of exactly who was making them.

Yet we will not always be content to define the "national interest" as whatever the head of state or foreign minister wants. When the popular feeling has even the slightest impact on foreign policy, we may wish to view the "national interest" as something like the "public interest," that is, related to the wishes of most or all the people.

If we insisted on majority rule on a one-man/one-vote basis as the determiner of the "national interest" for foreign policy, however, some major problems of definition would still remain. On most issues of foreign as well as domestic policy, specific minorities will feel much more strongly and intensely than the great "silent majority." Perhaps we will wish simply to overrule such intense minorities on such issues, on the grounds that no one's special or moral feelings can be interpreted to allow more than an equal voice on national policy. Yet what if the majority, while disagreeing on substance, itself endorses a procedural rule whereby intense minorities should be given special consideration? Most Americans probably do not feel that the preservation of Israel comes ahead of American prestige in the Arab countries. A minority of Americans share the directly opposite opinion—that the security of Israel comes far ahead of friendship with the Arabs. American Zionists probably place this issue at the top of their list in terms of priorities and importance; most Americans, while feeling opposite on the substance, do not regard the issue as of supreme importance. There thus arises an implicit sense in American politics that the few who feel strongly should get consideration ahead of the many who are close to indifferent.

Similar feelings may apply to the majority of Americans and the younger radicals who first openly opposed the Vietnam War. The young are interpreted as being more moral, more sincere, perhaps as the conscience of the country. Even if their mature parents did not yet agree with their opinion, many would regard the agitation and power of the radicals as good for the country. "It's good for dissidents to have some influence."

Yet there are obvious dangers in procedural accommodations by which the majority, while disagreeing with an intense minority, regards that intensity as a sign of some special moral qualities which require that national policy be accommodated to it. The majority in Hitler's Germany never voted Nazi, but the zeal and moral self-confidence of the Nazis was regarded as proof that the flabby remainder of society should submit to its leadership. Who could show that the Nazis did not indeed care more than the average German about Germany's future and destiny? In 1944 and 1945, the Allies had to define their plans for Germany's postwar political rehabilitation. Obviously Germany would have to be a democracy, but a democracy in which the majority did not submit itself meekly and voluntarily to some minority's rule.

In Israel today the "great silent majority" may oppose Jewish settlement and expansion into the Arab lands occupied on the west bank of the Jordan in 1967. Yet small zealous groups are able to force the government's hand by moving onto such lands, and by citing their special religious or political zeal as a reason to defy policies adopted through democratic processes. Faced with such faits accompli, the government has been reluctant to evict these settlers, despite the damage done to hopes of peace with the Arabs, since the majority of Israelis will respect the special zeal of the minority defying state policy.

Given such difficulties in sorting out procedural and substantive levels of consensus, one will be even more tempted to accept foreign policy, however it emerges, as the "national interest." Why worry about what the policies of country X would have been if its whole population had been less excessively solicitous of the wishes of some small subsegment? It is the other nation's foreign policy as it is, not as it should be, that will set the problems to which our own foreign policy must adjust.

Shifting focus a little, we can wonder whether the "national interest" indeed even requires what we call a foreign policy. "No man is an island," some philosophers would remind us, and we all have a duty to take an interest in everything that happens on this globe. Yet a more detached commentator might respond that Iceland is an island, as is Jamaica, Ceylon, and Singapore. To decide to have a serious involvement in international affairs, a nation must be large enough and entangled enough to bother. Isolation can thus not be ruled out so quickly as a policy alternative for a nation, for there are indeed states which carry on successfully without armed forces, with minimum investments in diplomatic services, with economies whose trade commitments do not generate political complications abroad.

A nation must, therefore, cross a certain threshold of international entanglement before it acquires a meaningful foreign policy problem. A second threshold might be defined on the distinction between status quo and revisionist foreign policies. The distinction is very arbitrary, to be sure, as all participants in the international system have some things they would like changed and some they would like to maintain. Yet if the amount of change desired becomes very great, states may become ready to overturn the entire procedures of the system in order to achieve their substantive ends, and their foreign policy style will indeed become noticeably different.

If nations thus elect to pursue their "national interest" in the international environment, does this require that such foreign policies will always be "selfish" or "greedy" or egoistic? The answer here must again be no, unless we are to define selfishness in a most tautological way. One can always argue that even the most altruistic behavior is selfish; "If I devote all my spare time to helping the needy, I am doing it only because I enjoy it." Yet the evidence offered for enjoyment here will typically only be that I chose to spend my time this way. Indian advocates of an independent nuclear force sometimes fall back on arguments similarly phrased, that "The United States will only defend India insofar as it satisfies its own national interest." The statement may be true by definition, but it hardly proves that the United States would not have responded if Communist China had dropped an atomic bomb on New Delhi.

The crucial question is obviously not whether all foreign policy is somehow geared to one's own happiness, but whether it is ever geared to another people's welfare for its own sake. Does a nation ever undertake a venture in foreign policy primarily or exclusively because it would make another people happy? The answer, for good or ill, is clearly yes. Nations adopt a foreign policy in part to head off military threats against themselves, and in part to collect material gains abroad. But they also intervene abroad because of genuine identifications with one national group against another, or one particular political, ideological, or religious cause.

FURTHER READINGS

Beard, Charles A. *The Idea of National Interest.* New York: Macmillan, 1934.
Morgenthau, Hans J. *In Defense of the National Interest.* New York: Knopf, 1951.
Tucker, Robert W. *Nation or Empire.* Baltimore: Johns Hopkins University Press, 1968.
Waltz, Kenneth. *Foreign Policy and Democratic Politics.* Boston: Little, Brown, 1967.

How "Coercive" Are International Relations?

How coercive are international relations? Can such relations, more than other forms of politics and human interaction, generally be characterized as one group imposing its will on another? "Coercion" is hardly a pleasant word. At the least, it suggests a denial of choice, where the addition of choice probably would open more desirable options. We may wish man to be "guided" and to have a "sense of purpose," if this means that some grander mechanism eliminates foolish or less happy choices. We may even wish to have choice narrowed to manageable or comfortable proportions simply for our psychic ease. Yet we hardly wish to have freedom narrowed toward the less gratifying end of the spectrum.

Sometimes we speak thus of nature coercing us. If the soil is barren, we may have to work long hours simply to survive, never able to attain the cash crop and savings which would allow us to choose the city as an alternative. Nature thus dictates our life-style, and we are more consciously than ever under its determination. Yet much more typically we speak of coercion in the context of human beings dealing with each other. Nature may be a cruel and demanding adversary, but she at least does not seem to be consciously manipulating us at her whim. When it is another human being who seems unilaterally able to dictate our behavior and fate, we find this considerably more obnoxious, and "coercive."

Coercion in human relations can take a purely physical form just as coercion by "nature." An obvious example is when a bully pushes some boy into a swimming pool. In an almost totally nonmotivational manner one is coerced into the pool. (A very different process, which we shall come to, is involved when the boy is forced into the pool by threats or promises of the bully.) A foreign soldier may kill us, or may simply wound us enough to hinder our physical movement, to hinder our ability to kill or wound him. Future psychedelic gases have sometimes been depicted as facilitating a most pleasantly coercive military disabling process, whereby our dreams would come to an end only after we had been disarmed and deposited in a POW camp.

We can coerce an enemy by killing or imprisoning him. We can also work through his mental processes, to motivate him away from harming us, or even towards service. Much of this mental manipulation involves a real effort to communicate, but some of it does not.

At a basic level, we sometimes can incapacitate an enemy by frightening him, just as effectively as if we had wounded him with a bullet. Such visceral rationalizations show up in much of the "psychological warfare" attempted around the world, especially between states of unequal economic development and prowess. Sonic booms over cities of the Middle East do not directly damage anyone's fighting capacity. They may demonstrate an ability to inflict damage on civilians, while at the same time signalling that such damage is being held in reserve as a deterrent. Yet their most serious objective is instead simply to reduce the mobilizable energy available to either side, through only partially rational processes of fear, intimidation, and discouragement. By waving my fist, I may cause the boy to fall into the swimming pool, just because his coordination was momentarily upset.

There are societies in which men lose much of their equipoise if their male prowess has been challenged. Being bested in any contest of strength does not then only lead to rational reassessments of options and costs, but also to an intense inner disturbance as one's whole station in life is challenged. Flights over Cairo or Damascus serve less as warnings than as insults, insults which might frustrate and enrage Arabs enough to hamper their war effort. Any other form of coercion (that is, any other means by which one human agency tends to dictate the behavior of another) may thus induce an additional form of power and influence (coercion) here in the psychological realm. If one's cultural background stresses manly independence, any hint of dependence in the more material or rational sectors can create an additional weakness (or dependence) in morale. By demonstrating how vulnerable your few cities are to my gunboats, you were made subject to my will in a way which far exceeds the practical importance you attach to these cities.

In today's world, however, the tactic of frightening an opponent into ineffectiveness probably will have limited application. Even if many military officers still portray their views of psychology in such terms, the bulk of coercion has to revert to the offer-of-gains/warning-on-costs format that addresses an opponent's rational decision process rather than his abilities. The mechanisms of truly communicative coercion can be separated into fairly rigorous categories. Each of them involves statements intended to induce or force a certain kind of behavior. An important difference emerges, however, between coercive statements which were true even before they were issued, and those which were not. The former can be labelled as "warnings" or "assurances," the later as "threats" or "promises."

An assurance/warning might simply be as follows: "If you want me to teach you how to swim, you must get into the pool." The statement was always true; it simply reminds the coerced person of a relationship that he might have forgotten. The functional equivalent in international politics might be, "If you wish to try to cross my territory to invade France, you will become entangled in my mine fields." If the statements are true, they are no more so for having been said.

A threat is something different. "If you don't get into the pool I won't talk with you." The threatener here presumably enjoys talking with the threatened, and is thus not describing some behavior which would follow naturally. Indeed, if his demands are not satisfied, he will carry through on the threat regretfully, only because he verbalized it. The statement is true, but only from the moment it is made, for it verifies itself. The equivalent on the international scene is "If you try to cross our territory to invade France, we will bomb your cities (even though it is something we would not otherwise do, for it means the total destruction of our cities in return)."

These last examples seem especially coercive in that the victim of the threat does not receive anything, but merely escapes punishment by giving in. The other form of self-verifying statement, a "promise," might seem deceptively less coercive at first. A promise might come as follows. "If you get into the pool, I will give you a dollar." The speaker will afterward only give a dollar because he has said he would. Having said nothing, he would have kept his money. The equivalent on the international plane is, "If you don't cross our territory to invade France, we will send volunteers to help you wherever the front is shifted."

Hence an exchange of promises might not seem "coercive." Each side to the exchange is better off; fair exchange is no robbery. Yet the initial distribution of power to exchange goods may have endowed one side much more generously than the other, in a way which we would regard as arbitrary and unfair. The rich country hires the young men of a poor Himalayan state as its soldiers; the soldiers fight well, and the rich state indeed then keeps its promises to pay monetary compensation. Yet the only occasion for these young men to risk their lives in the service of others may be a poverty which coerces them, a poverty which indeed allows foreign nations to have their way with them. If one must work to live, one can negotiate a "free exchange of labor" with some employer, but may yet feel considerably more coerced than in other situations where one was "threatened."

There are indeed even ways of "coercing one's self," of denying one's self options by attaching additional penalties to them. There will be arguments that men do so out of actual psychological need, that unlimited choice produces anomie, so that constricted choice is more comfortable than unlimited choice. Leaving aside this area of speculation, one can easily demonstrate bargaining situations as in the pioneer work of Thomas Schelling in which one is coerced less by others if one has precoerced one's self. I have $25,000 with which to buy a house that I want very much. The seller would sell for $20,000 but knows how attached I am to the house, and is holding out for $25,000. To upset his calculations, I bet someone $5,000 that I will not pay more than $20,000. The seller now knows that I can not possibly offer more than $20,000, no matter how much I like the house; and he must come down in price. In international politics, one sees this phenomenon repeated often. Since Congress coerces the president into being less generous with American money, the prospective landlord of a military base we seek to rent knows that he can not extract as large a rental from us.

Do these various forms of coercion occur more often in the international sphere than in domestic politics and social relations? Beginning first with the brute force example, whereby one person physically incapacitates another, we might speedily conclude that this is much more prevalent in the anarchic arena we know as international politics. To be sure, brawls still occur in barrooms in which men are knocked unconscious or have their arms broken. Criminals or policemen occasionally shoot someone, and criminals are held in prisons. Yet none of this compares with a war, a process in which thousands or millions are killed, wounded, or captured. It is indeed the absence of such physical coercion that we regard as law and order, as government instead of anarchy, as peace instead of war. If we are asked to explain our longing for a world government to replace the tangle of separate sovereignties, it is largely because of the possibility of war that hangs over the international system.

Turning to our second form of coercion, the physical incapacitation induced in psychological signals, the domestic-international comparison might be much more debatable. Israeli military feats perhaps thusly incapacitated some Arabs by intimidation, and the European states applied the same mechanism in their campaigns of colonial conquest. But the latter campaigns in fact illustrate our dilemma, because relations between British and Somalis were no longer international after the British had demonstrated their psychological mastery, but rather domestic (that is, colonial). Policemen in all our societies wear uniforms, in part to be recognizable, but in part also to exploit reflexes which have been conditioned to submit to authority. In sum, one might argue that this form of incapacitation plays the greater role in domestic affairs, in that almost all societies depend somewhat on citizens being cowed by established authority. Dissidents in various societies will claim that this unnerving effect goes very far. Persons more agreeable to such societies will counter that it is merely a useful supplement to the basically rational calculations that hold citizens to their states.

Some other dissidents will argue that this incapacitation phenomenon plays the much larger role in international affairs, however, so that smaller nations must take positive action to avoid being dominated by it. In this view, it is not only Israel that psychologically incapacitates Lebanon, but the United States that similarly manipulates Ecuador and India. At all points the alleged effects are extremely difficult to differentiate from the latter coercive models of rational warnings/assurances, threats, and promises; what one man claims to see as subliminally or viscerally irrational, another will find to be consciously rational. If the American radical thus sees Americans as the primary victim of United States governmental emasculation, the Peruvian radical will counter that Peruvians are the primary victim, and that international rather than domestic politics is the normal medium for this form of coercion. Nonradicals would say it is emasculation in neither case, but "persuasion," or "community of interest."

As evidence of the psychology factor, the world indeed seems extremely sensitive on this question of international coercion, with a great concern that any such coercion be kept invisible and unacknowledged. The sovereign independence and territorial integrity of states is almost the only legal "principle" that both the Communist and Western worlds have consistently paid lip service to since 1945. This atomistic notion that each nation should sense very little or no control of its destiny by any other nation might have struck a very responsive chord amongst laissez-faire classical liberal theorists of domestic society in the 19th century. Yet one could raise the same objections now at the international level as were raised against them. Can it really be that nations decide their own destinies? If man is a social animal, are not nations international structures? Why require the United States or the USSR continually to deny that they are ever imposing on the affairs of another country, but only trying to restore political processes to the way they would have worked before anyone else intervened?

Our third mechanism of human coercion, the ploy of assurance or warning, indeed plays a great role in all forms of human exchange, nonpolitical, domestic political, and international; the natural automaticity of the persuasion (or coercion) involved makes it extremely useful. If I do not wish to sing, the choral group will not invite me to join; if I do, they will. What could be simpler? The head of the group may remind me of this inexorable truth if I seem to have forgotten it, but he hardly has to go to any elaborate posturing to make his statement credible. It was credible all along because it was always so true. So similarly in domestic politics. If you do not leave a new address, the post office will not forward your mail; if you do, it will. So similarly in international politics. If you invade my country and shoot at my troops, my troops will have to shoot at you; if you don't, they won't. If you do not buy our goods, we will not be able to buy yours.

The very naturalness of these relationships makes them powerful motivational instruments. Because of this power, therefore, we see the smaller nations of the world so prone to resenting them. The unrealistic assertion of total independence (total lack of trans-boundary causation, total lack of coercion?) by various nations is simply intended to suppress the psychological intimidation discussed above.

This common-sense mechanism of cooperation explains the handling of a host of ordinary questions in international relations. Location of border crossing points, management of rivers, allocation of radio spectrum, and so on, often require nothing more than that each side make clear its real preferences, whereupon the other side serves its own interest by adjusting to them. Much of trade regulations and rules for commerce at sea are straightforwardly of this nature. The power of this mechanism is great; if it sometimes seems to serve one side of the boundary more than the other, it will therefore also be labeled as coercion. Indeed, the seeming "coerciveness" of any aspect of international politics is very much a function of the background conditions which seem to make exchanges unequal rather than equal.

There is one aspect of international relations, however, in which this particular coercive mechanism is diminishing in importance: military defense. As suggested above, what dissuaded an attacker in the past was simply the prospect that the defender would very naturally turn to his defending forces; these forces might repulse the attack, or at least might inflict costs sufficient to make the conquest unprofitable in the net. A major power in today's world dissuades attack instead by *threatening* a nuclear response that might make no sense at all: "If you invade me, it means World War III and the destruction of us all."

This of course brings us to the fourth form of coercive technique outlined above, the "threat." States threaten us with death or imprisonment in hopes of dissuading us from various actions. If we nonetheless engage in such acts (crimes), the state will punish us primarily because it said it would, because its honor is on the line, because other erstwhile "criminals" would no longer be deterred if it failed to impose the penalty. The officers of the state most probably do not enjoy killing or incarcerating us, but do so nonetheless when their honor has been coupled to the act by the oaths they have taken and the laws they have proclaimed.

Most of domestic law is thus in the form of "threats." The state will act contrary to its normal humane outlook, if we committed acts it intends to discourage. Individuals in normal nonpolitical interaction apply similar mechanisms to each other, but in a much less regular fashion, as "cutting off one's nose to spite one's face" has only limited acceptability and efficacy. We might indeed generalize that cultures differ on the necessity or acceptability of threat-fulfillment in interpersonal relations. Some cultures severely disapprove of the man who will not punish an unfaithful wife, even if he still loves her and wishes to forgive her. Other cultures, especially modern ones, tend rather to disapprove of punishment in such cases, unless the aggrieved husband has genuinely thereby fallen out of love with his wife. In short, our more modern and humane society endorses the naturalness of the warning/assurance mechanism by which spouses are induced (coerced) to stay faithful, but not the revenge mechanism.

Threats almost always cause anguish when they have been challenged, precisely because the threat thereby has failed, precisely because the threatener must now contemplate doing something against his natural inclination. Even at the domestic politics level, we are in anguish about the inhumanity of the death penalty, and about the inhumanity of imprisonment, even imprisonment under ideal conditions.

At the international level, the anguish can be all the more acute. We have hinted that we would escalate to nuclear war after our enemy sends troops into province X. If we suddenly discover that he has defied our threat, can we indeed move to execute it? Analysts have long argued that threats at such great variance from the basic inclinations of the threatener would be incredible, and thus ineffective as coercive mechanisms. Who will believe that Eisenhower would really have bombed Moscow because the Russians had just seized West Berlin?

Yet Latin American husbands do indeed shoot their wive's lovers, and the most civilized countries do indeed execute murderers, or send burglars to a prison which only intensifies their inclination to burglary. The honor mechanisms may depend somewhat on a rational perception of repeated instances, but it then takes on a life of its own. A judge may well say, "If I condemn this man to death, other men will feel less free to commit murder." Eisenhower would not have said, "If I launch World War III, other Russians will feel less free to seize other enclaves." Yet the president's escalation was hardly so incredible as to eliminate the coercive force of American declarations. Russians have indeed been coerced into tolerating the existence of West Berlin, into tolerating air and ground traffic across the Soviet Zone of Germany.

One can easily show that coercion in politics is not very different from the coercion of a criminal syndicate, or of a bully inflicting his will on fellow school boys. In all such cases, one human being is driven to serve the will of another, in a manner which an outsider would see as relatively one-sided. Warnings, promises, threats, or straight physical force are used.

Yet when the coercive mechanism becomes that of a "threat," some special problems arise in this international arena in which contending political bodies interact. To begin, most or all of "political activity" is at least nominally on behalf of some human group. Perhaps the Somoza regime in Nicaragua or the political activities of the Mafia in New Jersey are so venal that one would have to interpret them as blatantly intended only for the benefit of those directly holding power. Most regimes, perhaps even the Mafia, have to pretend to be defending some larger group of human beings. As in much of politics, pretense then becomes self-fulfilling. If the propaganda claims of higher purpose do not seem to be fulfilled even a trifle, the subterfuge involved becomes apparent, and the politician loses power.

Men can threaten anonymously, without being counter-threatened. Nations can not. Once a cause identifies with a human object, for example, "Spain," "the proletariat," "French-Canadians," it exposes a target for retaliation. The blackmailer who threatens to report me to the police if I do not pay off is only swearing to subject himself to an unpleasant walk to the nearest mailbox. Nations that swear to destroy some foreign city automatically invoke counter-threats against their own cities. Nations must, therefore, pursue even more seriously the myth of homogeneity and unity if they are to avoid the anguish of having their threats challenged.

The nation thus accomplishes more internationally if it coerces its individual citizens into a sharing of the risks and payoffs, if it accomplishes some reality for the myth of a single homogenous country. Is there doubt that the United States would retaliate against Moscow after a Russian air raid on Paris? Pierre Gallois and many other Frenchmen argue that this will be very much in doubt. Is there doubt that we would similarly retaliate for a raid on Bangor, Maine? Very little doubt at all, for the retaliatory threat presumably is conditioned to respond to attacks on *any part* of the United States.

One might question whether this blanket coverage would have extended to Alaska and Hawaii had they not been admitted to statehood. Perhaps not even statehood is sufficient, if the analogy of Algeria or Angola as "domestic" parts of European countries is brought to bear. (Perhaps physical continuity and contiguity will be required to establish the deterrent to invasion or nuclear attack.) Yet the deterrent could certainly be challenged if the myth of political homogeneity were not enforced across the geographical contiguous land mass. An attack on Churchill, Ontario, is not quite the same as an attack on Bangor, Maine. The nation that stays together deters together, and reaps international returns together.

States will thus be driven by the exigencies of the international environment to coerce component parts and individual citizens a great deal more than might otherwise be the case. India can no more let a state secede than could the United States under Lincoln. Young men are called into military service to fight wars of which they disapprove morally, or against armies in which their European or Asiatic cousins and uncles may be fighting. Coercion at a domestic level is required to reverse the direction of possible coercion at the international level.

Our last motivational phenomenon, that of the "promise," seems generally to be a happier one, and perhaps therefore is more rarely labeled as "coercive." If promises are executed, each side goes off wealthier than before the exchange was initiated, and the promises can be renewed again and again. If threats, on the other hand, must be executed, the outcome is disappointing and unhappy, with none eager to renew the relationship. Since both sides are better off in the exchange of a promise, moreover, why should anyone feel coerced?

We exchange promises in all aspects of life. "If you build me a house, I will repay you the cost over 25 years." "If you Russians build a dam for one of our rivers, we will repay you over 25 years." But when the dam or the house has already been built, why not then refuse to pay? Hobbes' classic dilemma was that whichever side has to deliver its part of an exchange second would have no incentive to do so, since its benefits had already been delivered; exchanges would be possible if, and only if, there was a higher force to coerce completion of the exchange.

In domestic politics, one does not refuse to pay, for one will be sued, the higher authority of the state will intervene to seize our property or even imprison us if we resist payment. Perhaps there is a constitutional arrangement of checks and balances within *domestic* politics that will also force any particular component of government to live up to its domestic promises, at least those dignified as law. Whether or not this form of "higher authority" is illusory, is there anything comparable once we reach the international scene? What would drive a state to deliver its half of an exchange to another state, if there were no higher authority intervening to punish perfidy? Won't the coercive impact of the contract be much less effective and relevant in this international arena of anarchy? Indeed, there is a logical paradox in the mechanism Hobbes uses to explain the establishment of the state contract-enforcer. This also is accomplished by contract; one can not be clear (by Hobbes' motivational logic) how this works; which came first, that contract or the enforcer?

There is in fact no higher enforcement authority for international law, but this may be an unimportant distinction, because the same powers that proclaim and enforce domestic law do so for international law also. In countries ruled by a single dictator, we do not typically have great definitional problems in determining what is law. The law is the code of conduct the dictator (or whatever government there is anywhere) proclaims himself as enforcing. There may thus be no higher physical authority forcing the dictator to go through with the promises and threats we call law; yet if he fails to make his "law" conform roughly with the practices he wishes to encourage and discourage, he is throwing away a valuable opportunity to achieve his will. In the same way, nations proclaim codes of conduct they intend to support with force in the international sphere. Again there may or may not be a higher authority to force them to fulfill their proclamations. Other things being equal, they will still be well advised to adhere if they are to be at all effective.

Other things rarely are equal. The absence of a higher enforcing authority indeed produces less adherence to international law than to domestic law. Yet cynical suggestions that most or all of international promises and international law are not of any significance are seriously mistaken. Most of the commitments made in the international arena are fulfilled; part of this is explained by the mechanisms already examined, but the rest illustrates the coercive efficacy of the "promise."

Reneging on an agreement simply runs the risk that other parties will not be willing to initiate similar agreements and exchanges in the future. It is true, this time, that the deal naturally occasioned the opposite party to deliver certain concessions first, after which we in turn would have come to make repayment. On a one-shot basis, we thus are naturally tempted not to carry through on our bargain, but rather to grab the goods and run without paying. No exchange can be exactly simultaneous; in every case someone has to deliver first and then (in the absence of a higher mediating authority) trust the other party. Yet most international interactions, and indeed many human interactions, comprise long series of repeated exchanges. The store that depends on "repeat sales" presumably is more reliable than one that does not; it can be pressured and "coerced" by its customers.

Any state will violate its international obligations if the alternative rewards are extremely substantial. If a state becomes powerful enough to brush off future distrust of other states as a binding constraint, it may even come to mock and ignore international law. Yet it is not only powermad great powers that sometimes exude skepticism about international law. Such states question whether voluntary contracts without higher enforcers can ever be binding, but other states will question whether such contracts will not indeed be "coercive."

FURTHER READINGS

Rothstein, Robert. *Alliances and Small Powers.* New York: Columbia University Press, 1968.
Schelling, Thomas C. *The Strategy of Conflict.* New York: Oxford University Press, 1960.
Vital, David. *The Inequality of States.* Clarendon: Oxford University Press, 1967.

Some Elementary Advice

As long as the world remains fractured into competing and potentially hostile states, advice will be set down on how to play this game, and how to win. The pursuit of successful foreign policy has hardly been a neglected subject in the literature accumulated over some six centuries, but we might still venture a few observations on how the post-1945 system should now stress certain maxims ahead of others.

To begin, there is today a greater need than ever before for motivating one's opponent, for considering his rational processes and seeking to work within them. The reason is simple. Nuclear weapons have clearly given several other major powers the means to destroy our cities, no matter how carefully we prepare our defenses. At an earlier stage, we might have put our trust simply in an army and navy which would win victories on the battlefields and never allow any damage to threaten our homes. Today, the enemy can always destroy us, even after we have won the greatest victories, and we must thus always make it to his interest not to do so; perhaps this will even require that we forgo winning that greatest of victories.

In game-theoretical terms, the world today is thus clearly not a zero-sum game. The worst outcome of any interaction on the international front is decidedly not the best for the other. The worst outcome is a nuclear holocaust which would destroy all the cities of all continents; everyone shares an interest in avoiding this, and must be prepared to communicate even in wartime to keep it from happening.

Yet everyone is also prepared to exploit the continuing risk of such a disaster to coerce and deter his opponents, indeed by threatening that he may actually unleash such a holocaust if certain concessions are not made. The effectiveness of deterrent threats illustrates somewhat the "rationality of irrationality." Having committed ourselves to impose some punishment, it indeed does not make sense for us to do so, it is "irrational" to keep our word. The possibility of such irrationality may still be quite effective in deterring our opponent from attacking us, and it is therefore to our benefit (it is "rational") to be known for such "irrationality."

Such a proclivity to fulfilling threats must always be harnessed within a basically purposeful constraint. When the stakes are so high, the rules of this new game can impose very delicate requirements on our foreign and military policy. A basic rule will be that one never kills his last hostage, that one never uses up his last option of imposing discomfort on the enemy, for then the enemy would have nothing left to fear and would impose damage on our side with impunity. An illustrative example emerges from the positions of Sweden and Finland vis-a-vis the Soviet Union. Why has Sweden refused to join NATO, when her defense spending per capita is indeed higher than that of NATO members Denmark and Norway? Why has the USSR never taken over Finland in the same manner as Poland, Czechoslovakia, or Hungary? The answer is largely that each has realized the unpleasantness of such a move for the other, and in effect holds it in reserve to deter the other. Sweden will not join NATO, unless and until a Communist regime appears in Finland. Moscow will not impose a Communist regime in Helsinki unless and until Sweden aligns itself openly with the United States.

Similar relations of bargaining standoffs explain many other arrangements around the globe. Indeed, cooperative bargaining of this kind has gone on for many centuries. What is unique about the nuclear era is that such bargaining can never be put out of mind.

If we accept the need for this cooperative/competitive mixture of bargaining techniques in the conduct of nuclear-age foreign policy, a great number of popular maxims on policy-making might have to be reexamined. Some of such maxims will prove to have been very wise and valuable, others erroneous or obsolete.

For example, it is often suggested that successful policy is advanced when the nation has succeeded in being "predictable," in giving friends and enemies clear signals of what its response will be to any and all of their initiatives. The Korean War may suggest an obvious case supporting this. It is entirely possible that confusing American signals left the North Koreans with an impression that the United States would not defend the regime in the South. The Pyongyang regime thus was led to blunder into a war with the United States it would have wished to avoid, and both sides lost in the unnecessary ensuing hostilities. When we are determined to defend some area, we may as well say so loudly and clearly, for deterrence of aggression is presumably preferable to defense against aggression.

Yet what if our defense of an area is unlikely or totally impossible? Should a state also be predictable here, clearly announcing to the world that it feels unable to intervene in such a region? There are obviously cases where a little uncertainty would work to one's benefit. Why not leave the other side uncertain of whether it can effortlessly seize control over some province or country? Perhaps even a small *unpredictable* risk of American intervention will deter the attack, and the United States would have come out ahead in terms of its policy goals. The American position on the defense of Quemoy and Matsu may illustrate this quite well. At no point has the United States clearly stated that it would defend these islands against a Communist seizure. Yet the failure of Peking's forces to attack has at least in part reflected an uncertainty on whether the United States would remain out of such a conflict.

Another well circulated maxim is that one should maintain flexibility in his foreign policy, avoiding a "rigidity" that might lose opportunities for real agreements or decisive gains. Sometimes this is described in terms of "room for maneuver," not having all one's resources committed and tied up, not being totally locked into a position.

Such room for maneuver and flexibility may indeed pay off handsomely at times. As a general rule, we want to be able to make concessions when they will close a generally good deal which otherwise would fall through. But what of cases where a deal is certain in any event, but the other side is merely delaying and pressing us to win the best possible terms for himself? In such cases, any flexibility and maneuver-space for our side merely weakens our position; if we could plausibly demonstrate that it was impossible for us to make further concessions, we might not have to make any, and we may still get all the terms of agreement we find necessary.

We are similarly accustomed to advice on appeasement versus resistance, in dealing with a potentially aggressive neighbor-state. Appeasement may have gotten an overly bad reputation in the light of its seeming failure vis-a-vis Hitler's Germany. Again, any general endorsement of one policy maxim over another may be premature. When one is dealing with territorial demands which are very likely to be finite, as for example, with Mexican claims on some acres of land along the border between Juarez and El Paso, the surrender of such lands buys much good will, and almost certainly does not inspire new demands on Arizona and New Mexico. If the demands are less finite, however, or if it seems that they will become extended and infinite once the first demands are met, then a tougher resistance may be in order, as in the instance of Hitler's demands for the Sudetenland district of Czechoslovakia.

The crucial issue in each case hinges on the delicate problem of momentum. To surrender too readily can suggest a total absence of resolve, inspiring hunger for much more territory and many more concessions. To resist for a time, when the grievances on the other side are genuine, may, however, also build up a momentum, if our resistance in the end collapses. Sure and steady resistance, or very quick concessions, tailored to particular grievances without implications of later precedents, are presumably what will be required to avoid such aggressive momentum. Some very interesting arguments have been advanced that the Anglo-French failing against Hitler was not pure appeasement, but rather a totally inappropriate mixture of and oscillation between appeasement and resistance, which may have made the Nazis even more aggressive than they would have been on their own.

The term "appeasement" suggests excessive reasonableness, excessive willingness to concede political questions to an opposing position in the interests of long-term peace. Why not advocate exactly an opposite policy, one of excessive unreasonableness? It is at least plausible that the world gives more than its proper share to those who demand more, to those who are especially obnoxious. The policy under consideration would thus be to answer all demands with larger counter-demands, always to be tough and unreasonable, and to cultivate this reputation. If Mexico lays claim to the Chamazal Tract, this policy would suggest asserting some counter-claims to the province of Chihuahua.

Stalinist foreign policy at its worst appeared to be molded along these lines, and many western commentators seemed envious of the results and advantages it apparently offered, sadly concluding that such policy would only be possible in a totalitarian state. Yet a closer look may suggest limitations to a tough policy, every bit as serious as the defects of an excessively agreeable policy. If one always makes counter-claims, in many or most cases quite preposterous in their substance, one's credibility will be challenged, and resistance to one's demands thereby encouraged. We well remember the many ultimata the Russians have issued on West Berlin, but we may too easily forget the willingness of the West to ignore them.

The tough line, if taken seriously, moreover, precludes cooperative ventures with the outside world. It is fully analogous to the grocer who charges higher prices for his wares. His profits per transaction may be higher, but customers will steer clear of him when they can, and he may thus garner a much more meager total of transactions. Sooner or later his net profits will have fallen in his unreasonableness. The USSR indeed has discovered that bluster alienates potential partners as often as it intimidates adversaries.

In the analysis and application of some aspects of game theory, some interesting if debatable maxims have been formulated by analogizing with the game of poker. Indeed there was a time when critics of American foreign policy expressed concern that the American national game was poker, with its encouragement of risk-taking and gambling, while the Russian national game has been chess, with its far greater determinism and deliberation.

A great deal of winning strategy in poker could be summarized as follows: Have one's hands challenged ("called") when they are strong, for this builds up the winnings on each round, but avoid being called when your hand is weak and you in fact are bluffing. The second part of the analogy might seem quite obviously applicable to defense policy and foreign relations; if we do not have sufficient troops to defend Singapore, why not let the other side believe that we do, so that he will not dare to challenge us and call our bluff.

The first part of the poker and analogy might draw more disagreement, however, for we normally will not prefer that an enemy challenge us, even when we have the weapons and troops to give him a sound beating. In a liberal democracy, the ideal would probably be never to have our hands called, to have all military attacks by the enemy deterred whether we have the military tools ready or not. Before rejecting the poker analogy totally, however, one might identify a few exceptional instances in which an enemy attack might be welcomed for the decisive rebuff it will receive. If one intends to impress the opponent and the outside world with one's military superiority for a long time into the future, there may be no more effective way of doing so than to lure the enemy into a short and decisive battle. Such was very probably the reasoning of the Israeli military command in 1967. Such was also probably the reasoning of American military leaders anxious to make Vietnam a test case proving that insurgency could be defeated.

When presenting such explicit analyses of strategy, the temptation is great to assume that something very new has been uncovered, something unknown to statesmen and politicians of earlier decades and centuries. Upon reflection, the international dealings of earlier centuries exhibit many of the same strategems and policies as those outlined here.

But does the quality of the strategic gamesmanship become improved in the process of explicating it? Is it possible that we previously were only intuiting and implicitly using strategies which we can now much more deliberately plot and execute? Explication increases the understanding and therefore very possibly improves the execution of strategic ploys, but it can also interfere with and confuse such strategies. Much of the success of a move of deception naturally depends on the deception being successful, that is, on keeping most people still unaware of its nature. When we explain and clarify strategy in ways that an enemy can read or listen to, however, we offer him the counter-strategy that undoes ours.

Explication of strategic moves can even upset the move's effectiveness at the performing end, as ploys become overly cute or exaggerated in sophistication. American strategy in the bombing of North Vietnam was intended to apply some bargaining lessons learned in the bombings of World War II. If the bombing tool was used inefficiently in 1944 because of insufficient awareness of tacit bargaining techniques, however, Americans may have exaggerated how many subtle distinctions could be communicated to Hanoi in 1967, and the extent to which Hanoi would care about or pay attention to such distinctions.

Excessive strategic manipulation on Vietnam bombing policy may thus exaggerate the ability of the other side to perceive the signals being sent. It may also underrate the ingenuity of the other side. If the North Vietnamese understand the reasoning by which the United States hoped to outlast the Hanoi regime in a contest of endurance, they could thus have known that American endurance would also be finite, and that a policy of one-upmanship here might indeed be successful. It may thus be very important for a practitioner of game-theoretical devices to disguise his perception of these devices. One lesson a reader might draw from having read Thomas Schelling's writings would be to deny having read Schelling. If the essence of the rational interaction game is to manipulate the other fellow's rational processes, this can be upset if he in the meantime discovers a way to manipulate yours.

Even if the other side does not outdo us in strategic cleverness, such cleverness may still be a drawback. When a reputation of deviousness and chicanery is once established, it will be difficult for other nations even as potential allies to develop the trust necessary for successful patterns of cooperation. Much of personal and international interaction is indeed straightforward and automatic. The person or nation that seems to give excessive calculation to each and every act frightens away potential partners.

Considerable attention in the past decade has been devoted to the modes of communication a nation must exploit in the international bargaining process. There was a time when the American ideal was stated as "Open covenants, openly arrived at," but greater experience in foreign policy has shown many limitations for this formula.

Open communications, to be sure, have some considerable advantages. Messages transmitted in this manner will be clear and less subject to misunderstanding. Being open, they will serve to reassure outside parties that their interests are not greatly in danger. Finally, in being open, such agreements will tend to be more binding, since each side's honor and reputation for further agreements will be explicitly at stake in any violations. Secret communications, as with the secret annexes commonly attached to open treaties prior to 1914, thus indeed have a disadvantage in frightening the outsiders whose interests may be damaged. Such agreements presumably are also more subject to a violation by either side, since their terms are published only in the event of a breakdown of cooperation between the parties.

Yet there are advantages to secret communications which may compensate for such drawbacks. Not the least of these is the opportunity for each side to explore the other's position, and to allow its own to be explored, without fear that this will produce embarrassment before the gallery of noncommitted spectators. A Russian willingness to consider forgoing an ABM system will be of interest to all outside powers. If the United States is to have the benefit of dealing with the USSR on this matter, however, it may have to be willing to receive a signal which it does not immediately share with other nations.

A third style of communications might be characterized as neither open nor secret, but rather tacit, exploiting a range of signalling that goes beyond explicit texts and phrases. It is certainly so that what nations do with their armed forces and economic policies can mean more than what they say or promise they will do. Every act in effect is thus an important signal on future acts, and some degree of tacit bargaining is thus almost inevitable.

The laws and political style of war may indeed enhance the importance of such bargaining, since many lines of explicit communication are broken. Ambassadors are withdrawn, and negotiations are typically terminated when war breaks out. For either side to propose the resumption of formal negotiations would be interpreted as a concession to the other. Important agreements on the limitation of war, on the treatment of civilian populations, and so on, are thus "bargained" simply as each side displays its restraint in ways which the other side will recognize. Similar exchanges of displayed mutual restraint may even be crucial to the halting of arms races in peacetime, and may be more important than any formal negotiations intended for this purpose.

Yet there are clearly some drawbacks to this form of communication also, drawbacks which may lead us back to alternative modes. Tacit signals may all too easily be misinterpreted or misunderstood. A subject as technologically cumbersome as ABM and MIRV missiles may require more explicit exchanges of proposals on paper or over a negotiating table. Tacit signals may similarly have to be as openly visible to third parties as to the intended receiver, with whatever embarrassment this entails. If the negotiations were intended to reassure these third parties, moreover, formal negotiations might still more clearly call it to their attention. Formal negotiations, if successful, are more likely to instill the superficial political sense of detente which is helpful in getting other negotiations, tacit or explicit, going.

Other maxims on good foreign policy practice remain to be examined in light of the strategic and communications analysis presented above. Are accessibility and clarity in communications always desirable, as the common sense would have it? Or could a device such as the hot line indeed someday be undesirable? A strategic analysis suggests that a nation might indeed sometimes benefit because its leaders cannot be reached. In cases where the other side is ready to give in, but wishes to try to serve us with one more ultimatum, we will spare ourselves this last threat in being unreachable. The family whose telephone is out of order may be a less inviting target for a kidnapper than the one that can always be reached to settle ransom terms. As earlier on the question of being flexible, the particular state of the bargaining would have to tell us whether unreachability was to our advantage. If peace will collapse unless we answer the phone, we will, of course, be better off for having it in working order.

It would be a mistake, of course, to become too engrossed in the communications process, and to assume that all utterances illustrate attempts to get a message across. Nations may still sometimes satisfy more of their aims in deceiving other nations, so that little or no communication and bargaining is intended.

Communist Chinese messages in the fall of 1950 have been analyzed extensively, in that the United States somehow failed to perceive that Peking was signally its intention to enter the Korean War. Misunderstanding the intense Chinese signal, it is commonly argued, the United States forces pushed to the banks of the Yalu River, and this unacceptable advance provoked the Chinese intervention of which Peking had been warning us. Yet the signals relayed by Peking were less than clear, to say the least, and it is not at all certain that communications incompetence at either end explains the failure of Washington to anticipate this intervention. It is just as likely that the Chinese Communists assumed a surprise intervention would enhance their chances of a military success, a success that would not only keep American forces away from the banks of the Yalu, but also might allow a new sweep southward to win the victory denied the North Koreans six months earlier. To achieve a tactical surprise of this magnitude, it is not necessary to communicate, but rather to dissimulate. If MacArthur and Truman and other American leaders did not realize that a Chinese attack was imminent, so much the better for Peking.

It is therefore inaccurate to assume that communications clarity should always be maximized in the international arena, just as it is inaccurate that the hostility and competition of this arena makes all communication inappropriate. Sometimes we get ahead in our national policies by cooperating and comparing notes; other times we do better by deceiving and double-crossing our partner states.

When we think of communications in international relations, we often focus on those particularly intense periods of bolstered message exchange known as negotiations. Messages flow back and forth at all times, in the various ways listed above, but when the importance of the issues seems to merit it, physical arrangements are made to allow representatives of the sides, usually face to face, to exchange many more messages in hopes that some special agreement may emerge. The erection of the negotiation structure thus presents each of its parties with the inherent three-part choice sketched out by Fred C. Ikle: to settle on particular terms offered by the other side, to continue the negotiations, or to break off the conference.

Breaking off negotiations represents a mutual loss to both sides, unless the entire conference was intended merely as a propaganda exercise. It is difficult to get a conference together after the delegates have gone home; convening it in the first place required a delicate sequence of invitations which compromised neither side from the outset, and this is hard to repeat. With the shadow of an unsuccessful conference hanging over both delegations, each will thus attempt to exploit this shadow to force the other to grant the concessions. Various kinds of advice emerge from our experience with formal international negotiating sessions.

It sometimes is argued that one should seek to move negotiations as much as possible to the other nation's capital, since this will place the opponent in a position of more easily amending his position. When deadlock threatens, one can therefore always plead that communications to win authority for new concessions will simply take too long on our side; the other merely has to walk down the hall to gain the concessions which will keep the negotiations alive. Yet this bargaining ploy is again subject to the limitations stipulated earlier for any tough position. When the nation hosting the negotiations will still not make concessions, we might wish to have given our negotiators authority, if we also prefer to have some deal go through, rather than letting the conference fail.

When dealing with governments and societies characterized by great internal suspicion, a second negotiating maxim has advised delivering written rather than oral statements of position when the message is intended to be relayed to higher authority. If a statement was in writing, the theory goes, the Soviet negotiator would not dare to withhold it from his superiors, lest he be accused of a secretive disloyalty. When the statement was oral, however, he would not dare to attempt to paraphrase it for his superiors, lest in the process he sound sympathetic to the position.

Where greater bargaining leverage is delegated to the negotiators, however, such advice obviously would have to be tempered. A verbal statement of position can be more convincing because it can afford to be more forthcoming and frank; we do not have to fear as much the verbatim quote intended to exploit our concessions to our disadvantage. In every society, negotiators moreover will tend to have a subtle vested interest in successful negotiations. Treaties signed most usually advance the delegates who negotiated them, advance them within their respective bureacratic hierarchies. Conferences that fail do not lead as naturally to promotion. Unless controls from above are extremely terroristic and effective, one's opposite number in negotiations may thus become a partner in quest of an agreement, and a formal document that must be referred back to the national capital might simply get in the way of mutual negotiating success.

Another bargaining maxim has warned against exuding too much confidence in the negotiations. A typical American position is that we surely can agree, if we all are only reasonable in our position. If this is true for much of the domestic bargaining process, it nonetheless gives important advantages to a foreign power confronting us in international negotiation. Our verbal assurances that negotiations will succeed presumably commit our side to making the greater concessions to avert failure. Yet again there may limitations to any tough-minded effort to shift the burden of success over to the opposing side. Not all international negotiations are conducted in an atmosphere which gives conflict great priority over cooperation. If the cooperative interest were already strong, for either side to stress it may convince the other, and may lead to a rapid disposition of the few issues on which disagreement remains.

Continuing on this discussion of bargaining styles in international politics, one might ask whether the outbreak of war does not indeed change all rules and practices drastically, so that most of the above observations would have to be qualified or dismissed. Does war not illustrate a pure conflict of interest, in which no community remains on which negotiation and exchange could be based? As noted earlier, some important communities of interest remain, if only because the nuclear age continually poses the horrendous consequences which all sides have an interest in avoiding.

The negotiating and bargaining here may have to be more tacit and less open, but it goes on nonetheless. Preagreed standards of reference clearly are of help here, and this accounts for much of the viability and relevance of international law on war. International law specifies rules on the treatment of war prisoners and of civilians, the kinds of weapons to be used, the kinds of targets which can be attacked, and so on, rules honored sometimes in the breach, but very often in the practice. Other agreements in wartime are worked out on a more ad hoc basis, without the benefit of prearranged agreements to fall back on, but again with some considerable impact.

The question of the morality or possibility of limited war attracted some considerable attention in the United States in 1950 and 1951 when General MacArthur in effect was arguing that war by its very nature must be prosecuted totally. Yet other military analysts had long ago noted how politics, life, and cooperation continue even if war has erupted. Clausewitz is quoted in many directions, but clearly did note that, "War was the pursuit of politics by other means."

If the tough-minded negotiation approach sketched out here is at all relevant to American dealings with the Soviet Union, does it apply as well to dealings with Allies—for example, with the United Kingdom? Or is there an entirely different "cooperative" approach that should be applied to cases where political or cultural ties draw two nations very closely together?

One answer would deny any significant differences. Anglo-American relations, just like Soviet-American relations, will be a mixture of cooperation and conflict, and one treats his allies with the same tricks and ploys as an "enemy." A counter-position would note that the variations in the mix of cooperation and conflict have to make some difference in the style one adopts, such that at least some ploys and devices will be more often appropriate for Britain than for the USSR.

A more significant difference, however, may relate to the extent to which "close" or "predominantly cooperative" relationships are accompanied by extensive interaction between the two bureaucracies at various levels, so that any strategic analysis of who is influencing whom gets enormously complicated by the infighting and conflicts within the two bureaucracies themselves. In effect, the fiction of national homogeneity becomes all the more of a fiction as the nations differ less in terms of "national interests," as alliances form between segments of each national government against other segments of the same two governments.

One might suspect that the process is enhanced when linguistic unity makes it possible for everyone in one government to communicate easily with everyone in the other. The "special relationship" between the United States and Britain obviously satisfies this condition, as did the alliance between Germany and Austria in 1914. Under such circumstances it may become extremely difficult to talk of one government having "offered," "advised," "threatened" the other, when possibly contradictory messages are flowing from person to person at so many different levels. Even if linguistic commonality is lacking, this process may yet occur if "cooperation" has generated a large infrastructure of joint committees.

Alliances and special relationships thus substantially complicate the application of strategic maxims derived from game theory or other sources. It may become appropriate to apply such theory at the bureau versus bureau level, rather than nation versus nation. Above all, it will require deeper research to unearth the actual constellations of conflicting interests and interest groupings from country to country.

FURTHER READINGS

Ikle, Fred C. *How Nations Negotiate.* New York: Harper and Row, 1964.
Neustadt, Richard E. *Alliance Politics.* New York: Columbia University Press, 1970.
Schelling, Thomas C. *Arms and Influence.* New Haven: Yale University Press, 1966.

CHAPTER TWO

Military
Power

If international politics is predicated on the possibility of war, military force deserves a great deal of our attention. When we talk of government, we are discussing agencies which are just as capable of violence as Hobbes contended. Where the violent capacity is monopolized, we are in the realm of "domestic politics"; where it is not, we have moved into "international politics."

Much political behavior is thus derived from potentials for violence, even where the violence is never exercised. International relations is not war, but the possibility of war. A host of other factors intrude, factors to be discussed through the rest of this study, so that international dealings often enough are conducted with the violent possibilities receding far into the background. Yet if they receded totally, we might no longer be discussing diplomacy, but some form of integrated domestic politics.

At the very least, then, one must set the stage by discussing the forms and structures of military force that cast such a long shadow across this field. There was a time when a discussion of military factors in international politics would naturally have begun with a measurement of comparative "national power," essentially addressing the question of "who can win?" for any war that might be commenced. Answers to such a question would be extracted from statistics on comparative manpower and industrial potential or gross national product (GNP), from an assessment of geographic and strategic location, and perhaps from a slightly more substantive assessment of the comparative military prowess of the national and ethnic groups involved.

There have always been difficulties of prediction here. Manpower and industrial potential have hardly been linearly convertible into indices of military strength, and it has been difficult to forecast how any particular mix would perform. A great deal of legend persists on relative national aptitudes for military campaigns, legend which may be false in its premises, but which might nonetheless thereafter be self-confirming. An army that believes itself to be superior may therefore become so, and vice versa. Germany, for example, is blessed or cursed with a reputation for producing superb fighting forces. Yet a more clearheaded and skeptical analysis of the West German Army has suggested that other NATO contingents would perform far better if war were ever to come, largely because of a chronic shortage of officers and noncommissioned officers in the Bundeswehr. Some other states have a negative legend of tending to lose battles and perform disappointingly in combat. If a well-done systems analysis now showed such a national army to be superior in equipment, training, and leadership, would this indeed be confirmed in wartime?

Some countries may feel happily perplexed by long histories of neutrality and peace, which have precluded their military forces from proving themselves. Sweden, for example, is credited with having a very first-rate army, air force, and navy, based on universal military training, but has not fought any wars or battles since 1815. It is thus hardly surprising that Swedish officers are quite willing to volunteer themselves for duty with United Nations peacekeeping forces; if nothing else, this has offered the practical experience of actual field operations. The Swiss Army is similarly in a position of having objective reason to trust its own competence, while lacking any memorable experience to prove it.

Apart from "who will win?", the military analyst classically addressed himself to "how to win?", putting together a collection of axioms and maxims presumably culled from the experience of history. Since the "lessons of history" often dated from the most recent campaigns, it would not be surprising if many of them proved mutually contradictory, as the successful tactic of one war was undone by the new tactic of the next.

Some strategists have therefore advised that the whole purpose of war must be to destroy the opponent's forces, while others have stressed indirect approaches, which might instead bypass these forces and somehow incapacitate them without the costs of a campaign of direct attrition. Ulyses S. Grant's campaigns in the United States Civil War could indeed be cited as exemplifying the earlier approach, on the notion that the Confederacy would never truly be defeated until its armies had been forced to surrender and disperse. Yet the legendary small team of operatives which penetrates enemy lines to disable huge armies is a staple plot of American war movies, showing how appealing may yet be the avoidance of attrition.

We similarly have historical disagreement on whether or not to take the offensive. The pre-World War I consensus in France and elsewhere indeed seemed to be that the offensive held the advantage, so that sitting on the defensive would only give the initiative needlessly to the enemy. In the aftermath of the gore of World War I trench warfare, the consensus indeed shifted, so much so that American maneuvers for a hypothetical enemy invasion of the Atlantic coast called simply for a withdrawal inland to prepared trenches.

The "old" questions of military strategy have assuredly not lost their political relevance. When choosing sides, many uncommitted persons will wish to know which side is more likely to win the military as well as the political contests. Money spent one way on defense is wasted, spent another way it may bring home political returns well worth the cost. Spent with total success, it might bring world domination and world peace, an end to "international relations," a resumption of "Pax Romana."

Yet if such "selfish" questions remain relevant, some other considerations of "arms control" may exact increasing fractions of our attention. If the old focus of military analysis was on "who would win?" and "how to win?", the newer questions in this field are a little more systematic and a little more world-concerned: Do all weapons, or weapons of a particular type, increase the likelihood of war? If war were to come, do all weapons, or weapons of a certain type, increase the costs and damage inflicted?

This increased concern for the prevention or moderation of war is obviously related to the enormous destructive power which has emerged with nuclear weapons, and the means of delivery which can inflict such destruction at the very end of the fighting even on the victor in war. Enhanced destruction requires that all of us, arms controllers, diplomats, generals, and heads of government, be more concerned about the costliness of war, even if this diverts attention from victory. It means also that each of us will be closely watching the motivation as well as the capability of other parties, for the simple superiority in capability can no longer shield us certainly against unacceptable destruction.

FURTHER READINGS

Earle, Edward Mead. *Makers of Modern Strategy*. Princeton: Princeton University Press, 1948.
Halperin, Morton. *Comtemporary Military Strategy*. Boston: Little, Brown, 1966.
Levine, Robert A. *The Arms Debate*. Cambridge, Mass.: Harvard University Press, 1962.
Wright, Quincy. *A Study of War*. Chicago: Chicago University Press, 1942.

Disarmament

One classic approach to the world peace problem might thus be to aim simply for as much disarmament as possible. A world totally free of arms might make wars impossible, as well as painless. Yet any quick perusal of the history of man's disarmament efforts suggests the enormous problems that remain to be overcome. American and Canadian school children are taught to cherish the agreement which demilitarized their frontier, widely heralded as an example to which all nations might pay heed. Closer study, however, shows a long string of American violations of the commitment to keep the Great Lakes and the frontier area unfortified, violations accompanied by repeated, but largely futile, Canadian protests. The real tranquility of Canadian-American relations should thus perhaps be traced instead to the disappearance of political issues between the two countries, an absence of issues which in turn has allowed some disarmament of sorts to occur. If the demilitarized Canadian-American frontier has been a myth, moreover, it may have been a very useful and even self-confirming one over time. "Almost adhering" to one's treaty commitments may be better for the world than never having entered into treaty commitments at all.

More serious and worldwide efforts at disarmament were undertaken at the Hague conferences of 1899 and 1907, which composed a number of rules of warfare, some of which were thereafter adhered to, and some not. While several governments participated only to please and satisfy the idealist aspirations of the Russian czar, the codification of rules on possible use of weapons in the future was a useful exercise, as long as no nation had acquired any substantial advantage in violating the rules. A ban on explosive bullets (dum-dum bullets) has generally been adhered to since, perhaps sparing the soldier in the field some of the more horrible wounds incurred in the American Civil War. A prospective ban on bombardment from the air was never generally ratified, and indeed was not adhered to as World War I broke out.

In the aftermath of World War I, the members of the League of Nations felt obligated to pursue arms limitation and disarmament much more seriously. In part this was because the world blamed the war's outbreak on the arms races that had preceded it. Fears had also emerged of a new naval arms race among the recent allies, Great Britain, the United States, and Japan, as well as France and Italy. A disarmament had moreover been imposed on Germany as the loser of the war, a disarmament which might be permanized with difficulty if other nations did not agree to match it.

The Washington Conference of 1921–22 and the London Conference of 1930 indeed succeeded in placing some limits on the number of naval vessels procured by the major sea powers. In disarmament, the problem is typically twofold—achieving agreement on fair ratios, and achieving assurance that agreed ratios will in fact be observed. The latter problem was inherently easier to solve on large naval vessels than on any other forms of weaponry, if only because none of the societies involved were "closed" enough to allow for secret and undetected construction of such ships.

Parallel efforts at comprehensive disarmament were undertaken at conferences sponsored by the League of Nations in Geneva from 1932 to 1934, but the attempts failed in a conflict between German demands for equality of status, British interests in serious disarmament, and French contentment with the unequal military status quo. If any compromise had been possible over a longer run, it was foreclosed by the rise of Adolf Hitler to power in Germany; Hitler directed the German delegation to withdraw from the negotiations in 1934.

Since World War II, a virtually continuous mandate for disarmament has existed under the aegis of the United Nations. At times nuclear disarmament has been discussed separately from conventional disarmament, while in other years the fields have been merged. Discussions have sometimes been shifted to small committees of only 5, or 10, or 18, or 26, or then again only two powers. Other discussions have been conducted within a General Assembly format allowing every UN member to participate.

Before discussing the prerequisites for success in disarmament discussions, one should attempt to be clear about what we are intending to avert in such talks, what indeed we mean by "arms races."

An arms race can mean a quantitative relationship of the policy preferences of two or more powers whereby no equilibrium of their military strengths can be found. Each side may regard the arms stockpile of the other side as the determinant of what its own stockpile should be, and makes its weapons procurement decisions accordingly. These decisions having been made, each side then revises its own decisions, based on the new weapons procurements of the other. If the graph below were accurately to portray the relative preferences of two such military powers, it is evident that no real equilibrium would be possible once the levels at point B had been passed, as each simply raced to purchase weapons as rapidly as its economy allowed.

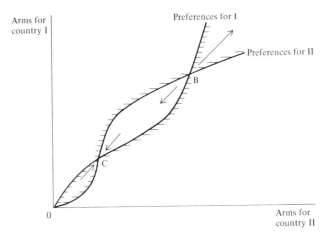

In the graph shown above, hope for disarmament might emerge if the two sides could once be induced to shift their armaments levels below point

B. Having dropped below this point, the two sides indeed would disarm further until reaching an attractive equilibrium at point C.

Yet there are other forms of "arms race" without the clear lack of equilibrium depicted above. The confrontation just discussed is characterized by an open-ended sense of extreme urgency in which each state is racing to spend as much as it can on arms. If we were in more of an equilibrium which precluded such urgency and panic, we might yet style it an "arms race," simply because large sums of money were still being spent year-by-year on armaments. An "arms race" here might thus simply be defined as any case of extensive expenditures on arms.

Apart from such arms races which can be measured and described quantitatively, we often also speak of qualitative arms races, as improved weapons each year replace existing ones. It might be difficult here to show that numbers of weapons had increased, but the fighting power of each arsenal certainly has, with the result that the power of the opposite arsenal also must follow suit.

Just as in the quantitative races noted above, qualitative arms races at the extreme may reflect a total absence of equilibrium, with each side instantaneously insisting on having better weapons than the other and racing to acquire them as quickly as possible. In a more subdued form this "qualitative" race may simply reflect the improvements that ongoing research and technology make possible year after year. Such improvements may result from research conducted under military auspices, or from "spinoffs" of civilian-oriented research, or even from pure science. If a new electrical storage battery is invented, each side will naturally wish to install it in its submarines, and thereafter will naturally have more powerful and effective submarines than before.

We may want to curtail or halt arms races in any or all of the forms just described, but doing so will not be easy. As noted earlier, agreement may be quite difficult to reach on fair terms. Perhaps more importantly, it will be very difficult to assure each side that the other is indeed adhering to terms once they have been agreed to. If information flows imperfectly back and forth, each side will see no assurance that the other is not cheating, and each will see no reason why it should not itself cheat.

A reasonable observer of the international scene would thus expect nations always to disarm only some fraction of what they have promised to, and the crucial question will entail estimating this fraction from society to society, and country to country. Both nations considering an arms limitation agreement might indeed prefer mutual disarmament to the continued arms procurement race, but each will even more prefer the unilateral disarmament of its opponent, and will be tempted to reach for this option whenever imperfect monitoring makes it possible.

As noted earlier, successful disarmament in the past has most notably occurred in categories which were self-inspecting, as with large capital ships in the Washington and London treaties. Since 1945, a most serious obstacle to disarmament has been the secretive nature of Soviet Russian society, which would have allowed production of nuclear weapons, tanks, airplanes, if not capital ships, without the outside world being aware of it. As the societies stood, the United States would have been markedly less able to engage in clandestine armaments production. The quotient of real to promised disarmament in the Russian case would thus have been much less than that for the United States, and disarmament agreements without additional inspection arrangements would have altered substantially the balance of military power.

The United States and its allies have thus consistently demanded the installation of an outside inspection agency to police Soviet compliance with disarmament agreements, thus to make mutually reliable disarmament possible. This demand has been made with regard to virtually all the reductions of armament discussed at Geneva since the mid-1950's, as well as to a ban on testing of nuclear weapons, where the U.S. in the end proved willing to accept only a partial test-ban, contending that the USSR would clandestinely test-detonate its weapons underground. Yet inspection arrangements have had political effects and costs of their own, especially in a society such as the Russia of Stalin. Even today, the Soviet leadership displays considerable nervousness about the impact of teams of inspectors from foreign countries wandering through factories, military installations, and Russian cities.

It is thus entirely possible that the political exigencies of a relatively totalitarian society have forced the Russian government to deny the need for surveillance on many disarmament agreements, even when it knew that many such agreements could not be effective without this kind of monitoring. It is also possible that some other disarmament agreements would not really have required supplementary monitoring arrangements over this period, in that information on infractions of the agreement would naturally have flowed back and forth between the sides. In some cases, the United States may thus have insisted on inspection arrangements where they truly were not needed.

In either of these cases, the side adopting the disingenuous attitude has expected to come out ahead regardless of what the other side does. When the Russians convincingly deny real needs for inspection, the U.S. must either submit itself to unequal disarmament or be branded before neutral opinion as the obstacle to arms control. When the Americans convincingly state a case for inspection which in truth is not required, they similarly confront the Russians with a choice of accepting the potentially unsettling presence of foreigners, or of accepting the apparent onus of preventing disarmament.

While the imagery of the secretive Soviet Union and the open United States has almost been taken for granted since 1945, this imagery is now changing in some interesting ways. It is indeed almost impossible to ensure that any nuclear power will now have totally divested itself of nuclear weapons, if it ever came to a question of agreeing to total disarmament. The United States would be just as suspect of having secreted away some nuclear warheads as the USSR. The more interesting question for the moment attaches to preventing the further spread of nuclear weapons to nations beyond the five that presently possess them, the U.S., USSR, France, Britain, and Communist China. On this latter "proliferation" question, the Russians, in the negotiation of the Nuclear Non-Proliferation Treaty (NPT), have come to insist on fairly thorough inspection, particularly of West Germany, to preclude a clandestine program for nuclear weapons manufacture. If nations on "our side" at last can be suspected of some significant secrecy, this serves to lift the abstract debate on the needs for, and merits of, outside inspection from a purely Cold War context.

Verification has moreover lost some of its significance with the appearance of unilateral information-gathering devices such as the earlier U-2 flights, and the reconnaissance satellites that both the U.S. and Soviet Union now regularly place into orbits around the earth. As each side can be more certain that the other is substantially limited in its force procurements, each can more easily relax its own procurement schedules. While the Soviet Union tolerated the U-2 flights for a time, it protested them openly after it acquired the interceptor capacity to shoot one down. With regard to the satellite reconnaissance, neither side has protested such "violations of air-space." While opponents of all military equipment may object to investment in reconnaissance "spy" satellites, along with the missiles they resemble, closer analysis suggests that the development of one has helped to constrict investments in and development of the other.

If substantial disarmament were possible, we would have to ask also whether it was indeed as desirable as is typically assumed. It seems clear that lower armament levels normally will mean lesser expenditures and costs, and therefore leave more resources free for civilian purposes. It is less certain that disarmament will always mean a lessened risk of war. We must also question whether disarmament indeed so surely reduces the costs of any war that might break out.

To turn first to the extreme case of total disarmament, sometimes labeled General and Complete Disarmament (GCD), such a move faces almost insuperable problems, including basic difficulties of definition. If we all agree to abolish our armed forces totally, are we agreed on what is an armed force? What of the police, which in some countries have at times displayed very military equipment and discipline? What of angry mobs which may be less spontaneous than they seem, or gymnastic societies which in their drills seem remarkably like soldiers?

Apart from definitional problems which can produce genuine or feigned misunderstandings, enormous problems of verification will emerge, especially now that so much destructive power can be packaged into small nuclear weapons. In countries which have already produced such weapons in the thousands, foolproof inspection to assure a return to the zero-level is almost hopeless. It is not even certain that inspection can assure that nations now at the zero-level will remain there. If the Soviet Union, the United States, Britain, France, and China were honestly to divest themselves of all nuclear weapons, it surely would be meaningless if some other nations were to refound the "nuclear club"; yet the political temptation to do so would be enormous, and the temptation to withhold a few warheads in the existing nuclear-weapons states would be similarly great.

It will thus be clear that partial disarmament is the best we can hope for in the near future; perhaps it is preferable to more substantial disarmament, even if the latter could be achieved. The atmosphere of total disarmament might be pleasant, but that of almost-total could be quite the reverse. Suspicions of deception and violation would abound, as the assured retaliatory potential of the major powers became less and less assured. Speculation would shift to other forms of weaponry, perhaps to chemical and biological substances that might double as weapons. Speculation would also shift to other nations as foci of military power; nations which never before had experienced such a grand role might feel tempted by any vaccuum so voluntarily created by the former "great powers."

Before turning to more limited and concrete arms control proposals, some alternatives of procedural approach should first be considered. As with other subjects of communication and negotiation, we can debate the merits of open or secret diplomacy, and of explicit versus tacit bargaining. Open discussions of disarmament proposals generate more explicit understandings and more binding commitments, but run the risk of leading the significant powers to play to the galleries of neutral nations in hopes of winning propaganda gains. Tacit agreements can bypass the formalities and publicity of the negotiating process, but may set up confusions which preclude mutual arms restraint even when adequate surveillance existed.

At times, the major military powers, moreover, will not by playing to the gallery of other states, but rather will wish to cooperate against them, as for example in containing the spread of nuclear weapons. Secret or tacit negotiations may make it easier for them to compare notes on arms control strategy without giving this strategy away to the "opposing side." Formal negotiations, as in the SALT talks, may be needed, however, to set up the image of mutual sacrifice and disarmament necessary to induce restraint by such potential "nth" powers.

The consideration of arms control negotiating procedures cannot be limited simply to what substantive accomplishments are thereby achieved. The mere appearance of agreement in such negotiations may have beneficial effects per se, serving in effect as an exchange of compliments, an exchange of compliments which can in turn trigger new waves of detente and an easing of political hostility. Thus even such meaningless steps as the demilitarization of Antarctica or outer space can be important in reshaping the images that the United States and the Soviet Union have of each other. Negotiation procedures must further incorporate an understanding of how bureaucracies function from state to state. Negotiations conducted explicitly rather than tacitly may well reflect credit and prestige and power on organizations such as the U.S. Arms Control and Disarmament Agency (ACDA) and its Soviet equivalent. If negotiations on some small item indeed advance someone within the Soviet bureaucracy who thereafter will have a vested interest in disarmament, it will be sensible to strive for any small agreement simply in hopes of encouraging further and more important agreements later.

FURTHER READINGS

Etzioni, Amitai. *The Hard Way to Peace.* New York: Collier, 1962.
Huntington, Samuel P. "Arms Races: Prerequisites and Results." Edited by Carl J. Freidrich and Seymour E. Harris. *Public Policy.* Cambridge, Mass.: Graduate School of Public Administration, Harvard University, 1958.
Spanier, John W., and Nogee, Joseph L. *The Politics of Disarmament: A Study in Soviet-American Gamesmanship.* New York: Praeger, 1962.

"Arms Control"

Total disarmament ("General and Complete Disarmament") may be undesirable even if it can be achieved, as it will produce great political tensions and mutual mistrust. It will probably be extremely difficult to achieve in any event. It may thus be necessary for us to choose among weapons, to develop rules of thumb to help us in steering away from the kinds of armaments that are most likely to produce more frequent or more costly wars.

For example, the superpowers may move to acquire weapons which allow calm deliberation rather than quick decisions in the event of a political crisis, as with missiles which can be kept stored underground rather than being left in the open. Certain areas may be declared out-of-bounds for the deployment or use of nuclear weapons. Without such a declaration, other areas may come under tacit restraints on the use of various weapons even when war has broken out. Arms suppliers may agree to curtail deliveries into certain areas, or to concentrate on defensive rather than offensive arms in such deliveries. Partial restraints may be arranged on military budgets and strategic weapons procurements in general, so as to save each side some amount of money.

Abstractly one must even consider removing bans on certain weapons, if these were to replace other, more obnoxious arms, or if they somehow made war less likely or less inhuman. For example, we might consider removing the taboo on chemical and biological weapons, or at least on some forms of poison gas, perhaps in exchange for placing a ban on the use of napalm. Proponents of gas warfare have often assembled their case on the argument that the crucial factor is the relationship of persons hurt and incapacitated in wartime. Ideally we should seek to prevent the enemy from killing or wounding us without in the process killing or wounding him. Experience suggests that this ratio of temporary incapacitation to permanent damage was higher for gas than for explosives in World War I, and research in nonlethal chemical warfare might carry this further.

One indeed already has borderline cases of gases being used militarily, albeit that these are nonlethal tear and nausea-producing gases. The distinction between riot control and counter-insurgency or conventional warfare has become obscured in the last decade, and partisans of chemical warfare could well argue that the taboo is unclear enough for us to consider discarding it.

Opponents of such a change could, however, point to some extremely lethal options that would be created hereby, as very small dosages of CBR substances can kill enormous numbers of people. Some of these most highly toxic agents are chemical, although the greater number are biological. Conversely, the more interesting possibilities of painless or even psychedelic warfare lie in the chemical rather than biological realm. Hence supporters of chemical warfare might yet try to split the CBW combination into a tolerance for chemical warfare (already partially tolerated anyway) combined with a renewed taboo on biological materials.

Yet the important point here is that all such analysis tends to ignore the heavy influence and momentum of any rule that has long been observed. Only part of the argument for any mutually observed distinction on restraints on warfare can be based on the substantive issues. Much of it must come instead from the simple awareness on both sides that tradition is behind a rule as it stands. As enunciated most clearly by Thomas Schelling, each side tends to grasp for salient landmarks to divide the field and to coordinate on what will be avoided and what will be tolerated. The saliency need not be as crisp in reality as it is perceived to be, for it is the mutual perception that accomplishes the restraining and limiting effect. If the United States has thus almost adhered to its commitments to disarm its Canadian boundaries, this is close enough to be described to schoolchildren as mutual adherence, and the restraints involved are self-perpetuating. Similarly, the United States and other states have *almost* adhered to a policy of never using chemical warfare; if close analysis shows that chemical warfare by any meaningful definition has indeed been carried on, this fact makes no difference as long as most of the world does not see it that way.

It would thus be quite difficult or impossible for any single state now to

win acceptance and recognition for a new line of restraint, whereby, for
example, napalm was outlawed and psychedelic gases were tolerated. Abstract reasoning on the pluses and minuses of particular weapons systems
must indeed be carried on, but this cannot be implemented apart from a
further consideration of the political and psychological background.

One of the more useful abstract rules for practicable arms control might
thus focus on the classic distinction between offense and defense. The
distinction has indeed also been distorted and propagandized a great deal,
so that many commentators today see nothing real anymore in the distinction. For example, almost no nation will admit that it ever is taking the
offensive in any grand sense. Why was the War Department in the United
States made part of the Defense Department? Japan, forbidden by its constitution from possessing armed forces, instead must be content with "Self-
Defense" forces. President Kennedy, in warning the Russians on the
deployment of Soviet military equipment in Cuba, specified offensive weapons as objectionable, while implicitly thereby tolerating defensive forces.

Occasionally the bias of verbalisms is reversed to advocate the offense,
as with advice that "The best defense is a good offense," or injunctions that
the nations should be "taking the offensive" in the same sense as showing
some initiative. Since many games lend themselves to analogy with military
battlefields, (for example, American football, but also the rest of the world's
soccer), the offense retains at least some legitimacy. In all such games, even
in American baseball, the offense presumably is the part of the game in
which one can change the score in one's own favor. Keeping the score as
it is, is the function of the defense, changing it is the offensive. Since no
one can win without at least once altering the score from 0–0 to something
better, the offense is indispensible.

Psychologically, people who are offensive are hardly respectable or over-
burdened with legitimacy, for they offend. Yet to be "defensive" is also less
than noble, betraying insecurities, excessive caution, a preoccupation with
warding off criticism which precludes the taking of any interesting initiatives.

The offense-defense distinction still has some reality for military analysis,
even when it has been confused and abused in other realms. It would seem
intuitivly obvious that the ability to move, when coupled with destructive
power, favors the offense. Yet a detailed explanation of this may be a little
more complicated. One link would be related to vulnerable sides of the
military force being attacked, the Achilles' heels, or blind spots. In the case
of the individual soldier, it is clear that he might be vulnerable to spear or
sword attacks from the direction in which he could not see. Even with
larger groups of men, if efficiency required that an entire company face
in the same direction in order to achieve a more efficient level of firepower,
this would only be at the risk that an attack coming from another direction
would not be rebuffed. Aside from blindness and the inability to fend off

the attack, there will be parts of the human body, or of the body of a band of soldiers, which are extraordinarily vulnerable, such that a wound incapacitates the entire unit. The supplies of a company of soldiers will thus invite destruction more than an equivalent mass of the soldiers themselves; the ability to move rapidly may enable an enemy force to strike at such vulnerable supplies, or from an undetected direction. In the case of aircraft attacking other aircraft, the angle of attack is all the more crucial; one airplane aloft attacking an airbase can destroy a great number on the base runways, and victory may depend on who gets his mobile airplanes over the other side's bases before the situation is reversed.

A second link between mobility and the offensive advantage does not depend on any such weak spots or angles of attack, but rather on the plausible mathematics of comparative attrition in straight combat—mathematics which suggest that one imposes far more losses than one suffers if one can first develop a numerical superiority. Whether or not the Lanchester Square Law states the relationship quite accurately, it suggests the drift of things, positing that the ratio of casualties suffered in land, sea, or air battle will normally be in inverse ratio to the squares of the forces involved. Thus if one side has 5 times as many airplanes as the other, the second side might suffer 25 times as many casualties.

Lanchester Square assumptions, of course, assume no complications due to terrain or fortifications favoring one side or the other, and no superior strategic decisions which cleverly exploit blind spots or weak spots. On such an abstract battlefield, victory will go to the side which brings its forces to bear most effectively, generally exploiting concentrations of force wherever the commitments of the country would allow. Thus we have the naval maxim of "never divide the fleet," which, of course, cannot be followed literally if more than one harbor is to be protected, or if merchant ships are to be convoyed, but nonetheless illustrates the drift of the considerations relevant to outright battle at sea.

It thus makes sense in winning wars to overwhelm parts of the enemy by suddenly massing one's forces to achieve vast local superiorities. If the enemy knows where such attacks are coming, he can counter by committing his reserves to the same sectors of the front. Increasing the mobility of the forces involved thus obviously allows for more effective surprises by such troop massings, with victory coming to whoever takes the initiative in attacking when he has a numerical superiority he can exploit. Lessened mobility, conversely, would give the threatened side more time in which to detect the threat and move troops to reduce it.

Some weapons help the initiator of combat more than the noninitiator; such weapons may be portable and thus allow attacks from unexpected angles, they may simply work better when away from their bases of operations. These weapons should be classified as offensive.

Other weapons help the initiator of combat less than the noninitiator.

They are typically weapons tied to a location which the enemy must enter to become exposed. These weapons can be classified as defensive. Examples of the latter type would include antiaircraft guns, trenches, and fortifications. In the offensive weapon category we might include bomber aircraft and tanks. A very sophisticated example of a recognition of this distinction came with U.S. congressional authorization for the arming of merchant ships in World War I. To assure that such armaments would not be used to commence hostilities, and thereby compromise American neutrality, cannons installed on such ships were sited only to fire backwards. The weapons thus would never facilitate the initiation of hostilities with, or pursuit of, another ship; the other ship would have to be in pursuit of the American freighter to become exposed to its fire.

One can base the distinction slightly differently in asking where weapons could possibly be used, regardless of their effectiveness. An antiaircraft gun or coastal artillery piece might be so permanently located that it would never have a target until the enemy had violated the nation's boundaries; clearly we would call the weapon defensive. An ICBM might only be usable against targets on another continent, as the name suggests, thus never finding a target within our own boundaries even if the enemy has violated the boundaries; it would then catch the label of offensive. Offense and defense were thus closely related here in terms of technology, but they may nonetheless all along have been at odds in terms of psychology, for development of the offensive might seem to be far more innovative than the development of defense.

In part this is because the defense basically seeks to preserve the status quo, while the offense seeks to alter it. Contentment with the political status quo one is defending may thus breed contentment with one's arrangements for defending it; great discontent with the political status quo may in its frustration breed continual revision in the approaches to attacking it. A second reason for such a difference is simply that the physical arrangements for the defense will stress permanent fixtures anchored to the ground in particular locations, reinforcing the ability of a force in that location to fight off a far larger force. Offensive preparations by contrast tend to stress mobility and movement. Having erected a fortress on a particular location tends to inhibit speculation about what newer model fortresses could have been put in its place. Marginal and incremental additions may be possible, but if one does not wish to leave this section of the frontier temporarily undefended, one can not easily tear the obsolescent redoubt down and lay a new foundation. Components of a flexible and mobile offensive force can be shuffled and rotated in ways which allow for a modernization while the force remains at close to full strength; this is much more difficult in a defensive line.

The probability of war is clearly affected by how effective offensive weapons seem to be, as compared with defensive, and by how much the rival nations invest in each. If both sides are primed to reap advantages by pushing into each other's territory, war may be extremely likely whenever political crisis erupts. If the defense holds the advantage, by contrast, each side in a crisis will probably wait a little longer, in hopes that the other will be so foolish as to take the offensive.

The balance of power system, to be effective, depended on some advantage for the defense in combat. If there had been no such advantage, one country might often have overwhelmed and conquered another before a third had time to intervene. The underlying principle of the balance was that disengaged third, fourth, and fifth countries would tend to intervene on the side that seemed to be losing. Even if country A had attacked B, clearly as an aggressor, aid would come to A instead of B, whenever B had repulsed the attackers and was itself advancing into A's territory. The object of intervention was thus not moral and judicial, but very power-political and practical. For A to absorb B or B to absorb A would equally be a disaster for C, D, and E.

If the advantage of defense over offense were absolute, there might never have been a need for intervention, as everyone would be able to defend his own sovereignty against absorption, relying on the defensive positions preestablished on his own territory. The balance of power system would thus never have appeared. If the offense had been very effective, there might never have been time for outsiders to judge who was going to win in a fast-moving war; other considerations would have had to determine the patterns of intervention, considerations different from the principles of the balance of power approach.

For many situations, the offensive-defensive distinction will hinge directly on the casualty exchange rate. With weapons of a certain kind, does one suffer fewer casualties (and impose more) by making the attack, or does one do better by letting the other side make it? The earlier intercontinental missiles clearly tended to be defensive by this criterion. If one fired off 20 missiles directed at the enemy's missile siloes, one could not expect, with the best of luck, to destroy 20, but more probably 10 or 12. Similarly, if the other side struck at us, he would expend 20 and we might only lose 12. In terms of force survival, such exchange rates favored taking the defensive, and discouraged initiating war. In a crisis they made war less likely by removing incentives to preemption and going first.

An obvious counter-example can emerge if each of these missiles is refitted with accurate multiple warheads, warheads which can separate from a single missile and can strike at several missile siloes at the other end. In such a case, 20 of our missiles with luck may destroy many more than 20 at the other end. If we waited, moreover, only 20 of their missiles might be expended to destroy many more than 20 of ours. The encouragement of war here is clear, in ambiguous crisis situations. The missiles, as "improved" with multiple warheads, favor the offense. Another example emerges, of course, in the confrontations of Israeli and Arab air forces in the Middle East, where the Israeli force, by taking the initiative, could destroy many more airplanes than it would lose. If Arab air forces could exercise even a similar advantage by hurtling themselves into Israeli air space, the encouragement to war in a crisis was only too apparent.

We do not have to advance beyond Sun Tzu or past Clausewitz to find classical recognition of the importance of the distinction between offensive and defensive. Clausewitz noted that if the defense were not generally superior to the offense, war would always have to be to the military advantage of one side or the other.

Thus far this definition of weapons has been almost entirely related to their "counter-force" effect, the ability of weapons-carriers to incapacitate the weapons-carriers of the opposing side. If a single bomber can destroy many bombers parked on airport runways across the border, the bomber in this reference is a weapons system that encourages taking the offense. If a single machine gun located in a concrete fortification or "pill-box" can incapacitate hundreds of soldiers who are crossing borders to carry rifles or machine guns toward it, this is a weapons system favoring defense and discouraging any recourse to the offensive.

Weapons can have a counter-value effect apart from the counter-force effect, the two at times being difficult to separate. Disabling the enemy's forces can include shooting soldiers, interdicting supplies, disabling munitions factories, and bombing the homes of the munitions workers to deny them the sleep required to be effective at their machines. Yet the same or similar weapons can be used to destroy cities and homes, and to kill civilians, where there is no material impact discernible on the enemy's ability to conduct military operations.

Aside from the impact on the war industry, is a weapon which can level residential areas of opposing cities offensive or defensive? If it has no impact on the comparative attrition of force levels, we might be tempted to define it as neither, as belonging to some third category. This would add to our precision here, but unfortunately it might require too great a departure from normal English usage. Since an atomic bomb *changes* a city by destroying it, the public normally would regard it as offensive without any semantic qualms about the use of words. Yet this kind of "offensive" which destroys civilians rather than soldiers drastically changes the wars that soldiers, disarmers, or arms controllers will have to contemplate.

FURTHER READINGS

Edwards, David V. *Arms Control in International Politics.* New York: Holt, Rinehart and Winston, 1969.

Schelling, Thomas C., and Halperin, Morton H. *Strategy and Arms Control.* New York: Twentieth Century Fund, 1961.

The Logic of the "Balance of Terror"

Aside from the likelihood of war, any modern arms control analysis must concern itself with the costs of war. It is not automatically true that all new weapons make war more costly; as noted, some might indeed have an opposite effect. Yet the weapons which we regard as most obviously "new," specifically atomic and hydrogen weapons, would certainly make any future war horrible beyond the most awful nightmares of the past. The advent of the airplane may have introduced the "permeability" of which John Herz spoke, whereby frontier forces will never again be effective enough to shield the population of any country against outside attack. Perhaps it was the addition of the nuclear explosive which made the air-delivered threat more saliently menacing, although one need only examine some casualty figures of the "conventional" bombing raids of World War II to see other forms of this increasing horror of war.

One is thus confronted with a relatively new constraint, that one's population can suffer greatly even if one's armies and navies win all the battles. Perhaps this was also true in the earlier times of city-states, with territorial extents so limited that they were always vulnerable to a "last-gasp" retaliatory raid by the other side. Coastal cities even in the 19th century felt themselves vulnerable to gunboat raids and thereby some forms of gunboat diplomacy. The airplane now extends this threat to all sizes of states, and to all cities within such states.

The combination of the increasing costs of war and the offensive-defensive distinction generates some complicated and interesting interactions; hopefully they may yet produce a new form of balance to preserve peace, a "balance of terror" rather than "balance of power." Even when the military aspect of some stage of weaponry encouraged the taking of the offensive, the costs which the winner would inevitably incur in the retaliation against his population might now conceivably deter and prevent such attacks. It thus is possible that increasing the costs of war has decreased the probability of war. Ideally we would desire to decrease both the likelihood and costs of war. Sometimes we can decrease the likelihood of war by avoiding procurement of the kinds of weapons which make war militarily attractive. If this should prove impossible from time to time, as technology perversely places offensive temptations before us, we might still hope that the enormous horror of war will itself prevent its outbreak.

To understand the strategic balance now operating in the world, we might first try to sort out the categories of goals of either of the superpowers, for example, the United States. A primary goal, of course, is to prevent general war, generally by deterring the nuclear powers from launching it, as well as by preventing and dissuading other states from becoming nuclear powers. Some commentators might claim that this should be the only goal of military policy, now that war has become so horrible, but actual practice would belie this as a description of any of the major powers' operating goals.

Related to preventing general war is reducing costs to the United States if such a war were ever to come nonetheless. Some costs simply reflect the mutual horror of war. If various practices can be outlawed, if various restraints can be enshrined, the costs to the United States and its enemy may be significantly reduced. Other costs for the United States relate to who "wins or loses" such a war, who has political control over the globe after all the missiles have been fired or destroyed, after negotiations have begun. Costs for the U.S. would be gains for the enemy, and vice versa, but decisions on the procurement of strategic weapons systems may still indeed be influenced by such potential outcomes.

Another goal of American policy obviously is to deter attacks on those industrialized countries with which we maintain friendly political and economic relations—Western Europe and Japan, to be specific. Perhaps the loss or destruction of Paris is not exactly equivalent to the loss of Pittsburgh, but the United States, since 1945, has indeed been ready to go very far in committing itself to defending these areas. Economic interdependence may explain some of this commitment, but such an economic interrelationship is also accompanied by a sense of cultural and political similarity that leaves Americans, in any event, reluctant to see these areas conquered by the Red Army.

There are various ways in which attacks on Europe, Japan, and Australia can be deterred or otherwise prevented. Yet again one can not terminate his analysis here with prevention of attack, for the U.S. has also had to be worried about reducing losses and costs if a war nonetheless were to break out. A defense of Paris or West Germany which destroyed these areas might seem somewhat fruitless. So also would be a defense which failed, allowing the Russians to move into Paris whenever they had decided that the American deterrent was no longer credible.

Another goal has extended American interests to deterring or preventing open military attacks on the rest of Asia and Africa, on areas not fully developed economically, but with political systems congenial with the United States. If American commitment here seems less strong than in the case of Western Europe, it has meant that nuclear responses would be less credible, so that some other punitive factors had to be arrayed to dissuade a potential enemy from embarking on aggression. Perhaps this would bring in conventional intervention and resistance as in the Korean War, or simply the superiority of American naval and air forces, as in the case of Taiwan. The strength of indigenous forces might indeed suffice so that little or no American participation was required, as in the Indian defensive position against Communist China in the Himalayas.

The last decade has finally seen the definition of another category of American strategic goal, the deterrence or prevention of "subconventional" attacks on regimes of which we approve, attacks using the methods of guerrilla warfare. Whereas the 1955 predictions were that South Vietnam would have to prepare for an armored attack from the North, similar to the North Korean attack on South Korea in 1950, events since then have shown the power of a much more diffuse offensive, using small bodies of troops which typically remain out of uniform and avoid trying to capture and hold territory.

Confronting this array of American goals to be served by strategic policy, an array which has a symetrical resemblance to the array motivating the Soviet Union, one must note how strains emerge within any pair of such goals, such that no one of them can be stressed without damaging the others. For example, does one stress deterring World War III, or winning it if it comes? Certain kinds of new missiles might facilitate vastly more effective strikes against Russian missile bases if war were ever to break out, but might stampede the two superpowers into such a war, simply because the USSR felt so vulnerable. There is a similar interaction between deterring Russian attacks on Western Europe and deterring World War III. American nuclear weapons deployed in West Germany greatly increase the chances of any local war escalating to all-out war. At the margin they probably reduce the chances of anyone launching such aggression from the Warsaw Pact side. Yet these tactical nuclear weapons also marginally increase the chances of all-out war.

Many commentators have expected West Europeans, especially West Germans, to be uneasy about the tactical nuclear weapons deployed for their defense, because of a fear that these would destroy most of the territory being defended, and indeed turn it into a desert. Yet the vulnerable parties involved have come to reason that this likelihood will also deter the Russians from ever attacking, since it will be pointless to conquer a totally destroyed territory. On the trade-off between deterring a European War and improving its outcome, the NATO countries have thus tended to stress the former over the latter, and have resisted American moves toward an opposite stress.

Since 1945, the prevention of a World War III and of other wars has thus depended very substantially on the threats of severe aerial bombardment. The conventional wisdom today is that the United States would destroy most of the Soviet Union in retaliation for any major attacks, and that the Soviet Union would similarly devastate the United States in response to any initiation of all-out war. This "balance of terror" is now almost taken for granted, but we still must spell out some of the prerequisites and implications of such a balance.

The balance depends, of course, on each side having the ability to retaliate, including massive explosives and the means of delivering them to target. It has further depended on each side's strategic forces not being vulnerable to preemptive attacks by the other side. The United States would hardly be as deterred from leveling Moscow, if on the same bombing raid it could destroy all the Russian aircraft that would have retaliated against New York.

The balance finally depends on such retaliatory responses being made credible. A skeptical analyst might wonder why the destruction of American cities rationally required the response of destroying Russian cities. The survivors in America would indeed be no better off because revenge has been exacted, and quite possibly would be worse off if the Soviet Union had been a potential source of relief supplies. Yet such analysis exaggerates the deliberate or rational quality of any decisions that would be made in the aftermath of such brazen and destructive war-initiation. Few observers can seriously doubt that the two major powers would go through with their "massive retaliation" threats if large portions of their population had just been murdered.

The credibility problem much more typically arises on other objects of retaliatory action. If World War III can be deterred by this threat, it is more debatable whether attacks on intervening real estate can be fended off in the same way. Some strategic analysts would concede simply that the threat to Moscow must be held in reserve to protect New York, and that it therefore cannot also be manipulated on behalf of Paris. Indeed, one argument frequently advanced on behalf of an independent French nuclear force is that the American deterrent logically can not be real or credible on behalf of Europe.

Yet the counter-argument can obviously be made that Paris is just as valuable to the United States elite as are most American cities, so that we will commit ourselves just as meaningfully (irrationally?) to destroy the Soviet Union in the event of damage to Paris. The Soviet leadership contemplating such an attack obviously cannot dismiss all possibilities that Americans would go through with such a commitment. If mere declarations of moral commitment did not suffice, the United States can reinforce this by deploying men or weapons into forward areas, in ways which would force an attack on the Soviet Union even if the United States were not attacked, even if an American president at the last moment preferred not to escalate to this level. Such a tactic of "wiring in" one's self is exemplified by the deployment of American tactical nuclear weapons in large numbers in Germany, as well as by the presence of American ground forces in West Berlin. Conversely, it may explain the Russian decision to deploy nuclear weapons to Cuba in 1962. Without such a deployment, observers of the international scene could well have asked whether the USSR would really expose Moscow merely to protect Cuba. The abortive move to deploy missiles forward might have served to couple the Russian nuclear deterrent to Cuba.

Another way to harness the nuclear deterrent to marginal areas is to devise a potential retaliation which would inflict only part of the damage of an all-out attack, thus reserving the rest of the destruction for the deterrence of attacks on the United States itself. For example, one can elect to use only conventional explosives in bombing raids, as in North Vietnam, or to bomb only the states which seem to be surrogates of the USSR, or to observe specific territorial restrictions within the country being bombed, possibly avoiding cities and aiming only at air force bases.

If none of these ways of deterring marginal aggression by threat of aerial bombardment can be made credible, a nation will have to find other means to deter such aggression, or to repulse it if it occured. The ability to repulse such attacks can *per se* be a deterrent to them, since nations do not typically like to launch attacks that most probably will be defeated. Yet an investment in graduated deterrents or conventional means of defense might also be the final signal that we no longer intended to respond to aggression with an all-out nuclear assault; by thus proving the inapplicability of the nuclear deterrent, one's preparations for conventional defense could serve as an invitation to aggression.

Since 1945, the relationship of defense to offense has thus been enormously complicated by nuclear weapons, weapons which might aid either the offense or defense in purely battlefield terms, but which can kill enormous numbers of civilians off the battlefield, imposing such retaliation and revenge even on the population of the side which was winning on the battlefield. Perhaps the relationship of offense to defense, on land or at sea or in the airspace, thus will make no difference anymore, as the mere horrendousness of war leads every state to forgo dreams of quick and decisive victories.

Yet such a calculation would be premature on several grounds. Not every defeat will bring nuclear retaliation from the losing side. If the U.S. cannot occupy Moscow without bringing on World War III in all its horror, it can occupy Pyongyang. Russian forces can not seize Paris or Washington, but they can occupy Prague.

Secondly, the balance that maintains peace can be upset if *defense of people* is improved to the point that the massive retaliation threat can no longer be carried out. Classically one judged the offensive versus defensive relationship in terms of who lost more troops, those attacking or those defending. If missiles are being fired at cities, it may be an attempt to immobilize some part of the war potential that emerges from these cities; but it may also, as noted above, simply reflect an attempt to be as frightful as possible in retaliation for some loss elsewhere. The relationship of "defense" to "offense" here thus simply relates to whether the missile warheads can indeed reach their targets and kill the people living there. If antiaircraft defenses can stop bombers from reaching their targets, or if ABM missile defenses can really stop missile warheads from inflicting damage on cities, the balance of terror might no longer be effective in preventing wars, and some other guarantee for peace would have to be found.

Thirdly, most importantly, the balance maintaining peace can be upset if offense recaptures too much of the advantage in the force versus force confrontation. For a long time it seemed that the expenditure of several missiles would always be required to be certain of destroying one on the opposing side within its concrete hole in the ground. As long as this is so, the defense will have enormous advantages in force terms, since one would always do better militarily by sitting back to wait for the other side to make the mistake of attacking. But if multiple warhead missiles enable one to fire a single missile to destroy a great number of warheads on the other side, then force-exchange calculations would again favor taking the initiative, with possibly very grave consequences for peace.

Peace thus depends in an important way on keeping people vulnerable to weapons, and keeping weapons invulnerable to each other. Greater accuracies for missiles threaten peace; greater concrete protection for missile silos bolsters peace. Concealment of missiles aboard submarines at sea reinforces peace; antisubmarine warfare (ASW) techniques threaten to encourage war.

Multiple warheads for missiles tend to encourage war, since only a few missiles, when fired, might immobilize and destroy many on the opposite side. ABM (anti-missile defense) becomes paradoxically difficult to evaluate, since it is stabilizing if it only serves to shield missile sites, but destabilizing if it also shields urban population centers.

FURTHER READINGS

Burns, Arthur Lee. "From Balance to Deterrence: A Theoretical Analysis." *World Politics*, July, 1957.
Green, Philip. *Deadly Logic: The Theory of Nuclear Deterrence.* Columbus: Ohio University Press, 1966.
Kahn, Herman. *On Thermonuclear War.* Princeton: Princeton University Press, 1960.
Snyder, Glenn. *Deterrence and Defense.* Princeton: Princeton University Press, 1961.
Wohlstetter, Albert. "The Delicate Balance of Terror." *Foreign Affairs*, January, 1959.

Superiority or Sufficiency

The balance of terror did not spring into being on the day the first nuclear weapon was produced. How, then, could we include the period until 1949 when only the United States had such weapons, when only one of the "superpowers" could "massively retaliate?" When indeed did the mutual deterrent situation come into being, and how?

We all may have exaggerated the impact of nuclear weapons on World War II, especially when we wonder why the United States did not exploit its monopoly of such weapons to force some sort of world government arrangement on the USSR. If the atomic bomb was the absolute weapon, why did we not terminate the anarchic condition we call international politics immediately, by threatening the Russians with all-out destruction if they did not submit? There are indeed revisionist commentators who find traces of such tendencies in American policy in 1945 and 1946, as Washington made demands with regard to Russian behavior in Eastern Europe, as the U.S. put forward the Baruch Plan for international control on atomic energy. Yet in truth the United States did not and could not bully the Soviet Union very much, precisely because there was as yet no guarantee that atomic bombing could force a country like the USSR to surrender. The Germans, after all, had borne up under quite horrendous conventional bombing attacks, and the Red Army might have rolled into Paris while the bombs were falling on Moscow. Atomic bombs, moreover, were in short supply in 1945, and would remain so for some years to come.

The nuclear weapon indeed becomes the absolute weapon somewhat later in the chronology with the development of the hydrogen bomb; the H-bomb emerged symmetrically enough on both sides so that, moreover, neither side could preemptively cash in on it for decisive political results. From 1952 forward, it was thus more definitely clear that war would be so horrible that no one could choose it with equanimity, and that either side could probably make it this horrible for the other. The major strategic question thus was less whether one side could brandish some advantage or monopoly over the other, and more whether the "balance of terror" now generated could be harnessed to stabilize the military balance in places like Berlin and Cuba, Quemoy and Hungary. President Eisenhower's working assumption clearly was that the nuclear deterrent would have this stabilizing effect, and the Republican administration hence did not invest heavily in conventional forces to defend against or deter local attacks.

At various points Eisenhower's critics charged that American retaliation for local aggressions would be incredible; at other times the very ability of the U.S. to retaliate was questioned because of Russian acquisitions of new bomber or missile forces. There were rumors of a "bomber gap" in 1955 by which the USSR would outnumber the United States in the means of delivering nuclear weapons. In 1957 came the orbiting of the Sputnik satellite. Many Americans thus came to fear that the USSR might soon be far enough ahead in missiles (perhaps 500 to 10) to launch a successful World War III, and thereby to command the world.

Neither the bomber gap nor the missile gap materialized, although the Republican administration was reluctantly forced to augment its bomber and missile procurement to rebut the charges of its domestic critics. Perhaps President Eisenhower was aware of Russian weakness all along as U-2 reconnaisance overflights kept him informed of actual Soviet procurement. His successor, John Fitzgerald Kennedy, nonetheless had campaigned for office on pledges to bolster strategic nuclear forces, as well as to generate conventional forces with which to resist local attacks, for which the Democrats had claimed American escalation to nuclear retaliation would be incredible. The incoming Kennedy administration thus significantly expanded the strategic weapons programs which had already been accelerated under President Eisenhower, with the result that the U.S. was in the end programmed to have 1,000 minutemen ICBM's and almost 700 polaris missiles (of which only a portion would normally be on station). The Russian inventory, by contrast, had fallen far short of the more pessimistic American predictions, with less than 50 missiles capable of reaching the United States by the end of 1961.

With a "missile gap in reverse," the United States thus held a commanding strategic position during the Berlin crisis in 1961, and a growing advantage in the next year. For this or other reasons, the USSR may have attempted a "quick fix" in deploying medium-range missiles (of which the USSR had produced more than 700) to Cuba in the fall of 1962. The ensuing reaction saw the United States prepared to threaten and risk all-out war, with the USSR withdrawing its missiles and adopting a markedly less belligerent line thereafter.

Perhaps at this point the United States might have been thought to hold a real "superiority" of nuclear weapons, rather than a mere "sufficiency." Yet even a small Soviet missile force might still have been able to inflict enough casualties on American cities to prevent any real move for U.S. domination. As the Soviet missile inventory slowly grew, such retaliatory capability would be all the less ignorable.

But the Kennedy administration was also characterized by a greater logical tidiness than had applied in the Eisenhower days, as it made an effort to "put the nuclear genie back into the bottle," and to prepare a series of graduated deterrents tailored to levels of violence from guerrilla insurrection to all-out war. This tidiness had advantages for some questions and disadvantages for others. If there had been any real risk of mutually unwanted preemptive war with vulnerable liquid-fueled missiles systems, the procurements and innovations introduced under Kennedy and McNamara substantially reduced this risk. If there was really a problem on the credibility of the American commitment to the defense of Europe, however, the Kennedy policies exacerbated rather than remedied it.

European reluctance to be defended "conventionally" quickly became apparent, since such a defense promised to require higher taxes and longer periods of military service on their own parts, as a conventional war in Europe would also inflict quite horrendous destruction, even if it was less than that of a nuclear war. Since West Germans and others were assuming that the Russians were already deterred by the prospect of American nuclear retaliation, the explication of the question by the new administration was seen as only aggravating any small doubts that might have existed before.

The Democratic administration now went further to conclude that Communist guerrilla tactics constituted the more serious menace to marginal areas of the free world, a menace against which the Eisenhower administration had not seemed adequately prepared. Such guerrilla tactics presumably would win control of territories for Communist regimes even where a majority of the people were opposed to Communism. A high level of abstraction of such theory can be found in the speeches of the president himself, and in the writings of advisers such as W. W. Rostow. Great importance was thus attached to including counter-insurgency capabilities in the expansion of the conventional or "general purpose" forces, and to expanding the "Green-Beret" Special Forces. At first it had been thought that much of the insurgency would be directed by Moscow, especially after Khruschchev's 1961 speech extolling "wars of national liberation," but it then seemed that Peking would be the primary instigator.

In the first years of the Johnson administration, the threat of guerrilla takeover led to the commitment of more than 500,000 American soldiers to the war in South Vietnam. As the American effort proved costly and inconclusive over time, popular support for the military commitment has continually dropped. Apart from the effectiveness or morality of American intervention, skepticism came to be expressed on the extent of the guerrilla menace, and the supposed insufficiency of U.S. nuclear guarantees by themselves.

The Republican administration which took office under President Nixon in 1969 seems to have concluded that guerrilla warfare of the Vietnamese pattern really reflects basically local conditions, such that American conventional force intervention typically will not be required. For much of the more valuable parts of the world, for example, Western Europe and Japan, such tactics offer no options at all for anti-American insurgencies. For these parts of the globe, moreover, the "sufficient" threat of American escalation to nuclear war is still sufficient to deter any invasions by Russian or Chinese forces.

The Nixon administration thus has placed greater stress on the deterring impact of strategic forces, in a more extensive balance of terror. Since 1967, several other factors have worked to draw attention back to the comparison of strategic nuclear forces. First, as American strategic force expansions were completed and leveled off in the middle 1960's, Russian missile procurement finally started to reach the higher levels which had been predicted much earlier. Hardenable solid-fuel missiles began to replace clumsy and vulnerable first-generation liquid fuel ICBM missiles, and submarine based systems at last were deployed at sea in quantity. Open discussion of arms control was somewhat inhibited (with the significant exception of the

Non-Proliferation Treaty) after both the U.S. and USSR had become more involved in Vietnam. While the numbers of Russian missiles at first still constituted only a fraction of the American 1700 missile inventory, the missiles were larger, such that the "throw-weight" available to the two sides might sooner become comparable. Since the Russians had tested larger bombs, with more explosive megatonnage per pound of warhead weight, the USSR even by 1968 might have been able to deliver more explosive power to the U.S. than vice versa, in what some more alarmed observers christened the "megatonnage gap."

Perhaps this reflected only a move toward parity or "sufficiency" for the Russians. But perhaps, if more and more missiles were procured, it might begin instead to amount to a Soviet "superiority," more in political terms than in strategic reality.

Second, the accuracy attainable in intercontinental missiles has been steadily increasing, with the prospect that missiles in underground silos may become vulnerable to incoming missiles in some sort of counterforce attacks. In the inevitable efficiency of Russian and American scientists, the efficiency of intercontinental and submarine-launched missiles is being drastically improved on each side. While previously missiles might have a 50 percent chance of landing within one mile of an enemy missile silo, soon they may come within 200 feet. With such accuracies, secure second-strike retaliatory forces may become impossible on each side, since no amount of cement hardening can protect a siloed missile against so close an explosion.

Similar problems are raised by multiple warheads now being applied to American and Soviet missiles. Such systems allow a single ICBM or submarine-launched missile to deliver warheads to as many as ten civilian or military targets, and may thus seem very desirable and efficient to any strategic planner. Yet a simultaneous deployment of such systems on each side, when combined with improved accuracies would restructure the mathematics of missile salvo exchanges again, so that whoever strikes first comes out ahead. Since accidental war is more likely when this is true, than when everyone feels it is better to let the other side strike first, these developments must be seen as highly undesirable.

Russian work on defense against ballistic missiles has also caused some considerable concern in the United States since 1967. Since the American administration's position has been to stress the "assured-destruction" we could inflict on the Russian populace after any Soviet attack, protection for that populace seemed threatening even at first glance. Considerable effort was thus expended to try to convince the Russian leadership that development of ABM was destabilizing and undesirable, with little or no evident success. The United States, therefore, invested heavily in penetration aids for ICBM's and submarine-launched missiles, aids which can mislead the defensive radars and thus get the warhead through to its target. Debates continue about the relative effectiveness of defensive systems versus penetration aids, and it now seems that confusing and bypassing such defenses will no longer be a trivial problem. It was once thought that each 100 million spent on defenses might be undone by a million on penetration aids; the ratio may now be closer to 10/1 or 1/1.

Since the beginning of the nuclear age, therefore, the maintenance of a balance of mutual deterrence never could simply be taken for granted. If the original U.S. monopoly was not decisive, there has always been the risk that the Russians might significantly move in front in one year, or the Americans in another. A strategic superiority would have become significant, of course, if either side could launch a World War III without having to fear unacceptable retaliation. But any strategic imbalance could become politically significant long before this if the world even came to suspect that one side might be able to escape retaliation.

Either of the superpowers will thus seek to avoid such political disadvantages. Both of the powers must simultaneously be anxious to avoid development of weapons which offer enormous advantages to whoever strikes first, for this could conceivably produce a World War III which neither side had wanted, as both sides suffer more damage than any rational political leader would accept. Both the superpowers must also be concerned lest great sums of money be spent in some arms race which only leaves the relative military strengths the same.

The above considerations help to explain the Soviet and American commitment since 1969 to negotiations on a Strategic Arms Limitation Treaty (SALT). The weapons balance of the early 1970's may offer the mutual assured destruction that we have linked to peace. If the two sides do not restrain themselves, however, one or another of the undesirable consequences spelled out above may emerge. A successful SALT agreement might freeze the offensive weapons strengths of the United States and Soviet Union at close to current levels, giving an aura of parity and equality, maintaining assuredly enough destructive power to deter war as it has been deterred. It will severely restrict the development of antimissile defenses, since the Russians, as well as Americans, now accept the logic that such people-protecting systems paradoxically are a threat to peace.

Finally, although this is less probable because of the difficulties of verifying compliance with any limitation, it might restrict the development of missiles with greater accuracies or multiple warheads, missiles which threaten to offer so much of an incentive to shoot first when political happenings suggest that the other side might be about to shoot. Perhaps the superpowers will be shifting the bulk of their strategic deterrent toward submarine-based systems in any event, independently of any formal agreement on missile characteristics; if antisubmarine warfare (ASW) does not make any grand breakthroughs in the next decade, this may yet reinsure the two sides against fears or hopes of successful counter-force offensives.

Chayes, Abram, and Wiesner, Jerome, eds. *ABM*. New York: Bantam, 1969.
Kaysen, Carl. "Keeping the Strategic Balance." *Foreign Affairs*, July, 1968.
Kaufman, William W. *The McNamara Strategy*. New York: Harper and Row, 1964.
Quester, George H. *Nuclear Diplomacy: The First Twenty-Five Years*. New York: Dunellen, 1970.

An Evaluation of Aerial Bombardment

The military balance as it exists today has thus depended on the threat of aerial bombardment by aircraft or missile, typically although not always using nuclear weapons. Ground strategy is now largely a task of making this threat more credible for the deterrence of attacks on marginal areas.

We have for a longer time been involved in a debate on the proper targeting strategy for such bombardment forces. What target options do we typically have? One could first aim at opposing strategic bombardment forces, on the theory that they may do whatever harm to us that we might do to them, and hence should be preempted. One can aim also, or instead, at all the rest of opposing military forces, the army, navy, or tactical air forces we would otherwise have to confront on the battlefield. One can aim instead at industrial production, hoping thereby to make the opposing war effort economically difficult or impossible. One can alternatively aim at the lives and residences of the enemy's civilian population. Finally, one could hold his strategic bombardment forces in reserve—once their existence and capacity had been made credible to the other side—as a deterrent to impose parallel restraints on the enemy's behavior.

What broader strategic goals would respectively support such disparate targeting policies? Preempting similar attacks on one's self has an obvious logical appeal, an appeal which would only fade if the opponent's bomber or missile forces seemed far less vulnerable than his other targets. Perhaps then one would have to concentrate on bombing the nonstrategic military forces of the other side, to win the war on the battlefield. Yet the same tonnage of bombs delivered to industry manufacturing tanks or warships might offer a greater battlefield impact. To be sure, bombs dropped on or near factories may incidentally kill some civilians. This might be lamentable from the attacker's point of view. Yet he might instead cold-bloodedly conclude that the enemy's military capacity will be crippled even more if bombs are deliberately aimed at the civilian industrial workers themselves, rather than the machine tools which they operate.

Residential areas may be easier to find than specific factories. A worker who has been killed may be more difficult to replace than a soldier who has been killed. Even if the greater part of the labor force survives in bomb shelters, war production still will suffer. Workers who are concerned about the safety of their families or have lost a night's sleep, will not be as effective as those who had escaped such intimidation. Loss of morale is itself incapacitating, and this loss of morale could spread from the cities being bombed up to the soldiers at the front lines.

Apart from reducing an enemy's capability for war, bombing attacks may be intended to reduce his willingness to engage in such hostilities, or at least to force restraints on some of his more awesome activities. Bombing raids could thus be used as punishment for bombing raids by the other side, or for any other particularly obnoxious acts. When such acts were terminated, the raids would also be stopped, and the proven unpleasantness of aerial bombardment would be held in reserve. Alternatively, such raids have been continued as simple punishment for the government's failure to surrender. The implicit message to Japan was simple: "As soon as you stop resisting, we will stop bombing you." Any such motivational operations have to leave something to the other side which he may yet redeem by giving in to whatever demands have been posed. It might seem that the blanket bombardments of World War II did not leave anything of this sort. Yet the mere limits to the efficiency of such bombardment implicitly left something. Since we have not levelled all your cities or killed all your people in previous raids, you will have some reason to bargain for their termination, to spare those who would be killed or made homeless in the future.

We have assumed, of course, that the regime in question identifies with its people enough to be motivated toward sparing them suffering. It is plausible that some regimes would be quite callous. A fifth kind of motive for bombardment might then hinge on the hope that the populace could thereby be driven to mutiny and rebellion against any regime which had subjected them to so much suffering.

Since so much depends on the effectiveness of the aerial bombardment threat, one might comment on some historical examples of such bombardment, examples which at times confirmed and at other times disproved the calculations which went into their planning. There were debates as early as World War I on whether the proper objective of an aerial assault was the weakening or instead the intimidation of the enemy. Bombing was far more effective and widespread in World War II, although it in some ways failed to be as awesome or terrorizing as interwar predictions had foreseen. It is generally remembered that the British bombing of Germany aimed directly at residential areas, while that of the United States was conducted by daylight and aimed at more specifically industrial targets.

The British "area bombing" campaign may simply have been intended to weaken war production by tiring out and demoralizing the labor force, or it may have hoped to inspire political discontent and resistance to the Nazi regime. Since no such popular revolt ever showed signs of materializing and since German war production rose during the war under the guidance of Albert Speer, it is thus common to write off the British effort as a misguided failure. Such a conclusion might indeed be premature, for the intangible effects of the bombings on the average German's willingness to continue the war are much harder to measure. Officers of the German Army did, after all, attempt to assassinate Adolf Hitler; the destruction of German cities being carried forward day after day could only have furthered their conviction that the Nazi regime and the war should be terminated as early as possible.

The United States Army Air Force indeed had shifted to area bombing in its assault on Japan after the German surrender, before the use of the atomic bombs on Hiroshima and Nagasaki. The criticism is sometimes made that the two atomic bombings were unnecessary since Japan may already have been on the verge of surrendering. Yet such an argument begs the question of what indeed was causing the Japanese to be so ready to make peace. The two major factors were the naval blockade of the home islands, and the conventional bombings already underway, bombings which on occasion did more damage than the Hiroshima and Nagasaki bombs.

The discussion of objectives in any bombardment campaign has been revived and intensified by the campaign conducted against North Vietnam between 1964 and 1968, in which a greater tonnage of high explosives was delivered than in all of World War II against Germany. Confusion on the objectives to be achieved in such a campaign was aggravated by conflicting rationales emerging from the U.S. government, rationales at times obviously composed simply for the benefit of world opinion. The intent of the bombings was not to preempt any corresponding air attacks from the North, since Hanoi never accumulated any significant air strength. Officially, the campaign was normally defined as an attempt to interfere with the flow of supplies south to the guerrillas fighting in South Vietnam, that is, to interfere with the Communist capability for fighting the war. Occasionally the motive was admitted to be instead to raise the costs to Hanoi of fighting the war, that is, to alter the Communist will to fight. If there was any expectation of inducing the North Vietnamese population to revolt against or resist the Ho Chi Minh regime, it was never expressed, and would indeed have been most unrealistic. Yet the possibility could not be excluded that some part of the ruling elite in Hanoi would have found the bombings particularly damaging to its own plans and vested interests, thus leading it to lobby for some compromise short of Communist victory.

Whatever its intentions, the American bombing operations against North Vietnam set a precedent which has been emulated several times since. The Turkish air attacks on Greek positions in Cyprus came almost immediately after the very first American air attacks on North Vietnam. These attacks have been followed by Egyptian attacks on Saudi Arabian towns during the civil war in Yemen, and then by repeated Israeli air attacks across the truce lines into Jordan, Syria, Lebanon, and Egypt.

What have been the objectives of the Israeli Air Force attacks? Only occasionally has there been a question of preempting the use or establishment of opposing military forces, as during the Six-Day War when early morning attacks virtually destroyed the Egyptian Air Force, and then in 1970 with attacks on the defensive missile installations being erected by the Egyptians with Soviet assistance.

Have the attacks been intended to deter any particular Egyptian or Arab practices? Here again the answer must be yes and no. In some sense the attacks have been reprisals for specific Egyptian artillery bombardments, or for Palestinian guerilla raids conducted from across the Jordan River. But more generally, many of the Israeli raids have been intended to intimidate the Arabs simply by the display of superior military prowess. Demoralizing any enemy contributes to defeating him on the battlefield, and this demoralization can sometimes be accomplished simply by flying patrols through his airspace at will, even if no homes have been destroyed or factories demolished.

FURTHER READINGS

Brodie, Bernard. *Strategy in the Missile Age.* Princeton: Princeton University Press, 1959.
Kahn, Herman. *On Thermonuclear War.* New York: Free Press, 1969.
Quester, George H. *Deterrence Before Hiroshima.* New York: Wiley, 1966.

An Evaluation of Guerrilla War

Military strategy since 1945 has thus become an exercise in contemplating extremes. The very prospect of the use of H-bombs in a World War III may intimidate one side more than the other, settling some crisis, determining some political outcome.

Yet such intimidation and deterrence can not effect every political movement or influence every issue. Much of what we have seen in the military sphere since World War II has thus occurred at the opposite extreme, with "sub-limited" or guerrilla warfare, the use of ambushes and assassination by forces small enough to conceal themselves in a backdrop of jungle and civilian population.

The 1960's in particular saw a greatly expanded discussion of the possibilities and problems of guerrilla warfare. A large part of this interest could be traced directly to the stress now placed on such warfare by various Communist regimes; at an earlier stage by the Russians in Khrushchev's distinction between "local wars" and "wars of national liberation," then much more significantly in the emerging independence of the Communist Chinese position and Chairman Mao's stress on guerrilla warfare, and finally with the theories and campaigns of the North Vietnamese Communists. In terms of written literature, particular attention has been focused on writings of Mao Tse Tung, which date from the 1930's and his guerrilla campaigns against Chinese Nationalist and Japanese forces; similar analyses have been published by other guerrilla leaders who credit Mao with inspiration, particularly General Giap in North Vietnam and Che Guevara in Cuba.

While close analysis can find some differences in detailed strategy and in the sequence or numbering of critical stages of the campaign, the basic analysis of such writers is very parallel, and can be sorted into three major contentions. First, the guiding principle of successful insurgency is stated to be the avoidance of combat until force levels and other considerations allow for a favorable outcome. Lines are not to be held, and territory is not to be defended. While some commentators have credited Mao with great originality here, military historians might recognize this as simply the classic principle of guerrilla war, practiced, for example, by George Washington in the American Revolution.

The second and third contentions advanced in Mao's theory are more recent in origin, and at the very least constitute brilliant political polemic and propaganda. Mao, as well as Giap and Guevara, assert that victory for the guerrillas is indeed inevitable, inevitable in the same sense that Marx found the destruction of capitalism to be inevitable. While earlier military analysts would have prescribed guerrilla tactics for certain situations in the *hope* that these would succeed, the new guerrilla theorists thus accompany this with a sociological and world-historical analysis purportedly indicating that victory is bound to come in time. One step backward, two steps forward; what seem to be defeats are only the forerunners of victory, what seems to be weakness is really strength.

This leads to the third major contention of the Maoist writers, that guerrilla victory reflects popular support, and that it could never have been achieved without it. A number of non-Communist analysts of insurgency have indeed accepted this proposition as the heart of the insurgency problem, that one can not defeat an insurgency without first winning the "hearts and minds" of the people. In effect, the guerrilla campaign comes to resemble a very brutal form of plebiscite; if the people are with the insurgents, the insurgents will ultimately win, if the people were not so inclined, the insurgents could not succeed.

One can see some great advantages in the Maoist insurgency analysis for the particular political position of the Chinese Communists. By combining Marxist dialectic with an analysis of guerrilla warfare, the Maoist account reconciles Marx with the Chinese experience, in which victory and revolution did not emerge from the proletarian cities but from peasants of the countryside. The Russian revolution indeed succeeded first in Petrograd and Moscow, and then moved into the country. The Chinese experience, as well as the Vietnamese, has been the opposite. The Lin Piao statement which portrayed all the underdeveloped world as a countryside which would wage guerrilla war against the "cities" (the developed countries such as the U.S. and USSR) carries this analysis to its most extreme abstraction.

A second important advantage of the Maoist formulation shows up in the encouragement it offers the guerrilla soldier. Since the dialectic model allows for, or almost indeed requires, some early defeats, it presumably bucks up soldiers who otherwise would be discouraged by early reverses. The doctrine of inevitability gives the ideologically motivated soldier an assurance of victory in the end. As with other forms of Marxist inevitability, doubt can be sometimes expressed about whether the message logically calls forth such heroic individual performance. If victory is inevitable, why should one risk his life on the barricades? Yet the same theory may explain that even our presence on the barricades is inevitable by the laws of class and revolution which determine all political development. With regard to the dialectic of one step backward, two steps forward, repeated defeats which are not soon followed by enormous victories might someday produce an impatience and shake some cadres' confidence in the overall model. Yet the counter-insurgents patience is also not endless, and Asian Communist guerrilla cadres have thus far shown themselves to be more confident and enduring than their opponents.

Apart from the Chinese and North Vietnamese guerrilla movements, the world has seen, and will continue to see, a number of derivative insurrectionary movements which attach importance to literal implementations of the Maoist outline. Whether such theory can be transferred so self-consciously is still subject to question. The Chinese and Vietnamese successes may indeed have been due to indigenous factors relatively unrelated to theory, such that they can not really be replicated elsewhere either through the analytical or propaganda impacts of the written word.

The United States itself has undergone an interesting evolution of attitude on the legitimacy and efficacy of guerrilla warfare. For a large part of its history, its position was predominantly on the antiguerrilla side, whether fighting against American Indians, or in the Philippines and Central America, or (stretching an analogy somewhat) when combating organized crime in the cities of the United States. A few campaigns of the American Revolution might have been characterized as guerrilla in character, and Confederate military forces had recourse to such tactics along various portions of the front in the Civil War. In the net, the United States, until 1939, remained disposed to condemn insurgent or irregular military activity as illegal and deceitful, as exposing innocent civilians to needless suffering when the uniformed army in the area had to protect itself.

Very much of this was changed in the special circumstances of World War II. Almost every recourse to guerrilla activity favored the Allies, since Germany and Japan had overrun so much territory at the outset of the war. The United States was thus disposed to encourage as well as to dignify

and glorify the activities of indigenous guerrillas from France to Yugoslavia, as well as indigenous and exogenous guerrillas in Burma and the Far
East. Such combat was generally believed and portrayed to show the
power of popular feeling as directed against the armed forces of an alien
power. Little doubt was expressed or tolerated that the FFI truly represented the majority of Frenchmen on whose behalf they were fighting and
inducing German countermeasures. The image of guerrilla insurrections as
a grand plebiscite was thus more than acceptable to the United States
public in 1945, confirmed all the more by the absence of similar resistance
in occupied Germany and Japan.

The implications of an American acceptance of successful guerrilla tactics as a popular mandate could be quite serious for the formulation of
policy. The United States, among other things, has favored representative
regimes over those which seemed to lack popular support. To have an
insurgency thriving in an area thus would seem to suggest that the regime
did not morally merit American backing. If the theory moreover stipulated
that popularly supported insurgencies were assured of victory, this could
unnerve even those Americans who regarded the representativeness of a
regime as unimportant per se. The first serious ambush of a column of
government troops would thus be taken as handwriting on the wall, handwriting showing that defense of this particular area and regime was hopeless.

The contrary propositions to those of Mao Tse-tung must at least be
considered—that guerrillas will not always win, and that victory by them
is far from totally determined by popular support. History indeed suggests
that guerrillas may operate effectively with far less than majority backing
in the theater of operations, so effectively that an opposing political force
will be deterred by the costs it is suffering. If the gimmickry of guerrilla
warfare can indeed award victory to a small but determined minority, some
important consequences emerge. First, an outside power intent on assisting
the most representative forces within the country need not be so dissuaded
by the apparent success of the insurgents. Secondly, the possibility will
exist that several insurgent forces could adopt the same guerrilla tactics to
counter and veto each other. One finds examples of dual insurgent actions
in Palestine under the British mandate, where Jewish and Arab insurgent
organizations applied guerrilla tactics to the British and to each other.
Denmark in 1944 would supply another example, with the Germans spon-
soring a Danish Nazi underground which retaliated clandestinely for clandestine attacks on German forces. Perhaps each side to a major political
disagreement can thus veto the workings of society as a whole by resorting
to guerrilla tactics; if so, one can not as easily justify such tactics on the
argument that they at least dynamically drive society to reach a political
decision.

Various suggestions have thus been advanced on how to counter the guerrilla, sometimes by adopting variations on his own tactics, other times by adopting countermeasures to make such tactics ineffective. The essence of guerrilla war in this view is not the winning of popular support, but a particular military tactic aimed at precluding the delivery of normal governmental and economic services, without establishing any counter-services of its own. The insurgents thus frustrate the operation of railroads and use of highways, but do not maintain and defend any railroads or highways of their own. Attacks are delivered against the most crucial or vulnerable points of the government's system, to veto the operations of that system. If popular support is required, in this view, we need not assume that it is anything like majority support. The efficacy of the guerrilla attack is merely a reflection of the physical vulnerability of the system, and not of either side's representativeness.

To counter such an offensive, one can move to raise the scale of operations. 10,000 government troops may be incapable of defending 1,000 vulnerable points against 1,000 guerrillas. But if the government forces are substantially expanded, these points can be guarded, even if the guerrillas are proportionately expanded, for the number of vulnerable points remains the same. An adequate garrison on each bridge, power plant, and hamlet might thus make ineffective the attacks which otherwise threaten to hamstring the regime. A second response is to resort to similar tactics, for example by aerial bombardment of the enemy's sanctuary areas. Here again one side is only destroying and not seeking to establish any communications lines of its own. Air raids in their infancy in World War I indeed were once challenged as violating the laws of war, that is, as being the equivalent of guerrilla activity.

There are serious problems, however, with both these responses to guerrilla attacks. If the general scale of military manpower is raised so that the government forces (and perhaps also the guerrillas) have been multiplied by ten, it is not certain that life in the besieged community will ever be the same. Given the likely inconveniences of hosting such large military forces, the guerrillas will have succeeded by default in preventing any normal life-style in the community under siege, succeeded therefore in alienating the community somewhat from the regime. Any such counter-tactic will thus hardly bring the state to a permanently tolerable or normal state. Rather it will simply be part of the more general contest of who has the greater endurance in guerrilla campaigns. Perhaps the introduction of large government forces has forced the insurgents back from Mao's Stage II to Stage I; perhaps this will, over time, disillusion the individual cadres who were in part motivated by a sense of inevitable victory. Yet it is also plausible that the government forces will tire of the prolonged state of emergency involved in saturating a country with forces, or that the protected populace will tire of the costs of being protected.

Drawing an analogy between aerial bombardment and guerrilla warfare may also seriously upset many onlookers and uncommitted nations, if only because the analogy has such major imperfections. However little indigenous support is required for guerrilla operations, few would deny that some local support is needed. Without sympathizers in the south, North Vietnam could not have engaged the Saigon regime as it has. By contrast, bombing a territory requires no indigenous support whatsoever. The bombing option is thus potentially applicable to any nation as a victim, while the guerrilla option is not, and Communist and non-Communist nations alike may see some threat and unfairness here. Bulgaria, for example, might wonder whether an insurrection in Greece will bring aerial attacks on itself.

The established regime might of course attempt to emulate guerrilla tactics in ways other than aerial attacks. Yet the limits here may be quite constraining. To a great extent, the regime in any society will have won the allegiance of, and will have become at least partially dependent on, the portions of society which require and use railroads, highways, electric power, and so on. If insurgencies typically pit those with the most vested interest in society against those with the least, the government is forced to maintain many of the trappings of an established regime, trappings which the "revolutionary" forces can do without. Commentators have noted how clever it has been for the Viet Cong in South Vietnam never to establish a "revolutionary capital," because they would then have been forced to defend it, at great loss to themselves. Yet any implication that the Saigon regime would have been wise to emulate this is substantially mistaken, for the regime's very nature requires it to attempt to administer the country as any normal government would.

This asymmetry might seem to enhance the legitimacy of the guerrillas, since they are prepared to do without health services, food supply, and other benefits of an established regime. The willingness of the insurgent to disrupt and to forgo maintaining functions for himself is thus to be taken as proof of his sincerity and moral intensity, of his depth of feeling. Why should one care whether some faction has the majority of numbers, when its members have obviously proven themselves so much more willing to make personal sacrifices?

The problem of comparing numerical votes with intensity of feeling is an old one in politics. Indeed, within the United States, as noted earlier, Zionists are a distinct minority whose feelings on the security of Israel are taken to be much more intense and deeply held than the feelings of other Americans on the same question; in a rough-and-ready calculus of the political process, most Americans regard it as proper that the minority in such a case should have its way. It is then not a tremendous jump to concluding that insurgents in most guerrilla situations have proven a greater commitment than the soft bourgeois seeking shelter behind the government's armies. History tends to dignify the side that wins such contests of endurance and willpower. Historians can indeed argue whether a majority of Americans desired independence from Britain in 1776, or whether a majority of Algerians desired independence from France in 1960. Yet such states, once independent, tend to erase the evidence, as well as the reality, of any challenge to their mandates.

The most serious charges that can be brought against launchers of guerrilla warfare, and then against the armies that elect to resist such campaigns, may well be that such warfare is extremely brutal for the civilian populations in whose midst it is fought. The risk of atrocities is increased because of the very nature of the insurrectionary tactic, avoiding any open stands on the battlefield against the government. As the guerrilla soldier thus dons civilian dress, civilians come to resemble guerrillas, and the army is inclined to inflict casualties on innocent persons in genuine confusion about who the enemy is. International law as codified in the later 19th century tended to recognize this problem and to legitimate punishment for any who used guerrilla tactics. As international law still reads today, a soldier caught engaging in combat while out of uniform is liable to immediate execution; he furthermore has no rights whatsoever as a prisoner of war, and is subject to most horrible punishments short of execution.

The acceptability of such executions and deterrents to guerrilla insurrection is heavily a function of the climate of political opinion, however. In 1900, most regimes and most public opinions would have frowned on insurrectionary tactics, and sanctioned punishments directed against those who fight out of uniform. In 1944, the western climate would have been far less inclined in this direction; as noted above, this ambivalence has persisted to the present.

If the army in uniform is within its rights in executing enemy soldiers captured out of uniform, the world will hardly be ready to tolerate large numbers of such executions. The regime may have to forgo its legal prerogatives here, if it wishes to induce any of the insurgent enemy to surrender or hopes to have its own soldiers kept alive when captured. Yet the temptation to brutality on the part of the state is enormous, just as it is to the advantage of the insurgents to encourage such brutality. The brutality which characterizes counter-insurgency campaigns is essentially of three varieties. Since information, as always, is valuable, the temptation is great to extract such information by torture, that is, by inflictions of pain short of death. The tactic of discouraging guerrilla attacks by calculated retaliation against local civilians may also often seem expedient. Finally, there is the irrational retaliation which occurs in the field when frustrated soldiers see themselves suffering casualties from an enemy imbedded and hidden among these civilians.

The history of such brutality is depressingly regular. German performances in the occupied areas of World War II included the most awful forms of brutality, sometimes spontaneously, sometimes by calculation. American performance historically has not been saliently better, when confronted with insurgencies. Hostages were taken in the pacification of Confederate areas in the Civil War, the treatment of the Indians at times verged on genocide, the pacification of the Philippines saw widespread torture and retaliation against noncombatants. For more recent examples, one has examples of torture by the French in Algeria, the British in Cyprus, and by Americans in Vietnam. The My Lai massacre, presumably reflecting spontaneous frustration and rage, nonetheless seems to weaken for all time the hope that American cultural and political styles have provided immunization against such infliction of atrocities.

Apart from its brutality, an even more serious criticism of guerrilla tactics would cite theories of such warfare as an important explanation of the continuation of the Cold War. When Khrushchev or Mao endorsed "wars of national liberation," when Communist China later placed great stress on "people's war," this may have reflected a sincere belief in the Marxist states that guerrilla war was logically linked to revolution around the globe, and that its success was inevitable. Yet such theories amounted to a challenge to the non-Communist world, a challenge quite at variance with any "coexistence" based on mutual toleration of the territorial status quo. As such it led to counter-insurgency theory and counter-insurgency efforts, and the clash of theories is an important explanation of the prolonged war in Vietnam.

Theories on each side may have been excessively abstract. There may be little in common between Vietnam and Palestine and Venezuela. A belated recognition of the local idiosyncracies here can help produce detente between Marxist states and non-Marxist. A continued fascination with guerrilla war conversely will stand in the way of detente.

FURTHER READINGS

Galula, David. *Counterinsurgency Warfare.* New York: Praeger, 1964.
Giap, Vo Nguyen. *People's War, People's Army.* New York: Bantam, 1968.
Mao Tse-tung. *On Guerrilla Warfare.* New York: Praeger, 1961.

"Conventional" War

In some ways, therefore, military power and war planning may seem enormously different today from what it must have been prior to 1945 or 1952, when the A-bomb and the H-bomb arrived. Much of war is deterred today, deterred by the knowledge that a major outbreak of fighting could all too quickly escalate into a nuclear holocaust in which much of the world's population would be killed, even much of the population of the war's "winner." Guerrilla war wins a partial exemption from this deterrence, perhaps because it is so spontaneous and gradual that threats of massive retaliation and nuclear escalation cannot be made credible.

However, this description probably understates the continuing significance of the kinds of warfare that lie between nuclear war and guerrilla war in the spectrum of violence. Even if such wars are not fought, armies still must prepare for them, and meaningful preparations here are politically important. Soviet armies have "conventionally" invaded Hungary and Czechoslovakia, and the threat of nuclear war was not interposed to cancel the operations; the threat of similar operations has kept other Communist regimes in Eastern Europe from asserting too great an independence of Moscow. The threat of such an invasion hangs over the politics of Finland. A similar threat would hang over Western Europe if NATO's conventional defense preparations were totally abandoned, and if the nuclear threat in NATO's defense were no longer to be credible; this possibility is sometimes described as the "Finlandization" of Europe.

Preparations for conventional war are thus meaningful wherever there is no nuclear umbrella, as between India and Pakistan, or Israel and Egypt, or the United States and the Dominican Republic, or the USSR and Hungary. Since 1945 we have seen conventional war occasionally appear in Vietnam (although the conflict here has much more often been of the guerrilla variety) and very clearly in Korea. Preparations for conventional war are even meaningful where the nuclear umbrella has been extended, as long as some inherent doubts have to remain on whether a nuclear power would actually go through with its threats. If the U.S. were unable to defend some area by conventional means against a conventional attack, would it launch World War III at great cost to itself, or would it surrender the territory at issue? The answer obviously depends on what territory is involved, and on a great deal more.

Conventional weapons thus still have to be assessed as in the past in terms of who is strongest, and so on. Could the Chinese Army hold its own on its frontiers with the USSR, or couldn't it? Does the answer change as additional divisions are moved east by the Russians? And what of the Israelis along the Suez Canal, or the Pakistani forces in Punjab or Indian forces facing the Chinese in the Himalayas? The political behavior on each side of these armed frontiers will reflect expectations of the conventional military power deployed. As suggested above, however, additional "arms control" questions need to be raised, at least on behalf of peace-loving outsiders, if not also for the hapless parties to some bitter conflict. Do certain kinds of conventional weapons—tanks, tactical fighters, motor torpedo boats—increase the likelihood of war by making the first-strike very attractive, while others favor the defensive and dampen down crises? Are some kinds of weapons more prone to uncontrolled escalation, drawing in the great powers, breaking down the conventional-nuclear distinction if great powers are already involved?

Having said this much about conventional war and the need to take it seriously, the fact remains that markedly fewer such wars have been fought since the dawn of the nuclear age than in comparable periods before. Has war thus largely become unthinkable, because of the H-bomb? Or is guerrilla warfare such a superb technique that its discovery largely precludes recourse to conventional campaigns? But guerrilla warfare as noted may have a very limited applicability. Can it be instead that the cultural and economic interdependence of the world is increasing enough to make war generally unprofitable? Perhaps, except that we might be on our guard since similarly optimistic predictions have been made in the past also.

A look at history may thus become quite relevant here, if for no other purpose but to note the ins and outs of warfare as a dominant characteristic of international relations. Perhaps men will have to ask the same questions as before on the "balance of military power," as the processes of history have not yet pushed us forward enough to forget such comparisons. Nuclear weapons, or the techniques of guerrilla insurgency, or the demands of an increasingly complicated world economy, of course will complicate the questions, but most probably will not outmode them.

FURTHER READINGS

George, Alexander L. *The Limits of Coercive Diplomacy.* Boston: Little, Brown, 1971.
Knorr, Klaus. *The War Potential of Nations.* Princeton: Princeton University Press, 1956.

CHAPTER THREE

*International Law
and
Organization*

It may seem strange that the discussion of as "tough-minded" a factor as military power should be followed directly by reference to something as "soft" as international law. International law indeed often seems to draw an excessive respect from "idealistic" interpreters of international relations, with an injunction that one's own county should set some kind of moral example for the world by being "law-abiding." Such advice may come from clergymen or international civil servants, or from lawyers who might be suspected of excessively stressing the merits of their own profession, while forgetting what may be some enormous differences between domestic and international law. "Realistic" political scientists in the international field almost as often tend to debunk international law, seeing the international arena as vastly different from the domestic, indeed as "lawless."

Yet it is difficult to focus on the military power sketched out in the preceding section without assuming that states will want to achieve some regularity and predictability in their exercise of such power. Military force is too dangerous to use randomly, it is too valuable in terms of getting one's way, in terms of coercing others. What, after all, is "law" anywhere, except the threats made by monopolists of violent power, threats intended to coerce and guide individuals down paths useful to the state?

A number of definitional problems must thus be confronted here. First, if international law is "law," where is its enforcer, the maker of the threats noted above? Yet the "enforcer" of international law may not be as lacking as is sometimes conjectured, for he might indeed be found in the same governments that enforce domestic law, the states of the world as we know it. One could thus contend that treaties are law in the same sense as all other law, proclamations of intent by the monopolies of violence we know as governments. The proclamations declare that retaliation will be imposed for specified acts, in the hopes that such acts will thus be deterred. Law simply becomes "international," therefore, whenever two or more states concur on its wording; the mechanism for this concurrence is known as a treaty.

Yet there is no "higher" enforcer of international law, its critics would argue, no higher authority to bind and supervise the states which contract themselves under it. It is sometimes contended that only states can be parties in actions under international law, and never individuals. There are cases which cloud this observation and distinction, for example, the penalties imposed on war crimes and piracy. Yet there might still be a meaningful question here on whether international law is created by states, or whether states are merely writing contracts under it.

As noted earlier, this distinction may again recede when one remembers that there are often no "higher" enforcers in domestic law either. A policeman who issues a speeding ticket on the Main Street of a small southern town may be punishing a civil rights agitator who had not exceeded the speed limit at all, while ignoring the transgressions of most other motorists. In short, he is not fulfilling the pledge he has made to punish certain acts and not punish the rest. Law is indeed what the policeman, or any state functionary, promises to enforce; his actual practice, as compared with what he has promised to do, is a function of politics and momentary interest. Whether or not he has superiors, this holds true.

Yet the constraints on adherence to law may still be far less durable in international politics than within nations. However willing domestic policemen will be to ignore the law they are sworn to enforce, this will not match the freedom statesmen have to ignore the treaties they have signed. But this again may overstate the skepticism we should feel about the power of international law. Several kinds of argument can be offered to explain why the treaties of international law will be taken with some seriousness by those who sign them.

To begin, an international rule may simply be a signal of coordination. British sailors perhaps would prefer to have ships pass each other on the left, just as their autos do at home. Having lost on the bargaining point of how one passes, it would be folly for British ship captains to betray their word when passing other ships in fogs at sea. The contract thus is self-enforcing once made; the British mariner is coerced by the simple logic that ships at sea must use a standard rule or else experience repeated collisions.

Aside from pure coordination, we may keep to our international legal obligations because others have made threats, threats to retaliate against anyone who does not keep such commitments. Retaliation involves more than simply failing to renew business relationships which we have now made precarious; that would simply make sense in its own terms. Retaliation involves their going out of their way to inflict punishment on us, as a warning for anyone in the future who might fail to keep a bargain. The forces I have cheated may send mobsters to assault me, send bombers to destroy one of my factories, or cut off trade relationships even where they had still been viable (for example, ones where we would have been trustworthy because we had to deliver the goods first).

Yet much of cooperation in international politics may not require such mechanism of coordination or retaliation, but may stem simply from the logic of the promise as defined earlier. There is inevitably somewhat of a pyramid-club or chain letter psychology about all this. Other parties semi-irrationally regard our trustworthiness at stage one as an index of our similar response at stage two. We confirm at stage two in order to induce their acceptance of stage three. When we get to the last transaction, where there is no longer a possibility of one more repetition, we should presumably cease to be honest. But we may never get to the end of the string.

A certain fraction of exchange in domestic society depends on the ability of the state to enforce contracts. Yet many "deals," as between college roommates, are adhered to without any reference to the state's authority. By comparison, almost all successful interactions in the international arena are necessarily independent of higher authority. Yet many deals are adhered to nonetheless.

The nature of any legal argument is thus an appeal to the militarily powerful sovereigns to adhere to their pledged word, on the grounds that failure to adhere will in the future confuse anyone the sovereigns are seeking to influence in one direction or another. "What impression would you have given to a reasonable man?" is the topic to which all arguments are addressed. The answers will depend on the meanings of words, and the meanings such words have conveyed in environments of the past. The very evolution of international law thus reflects all the varied sources of evidence that can be cited here. Unless a sovereign revises the general understanding on how sovereigns behave, others will assume that he intends to behave again in the accustomed ways.

Roman law is probably the earliest source to be cited here. It had the advantages of being well developed and clearly articulated. Its legitimacy in part reflected the slow erosion of the myth that a Roman Empire was still in existence into and through the Middle Ages and Renaissance. With the recognition of multiple sovereignties thus postponed, the fiction of political union provided a functional form of international law. It was indeed not until Napoleon's time that this fiction was definitively terminated. Since states so clearly need and value benchmarks of coordination in their international dealings, the presence of Roman law was quite welcome.

If the physical source of much of early international law is the law of Rome, the logical source is philosophically interesting. The Romans were indeed not so vain as to portray their law simply as an artifact of power, but rather utilized a natural law reasoning which can be traced back in time to Aristotle and Plato. The lawgiver was thus purporting to be discovering rules of conduct inscribed in the very nature of the universe, rather than merely composing directions to suit his own interests. "I call them as they are," was the message of the Roman umpire, rather than "They are what I call them."

The difficulty with natural law is, of course, that some observers will today deny that any such thing exists, while others disagree on what its dictates are. If any broad agreement were possible on what most men found "natural," this would be useful again as a coordination point, even if individual men or states wished that the consensus were substantially different. One can ask whether natural law supplied any "higher enforcer" such as is commonly argued to be essential for meaningful law. Since natural law's dictates are typically stated to lie within the nature of the object itself, one can argue that no additional sanction is applied. The "punishment" of natural law lies in the very "unnatural" quality of any act contrary to it. Yet when elaborated, natural law was also construed to dictate that there should be a state, and that this state should guide individuals toward adherence to natural law by means of a reinforcing set of punishments and rewards.

The onset of Christianity supplied a new body of "law" around which states might coordinate the rules they make and the punishments they impose. Christianity differs substantially from some natural law philosophies, in imputing a consciousness to the higher lawgiver and enforcer, specifically God. "God commands," "God wants," "God will punish," and so on, thus supplying a "higher enforcer" that individual sovereigns might ignore only at their peril. If doubts moreover arose on some point of God's will, as it affected several Christian sovereigns, there was a generally recognized Vicar on earth, the Pope, who could interpret God's will on international, as well as on other, political questions. Christianity came to dominate all the European world, while this world remained generally in isolation of, and occasionally at war with, the rest.

The breakup of the unity of Christendom, together with a diminished credibility for the Roman inheritance, cast doubt on the legitimacy and relevance of the traditional international law. The breakup induced efforts to codify tradition as it had been handed down, to retain a benchmark of coordination and trust. The most significant of these efforts at codification comes with the writings of Grotius. Grotius' effort illustrates a very changed basis for international law, as agreement on natural law or on the dictates of the Christian God no longer could be achieved. If men and nations cannot agree about substance, they can at least agree as to what has been agreed on in the past. Grotius indeed hoped to reestablish natural law as the logical foundation of international law, a natural law that even warring Protestants and Catholics would agree upon, a natural law that even "God could not change." The need for a codification of international law had been made clear in the general absence of mutual restraint and the barbarism of the Thirty Years War. The ensuing century indeed saw a reestablishment of the more civilized usages with regard to the treatment of prisoners and civilians in wartime, but this reflected changes in the political environment as well as the clarification of the usages of law.

The usages of the Roman Empire and of Christianity, as modified and reworded over time, thus today explain much of the international law known over the entire world. The world's acceptance of this body of tradition and usage is hardly a testament to the intellectual or moral superiority of this particular legal tradition, however; it is rather a by-product of Europe's conquest of the world in the 19th century, whereby almost all the globe was nominally subjected to the political domination of one European nation or another, while the remainder—Japan, China, Thailand, Ethiopia—was forced to adopt western styles, if only to protect its independence. Even unhappy customs are custom, and two recently independent nations today will turn to the legal heritage saddled on them by colonial conquerors, if only to exploit the community of experience that can be found only there.

To be sure, the acceptance of western legal modes could not be total, and it would be unrealistic for western observers to expect that it was. At the trial of various Japanese leaders for war crimes at the end of World War II, it was an Indian judge who demurred from the findings of guilt, on the grounds that Japan, and most of Asia as well, had never bound itself to the laws of war as understood in the western world. As more and more non-European states participate in the deliberations of international law as at least nominal equals, moreover, the international law they generally accept will have to undergo further accommodation and modification in the process.

Returning to the nature of international law itself, one can inquire about the substantive forms it takes. Where indeed does one go to determine the proper answer on any disputed point of the law? As suggested above, there has to be a heavy reliance on custom, tradition, and precedent, a notion which may be quite congenial to Americans and Englishmen accustomed to the Anglo-Saxon legal tradition of the Common Law, but perhaps less so to continental Europeans with their more fully codified legal systems.

Traditional international practice is something nations implicitly swear to uphold in the very process of being or becoming nations. To deviate from this tradition, without prior warning, would be to surprise the outside world, and surprise can be very upsetting. Amendments to the body of tradition will thus appear in specific declarations of deviation, some of which show up straightforwardly in the unilateral domestic law of the countries involved. Since the acquiescence of other nations involved may become an issue, such a deviation can be handled much more tidily by a treaty among two or more nations. The treaty always had a place in the natural law legal tradition itself, since it seemed "natural" that "Pacta Sunt Servanda," promises were to be kept. For the observer of the present, it may no longer be intuitively obvious why promises, once made, are ipso facto "naturally" to be kept. Yet if the proposition was always somewhat of a non sequitur, it was nonetheless a quite useful one if most countries and sovereigns felt driven to adhere to it. Indeed, it could thereby have become self-supporting.

Treaties are just one more form of law comparable to the domestic law of the states involved, but they do have a contractual quality which must be taken into account. Two states composing a treaty are doing more than simply comparing notes on and standardizing their respective domestic laws. To some extent, each is making its proclamation of the treaty text conditional on the other's making and adhering to the agreed proclamation.

Treaties thus become part of the international law, and modify it as they are incorporated into it. A most useful principle of "equity" somewhat expands the impact of any particular treaty, stipulating that either party's deviation from the terms of the treaty can sanction an approximately even deviation by the other.

Do treaties retain their effectiveness forever into the future, or is there some understanding that they may terminate themselves? The international convention on this point is itself rather well developed and commonsensical, although on fine points some disagreement can emerge. Does war between the parties terminate a treaty, for example? The answer obviously will have to depend on the substance. If the treaty concerns a cultural exchange program, it probably would ipso facto be terminated. If it concerns the treatment of prisoners of war, it naturally enough should remain in effect. The test of whether the principles of wartime treaty termination are generally understood and accepted has come before two sorts of tribunals. After wars have been ended and peace reestablished, recourse may be had to international courts for opinions on whether certain treaties were or were not in force at a certain time. Similar recourse will be taken on related matters to the domestic courts of the nations involved. Some of the most meaningful tests of the impact of international law thus still occur in the extent to which such domestic courts interpret treaty obligations as part of the domestic law.

What about the passage of time as a terminator of treaties? The United Kingdom and Portugal are technically bound by a military alliance which dates back seven centuries. Although the alliance was invoked as recently as World War II to explain British military bases in the Azores, Portugal did not find it advisable to try to invoke it in 1960 during its military difficulties with India. If nothing else, the example suggests that political realities still will determine much of the potency of international law from case to case.

Some treaties terminate themselves quite logically in their own terms, as when a fixed time-limit is reached, or when all the provisions promised on a specific and finite list are fulfilled. Treaties may similarly be terminated by mutual and explicit agreement of all the parties to it, or by one nation denouncing its provisions and the other party acquiescing to the denunciation. If the original parties to a treaty negotiate a new one on the same subject, this similarly can be taken to have terminated the original by either amending it or making it redundant.

How do treaties become the official statement of legal policy for particular nations? Today it is typically true that treaties must be ratified somewhere within the national legislative process before they become binding, and the text of the treaty may well so specify. In the 18th and early 19th century, ratification would have been understood ipso facto in the process of negotiation and signature, being at most a formality. To some extent the United States pioneered in the process of making ratification a separate meaningful step by the Senate's failure to ratify several treaties which the president had quite confidently negotiated. As governments have become more and more democratized, especially when this has brought in the checks and balances of the presidential rather than parliamentary system, the requirement of ratification has become almost universal. Even countries with totally unified and unrepresentative systems, as the Soviet Union, have imposed this "requirement" on themselves. The explanation for this last affectation is quite simple. International relations continues to be a tit-for-tat bargaining process until the moment the goods are delivered. If the United States Senate can hold up the Non-Proliferation Treaty, the Soviet Union must have a body similarly capable of withholding approval, lest it have no more bargaining cards to play.

As additional material to be cited on the substance of international law, we have commentaries on the law authored by distinguished professors of the subject. The authors themselves have no legal standing, but their scholarship is widely accepted as to what tradition had required on the subjects in question, and their commentaries are thus regarded as good evidence to be cited on any question in dispute.

Having a slightly more official standing are the codifications of international law undertaken by conferences convened at the request of some number of governments. Typically these have been convened when the pace of technological improvement had increased the costs of confusion on legal questions, such that all parties would benefit from having such confusions reduced or dissolved. An example of this is the Conference on Telecommunications convened to determine legal rules that would apply to cables placed on the ocean bottom.

Law is generally more manageable when specified individuals are assigned the task of interpreting what governments have declared. If states pledge themselves to be bound by whatever these "interpretative" individuals declare, the "Judges" involved ipso facto become lawmakers themselves. The international system has seen the establishment of various ad hoc tribunals, sometimes pertaining only to the interpretation of particular treaties. Since the end of World War I, an effort has, moreover, been made to supplement these with more general courts to deal with all of international law, first the Permanent Court of International Justice, since 1945 renamed as the International Court of Justice. As everywhere else, judges on these courts maintain a useful fiction in pretending that they are only interpreting laws established from other sources. As everywhere else, these judges are indeed expanding and supplementing the body of international law in the process, with the result that decisions of these courts are to be cited along with, or ahead of, the commentaries of private legal scholars.

Yet the commitment of individual states to accepting the decisions of any particular court has been quite uneven, varying from country to country and subject to subject. Some states have accepted an automatic and obligatory jurisdiction of such courts for specified kinds of cases, while leaving themselves the option of rejecting its jurisdiction on other cases. The court's stature has also faced an obvious risk that individuals serving on it would see themselves as serving the particular interests of the nations from which they came, as they composed their decisions and cast their votes. Such charges were directed, for example, at French justices serving on the court between the two world wars.

The international court question indeed introduces a broader problem—whether nations can still consider themselves unbound by any aspects of international law to which they have not specifically assented. Does a rule of international law require unanimous affirmation by all the states which it purportedly binds?

Traditional analysts of the limitations of international law would indeed conclude that a nation still cannot be bound unless it has declared itself bound. Yet couldn't a state bind itself to whatever rules some higher process came forth with? Most of developing international law and treaties indeed still deal directly with substantive matters, rather than binding the parties to any new procedural forms which might compromise their rights of review or dissent in the future. Logical analysts may now enter the fray to note that the distinction between substance and procedure is an extremely illusive and difficult one to maintain, so that any treaty whatsoever indeed implies a little of each, and hence a little bit of surrender of sovereignty.

Legal tradition has not allowed nations to withdraw from treaties except under certain circumstances. If "Rebus sic stantibus," the conditions originally applying, having undergone change, nations classically are allowed to withdraw; some treaties, for example, the Nuclear Test-Ban, allow nations to withdraw with specified procedures and submissions of advance notice. A few treaties, indeed, provide for amendment with less than unanimous consent, with the proviso, however, that nations need not accept the amendments, and can withdraw from the treaty as a whole if they have not agreed to the changes. It may nonetheless be difficult or embarassing for a nation to exercise its rights of independent sovereignty in such cases, and it may thus feel driven to follow the majority's wishes even if it had disliked them on substance.

To note that international law cannot bind except by consent is thus a misleadingly pessimistic statement. All international law and treaty impact is to some extent involuntary. One keeps a promise not because one wants to deliver the goods, but because one's reputation is on the line and would suffer if the goods were not delivered.

In the aftermath of World War II, an argument was developed that nations were bound by international law even if they have not consented to or ratified the particular provisions in question. To judge the validity and relevance of such a proposition, one must again ask what it means to "be bound" by international law. The argument as stated above emerges from prosecution of Japanese leaders for failure to adhere to the Geneva Convention, albeit Japan had never ratified the convention. Yet it is obvious that prosecution in this instance resulted from the near total defeat of Japan in World War II. If any country again loses a war to the same degree, its leaders will probably also be placed on trial, for violations of some sort of law, whether or not it was law they had ever acknowledged. Yet it is unlikely that defeats or victories in the future will be as total, now that several nations possess nuclear weapons, and the precedent of 1945 may see very little repetition.

If "majority" international law cannot anymore be made binding by trials, how binding will it be? Other nations may retaliate for "violations" in smaller ways, just as they now retaliate for undesired behavior which has no relation to law. If most countries have agreed to limit themselves in a certain way, a nation which elects to act differently always runs some risks in not matching such restraints, in terms of world distrust, or resentment, or simple confusions standing in the way of cooperation and coordination. As always, these costs will have to be balanced against the gains of the act being considered.

In summary, international law exists, if we bear in mind what we generally mean by the term "law." Lawyers and others must be prepared to decipher its wordings and its inner logic, while politicians and others must reflect on the power context to determine how much such wordings will motivate themselves and others. To say that something is illegal under international law in almost every case, is to say that it is less likely. Little more can be said, but not so much more can be said for domestic law either.

FURTHER READINGS

Brierly, James L. *The Law of Nations.* New York: Oxford University Press, 1963.
DeVischer, Charles. *Theory and Reality in Public International Law.* Princeton: Princeton University Press, 1957.
Hoffmann, Stanley. "International Systems and International Law." *World Politics,* October, 1961.
Kaplan, Morton A., and Katzenbach, Nicholas de B. *The Political Foundations of International Law.* New York: Wiley, 1961.

The Issues of International Law

To what kinds of questions does international law indeed address itself? What subjects necessarily emerge in the extranational or international sphere which would not have been settled adequately within the framework of domestic law?

One issue obviously to be settled is the declared geographical extent of exercise of power for the various states of the system. In effect, when states proclaim laws, they are warning that they will punish specified conduct. With the exception of certain imperial systems with limitless aspirations, such states normally will specify some geographical limit over which this policy will apply. The United States will punish sellers of pornography within certain defined geographic limits. It will do nothing to persons engaged in such sales in Denmark. Nations can declare their borders unilaterally, but it simplifies life for all concerned if the two or more nations sharing a boundary indeed agree upon this boundary, and thus we tend to look to treaty declarations rather than unilateral declarations for the most meaningful clues in this kind of law. If the direct parties to a boundary agree on its location, the rest of the world traditionally will tailor and adjust its legal practices along the same boundary. An interesting exception today appears in the status of the Oder-Neisse line, which is agreed to by the German Democratic Republic (East Germany) and by Poland. Despite the Communist world's contention that the German Federal Republic (West Germany) does not in any way have authority extending up to this boundary, Moscow and Warsaw have devoted much effort to getting Bonn to acknowledge the Oder-Neisse line.

It is relatively easy to demarcate a boundary on the ground surface of the earth; sometimes the last inch may be contested, as on the boundaries between Communist and nonCommunist countries, along which great effort is expended to prevent the escape of persons wishing to leave Communist rule. Yet even land boundaries classically can become complicated, as when a coal mine from one country tunnels under the boundary into the other's territory, or when special arrangements have to be made for passage of some commercially crucial rail lines or highways. The best known example today of such a compromise of neat and clean territorial integrity is the western access to West Berlin by means of railroad and Autobahn highway across East Germany. In today's world, such a compromise of political control over any area indeed seems unnatural; before 1939, the separation of East Prussia from the rest of Germany by the "Polish Corridor" was similarly depicted as violating the natural unity of the whole, despite the existence of semi-extraterritorial road and railway rights for German transit across the corridor. In some ways this cartographic fixation on homogeneity and security is of more recent origins, since central Europe in the 18th and 19th centuries would indeed have shown many examples of countries splattered in a checkerboard fashion across the map. When President Eisenhower agreed with Premier Khruschchev in 1958 that the Berlin situation was "abnormal," he nonetheless echoed feelings most 20th century analysts of political events share when they examine the map.

It is much more difficult, of course, to delineate clear boundaries over water. A practical rule once made sense that a nation's sovereignty out into the high seas should extend "as far as cannon could shoot," which perhaps amounted to three miles. The three-mile limit, while generally accepted for some long time, itself could cause disputes on the mode of calculation, with entire bays sometimes being included or excluded. Over time, nations with valuable underwater coastal resources have increasingly come to claim and demand a 12-mile limit, and at times much greater extensions of legal sovereignty, as far as 100 or 300 miles out to sea. The claim has sometimes been based on the shallowness of water over a continental shelf, rather than simple proximity to the shore, so that nations may control the exploitation of oil resources and specified fishing areas, but also with the implication that national extents of sovereignty would vary with the peculiar configurations of an ocean bottom. Countries with a relatively steep dropoff on their shores, such as Chile or Norway, would thus gain relatively little.

Some similar uncertainties have arisen on national sovereignty extending upward from the earth into the airspace, and then into outer space. It is now generally agreed that nations have legal monopolies over their airspace, although Great Britain flew bombers across Switzerland in World War I to attack German targets, and rejected Berne's complaints on the ground that there was no clear international law on the subject. (The RAF did the same in World War II, attacking targets in northern Italy, but the British government this time made no pretense that this was legal.) More recent challenges of the sovereignty over airspace came with the American U-2 overflights of the Soviet Union from 1956 to 1960, which President Eisenhower promised to terminate after one of these aircraft was downed.

While this in effect seemed to concede the illegality of such flight, it more clearly signalled respect for the feelings of an opposite superpower, for such U-2 flights continue over Cuba and the Middle East, without the permission of the countries involved.

The Russians quite consistently asserted that overflights by manned aircraft constituted a violation of sovereignty as understood in international law. Yet Moscow has been willing to take a very opposite tack on orbital satellites, even those used for reconnaisance purposes. In part this must be attributed to the Russian pioneering in the orbiting of artificial earth satellites with Sputnik, and to the existence of Russian "spy" photographic-reconnaisance satellites performing the same function as those of the United States. One Russian legal argument somewhat shamefacedly advanced is that orbiting satellites are different because they do not drive themselves into the space of the country being crossed, but rather hang in orbit as the earth turns underneath them. If nothing else, such an argument illustrates the inventive imagination often required to establish and make workable the distinctions of international law.

Coordinating claims and acknowledgements of jurisdiction can cause problems also at the polar regions of the earth, or on the moon. In earlier days of European discoveries and colonizations of outside territories, international legal usage awarded territories to those who sighted them or discovered and explored them, on a first-come/first-served basis. As in many other aspects of life, the advantage of this principle is that it precludes belligerent competition for the territory at later stages, where hordes of settlers from each side might be racing to beat other hordes to the ground in question. Races between explorers promised to be manageable and nonviolent; indeed they were to be encouraged in terms of furthering European knowledge of various "new worlds." Races between larger groups almost certainly would have turned violent.

One obviously cannot allocate the moon on the basis of who first sighted it, and the world today is not especially prepared to award it to whoever first sets foot on it. The first landfalls on the moon will continue to be extremely tenuous, without any of the potential for permanent colonization and inhabitation that characterized territorial claims on earth. The world, having allocated almost all its territory to one generally recognized sovereignty or another, is, moveover, not attuned to such special principles of extension of sovereignty as were required in earlier centuries. It is thus likely that the moon will long remain internationalized and belong to the entire world. Perhaps this will mean that the laws of the sea will have to be applied, to determine, for example, who gets to punish persons committing homicides on the moon's surface. Perhaps other forms of international law will have to be developed or created.

A similar aversion to the first-come/first-served principle now characterizes the world's attitudes on its polar regions, again because landfalls have been tenuous and colonization unlikely. For the northern polar cap, the principle of "pie slices" has seemed attractive, whereby each country adjacent to the polar region acquires sovereignty over the zone running north from its shores to the North Pole itself. The Soviet Union and Canada thus acquire the bulk of the region, with much of the rest going to the U.S. (by way of Alaska), Denmark (by way of Greenland), and Norway. Since the Arctic region is an ice cap over water, however, this division might be challenged simply on the argument that the law of the high seas applies over the entire region. The threat of American oil tankers polluting the ice flows has made this a real issue.

The pie-slice rule seems less attractive for the southern polar region, albeit that "dry land" is involved here in the Antarctic continent, so that the law of the high seas has a much weaker claim. Unlike the northern cap, however, countries like Argentina and South Africa are not so close to Antarctica that they will be conducting the bulk of exploration and human activity in their regions. Law proclamation and law enforcement do not naturally fall in the shadow of these states, or of Australia, Chile, or New Zealand, and many nations have already conducted explorations or made claims on the Antarctica continent.

The claims to Antarctica typically resemble slices of pie, radiating out from the South Pole along lines of longitude, but the slices are only occasionally related to the longitude on which the home country rests. American claims, less formalized, have indeed effected a coastal region without being extended in to the pole. As with the moon, it is likely that Antarctic law will ultimately be developed from some notion of international condominium and world ownership rather than being parcelled out into jurisdictions based on earlier precedents of colonial discovery and conquest.

Related to detailed boundaries is a second area of international law, declarations of cooperation for areas which are not assigned specifically to one country or another, the high seas, outer space, Antarctica, some undemarcated deserts, and so on. Ingenious rules have been developed to determine who will have the authority to punish whom on board airplanes or ships. This has a very practical result in that individuals can discover which state forces can threaten them, which laws they must obey to avoid punishment; an equally useful result is that state forces do not become entangled in conflicts with each other.

Apart from standardization of rules for commerce on and over the high seas, and in unclaimed areas of land, the nations endorsing international law furthermore proclaim broader policies on mutual commercial penetration of each other's territories and airspace. A third category of international law, the "law of reciprocity" thus covers such things here as the presence or absence of tariff barriers, commodity sales agreements, and commercial and technical cooperation, as well as airline routes and shipping privileges in coastal waters. In effect, each nation is writing or modifying its domestic law to take into account and accommodate the matching concessions by some other state in its own domestic law. Once again the distinction between what is international and internal is somewhat shaky. The United Nations Charter, for example, forbids the organization from interfering with any internal matters of its members. Yet some commentators on international law have argued that any subject covered by treaty ipso facto becomes "international." If this were accepted, the members of the UN would hardly stand pledged at all to contain or limit their inquiries into the internal affairs of individual states, since treaties can cover items as prosaic as the exact number of airplanes to land at specified cities in any particular day.

There was a time when stronger nations would simply demand "most-favored-nation" clauses in treaties with smaller countries, clauses which automatically granted each and every privilege conceded to any other state. As the world moves toward at least a greater nominal equality in interstate relations, these have become much more rare. Also eliminated have been most vestiges of "extraterritoriality," whereby larger or more advanced states won substantial exemption for their citizens from the legal processes of the country involved. Like "most-favored-nation" clauses, extraterritoriality was rarely, if ever, reciprocal.

The generally one-sided nature of many of such treaties has generated the legal doctrine of unequal treaties, treaties which in the past committed one nation to permanent concessions only in exchange for an absence of violence by the other side. The doctrine contends that such treaties have lost their validity, even if their text would not have suggested any termination as yet.

Considerably complicating international law on commercial interaction is the generally enhanced participation of governments everywhere in economic activity. In some socialist countries almost every commercial venture may belong to the state. Most countries at least regulate their industry, if not also purchasing ownership of a great deal of it.

Some state commercial activity is thus "positive" in the sense that the government actually produces goods and services. When this is done outside the borders of the state, it creates at least a few problems for international law. Obviously the immunities granted the Netherlands Embassy can not be extended to KLM, the Netherlands government-owned airline. Where previously it would have been simple to design a rule that reciprocated special treatment for diplomats, embassies, and government delegations, the rules must be more elaborate and complicated now.

Much of state economic activity is a little more "negative" in the sense of regulating industry, forbidding certain practices while in the process encouraging others. Since corporation activities tend to overlap national borders, questions will then arise on whether such regulatory powers can follow along. Do decisions rendered in accordance with U.S. antitrust law, for example, apply to the affiliates of American companies abroad, as in Canada? The emergence of the "multi-national" corporation will make the problem of regulation all the more complicated, since it is difficult to define the "home" of the corporation from which it is to be regulated and controlled by government. Until international legal practice develops more polished procedures for such questions, it is very plausible that such corporations indeed will tend to escape effective regulation. Even a little more complicated is the case of multi-national government corporations, as for example, Scandinavian Airways System (SAS), which combines a multi-national home with a blend of public and private ownership.

This third category of international law further departs from the agreed declarations of territorial extent as nations reciprocally grant personal exemptions because of individuals' loyalty or attachment to another country. If a person normally resident in Argentina thus spends time in France, he may be exempt from military service or from paying some or all taxes, and so on. By the same token, he may not be allowed to vote or to hold public office or to purchase land in certain areas. Exemptions from duties or privileges in such instances essentially result from bargaining between the countries from which such persons come. With the possible exception of diplomatic representatives of one government to another, no foreigner is totally exempted from the laws of the state in which he is geographically present. Yet the encouragement of trade and personal interaction has long suggested special dispensations, dispensations which in effect introduce such concepts as "nationality" and "citizenship." More barbaric political units might simply have drafted everyone within their reach, even tourists, into their armed forces. Peaceful interchange instead requires that states treat some humans within their physical grasp differently from the rest.

Nations of the world are not necessarily consistent in their interpretations of personal citizenship, with the result that individuals occasionally possess more than one citizenship, to their pleasure or displeasure; some countries, typically "frontier societies" such as the United States, have been quite generous with their citizenship, granting this on the basis of either parentage or birth. Others have been much more restrictive, requiring that one or both parents of the child be X for the child automatically to become X. A child born in Sweden of American parents is therefore not ipso facto entitled to Swedish nationality. A child born in America of Swedish parents is conversely an American citizen until he renounces this birthright. Frontier societies, anxious to acquire additional population, have also typically been more flexible in "naturalizing" immigrants and admitting them to citizenship.

Similar ambiguities arise on whether nations are willing to surrender their claims on persons who have acquired citizenship elsewhere. Individuals are sometimes shocked to discover that the country of their birth will still impose compulsory military service, taxes, and other duties if they return to its territory. Confusions of this sort thus can establish dual citizenships with doubled responsibilities or privileges. The United States has historically frowned on such dualities, for a long time penalizing Americans who served in foreign armed services or participated in foreign political processes. When it was expedient, however, the American government has been willing to swing in the opposite direction, as, for example, during the Italian 1948 elections, when Italian-Americans were urged to cast ballots by mail to help stave off a Communist victory.

Perhaps the saddest abnormalities of nationality appear with various categories of "stateless" persons, to whom no one is willing to grant the full prerogatives of nationality. This condition has sometimes been inflicted on nationals of defunct countries such as Lithuania. A more recent example arises with Asians resident in Kenya who possessed only some of the privileges of being British nationals. It is indeed difficult to imagine any greater disability than to be denied a national location in which one can reside. Most states will not admit persons as guests or visitors unless they have a specified home to which to return, a home perhaps signified by valid passport. The stateless person thus loses visitor privileges when he loses the domicile privileges of specified nationality. In the most tragic circumstances he may find himself on an airplane between Kenya and Britain with no rights to leave the plane or airport at either end. With more numerous refugees as at the end of World War II, or the Hungarian Revolution, statelessness may require long domicile in camps, waiting for immigration permits from some state or another.

Apart from such confusions on the particular nationality of individuals, provisions of international law do not so perfectly settle whether a state can extend its jurisdiction to its own citizens outside its borders. If an American engages in espionage for a foreign power while abroad, is he liable to punishment under the laws of the United States and international law as declared? Similarly, if he had purchased and sold liquor abroad during the period of Prohibition, would he have been liable? If the former be construed as "treason," international legal practice will indeed distinguish a liability to punishment which might not exist in the latter case. Yet the Swedish government has even considered making it a crime for a Swedish nationals to contract for an abortion abroad that would not be permitted at home.

It is more generally acknowledged that states cannot attempt to inflict punishment on their subjects while these are resident abroad, for this would serve to confuse and challenge the territorial monopolies of violence that are the heart of the political institution of states. Rather the states hosting these foreign nationals more typically will have pledged themselves by the treaties of international law to arrest and extradite such persons to the countries which will try them. Yet the very process of extradition itself is substantially circumscribed. The crime typically would have to have been committed on the territory (within the jurisdiction) of the country and courts to which the person was forcibly being returned. Secondly, the crime would have to be of a nonpolitical nature, for the purpose of altering the form of government has classically served as an exemption from extradition. The crime involved would probably also have to be a crime under the domestic laws of the country doing the extraditing. A murder charge would thus have induced Canada to send a fugitive back to the United States for trial. A charge of having violated the 1920's laws against production of liquor would not.

All of such law is "international" in that it affects several nations at once, and pertains particularly to persons who have crossed from one nation to another, but only some of it will be "international" in the sense of appearing in treaties between nations. Some provisions simply appear in domestic legal codes to reflect general understandings on how nations cooperate and interact with each other. Here, as elsewhere, the distinction between the nature and potency of domestic and international law become a little less pronounced than we sometimes have seen them to be.

A fourth category of international law simply relates to identifying which persons within a state will be recognized as holding governmental authority by other states, for purposes of the long series of regular interactions which must occur between governmental authorities. A distinction is drawn in some cases between recognition *de jure* and *de facto*, the former presumably suggesting much clearer legal title for the provisional government in question, with the understanding that the recognitor is prepared to argue legally for the validity of such title.

Between countries that have little or no physical interaction, recognition may at best entail the presence or absence of ambassadors, perhaps votes for seating at international assemblies, and the legal award of governmental assets which may be resting abroad in bank accounts. Between countries which interact more completely, perhaps sharing a common border as the United States and Mexico, recognition will touch on thousands of daily problems on which the government officials of one side must give special treatment to the government officials of the other, and must therefore express an opinion on who these officials are.

Some nations indeed draw no distinctions between de facto and de jure diplomatic recognition; France, for example, drew the ire of the United States in 1965 for recognizing a rebel government in the Dominican Republic. The problem of recognition is obvious far more severe when two rival regimes are claiming the status of a country's government, when each has some viable portion of the territory under its military and political control. The case of China since 1949 fits this class, as did some other countries in the periods of their civil wars. It is common to criticize the United States government for naive unrealism in "pretending" that the regime in Taipei governs all of China. Yet there was no similar criticism during World War II of American recognition of the exile governments of Norway and the Netherlands, albeit their control over Norwegian or Dutch nationals was far less than the Nationalists' control over some Chinese.

It is misleading to interpret "recognition" in its nondiplomatic meaning simply as the acknowledgement of physical reality. Diplomatic recognition by any state carries with it title to property within that state, as well as the host of diplomatic and legal prerogatives that countries grant each other. Regardless of physical reality, it would have been politically foolish for the United States to grant such recognition to the Quisling regime in Norway, as the political problem of winning World War II suggested an entirely opposite policy. Similarly, concern for the political future of the 14,000,000 people who live on Taiwan may have given the United States good political reason to continue according diplomatic recognition to the Taipei regime as the legal government of all China, although this in no way accords with physical reality.

Diplomatic recognition in any event does not necessarily coincide with the maintenance of diplomatic relations or channels of communication. One can have consulates in an area without recognizing the regime, as Britain has done in Taipei. When diplomatic relations are formally "broken," we can maintain contacts through economic missions, as West Germany has done for many years in Eastern Europe, or through "sections" of another embassy charged with representing our interests, as with a staff of Americans attached to the Spanish Embassy in Egypt which has remained in place ever since Egyptian-American relations were "ruptured" in 1967. One can also obviously have diplomatic recognition without any meaningful contact. The United States "recognizes" Castro as the ruler of Cuba, but has had less of a negotiating relationship with him than with the unrecognized Peking regime through the ambassadorial talks in Warsaw.

As noted above, there may be some very legitimate confusions on whether a government qualifies for diplomatic recognition. Rival regimes may even be contesting control of a country in civil war. One regime may suddenly succeed another in a military coup, always with the threat, however, of a counter-coup. Two preexisting countries may merge voluntarily, as with Syria and Egypt into the United Arab Republic, or only semivoluntarily, as with the Anschluss of Austria to Germany in 1938. At other points a nation may divide, as with India in 1947, or the UAR in 1961 again, either by common consent or without it.

Apart from such general confusion about the viability of governments, the world will typically condition diplomatic recognition on whether a candidate regime swears to uphold the prior regime's treaty obligations, usually including its financial debts and obligations. A revolutionary regime might incrementally at later stages elect to default on one agreement or another, but it will typically be persuaded to begin its tenure with a general reaffirmation of obligations, so as to leave the benefit of doubt with traditional practice until explicitly amended.

A final category of international law deals with states' behavior once they move out beyond the territorial limits to which they have bound themselves. This is, of course, what we refer to as war, when violence is inflicted on territory outside the boundaries that were mutually agreed. As noted above, some other treaties logically lapse when wars are undertaken, but the declarations that states have issued for the contingency of war do not lose their relevance, serving now as important signals of the rules these states wish to follow while they pursue military victory.

Such international law establishes categories of civilian persons and property which are not to be attacked or damaged except for very special circumstances. It simultaneously removes these protections, and all protections, when civilians serve as soldiers, but out of uniform. The same pledges of international law deal with the treatment of prisoners of war after they have surrendered themselves. Rules that have been generally, but not universally, agreed to concern the treatment and nourishment of such prisoners, the types of employment that are forbidden or permitted, and a requirement that information about their health and condition be relayed via neutral agencies to the homes of the prisoners.

As with other areas of law discussed, some provisions of international law here have been honored more often in the breach than in practice. Yet even honor in the breach has meant modifications of behavior for the sake of outside appearances, modifications quite meaningful to innocent bystanders spared additional suffering. Even at the height of World War II, for example, the mutual treatment of war prisoners between Germany on one hand and Britain and the United States on the other approximated the standards ordained by law. By contrast, mutual treatment of prisoners between Germany and the USSR was far worse, as was Japanese treatment of POW's. Yet Japan had indeed never ratified the Geneva Convention on the subject, and expected its own soldiers to die in battle rather than falling into captivity.

The laws of war also identify proper "laws of neutrality" procedures for nations not participating in the war. Combatants in any war implicitly have pledged themselves to abstain from inflicting damage on the territory of countries remaining neutral, not to pass across their territory or through their airspace, not to have their warships pass into the territorial waters except under sharply specified conditions. The respect for a nation's noncombatant status imposes or implies a reciprocal requirement that the neutral nation not offer bases to the opposing side, that it not commit its military forces to military campaigns, that it intern military forces of either combatant when they stray into its territory.

The law also will go into great detail as to what kinds of commerce are permitted on the part of neutrals, and what kinds of interference combatant nations can impose on such commerce. It is true that these provisions are commonly violated along with the rest of international law, yet it is again not clear that such violations should be viewed as a failure. If neutral nations wish to abstain from a war in most respects, but elect to participate and thereby violate international law in one or two instances, the aggrieved nation could choose to interpret this nation also as enemy, or to tolerate this quasi-neutrality in preference to extending the legal state of war. Thus Portugal was neutral in World War II, but let the Allies use bases in the Azores. Spain was neutral, but dispatched the "Blue Division" to fight against the Soviet Union as part of the German Army. In each instance, the pure case of neutrality was thus a useful benchmark by which all the nations could guide their behavior, choosing to keep hostilities limited and far short of actual war.

It is also generally true that combatants have not totally respected neutral rights in wartime, especially on matters of commerce. The extent of adherence to neutral rights here very closely reflects the relative number and weight of neutrals versus nations at war. When only a few states have chosen to remain neutral, as in World Wars I and II, their potential weight on either side is rarely enough to frighten anyone into appeasing their interests.

Standards of neutral behavior have generally been eroded since 1945, in part because of the enhanced role of ideology in motivating countries in war or in peace, in part because the delicacy of the nuclear balance has caused nations to be more tolerant and innovative in limiting warfare when it can be avoided. It is now much more general "neutral" practice to offer weapons to combatants. It is common to offer training camps and supply bases from which guerrilla forces may operate, and even air bases from which missions may be conducted into the airspace of the powers officially at war. Ideological formulations of communism, or resistance to communism, or the elimination of imperialism and colonialism, have substantially replaced the particular issues of France versus Germany, or Spain versus the United States.

When a combatant notes that an allegedly neutral country is actively aiding its enemy, the response today is hardly to declare war against this nation also. For one thing, declarations of war have fallen into disuse, simply because the world's condemnation of war has made it embarrassing for either side to admit that a state of war exists. But even extending a policy of de facto armed hostility to any pseudo-neutrals would often be bad policy today. If this pseudo-neutral were one of the major powers, the response of "treating all enemies alike" would simply constitute escalation from what had been limited war to all-out war. Even if the supporting state is not one of the major powers, the aggrieved party may see considerable advantage in keeping the degree of international hostility under control at this point.

We can attempt to summarize some definite trends now underway in the style and impact of international law. As noted, the general democratization of political systems since the 19th century has increasingly required ratification and openness in the establishment of treaty law. The general technological complexity of our times has simultaneously forced greater codification and explication of the law. Economic intervention has become the normal practice in most countries, thus forcing us to discriminate among differing governmental functions, some of which receive the special reciprocal treatments governments accord to each other, some of which do not.

In some ways the most important development has been the addition of new states, states which have interests and attitudes sharply varying from those of the older European members of the system. The conflicts here emerge most clearly on the law's protection of foreign-owned property within any particular nations' territory. When leases for mineral development have earlier been granted for extremely long durations, the hosting states are now often governed by regimes considerably less willing to tolerate such foreign exploitation of indigenous resources. The "laws of property" and of contract will thus receive less certain support and endorsement as more and more nations turn to expropriation as a means of remodeling their economies.

Newer states will similarly argue for territorial limits extending further into the seas than the older "sea-faring" nations are willing acknowledge. Countries like the United States and Britain, with large navies and merchant and fishing fleets, have a vested interest in arguing for the 3- or 12-mile limit when much of the world is coming to favor much more, perhaps even 100 or 200 miles. The discovery of exploitable natural resources on the beds of the oceans, as with oil and natural gas in the North Sea, raises new problems of demarcating international jurisdiction and regulating national practices on the seabed.

Newer nations, many or most of them fairly recently freed of colonial regimes, will be far less tolerant of intervention from outside wherever this seems to reproduce the aggressions of the colonial period. Yet the same nations will refuse to allow this rigorous defense of "national integrity" to apply to any regimes which are still left over from the colonial period, as, for example, the Portuguese colonial governments in Angola and Mozambique. This "double standard" on nonintervention in nations' internal affairs may be transitory, and may thus not do permanent damage to the fabric of understood international law. Perhaps the distinction drawn between colonial and noncolonial regimes can even be made consistent and clear so that it would not be redefined on an ad hoc basis whenever a state wished to justify intervening against another. The risk remains, however, that some truly independent and moderate regimes will be slandered as surrogates for the former colonial powers, and that the vehemence of new nations on national autonomy and integrity is not as meaningful as it appears.

As noted earlier, the legal duties of neutrality are likely to fall into repeated disuse and violation now, as a more ideological base for national policy almost seems to require some intervention in every conflict. Neutrality in the sense of international law should, in any event, not be confused with "neutralism" as a contemporary label for a particular political stance. Neutrality refers to a code of conduct which may have little to do with the sympathies of the country, but rather reflects a strict adherence to legal rules, as in the practice of Sweden or Switzerland. "Neutralism" rather tends to describe a set of stands on the substantive issues which accidentally or deliberately sees itself more or less midway between the two "superpowers," the United States and Soviet Union. This latter is, of course, not a legal concept at all, but rather an astute political position reflecting an adjustment to postwar distributions of force and strength.

Since all-out war is so horrible as to be almost unthinkable, the likelihood of any recourse to the formal declaration of war is considerably less in the present international environment, in part also because of the tone of the United Nations Charter. Arab states in the Middle East from time to time have described themselves as being in a "state of war" with Israel to justify constrictions of Israeli traffic that would otherwise seem illegal, but presumptively it was Israel that initiated and first declared this condition. If nations have thus in effect been hypocritical, this has advantages as well as disadvantages. Among the disadvantages are the bypassing of domestic processes which otherwise would have been required if a declaration of war had been involved, and a general obscuration of whether the legal conditions and protections of war will apply. The advantage is that the emotional and legal style of all-out war here is muted, making it easier to limit warfare to less than total activity on each side.

FURTHER READINGS

Coplin, William D. *The Functions of International Law.* New York: Rand McNally, 1966.
Friedheim, Robert L. "The 'Satisfied' and 'Dissatisfied' States Negotiate International Law: A Case Study." *World Politics,* October, 1965.
Scheinman, Lawrence, and Wilkinson, David. *International Law and Political Crisis: An Analytic Casebook.* Boston: Little, Brown, 1968.

International Structure

International relations has unhappily seen repeated intrusions by the armed forces of one country into the territory of another. More happily, it has seen some coordination in declarations of law, which ultimately help to reduce the number of such intrusions. Yet military operations and international law hardly comprise all there is in meaningful international political activity, for we have become accustomed to mutual intrusions by a host of unarmed agents, in what is known as diplomatic relations. Some of this mutual penetration has further seen such individual agents surrendering their national allegiances and identities, to become part of an international bureaucratic structure with loyalty to the world as a whole.

Has there ever been a total absence of such peaceful international activity? Are diplomatic relations indeed something new in the history of international affairs? History as far back as the Greeks and Romans records the existence of "embassies" on an *ad hoc* basis, but these were more precisely delegations sent to conduct specific conferences. The conventions of the time most certainly had to exempt such delegates from being treated as hostile soldiers or as prisoners of war, but the "embassies" did not remain in place to represent their home countries on any continuing basis.

In general, the generation of a true embassy structure presupposed the existence of a multiple of well oriented states, which can not be said to have emerged until long after the Roman Empire. Further required were regular and serious interactions for which such states had to negotiate across a barrier which was typically ethnic and cultural as well as political. In the case of the Greek city-states, the cultural links among these states were already so strong that supplementary diplomatic channels were not really required at the governmental level, except for the ad hoc delegations that appeared from time to time. The very dominance of the Roman Empire conversely precluded recognition of any diplomatic equality for delegations from neighboring territories; these often were accorded only the status of delegations coming to surrender and plead for terms. Perhaps an apt analogy would be with the 19th century reception of delegations of American Indians in Washington D.C., "embassies," to be sure, but with no equal status or permanent function, invited to the capital primarily to be intimidated by its very size.

Sometime after the resurgence of Europe at the end of the Middle Ages, the functional need became clear for more permanent governmental representation abroad. As often happens, the first satisfaction of the need came through the adaptation of an otherwise vestigial organ. The Byzantine Empire, with its own claims on the Roman inheritance, still maintained the pretenses of dispatching governors to various territories in Italy, territories which in fact had achieved real independence. What nominally were viceroys in fact thereby came to be ambassadors. A present-day analogy might appear in the labeling of ambassadors within the former British Empire as High Commissioners. Other parts of Italy came to copy the practice of maintaining permanent representatives abroad, and of tolerating such ambassadors in their own capitals, and the practice spread throughout the European system.

As communication from government to government thus came to be recognized as extremely important, other standardizations of practice occurred to facilitate this. Latin was the unitary language upon which diplomatic practice standardized, although French would later replace it. Rules of accreditation and precedence began to be developed and codified. Diplomatic immunity was made standard, thereby enabling each state to recruit better people to go to nations which might someday turn into military enemies. In some ways this might be interpreted as a grand conspiracy among all the diplomatic services or political elites of the world to protect each other. At the extreme, we have the contemporary Latin American practice whereby the embassy is treated almost as a geographic part of the country which has dispatched it, such that deposed dictators regularly seek and find sanctuary in such embassies. The respect revolutionary governments show for such sanctuaries presumably reflects a foresight that the same privilege might be used when another revolution has deposed the new regime. Apart from bureaucracy protecting its privileges, however, it seems clear that diplomatic agencies could not serve mutual interests as well if the host country did not accord immunities to the persons, communications, and property of foreign embassies.

Diplomatic activity abroad has classically involved two kinds of risk, mistreatment of the persons sent, and humiliation of the country in a derogatory application of the formalities. Especially when the legitimacy of European states still often seemed to depend on residual claims of inheritance from Rome, a denial of precedence or equal treatment when compared with other ambassadors might force a nation to protest by withdrawing its embassy, lest it implicitly otherwise acknowledge a flaw in its legal claims to authority. The quarrels of diplomatic practice on occasion required that duels be fought; at other times ambassadors would have their coaches race for primary position in some procession. The very title of "Embassy" was for a long time reserved only for missions to the most important countries. The United Kingdom at the beginning of the 1840's had embassies only in Paris, St. Petersburg, and Constantinople; all the rest were missions or legations. Washington D.C., Americans will be bemused to discover, was elevated to the rank of embassy only in the 1880's. To resolve the many quarrels over the precedence of envoys, the Pope drew up a list of priority, a list, however, never really accepted by Protestant countries or even by all Roman Catholic states.

As states became more organized and professional at home, this efficiency was reflected in the organization of international activity. The epitome of this in the 17th and 18th centuries emerged in France under Louis XIV, and the proof of French excellence might thus be found in the replacement of Latin with French as the normal language of diplomacy. French diplomacy was marked by a stress on privacy and confidence, on communication with the national government involved, typically forgoing opportunities for intrigue with dissident factions in the hosting country, as had often been the practice in the Italian system. The stabilization of regimes from country to country thus perhaps inevitably required a stability in relations between regimes, forgoing the opportunistic pursuit of intrigue, cultivating a professionalism about the post of ambassador.

The consolidation of national sovereignty in time had to terminate the supposed legacies of hegemonic Roman sovereignty and authority, although it required the final blow of the French Revolution and the Napoleonic onslaught to bring an open admission of this. The last vestige of the Holy Roman Empire was thus declared terminated in 1806. The peace conferences reestablishing a legitimate Europe after the defeat of Napoleon in 1815 chose to redefine precedence of missions and embassies entirely on priority of the individual's arrival in the country, thus laying to rest implications of one country's primacy over another. In diplomacy, as in other questions, Europe after 1815 thus gave up the notion of being united in the inheritance of Rome, and thereby rescinded one classical invitation for sovereigns to lay claim to the post of unifier.

Yet why do nations still indeed bother to locate embassies abroad today, and to tolerate them from abroad, when this physical arrangement still so much serves as the object of a great deal of abuse. Ambassadors are kidnapped, embassies are picketed or more violently attacked; the very location of embassies becomes a perennial issue in the city-planning of national capitals, as the host government, the foreign government, and the local residents typically have three different ideals on where this foreign presence should be sited. Why indeed would it not suffice to have governments deal through such neutral media as the mails, or today through telephones and telegraph lines on the order of the "hot line"; at least delegates might meet on some neutral ground such as the United Nations, or as the Communist Chinese and American representative used to sit down together in neutral Warsaw.

In earlier days, of course, the flow of communication back and forth between national capitals would simply not have been fast enough. Rather than waiting for a message to travel all the way from Paris to Washington in 1810, and then to return, it made far more sense to deputize a trustworthy American to Paris, to answer French questions in a way which very probably would duplicate any answers that would have come from Washington. Deploying a representative of one's government forward thus allowed messages to be turned around before they had to travel the lengthy distance between capitals. There is surely no such time lag today, when messages can flow from Paris to Washington in seconds. Yet the same technology which has so drastically increased the speed of communications has also tempted us to expand the volume; having a staff of the American government in Paris thus still markedly reduces the time and effort required for the two governments to coordinate and compare notes on items of mutual interest.

Even when the message originates in Washington, the American ambassador who delivers the note in a foreign capital eases the physical communications problem by being ready to amplify and explain its meaning as questions of interpretation and significance are directed at him by his host government. In terms of relaying information back to his home capital, it likewise might have seemed that the government could simply have asked all its questions by mail or telephone. Having an ambassador in place, however, allows the composing of follow-up questions on the spot, in response to the preliminary answers.

The telephone and cable, therefore, still cannot carry information quite as well as the human being who is physically dispatched abroad. Fuller exchanges of information are facilitated by sending ambassadors and allowing other nations to send ambassadors in return. Yet each side might become concerned lest it is getting less of the benefit from such information exchange than its opposite number. If Paris locates a mission in Washington, therefore, the U.S. will probably wish still to have its own mission in Paris.

The same men who ask questions of the government can also collect information about their hosting country independently of its government, and one clear function of all missions abroad is thus simply intelligence. The embassy staff will try to report back the capabilities and preferences of the country they are watching, and this is parcelled out among political officers, scientific attaches, cultural attaches, and military attaches. The military attaches indeed are engaged in a legally tolerated form of espionage; if too zealous in their activities, they may be expelled as persona non grata, unlike other spies who will be shot when caught.

To some extent the host country will welcome being observed, if it feels that accurate reports of its inclinations will bring a cooperative response from the country with which it is dealing. The host country will obviously hope that the embassy's reports will reflect as favorably as possible on it, inducing more cooperative interactions rather than less. Yet this hardly leads to the conclusion that a very sympathetic ambassador will be regarded as ideal from the host's point of view, for there may then be doubts on how seriously his reports are taken by his home government.

Past a certain point, moreover, the host country may not wish to be watched too closely or carefully. There may be some irreducible conflicts of interest between the two states, where accurate reporting of the military, economic, political, or social condition of the country would only worsen relations, or help the adversary win more of the disputed points. In Russia and China, therefore, diplomats are not allowed to wander freely, but rather are substantially limited in what they may see and to whom they may talk. Embassies are tolerated because the government indeed wishes to compare notes with other governments; but the same state does not wish these other governments to compare notes with ordinary citizens, or to wander about reaching conclusions differing from those presented by the state.

Another part of an embassy's function is, of course, supplying information, rather than collecting it, in a way which will produce the response most desired back home. The supply of information may include simple information services, the promotion of industrial exports or tourism, cultural exchange programs designed to highlight what is common to and attractive in the two ethnic heritages, and straightforward political propaganda.

Again, there may have to be limits to what the host nation will tolerate in such activity. Some distribution of information by embassy directly to citizens may seem perfectly natural and desirable in the more open societies, but very threatening in the more closed societies. Part of any tolerance for such foreign propaganda emanating from a camp on one's own soil relates to reciprocity; if the USSR wishes to publish an English-language magazine in the United States, it must allow distribution of a Russian-language magazine of the U.S. Information Service in the USSR. Even as democratic a country as India will be reluctant to see itself inundated with Russian or American information outlets or "libraries," in part out of sensitivity to foreign propaganda battles being waged in its cities, in part because a toleration of overt activities may inevitably produce a greater volume of covert activity issuing from the same buildings.

A third major function of the embassy is quite symbolic, as the very presence of a stately building with a foreign national flag flying over it suggests that relations between the two countries are normal and friendly. It was earlier noted that the explicit embassy can be the object of a great deal of symbolic abuse coupled with physical attack; yet this only illustrates the extent of the normal symbolic reinforcement that the institution of the embassy supplies to the image of friendly and cooperative relations, since opponents of such friendship must go to such extremes to tear the image down. The significance of the symbolic function is well illustrated by those special cases where normal embassy functions are exercised without the symbolism, when "diplomatic relations have been broken." For years, the West German government had "trade missions" in various Warsaw Pact countries which handled most of the normal functions of an embassy, but were accorded none of the honorific trappings. Credentials were not presented to the nations' presidents, diplomats were not invited to and toasted at national day celebrations. A similar situation applies to American diplomatic presence in various Arab countries, where an "American Interests Section," manned by American State Department representatives, is attached to the Spanish embassy in Cairo, often still working out of the American embassy building, even holding conversations with Egyptian presidents, but not symbolically suggesting that any normalization of relations with the United States has occurred.

By contrast, there are places where the United States has had no diplomatic presence at all, either symbolic or real; Communist China has been an obvious example, East Germany is another, a few of the Arab states with more radical regimes are in the same category. The absence of any American governmental presence serves to illustrate a fourth major function of having a governmental presence overseas, which might generally be labeled as the consular function. Governments which can afford to deploy consulates and embassies abroad thereby try to supply their citizens abroad with many of the same services to which they would be entitled at home. Advice on how to do business, or on how to renew or replace a passport, or on how to pay one's income tax is to be had, along with warnings and advice on local laws and customs. This may seem a most mundane part of the explanation of the ambassadorial function, but it is hardly trivial for most embassies of the world, as judged by the volume of their daily business. For much of the 19th century, the American diplomatic presence abroad dealt predominantly with such matters. One should note, for example, that Norway's final decision to seize independence from Sweden was caused by the failure of the Swedish government to supply sufficient consulates abroad for the service of Norwegian seamen.

It is therefore important to be careful in rendering judgments on the performance of particular embassies or ambassadors. We are prone to credit ambassadors with high visibility as having done especially good work, but such visibility may only be desirable when the symbolic message to be transmitted is one of cooperation and agreement. If inevitable conflicts of interest have to surface during the tenure of an ambassador, it may be best if he appears in the nation's press as little as possible.

Similarly, on the question of credibility of information-gathering, the Israeli public might welcome the idea of an American ambassador who was of Jewish religion, or in addition a dedicated zionist, but the Israeli government would probably be concerned immediately about his effectiveness as a deliverer of messages. Won't Washington instinctively discount all his reports on the grounds that his religion has biased him toward the Israeli position? To be sure, the Israelis also will not welcome an ambassador with a history of skepticism or hostility toward zionism, not because his reports would lack credibility, but because they would tend to be unsympathetic to the Israeli viewpoint. Just as the balance is delicate in terms of the kind of ambassador the hosting country would like to receive, it will be delicate in terms of the interests of the country dispatching him.

Even harder to judge from the outside are questions of personality, whether or not a certain ambassador has antagonized or alienated important political figures by his boorish style or arrogant manner. Here the greatest variance may appear between political reality and press image, for a man could be very successful at capturing the admiration of the masses of the Indian population, and at the same time succeed in alienating individuals who have much more political impact.

The communications function of embassies has obviously been altered by the rapidity and volume of communications which are available to governments today. Americans will be amused to read of President Jefferson pleading with one of his ambassadors to correspond more often, since nothing had been heard from him for several years. With speedy and voluminous communication today, the stress on the diplomatic side would have to go to credibility and acceptance, ahead of simple delivery of the messages involved.

Any generalizations one makes about diplomatic activity obviously will also have to be conditioned on the size of the countries involved. Large nations can maintain enormous embassies abroad, posing substantial management problems of their own. Some of these staffs will be devoted to the consular functions, but the rest will be propagandizing, spying, reporting, and functioning as a symbol of two countries' close and good relations. A significant portion of the embassy staff, especially at clerical levels, will be nationals of the hosting country.

At the other extreme will be the mission of some small country which has relatively little political, economic, or other business to transact with its host. The mission may comprise one or two persons, sometimes only on a part-time basis, perhaps serving as the mission simultaneously to several countries, often on a budget so constricting as to preclude telegraphic communication with the country back home. Any study of international behavior which focuses on the "objective data" of who maintains diplomatic relations with whom might thus be misleading, if many of these relationships are mostly symbolic and nominal. It is hard, for example, to imagine really significant diplomatic exchanges occurring between Burma and Norway.

The costs of embassy maintenance illustrate once again the economies of scale which can favor larger nations, economies which mean that a state ten times as large may decide to maintain a diplomatic staff much more than ten times as large or effective. Much of small nation diplomatic presence will thus lack real substance, because it is costly, and because the political gains are not substantial enough. A good number of "consulates" or "embassies" are thus even staffed by itinerant businessmen, sometimes not even of the same nationality as the country they "represent," businessmen willing to discharge a few functions such as issuing visas, in exchange for some of the privileges of diplomatic immunity.

As a substitute for real state-to-state contact, an obviously efficient arrangement is a single assembly to which each nation need send only a single delegation which can deal with any of the other delegations. Participation in such bodies as the U.N. General Assembly serves prestige purposes, serves them so well that almost no member of the organization ever economizes so much as to dispense with sending at least a single delegate, albeit many countries assign this duty to their envoy to the United States, who must shuttle between New York and Washington D.C. The assembly is also a potentially important means for communication. Where else could Iceland and Paraguay compare notes on any issues, since neither is likely to send an embassy to the other's capital.

The existence of such an assembly can thus compensate somewhat for the disadvantages of small size in nationhood. Yet some problems will remain. First, neither the envoy from Iceland nor from Paraguay is in a position to savor opinion in the other's country as a whole. Each is capturing only what the other's envoy can transmit. Second, Iceland and Paraguay may indeed have had almost nothing about which to communicate. Third, even at the United Nations, small nations may still be confronted with austerity budgets which prevent communication with their home capitals, so that their opinions as expressed and votes as cast are not authoritative.

Yet problems of coordination between home capital and embassy in the field are not limited to small countries. Virtually every memoir of an ambassador or foreign service officer of a major country complains about the amount of "paper work" he must complete to satisfy his superiors back at his home capital. Indeed, Mark Twain's aphorism might easily be revised as "Everyone complains about paperwork, but no one ever does anything about it." If the completion of detailed forms and cables comparing notes on the details of foreign policy is such a universally condemned chore, why indeed does it manage to persist with no one to defend it? Many of the same commentators who condemn excessive "paper work" would be quick to demand that the embassies abroad be "more fully coordinated" with national policy as defined back in the home country. Yet it seems clear that "paperwork" and "coordination" come close to being functional synonyms here, the one being a pejorative term while the other is a euphemism. Why shouldn't Germans ask for a maximum of coordination between Bonn and their embassy in Malaysia? Who can be against the "right hand knowing what the left hand is doing?" Won't a lack of coordination threaten the embarrassing possibility that two parts of the same government may inadvertently or knowingly be working at cross-purposes, the one undoing the work of the other?

Coordination has a price, and there will thus be times in a foreign service, just as in a domestic government, where the risks of a lack of coordination are to be accepted, since the effort to keeping everyone in touch with everyone else will far outweigh the savings thus provided. Just as we trust individual officials of a city government to suboptimize some part of the entire city's necessary functions, when deputized to do so and left on their own, we might thus grant the same trust to our ambassador in the field. We originally chose him, after all, on the basis of his proven loyalty to the country and the government, and on his intelligence and competence.

Before coming down too heavily against the paperwork of coordination, however, we will probably have to stipulate that some degree of note comparison will still be required. In part this will simply be because foreign policy as determined in the national capital is itself continually undergoing change. Even the most gifted mission abroad will not be able to adjust to the details of very important policy moves if it has not been briefed, it it has not been induced to respond with details on how the policy can be applied in the particular country involved.

Yet there will also be reasons to distrust the ambassador and staff we chose ourselves. Not only will being out of Washington leave such people unfamiliar with the intricacies of policy as we are conceiving it, but being immersed in a foreign capital may cause such people to become overly sympathetic to the country they are in. Many foreign services have rules to guard against the more straighforward complications which emerge when a diplomat falls in love with and wishes to marry a local national. Marriage will be forbidden in a few cases; more typically, the diplomat and his new wife will be transferred to a very different post where conflicts of interest might not apply. Much more subtly, however, it is possible that diplomats more generally will fall in love with the country and culture to which they are assigned, thus presenting an overly sympathetic image; closer coordination and more paperwork will thus be required to counter-act this effect.

Finally, our distrust could be aroused simply because of the bureaucratic imperialism which we have come to expect from all parts of our government back home. Whatever the personal ideology of the individual, or whatever the broad national policy of the government, it is predictably true that ambassadors and their staffs will tend to try to enhance the importance and activity of the particular mission they are staffing. If Guinea can be brought to the forefront of American policy while one is the ambassador to that country, one has moved into a position of greater status and promotion possibilities, with more of the sense of political power.

There are thus at least two kinds of issues on the role and personality of the overseas mission. One continuing issue pertains to simple compe-tence; regardless of what the ambassador most wants to achieve, the na-tional interest or his personal interest, is he capable of doing so? A second issue, of course, is one of the loyalty of the embassy to the home country, whether it will try to serve exactly those goals that the national govern-ment would have wished.

As with other examples of tension between a chief executive and his subordinates, each side has a number of tools at its disposal. The ambassador can secretly ignore the orders it receives from the home capital. It can even openly engage in insubordination, if the home government would be politically embarrassed by having to remove an ambassador it had chosen itself. The mission in the field can play the game of deliberately misinterpreting the sense or the spirit of its orders. It can report back the options for policy in ways which seem to leave the home country a choice only between disaster and following its embassy's advice.

The home country, in the person of a president or a secretary of state, can conversely devote greater attention to any particular country, giving very explicit instructions which brook of no misinterpretation, clearly warning personnel involved that bureaucratic punishments will follow if the government's wishes are ignored. While the central government can always invest such energy in a particular country if the priority seems to merit it, such energy would be drained from other areas, leaving other country-desks and embassies all the more free to do as they wish.

The alternative of choosing noncareer ambassadors, perhaps old friends or political associates of the president or secretary of state, is a practice often resorted to in the United States. Such appointments obviously run the risk that the individual will lack personal experience and competence with regard to the country to which he has been dispatched; if he was chosen merely to reward his personal or financial contributions to an election campaign, foreign policy considerations may indeed have been given a low priority. Yet the same kind of appointment might advance foreign policy, if it gave the president a man of greater loyalty than those who have risen through the bureaucracy of career diplomacy, a man who will not be interested in protecting or serving the particular interests of this bureaucracy, since his own career future is not tied to it.

Such individuals presumably have been recruited by their admiration for the president and their love of country; when reporting back to Washington, the president will find it all the easier to exchange communications with them because of his personal friendship, and because of his trust. Yet even here there can be conflicts of interest which leave the embassy imperfectly representing the nation as a whole. We are discussing individuals who enter and leave the government, ins-and-outers, who typically leave much more remunerative positions in private industry to serve their president. The psychic return that attracts such highly qualified people is probably the chance to have interaction with the president, and to do something important and valuable for the country as a whole. If such a person is sent to some country in Africa, it would be entirely possible that this country would receive excessive attention as a result, compared with nations where more ordinary diplomats had been sent. Not only will the president be more receptive because of his personal attachment to the ambassador who sent the message, but the ambassador will subtly be conducting policy so as to have excuses to send more numerous and more interesting messages, and to return to the capital periodically to have a personal chat with the chief executive. The pleasures of an old friendship can thus stretch a president's energy, but it can also misallocate that energy.

A capital has additional ploys to check the independent tendencies of its representatives in the field. All such ploys can be effective; all of them also have some price which may have to be paid. By the very nature of the embassy system, each head of state has at least two formal channels for communication. An American message to London can be sent by way of the American embassy in London or the British embassy in Washington. Where the personality failings or other drawbacks of one channel make it unusable, the other may suffice. Special envoys may also be dispatched, ad hoc delegates with a formal and real authority higher than that of the standing ambassador. The dispatching of a special envoy may attract a great deal of attention, which may be desirable in some circumstances, but not in others. The home government might thus instead rely on subordinates within the embassy whom it trusts more than the ambassador. Just as the foreign service as a whole is imperfectly coordinated and loyal through all of its chain of embassies, any particular embassy will be imperfectly coordinated or under the control of the titular ambassador. Occasionally the home government might even have recourse to totally clandestine agents, perhaps not even known to the ambassador, to engage in espionage or sabotage, or to engage simply in the exchange or proposals and advice.

In principle, it is also always possible for nations to dispense with or bypass their diplomatic organizations entirely in bringing together the two heads of government at the "summit." The advantages of such a procedure would seem obvious. The imperfect loyalties of delegated representatives are bypassed, as are the confusions which presumably enter into communications which are transmitted and retransmitted back and forth. Rapid, authoritative, and binding decisions can be rendered on each side, in exchange for equally binding concessions on the other. The apparent clarity of these advantages generates another, for the entire world's attention is captured during a summit, with the implication that each party to the conference is now likely to be friendlier to, and more cooperative with, the other. For publicity value alone, the summit must be characterized as a most useful tool of diplomacy, or substitute for diplomacy.

Yet, apart from appearances, the use of the "summit" has some definite practical disadvantages. Few heads of state can operate effectively when far removed from the bureaucracy which runs their government on a day-by-day basis, which briefs them on opportunities and risks. By definition, a summit requires that at least one of the heads of state leave his capital, and perhaps both, if some "neutral" meeting place has been chosen. The ability to render decisions instantly may also be a disadvantage if agreement were better served when each side had time to mull over its responses to its adversary's proposals. The mere confrontation of personalities may lead either side to an excessively anthropomorphic interpretation of the opposing state colossus; if the single human being heading the conference delegation should happen to seem weak, will this mislead his opposite number, in a way which would never have happened when messages are composed and read at a greater distance?

As noted, the summit has diplomatic value per se, simply as a symbolic gesture. As President Nixon's visit to Peking shows, it can completely take the place of day-to-day diplomatic relations. While some important substantive agreements can be achieved in this medium, however, the bulk of international business will require the more normal channels that do not tax the attention or capabilities of a single man.

If a corporation in private business expands in size and payroll, one assumes that it is efficient and successful. Should not the same yardstick apply to embassies that one country sends to another? Fear of excessive bureaucracy, or of excessive annoyance to the local public, make us cautious in assuming that a large U.S. embassy in Brazil will prove the success of American policy there. Yet perhaps some of this caution should be contingent on circumstances.

Is it really necessary to coordinate all the activities of an embassy, to worry that excessive size will make such coordination impossible? The U.S. government, after all, has all its agencies represented in Boston, Massachusetts perhaps grouped into a single complex of "Federal Buildings," but no effort is made to call weekly or monthly meetings of the various agency heads to be sure that the U.S. approach to Boston is "fully coordinated," as a "country team." Why should the multifarious activities of the U.S. government in London or Bangkok require coordination any more than those in Boston. Boston, to be sure, is not an alien city, but is it only alien hostility that requires "team coordination"?

Like many other things, coordination is a positive good, easily defended as long as there is no price. If the effort at coordination seriously runs down the energies and resources of the officials involved, however, then coordination may have to be dispensed with here and there; if the U.S. is heavily involved in the affairs of a foreign country, it may be necessary that the right hand often does not know what the left hand is doing.

With regard to the obtrusive visibility of the U.S. government's activities in the host country, judgment will again depend on whether the background of the two countries' interests leans toward cooperation or conflict. Where there is widespread agreement, increased visibility may simply serve as a beneficial reminder of how good relations are, rather than as an irritant.

As nations establish embassy structures which project out beyond their borders, the next step might appropriately come in the form of joint staffs holding nations together, as in military alliances. Some of the earliest secretariats of what later became truly international organizations were thus indeed outgrowths of wartime alliances and of the need for military cooperation and coordination.

There will always be some confusion on what one means by an alliance, and what is crucial to such political relationships. For example, is there still an alliance between the Soviet Union and Communist China? We have read explanations and accounts of Sino-Soviet "disputes," "rifts," and "conflicts," and yet certain kinds of legal reasoning would suggest that the earlier "alliance" has not yet been terminated. Military alliances indeed typically begin with a formal treaty, and the treaty in the Sino-Soviet case (as also in French membership in SEATO) has not been formally terminated. But such treaties are mainly significant in the infrastructure they lead to, an infrastructure which amounts to binational or multinational bureaucracy transcending national frontiers. The infrastructure reinforces and reifies the alliance in two ways: By bringing many nationals of each country into closer contact with many nationals of the other, it tends to foster an augmented sharing of values. By fostering extensive communication, it precludes the kinds of conflict and counter-productive activity which stem from simple misunderstanding or "prisoners' dilemma" situations.

No alliance can eliminate all "conflicting goals"; even the United States and Canada disagree on direction or on emphasis on many issues of foreign policy. An alliance can, however, largely prevent a conflict of efforts, whereby the military, economic, or political resources of one country are expended merely to counter the similar efforts of the other. As with some other international interactions, a threshold phenomenon occurs in this case. If the interests of two countries autonomously become close enough, the establishment of infrastructure may become advisable, an infrastructure which then occasions the nations to cooperate and agree all the more. In reverse, an erosion of basic agreement may lead to a breakup of alliance structure, with the result that conflicts reappear or worsen. Such would seem to have happened since 1958 between China and the Soviet Union, even if the legal mandate for alliance remains in effect. The infrastructure of military alliances, if developed further, can be transformed into the secretariats of still more international and peaceful organizations. In effect, this would give us almost a completely inverted version of functionalist theory. Functionalism assumes that the demands of peaceful activities will generate a coordinating apparatus which also incidentally precludes outbreaks of war. The process cited here sees cooperation on peaceful pursuits conversely emerging as the by-product of cooperation on military matters.

When we refer to any form of "international organization," we are normally discussing structures which go beyond the embassy structures of "diplomatic relations processes," in that the loyalty of personnel is no longer pledged to one nation or another, but somehow to the organization as a loyalty-holding entity in its own right. Such "international" organization at the same time must be distinguished from "supranational" governments, for as long as the approval of every member state is required to general mandates for action.

By comparison with domestic political structures, what forms have these international organizations taken? One could expect to discover legislative bodies, and judicial bodies which purport only to be interpreting the legislation of others, and executive agencies with single or collective leaderships, and perhaps some structures which can only be labeled in the end as "administrative." Yet some severe difficulties of interpretation can emerge here, as illustrated in the case of the European Economic Community (The Common Market).

The European Communities today have a "legislative" Assembly which in fact has had little or no real influence over policy. They have a judicial Court of Justice which has executed its relatively limited function without serious challenge. Real power indeed rests with an "executive" Council composed of representatives of each of the member states, and with an "administrative" Commission. Since unanimous consent has been required within the Council, we might thus elect to describe the EEC as an "international" rather than "supranational" organization. Yet the Commission has been able to affect policy by presenting the Council with faits accompli from time to time, and we might thus find it quite meaningful to see the Council really serving as the legislature of the European communities, with the head of the Commission being the real executive.

Any time an "international" agency is created, some "supranational" attributes thus tend to slip in, if only because bureaucratic loyalties can generate certain kinds of political activity and political momentum that are difficult to stop, even with a constitutional or legal mandate on one's side. Assessments of the degree of international government must thus look beyond legalism and formalisms, to the more real motives and drives that tend to explain political behavior as we know it. Functionalist theory is indeed one form of such a "realistic" outlook, arguing that the economies of scale in economic cooperation would naturally force an expansion of the central organizations, until some political unification functions, for example, the prevention of war, had ipso facto been assumed.

Functionalist theory may indeed be too deterministic to account for whether international organizations will develop supranational elements. A different "realistic" theory will extrapolate from our experience with the practices of bureaucracies on the domestic scene. The crucial variables to be watched thus become the longevity of careers (or security of job-tenure) of the individuals staffing an international organization, and the degree of their protection against pressure or reprisal by their own home governments or other governments. Do they have to worry about having no home to which they can safely return, or no sure careers? Once such worries are eliminated, the international civil servant will be able to turn with gusto to (perhaps literally) "building empires," to making his bureau as big and as important as possible.

International organizations, like domestic governmental bureaus, will thus strive to expand their mandate, their patronage, their budgets, and their staffing, because this leads to more rapid promotions and pay increases for the leaderships and for all concerned within the bureaus, because this tends to satisfy the lust for power and importance that historically has attracted so many people to politics in the first place.

Within domestic governmental structures, differences have sometimes been noted between "younger" and "older" organizations, the younger being all the more prone to seek expansion, the older being more staffed by persons closer to retirement, accustomed to standard operating procedures, such that some of the drive for innovation and aggrandizement has been tempered. These factors thus generate a typical bureaucratic life cycle which sees agencies grow quickly and then later become dormant. Some of the same dormancy, after an initial period of zeal and enthusiasm, might presumably be found in international specialized organizations, although events as momentous as two world wars could easily complicate the pattern.

As part of this bureaucratic politics pattern, one notes some other regularities. Bureaus tend never to die or dissolve or disappear, presumably because those who would have to pronounce them dead have a vested interest in not doing so. Subtle forms of competition and infighting will appear among bureaus competing to assume the same function, as, for example, between the World Bank and the Food and Agriculture Organization (FAO) about who will administer an aid program in some country, or between the United Nations Secretariat and the International Atomic Energy Agency (IAEA) about who would have jurisdiction over peaceful nuclear explosions. For various reasons, such struggles have to be kept behind the scenes, because of the unseemliness of an open conflict between international organizations, all presumably dedicated to the same high purposes. Yet, as within national governments, these interbureau conflicts are often more real than the international conflicts of interest we are all accustomed to noticing. Since sovereignty is regarded as legitimate, it will often seem appropriate for a diplomat or statesman to stress or even exaggerate the conflicts of interest between his own country and some other. Pretending to be very unhappy about some proposal sometimes increases the concessions one wins, over what a more honest statement would produce. In the arena of international bureaucracy, however, conflict must be hidden rather than declared, and it is the cooperation, coordination, and agreement of the various agencies that must be exaggerated.

FURTHER READINGS

Attwood, William. *The Reds and the Blacks.* New York: Harper and Row, 1967.
Galbraith, John K. *Ambassador's Journal.* Boston: Houghton-Mifflin, 1969.
Nicolson, Sir Harold George. *The Evolution of Diplomatic Method.* London: Constable, 1954.

International Organization

The first modern international organizations appear in the 19th century in the aftermath of the defeat of Napoleon, in the form of secretariats with continuing staffs, thus to be distinguished from the staffs set up on an *ad hoc* basis for specific international conferences. One category of these emerged with the various river commissions, some of which, as on the Rhine and Danube, continue to the present. Such commissions were entrusted with the regulation of commerce on waterways passing through a number of distinct sovereignties, waterways which in the age of canals and the steamboat might otherwise have been difficult to regulate and use; operational responsibilities would include locks and subsidiary canals, and perhaps various flood control structures. The river commissions seem almost to support Professor Wittfogel's general theories again, that large water systems require coordination and therefore occasion the centralization of political authority.

One might have predicted greater and greater extensions of authority for such commissions, as canal-building boomed in the 1830's, perhaps extending all across Europe. The replacement of canals by the railroad as the dominant mode of transportation limited any such grand functionalism here, however, as the international bureaucracies that had been established settled back to a more finite role.

A second kind of international organization appeared in the latter 19th century to exercise a transitory jurisdiction over various territories outside Europe, territories soon to be divided into distinct colonial segments, but for the time requiring temporary exercise of multinational authority. By the very definition of their function, these organizations were not destined to expand or persist.

A third and more significant form of international structure emerged at about the same time, in the regulation of various kinds of internationally relevant communications and economic functions. Among the most prominent of these are the International Telecommunications Union, dating in some sense from 1865, the Universal Postal Union from 1874, the International Labor Bureau (later to become the ILO) from 1901, and the International Institute of Agriculture from 1905. Most of these coordinating organizations offered memberships only to governments, although a few combined governmental and private organizational memberships on an international basis. By 1914, according to one count, 222 such unions had been established.

The ITU and UPU were manned by employees of the Swiss government until well into the 20th century, but the bureaucratic motivation of the individuals involved nonetheless already displayed a certain kind of the "statelessness" that we have come to expect of more multinational secretariats since; this was possible in particular because Switzerland as a country could be said to have pursued no foreign policy in this time. As Swiss soldiers were the mercenaries of earlier centuries, the Swiss civil service was, in effect, offered on a mercenary basis to serve the purposes of international coordination.

An important legal distinction first appeared with the International Institute of Agriculture, based in Rome, which was granted diplomatic immunity for its functionaries by the Italian government. Within a short time, this grant of immunity became the general practice with regard to international organizations, thus rounding out the personal security prerequisite for a motivation substantially independent of particular nations.

One might have held hopes that the functional basis of organizations like the UPU and ITU would become dominant and important; perhaps this would lead to organizational expansions and would ultimately amount to so much "international government" as to make war impossible. Yet the experience of such organizations again suggests that such functions do not flow in a wider and wider stream, but rather reach natural limitations whereupon they are dammed in. Observers take pride in man's ingenuity as illustrated in the UPU in somehow arranging that wars lead to very little interference in the mails, but not in having made war any less likely. In time of war, nations may cut each other's cables lying on the ocean bottom, but the functions of the ITU otherwise are preserved.

Yet these organizations at least set the precedent for international secretariats and an international civil service, a precedent which might pave the way for other organizations with different functional bases, organizations which might accomplish more in terms of making war unlikely.

Obviously the first organization of the latter type emerges with the League of Nations in 1919. If the League had a "function," it was now explicitly to be the maintenance of peace. The assumptions underlying the League's formation indeed were that World War I had in large part been due to the major powers' inability to coordinate with and reassure each other. A permanent conference system would thus be required, backed up again by a permanent secretariat. In times of crisis, this would mean that no one had to take the embarrassing initiative of convening a conference, since the organization itself would be almost automatically geared to doing so. It sometimes has been argued that the death of any sovereign in 1914 would have been most fortunate in generating an automatic excuse to bring heads of state and heads of government together. Since no such occasion arose just prior to the outbreak of war, mutual misunderstanding presumably made war so much more likely.

This reasoning on the need for relatively continuous communication thus explains much of the League's constitutional structure. The Council of the League might be compared with the old congress system of the 19th century, entailing representation for all the major powers plus a number of memberships rotating among smaller states. The League's Assembly, conversely, convened representatives of every member of the League. There was indeed to be no rigorous division of duties between the Council and the Assembly, merely an assumption that the Council could be convened on shorter notice if an emergency had arisen. Decisions were to be reached in the Council by unanimity, with the understanding, however, that parties to a conflict would not be voting on it. This provision illustrates, as much as any other, the assumption that conflict typically would emerge from ad hoc misunderstandings, rather than from deep-rooted contests between ideological blocs or permanent military alliances.

In practice, the unanimity rule, which would have provided every member of the Council with a veto, was watered down somewhat. There was no veto, for example, on expelling a nation from League membership. A great number of issues were redefined as "procedural questions," on which unanimity was not required.

The League's covenant also established a Permanent Court of International Justice, again reasoning that legitimate misunderstandings on the dictates of specific treaties or of international law in general, might explain much of the threat of war. If a respected and impartial body of legal expertise could be brought in to focus on such disputes, they might be settled with enough mutual satisfaction to prevent any recourse to war. The League did not therefore presume that no changes would ever be required in frontiers or other international disputes. Rather such changes could be handled peacefully, so as to settle the dispute in ways which did not inflict enormous costs on everyone involved.

The League Covenant finally provided for a Secretariat, headed by a Secretary-General, who might indeed have become a powerful figure. The persons holding this position varied markedly in ambition and personal ability, however, with the result that none have become as memorable as their successors in the post of United Nations Secretary-General.

The League of Nations was given a loose authority over the other preexisting international organizations, such as the UPU and ITU, as part of its function of coordinating affairs relevant to peace. While these organizations and bureaus were thus nominally subordinate to the League, in the respects that matter most they remained independent, having their own sources of financing, and their own staffs with separate paths of career advancement from those of the League itself. It comes as no surprise therefore that relations between the League and the specialized agencies exhibited a fair amount of friction and infighting between the two world wars, always within the bounds of a general decorum befitting international organization. Similar disputes persist today between the secretariats of the United Nations itself and of the specialized agencies. Indeed, it would have surprised students of any national bureaucratic process if such disputes had been totally absent.

Why did the League of Nations "fail," from the viewpoint of supplying peace in the world, from the viewpoint of supplying the services its "customers" were seeking? One adds the latter qualification, only to note that the League was hardly a failure in terms of getting an international bureaucratic function going, since the UN in fact assumed the role of the League, indeed with bigger and better job opportunities for the civil servants involved.

Part of the difficulty of League peace-maintenance could be attributed to the limited participation of the really great powers of the world. The United States abstained from membership from the very beginning. Soviet Russia was long denied membership, was then admitted in the 1930's, and expelled after its invasion of Finland in 1939. Germany, Italy, and Japan all withdrew from membership as a sign of their contempt for peace-oriented indictments of their drives for territorial expansion. Only the United Kingdom and France were members of the League organization from beginning to end, so that the great-power fraction of the Council never was really stabilized. The smaller powers at several points demanded greater representation in the Council, for prestige reasons if for no other. The total membership of all nations in the League reached its high of 60 in 1934 before the German withdrawal. Twenty states in all were admitted to membership after the League had first been launched, while 17 withdrew voluntarily, and one, the Soviet Union, was expelled.

Yet mere membership or nonmembership does not fully explain the failings of the League at peace-keeping. It simply was not the case that nations could always put the coordination of national policy toward peace ahead of other national interests. Even the United Kingdom at points was unenthusiastic about such an absolute principle, for example, with regard to the Japanese seizure of Manchuria from China, a military intervention which was hardly the simple fruits of misunderstanding, but an intervention on which many individual Europeans might have identified with the Japanese. The League in the end failed to prevent war because its underlying assumptions about the causes of war, in effect that a secretariat could coordinate the possible antagonists to head it off, were wrong.

The United Nations Organization, which succeeded the League after World War II, was predicated on somewhat different assumptions about what was needed to preserve peace. Indeed, it is sometimes charged that the UN was formulated to prevent World War II, just as the League was designed to prevent World War I. If generals always prepared to fight the last war, in this view, diplomats always prepare to prevent it. The central assumption in the planning of the UN was that continued peace would depend on cooperation among the World War II Allies in resisting aggression by the Fascist states, and by any later states which had adopted a similarly aggressive world outlook. World peace was no more likely than Soviet-American cooperation, in this view, and the Charter of the UN reflected this. The major aim of the UN would be to maintain a purposeful unanimity among the powers which had defeated Germany and Japan in World War II, rather than any prevention of the misunderstandings which might have caused the war. Misunderstandings indeed had not caused World War II, as much as the naked aggressiveness of Hitler and the Japanese regime. Any decisions of the UN which lacked the acquiescence of the major powers, the "permanent members" of the Security Council, would thus be ineffective in any event, and the veto was seen as merely acknowledging this. The anti-Axis bias of the Charter is illustrated in Articles 53 and 107, which despite the general Charter tone forbidding assumptions of military initiative, explicitly sanctions such armed intervention where a resurgence of Fascism is involved.

As mentioned, the UN replaced the League's Council with a Security Council, initially composed of five permanent members (The United States, United Kingdom, France, Soviet Union, and China) together with six nonpermanent members. This was later expanded to ten nonpermanent members after the overall membership of the UN had been greatly expanded. For any substantive decisions of the Security Council, unanimity was not required, but a majority including the affirmative votes of each of the permanent members, even if one of the permanent members was a party to the issue that had been raised. The United Nations differs from the League in having security functions assigned more explicitly to the Security Council, instead of being simply shared with the General Assembly, but this provision indeed has been bypassed.

The General Assembly of the United Nations corresponds to the League Assembly, and the Permanent Court of International Justice was renamed the International Court of Justice. Most of the specific specialized agencies of the League of Nations were simply transferred over to the jurisdiction of the United Nations, with many of the same independences and rivalries persisting. Within the United Nations itself, an Economic and Social Council was established to exercise a loose jurisdiction over these agencies. A United Nations Trusteeship Council was given responsibility for monitoring the administration of former League of Nations mandate territories prior to their independence.

If lack of great-power participation was an important cause of the failure of the League of Nations, brighter hopes might have been entertained for the UN, for it began with a virtually total roster of significant states. Germany, Italy, and Japan, as recently defeated Axis powers, were, to be sure, not admitted to membership, but for the moment they were nonexistent as internationally significant actors. By 1948 or 1949, a more serious omission was to emerge as the defeat of the Nationalists in China left the mainland to a Communist regime which was not awarded the Chinese seat in either the General Assembly or the Security Council.

Membership in the organization was originally offered to all states which had participated in the war (in fact merely declared war) against the Axis. As the more flagrant example of an effort to capture membership by mere formality, Argentina declared war on Germany virtually at the end of World War II, and thereby was accorded access to UN membership.

The 51 original members were augmented by miscellaneous admissions, of which the most significant was Israel's in 1948, until the total membership had reached 60. At this point, the United States and the Soviet Union became involved in a deadlock on new memberships, with the United States consistently vetoing applications on behalf of former-Axis East European satellites of the USSR, and the Soviet Union insisting on a package approach, vetoing all other memberships.

The logjam on new membership was broken at last in 1955 and the roster has since grown steadily, with a total of memberships now surpassing 130. The membership question has almost now become a problem of defining which states are too small for membership, as miniscule island territories now achieve their independence of former colonial powers, barely able to send a delegation to New York, grossly distorting representativeness if they are accorded a single vote equal to that of each of the other delegates in the General Assembly.

In the end, the major unrepresented states have been Communist China and the two Germanies, together with the two Koreas and the two Vietnams. In every case except China's, the issue presumably was one of a new membership, to which the great-power veto in the Security Council clearly applies. In the case of China, the issue has instead seemed to be one of credentials; other issues of credentials have been settled rather smoothly as simple procedural problems, even when relatively abrupt and violent changes of administration occurred. But the Chinese case has been complicated by the persistence of a Nationalist government still controlling Taiwan and a few off-shore islands, a government quite insistent on sending delegations to the General Assembly and Security Council. It is also complicated obviously by the real importance of China as a country, as well as by the special importance which was originally accorded China as a permanent member of the Security Council.

For a time it seemed that the United States year after year would expend much of its political credit in preventing the seating of the Communist regime in the UN. Perhaps this stemmed from fear that the unseating of the Nationalist regime would complicate the legal basis for the U.S. defense of Taiwan. Outsiders planted suggestions for the seating of "two Chinas," or "one China, one Taiwan," suggestions rejected by both the Communist and Nationalist regimes, and by the United States.

For a time it seemed also that the Communist regime was not really interested in being admitted to its seat in the UN, or would gravely disrupt proceedings once it was admitted.

All this was abruptly changed in the summer and fall of 1971 with the announcements of the Kissinger and Nixon visits to Peking. The United States now officially supported the retention of a General Assembly seat for the Nationalist regime, while the Communist regime would take a seat in the Assembly also, and take the Chinese permanent seat in the Security Council; but the intensity of American support for this fall-back position was in great doubt, as the President's national security advisor Dr. Kissinger was in Peking at the very time that the UN vote was taken to expel the Nationalists. If this reflected a backing down by the U.S., the Chinese on their part have taken very moderate positions within the UN since assuming their seat, while in earlier times Peking had demanded wholesale changes in the organization, and the rescinding of resolutions in the 1950's which had condemned the Chinese participation in the Korean War.

The United Nations' procedures and rules have undergone some interesting changes in the 25 years of its existence. While great attention has been focused on the veto held by each permanent member of the Security Council, the ruling was rendered at a very early stage that abstentions did not constitute a veto, although the Charter itself required "the affirmative vote" of each of the permanent members. In the early years of the organization, the Soviet Union was repeatedly outvoted by huge margins in the General Assembly and the Security Council, thus presumably suggesting that the organization was doomed to ineffectiveness simply because its initial premises had been unfulfilled. If the Russians were to veto any serious Security Council resolution on war or peace, would this not render the UN even more meaningless than the League?

For a time it seemed that the veto would be applied to every action of the Security Council, even though procedural issues supposedly were exempt. The Russians simply would challenge any interpretation that a certain matter was procedural, and could presumably veto such an interpretation, then following with a veto on "the matter which had become substantive." While the Soviet Union was able to exploit this "double veto" for a time, a precedent was set in 1950 to deny this veto to the Nationalist Chinese, as the chairman of the Security Council simply ruled that a matter was procedural, whereupon it would take more than the single vote of a permanent member to upset the ruling. The precedent was then invoked against the Soviet Union in 1959, on the question of whether to send a UN observer team to Laos; the Russians might have been able to argue (quite correctly perhaps) that this was already a substantive rather than procedural decision. Since the chairman had established a status quo by ruling it procedural, however, the Russians were not able to veto the finding.

At the outbreak of the Korean War, the Russian veto in the Security Council did not prove a problem, for the Soviet Union had elected to boycott the Council's deliberations in protest against the continuing presence of the Chinese Nationalist delegation. Having perceived their tactical error, the Russians soon returned to the Council, however, so that any future Security Council actions with regard to the Korean War were now to be stymied. Late in 1950, therefore, the United States moved to the General Assembly where no veto would apply to secure passage of a "Uniting for Peace" resolution. The resolution in fact claimed no increase of powers for the Assembly, but merely authorized the creation of staffs to handle problems related to preserving the peace, and provided for emergency special sessions of the General Assembly. The staffs in fact were never to be constituted, but the Assembly's action opened a greater role for itself on this kind of issue, and the precedent was to be significant for at least the next decade.

For a time, majorities in the General Assembly continued to be heavily in favor of the West, but a shift in this vote distribution was likely to occur once the bar to new memberships had been lifted. Over time, therefore, the General Assembly became as prone to resolutions hostile to the West as to the Soviet Bloc. A crucial point was reached in 1965 with an American effort to compel the Soviet Union to pay its share of peace-keeping costs for UN operations in the Middle East and the Congo. In firmly resisting the invocation of Article 19, the Soviet Union maintained its insistence that such activities were reserved to the Security Council under the Charter, and in the process brought the organization close to the edge of disruption. In the end the United States proved irresolute on the question, in part because many of the neutral nations had proven irresolute in face of Soviet intransigence. The aftermath saw a more general consensus among the major powers that the Security Council was again to be emphasized ahead of the UN General Assembly, at least in part because the fluid majorities of the larger body could no longer be counted upon by any of the major powers. This did not so much endorse the thesis of 1945 that majorities were meaningless when the major powers were in disagreement; rather it reflected the powers' aversion to bidding against one another in pursuit of small-state votes.

In the aftermath of the Article 19 crisis, the permanent members of the Security Council seemed agreed on returning matters of peace and security to the Council, and avoiding recourse to the unpredictable General Assembly. Yet the final resting place of power is hardly clear yet, since the rest of the General Assembly membership may have other ideas, and may still wish to assert the Assembly's prerogatives on matters of war and peace now that the precedent has been set. It is clear now that the Assembly can not compel such countries as France and Russia to pay for peace-keeping operations it has not approved, but the moral force of a UN vote may be strong even if financial support is thin.

Power within the UN organization will thus remain somewhat uncertainly distributed between the Security Council and the General Assembly; in important ways it will be shared also by the Secretariat headed by the Secretary-General.

One can speculate about voting reforms within the General Assembly to make it more representative of the real significance of the various states. It is obviously a distortion of sorts on the simple basis of population to accord the same single vote to the United States and to the Maldive Islands. Perhaps delegations could be given weighted votes in accordance with the number of people represented. If this were adopted, however, it would not immediately make the General Assembly much more disposed to the wishes of the great powers, for the Indian and Chinese delegations would grow even larger, as would that of Indonesia. If one examines the actual votes cast in the Assembly, moreover, they do not show any such great distortion of representativeness as could be imagined in the worst possible case. Large states typically appear on both sides of the issue, as do small states.

A few international organizations accord voting strength on bases other than population, for example by financial contributions to the organizational treasury, especially when financial assistance or economic development will be the principal purpose of the agency. If this procedure seems redeemingly logical for organizations such as the World Bank, however, it would hardly be acceptable for any international body which went beyond the financial realm; indeed it would be a standing irritant in reminding underdeveloped countries of their plight. In effect, the allocation of permanent memberships in the Security Council already recognizes a priority for those states with economic muscle, although the distinction is never explicated that way.

FURTHER READINGS

Alker, Hayward R., Jr., and Russett, Bruce M. *World Politics in the General Assembly.* New Haven: Yale University Press, 1965.
Bailey, Sydney D. *The Secretariat of the United Nations.* New York: Praeger, 1964.
Kelsen, Hans. *The Law of the United Nations.* New York: Praeger, 1964.

International Military Forces

Peace-keeping as accomplished by international military forces amounts to something distinctly different in the development of international organization. If we think of a state as being defined by its access to military force, partisans of world government might have regarded this military establishment as an indispensible prerequisite to world statehood. An international organization with tools for fighting wars and inflicting death and destruction is clearly something quite different from a mere coordination organization afflicted with the inevitable bureaucratic drives to expansion.

Yet one must be quite cautious in interpreting any of the international military force experience to date as the precursor of true international government; if there are hints of world government in this experience, the evidence also suggests some problems for such a government when it should ever come into being.

The League of Nations itself had a series of experiences with international military force, experiences which might be interpreted as forerunners of the UN efforts. In the aftermath of World War I, League plebiscites were conducted to determine the future of a number of territories along the borders of Germany. Outside military forces were deployed to assure the fairness of the elections, and to preclude interference by any other military forces. While wrapped in the mantle of the League, however, such forces were really nothing more than the agent of the victorious powers in World War I, imposing their will, which in this case tended toward self-determination for the areas involved. While the plebiscites went fairly smoothly in some territories, violence erupted in Upper Silesia between ad hoc armed forces favoring the German and Polish sides, and the French troops deployed to assure a fair plebiscite were soon suspected of favoring the Polish side. British battalions were in the end dispatched to the territory to counterbalance the apparent bias of the French units who seemed to be serving the interests of Paris ahead of those of the League.

The experience in Upper Silesia suggested that troops on loan from their home governments might not be trusted to serve the international rather than their national mandate. But the experience of League forces in the Memel territory might have been even more disturbing. As litigation continued over whether the port should be given to Germany, to Lithuania, or to Poland, or should simply be internationalized, French troops representing the League were forcibly expelled by Lithuanian troops with little dignity for the international organization.

The last international force assembled under League auspices completed its tasks with more dignity, in conducting the plebiscite by which the Saar territory voted to return to Germany in 1935. Troops from Britain, Italy, and Sweden policed the polling booths with no hint of partiality, and with no challenge or interference from the armed forces of states bordering the territory. The plebiscite's outcome was so certain to be in Germany's favor, of course, that neither Nazi Germany nor France would have wished to try to tamper with it.

The United Nations from its inception saw plans for a more extensive international military force, but little agreement was achieved in the early years on any moves to go ahead with such a force. The emergence of peace-keeping military forces was thus the product of a more gradual and incremental drift into such ventures, dictated by the logic of particular situations rather than by any overall plan.

The development of such forces begins with various observer missions dispatched by the UN in the latter 1940's to report on armed conflicts in various parts of the world. Without detailed information on such conflicts, it would be difficult for the Security Council to reach findings on who was at fault in initiating or prolonging combat. For various reasons, it made sense almost from the beginning to dispatch trained military officers on such missions rather than civilian bureaucrats, military officers on loan from the armed forces of their home governments. Such officers would be better able to judge the nature of the fighting than untrained civilians. They probably would be in better physical condition if their observation task required their moving around battlefield areas, up and down mountain-sides, through jungles or deserts. Their status as professional soldiers, more-over, would win respect and cooperation from the military officers commanding the two sides in a conflict, an important consideration if diplomacy was to be harnessed to the halting of battles, a diplomacy with little or no military sanctions to back it up.

UN observer missions of this sort were thus dispatched to Greece and Indonesia in 1947, and to Palestine and Kashmir in 1948. From such missions it would therefore not be so difficult to move up to borrowing actual national military forces for use by the UN. The organization at least would already have a cadre of officers used to working with the organization and familiar with its procedures and outlook.

The first instance of such a force deployment came, of course, with the United Nations Emergency Force dispatched to the Middle East after the Anglo-French-Israeli invasion of Egypt in 1956. The logic for dispatching such forces, instead of simply sending individual officers, still did not ap-proach the original rationale for a world government military force, how-ever. The forces were not intended to engage in combat on either side, or to punish or defeat aggressors. Rather, it was expected that sizable forces of such military men could be interposed to halt fighting between the two sides, since neither would wish to accept the onus of having attacked and wounded these representatives of the outside world. If UN forces in this case were armed, it would only be for purposes of professional self-respect, or to protect themselves against attack by some isolated individuals disre-garding their nation's orders. If the UNEF had become engaged in full-scale combat with either side, it would have been a failure; had this been at all likely, the force would never have been dispatched. One could ask why a group of civilians could not have been dispatched for the same purpose. The answer again was that only a military unit was physically in the proper condition for such duties, and logistically and organizationally prepared to move as units in response to orders. To have the proper effect, it would be important moreover for the UN units to be in recognizable uniforms. The men of the UNEF, and of subsequent UN peace-keeping units, have worn their national combat uniforms, with the addition of UN light blue headgear and insignia. The latter, distinctly unmilitary in its incompatibility with field camouflage, indeed completes the visibility effect desired for the peace-keeping role.

The Middle East expedition had the backing of a consensus of the United States and the Soviet Union, thus conforming with earlier expectations that nothing could be achieved through the UN except in the presence of such a united front. Yet it is not clear that the freedom of maneuver of the UN Secretariat is so constricted. The UN, when intervening in the Congo in 1960, was to include operations which distinctly lacked the backing of the Soviet Union, operations which for the first time saw UN forces engage in combat against one of the parties to the conflict. Also to arise, perhaps most disturbingly for the long run future of international military forces, are possibilities of insubordination by military officers in the field.

The Congo operation saw UN forces having to defend themselves against attacks from Katanga secessionist forces, and then perhaps at a later stage even taking the offensive against these forces. Lacking an air force when first deployed, the UN force was harassed and embarrassed by the attacks of some Katangan jet trainers, and a UN air force was then dispatched to counter this, composed of aircraft from India, Sweden, and Ethiopia.

Apart from the precedent of violent combat operations, the Congo operation saw several national contingents accused of pursuing the policy goals of their home governments, rather than of the UN organization itself. When the UN finally disarmed the Katangese forces, the accusation has moreover been advanced that this operation was launched without authorization from UN headquarters in New York, but rather at the instigation of UN military officers smarting under the humiliation of earlier encounters with the Katanga forces.

Since the Congo, the UN has adopted a somewhat more constricted role in deploying military forces, in part because the opposition of the Soviet Union in the Congo case finally had threatened to align the UN Secretariat too firmly and permanently with the West. To facilitate the handover of Western New Guinea (West Irian) from the Netherlands to Indonesia, the UN assumed territorial control over the territory for a year, with units of the Pakistan Army dispatched to police the area in the UN's name. After the outbreak of civil war in Yemen, a UN observer mission was dispatched to report on the fighting and perhaps thereby facilitate a truce, but this effort was much more on the lines of the UN observer missions of the 1940's.

The eruption of serious violence between Greek and Turkish communities in Cyprus saw a UN force deployed to that island in 1964, in place of the NATO force that President Makarios had deemed unacceptable. Since the net effect of the intervention was to protect the Turkish enclaves, and also to stabilize the political situation on an island supporting British NATO bases, the Soviet Union was less than enthusiastic about this operation also, and in the end refused to pay the portions of its assessments deriving from either the Congo or Cyprus expeditions. In addition to the strain thereby presumably incurred for the presumed neutrality of the UN, the Cyprus operation saw some incidents of insubordination of a different sort, as individual Swedish soldiers were convicted of having smuggled weapons to the Turkish Cypriots.

The UN Emergency Force had been deployed in the Middle East ever since 1956, keeping military operations from being conducted across the Egyptian border into Israeli territory, safeguarding Israeli passage up the Gulf of Aqaba to the port of Elath. In May of 1967, President Nasser chose to expel the UN force from some of its posts, and to announce the closing of the gulf. In what may have been an overreaction to Nasser's move, Secretary-General U Thant then ordered the immediate evacuation of the entire UNEF from the Sinai Desert area; the ensuing war between Israel and the Arab states saw large areas fall into Israeli hands, including the entire Sinai peninsula. Some sources today suggest that Nasser had not intended to drive the UNEF out completely, and merely wished to make a gesture of solidarity with the Syrians by announcing the closing of the Gulf. If so, Secretary-General Thant may have mistaken the signals he received from Cairo on the Egyptian moves. Alternatively, Thant may have decided that too great an indignity would be incurred for the international organization if the Egyptians were to dictate when and where the UNEF could base itself, and thus have withdrawn the force despite Nasser's intention that it remain.

In the event, some part of the UN force were caught in the middle of the ensuing combat, and some 11 Indian soldiers were killed when their evacuation convoy was strafed by Israeli planes presumably mistaking them for Egyptians.

With this historical experience behind us, one can note various kinds of problems which will appear on the handling of UN military force operations in the future. It generally has been found advisable that the force be a mix of troops from several different nations, with one exception always from nations which are not permanent members of the Security Council. (The exception in the Cyprus case was Great Britain, which already had forces in the country on the military bases it had retained after granting Cyprus independence; one can also mention the "UN" intervention in Korea, of course, but this was a very nominal UN presence not really under the control of the Secretariat, an experience unlikely to be repeated in the future.) Several smaller countries have indeed taken to earmarking part of their armed forces for duty with the United Nations, particularly the Netherlands and the Scandinavian countries, and Canada.

The combination of various forces into a single unit may reduce suspicions of political partiality in any international military force, but it raises some logistical problems significantly greater than those of any ordinary army. Standardization of language may be a serious problem, and in the Congo was eased only by the availability of some bilingual French-English Canadian signal operators. Dietary problems based on religious or national background can make the provision of food vastly more complicated. Incompatabilities of military equipment can be a serious failing, if combat operations were ever to arise. The gross inequalities of pay from one armed force to another nation's forces may cause unhappiness and friction, as for example pay is much higher in the Swedish army than in the Indian. Differences of pay, or of operating style, may cause the UN itself to worry about the cost-effectiveness of different units, since standardizing on the cheaper units can reduce expenses, but with a resultant loss of broad representation. Highly motorized units, for example, consume much more gasoline, and are therefore more expensive to keep in the field, in Cyprus or in the Sinai desert. For purposes of showing the UN flag in Cyprus, however, motorization may be very desirable.

While it is indeed desirable that the actual ground forces of any UN force be drawn from states other than the major powers, transporting such a force from home country to particular theater has required equipment beyond the means of small countries; until recently, it was indeed only the Unites States that possessed air transports large enough to ferry troops from India or Scandinavia to Africa in any short period of time. In effect this might have seemed to give the U.S. an implicit veto over most peacekeeping operations, a veto very undesirable from the UN Secretariat's point of view. More recently we have seen the Soviet Union also develop and equip itself with huge tactical transport aircraft so that it would be plausible to see the UN turn to Moscow for logistics support for some operation of which the United States disapproved.

Financing of UN peace-keeping operations was, of course, the core issue in the Article 19 controversy of 1965; in the aftermath of that abortive showdown, operations such as the one in Cyprus now depend on voluntary contributions from interested nations, rather than assessments through the normal fiscal procedures of the UN. Since many other UN functions draw their support on a similar basis, this is not such a drastic departure from practice, but it again may limit somewhat the UN organization's autonomy and leeway in deciding what operations should be undertaken.

In the end, one confronts the question of who gets to direct peacekeeping operations once they are launched. As noted above, serious doubts remain on whether donor nations will indeed abstain from attempting to control the movements of their forces on UN duty. Even in the relatively quiet periods of tl.: UNEF presence on the Egyptian-Israeli frontier, Israelis claimed that some detachments were much more willing to tolerate Egyptian border incursions than others, singling out the Indian and Yugoslav contingents as being especially biased in Cairo's favor. Transcending national interference, there is the risk that "multinational" units in the field may spontaneously decide to alter UN policy, as with Swedish soldiers who came to sympathize with Turkish Cypriots apparently in danger of being overwhelmed by Greek forces. Perhaps instead the "multinational" field leadership of the UN may become insubordinate, whereby the generals of the UN ignore orders from its civilians in New York.

A more immediate ambiguity remains on who will get to authorize such international military operations, given the effort to return such authority to the Security Council. It is certainly not inconceivable that the General Assembly will in the future try to require the launching of such a force again, even if France, the USSR or even the U.S. refuse to pay any of its costs. A closer look at any policy process will moreover attach overwhelming significance to the "faits accompli" with which any executive such as the Secretary-General and the Secretariat can confront the "legislative" bodies, in the face of unexpected events. Both the Middle Eastern and Congo operations reflected considerable personal initiative on the part of Secretary-General Hammerskjold, the kind of initiative that can set world public opinion into a mood to support the operation, and thereby make it diplomatically much more difficult for the great powers to object.

FURTHER READINGS

Bloomfield, Lincoln, ed. *International Military Forces.* Boston: Little, Brown, 1964.
Fabian, Larry L. *Soldiers Without Enemies.* Washington: Brookings Institution, 1971.
Von Horn, Carl. *Soldiering for Peace.* New York: McKay, 1967.

The Impact of International Organization

In assessing the impact of the United Nations we might devote some attention to the bureaucratic practices and personal styles of delegations to the organization in New York. Every member nation, as noted earlier, manages to afford an ambassador to the organization, albeit sometimes doubling up with the same person as ambassador to the United States in Washington (or also as ambassador to Canada in Ottawa). Studies have been done on how votes are cast, and on association patterns, in terms of which delegates talk to which others; the latter statistic is unhappily warped by the simple alphabetical pattern of seating in UN sessions, whereby Brazil and Burundi exchange pleasantries far more often than any mutual interests of the two countries might have required.

It is clear that duty with the organization educates and broadens delegates, thus perhaps fulfilling the original goal that information and views be exchanged among the nations. Yet problems remain in the significance of all this, since in many cases communication to the governments back home is much less than might have been thought appropriate. On questions related to the Congo, for example, delegates of countries with troops on duty often expressed opinions in New York greatly at variance with the opinions of their soldiers and civil servants in the field. The governments in the home country might have presented yet a third view at times, thus illustrating the impact of imperfect communication. This is, of course, as true of embassies and delegations elsewhere as in the UN. Yet the net effect can be to have created a new vested interest around the delegations of the organization, a vested interest which mostly talks to and compares notes with itself. An interesting example of this came with Khrushchev's proposals in the early 1960's that the UN headquarters be moved from New York to Geneva. If the Russian leader expected that the smaller "neutral" nations would favor such a move, he was dreadfully mistaken. Regardless of the views of the governments back home, the actual delegates clearly much preferred cosmopolitan New York to small-town Geneva, and assuredly were telling their governments that a move would be very undersirable.

The Secretariat of the United Nations is considerably larger than that of the League, and has been confronted with greater difficulties in establishing standards of institutional rather than national loyalty, principally because Soviet-American hostility has been evident almost from the outset of the organization. Difficulties arose because Soviet nationals tended to act as agents of their own government rather than of the organization. Other difficulties arose when various American nationals employed by the UN were accused of being members of the Communist party. The American attitude as expressed in the latter case was not necessarily that such nationals should be loyal to the American government, but that they should at least not be identifiably loyal to the principal adversary of the United States.

The UN has thus had to maintain a continuing search for middlemen, for competent nationals of nonaligned countries whose loyalty can not be challenged from within or outside of the organization. Despite earlier difficulties, and challenges as late as 1961, the UN organization had generally been successful in this endeavor.

The Secretaries-General of the League of Nations did not have such personal charisma as to capture the imaginations of much of the world. With regard to UN Secretaries-General, the four men who have held the post have each exhibited different strengths and weaknesses. Trygve Lie, the Norwegian who first held the post, was burdened by a lack of middle-nation constituency, as well as by an outspoken personal style. Dag Hammerskjold at first seemed to typify greater discretion; when coupled with the support of the many new members admitted to the organization in the late 1960's, this allowed him to expand the prestige and role of the organization. With considerable initiative and finesse Hammerskjold played a principal role in launching the UNEF into the Middle East in 1956, and the UN force into the Congo in 1960. The latter lead to difficulties in the end, however, as the Soviet Union became vehemently opposed to the manner in which the Congo operation was developing. The UN's finances were severely strained by this process, as was the reputation of the Secretariat for itself being "nonaligned." Khrushchev's drive to weaken the Secretary-Generalship by installing a "troika" of advisers was defeated, however, as the Afro-Asian bloc of nations rallied to Hammerskjold's support, despite Khrushchev's charge that "there are no neutral men." The rank and file of the UN Secretariat naturally supported the Secretary-General also, when its political and institutional integrity was thus threatened.

Hammerskjold's tragic death brought U Thant to the office. Thant has been generally criticized for being less innovative and able than his predecessor, although his Burmese nationality made him much more representative of the bulk of the middle-nation bloc whose support was required. Whether because of his caution, or background, or because the efforts to weaken the post were decisively defeated, the Russians did not launch attacks on Thant parallel to those on his predecessor.

The election of Kurt Waldheim, an Austrian diplomat, as the fourth Secretary-General in 1972 followed Russian vetoes of several candidates who seemed likely to be more assertive in the post. Yet many prime ministers and presidents in this world have been elected as supposedly mild and controllable men, only thereafter to become very pronouncedly power-hungry and bureaucratically imperialistic. It would thus be dangerous to predict any continued recession in the independence or assertiveness of the Secretary-General position on the basis of personality alone.

In summary, one can thus ask what difference it has made to have a UN. Since it has not seen the maintenance of super-power agreement on which it was originally premised, has it therefore been a failure? The answer most certainly would be no. The UN forum provides a handy mechanism for coordinating the activities and opinions of the smaller and medium-sized states of the world. Coordinated opinion is stronger opinion, and while moral condemnations are rarely decisive all by themselves, they are also not without effect. Presumably the existence of the General Assembly might have suggested also some coordinated physical action by the nonaligned states, but for various reasons the probability of this has been much smaller.

The smaller states, as a mass coordinated through the UN mechanism, offer the great powers an honest broker to help settle disputes, to help assure each side that the other will not dare to violate its part of the agreement. In effect, this validates some of the premises of the League of Nations rather than of the UN. If the threat to peace emerges from some deliberately aggressive force, a coordinating organization, as with the

League in 1938, will be quite ineffective. If misunderstanding and distrust breed conflict in and of themselves, however, then a coordination mechanism can be quite useful.

It might be a mistake however to label the UN straightforwardly as an "honest broker," because this broker, as others, will wish to rake off a commission for itself. The UN thus serves as a vehicle for demands of the "third world," whenever the other "two worlds" are prepared to meet such demands in exchange for whatever stabilization is accomplished. The UN organization rakes off a share for itself, moreover, in addition to pleading the demands of the third world. Like other organizations, it seeks to increase its organizational dignity, size, and power. If this normally conforms with the interests of maintaining peace, it occasionally may conflict. If U Thant really withdrew the UNEF because of the threat to the UN's dignity in 1967, dignity was preserved at a price of making the Six Day War much more probable.

The change in function of the UN raises a basic question on why the U.S. and USSR are so prepared to tolerate dictates they would not have composed themselves. Part of the explanation is obviously the risk of alienating states in the third world and the USSR remained in the organization, therefore, even in the years when it was regularly outvoted. With India and the Latin American countries already in the organization, quite idealistically attached to it, Moscow would have been making a mistake to be the first openly to label the organization as objectionable.

Apart from sensitivity of neutral nations, the super-powers indeed recognize the value of the honest-broker function. In the "anarchic" international relations of today, virtually all the powers that matter must still be interpreted as genuinely desiring peace. In part this is because of the internal natures of the nations involved, in part because nuclear weapons would make war so much more horrible than it seemed in 1936. Hitler may have thus been quite exceptional as a political phenomenon, someone relatively cold-bloodedly ready to pay the costs of war. The UN might have "failed" against Hitler, and the League of Nations conversely might have done fairly well in today's world. The inference might thus be that politics determines peace or war more than the particular design or structure of international organizational bodies.

There are nonetheless limits to what the UN organization can undertake to do. The organization, to be clear, is not limited to acting only when the great powers agree, as on Palestine in 1948 or 1956, or in Indonesia in 1948. The organization can act also whenever the super-powers disagree, as long as they do not disagree enough to make the organization expendable for either of them. One can draw a rough analogy with each side's tolerance for limited warfare strikes in the shadow of World War III; the larger threat is to let the world organization collapse, but Moscow and Washington are prepared to tolerate a great deal before invoking retaliation of this magnitude.

Yet the demise of the United Nations at any point would not be nearly as costly as an outbreak of World War III, so that the threshold of compliance with UN procedures will have to be narrower before either Moscow or Washington would angrily break free. The great powers have bowed to world opinion in places like Lebanon and the Congo, but have defied world opinion just as clearly in the Dominican Republic and Hungary.

Is there any hope that the United Nations will now advance to becoming the kind of effective international government that would produce and guarantee real peace? It should always be remembered that this is not what the planners of 1945 were aspiring to, as their images of what was possible were considerably more realistic. Perhaps the more idealistic devotees and propagandists of the organization sensed such hopes in 1946, but nothing like this has ever been in sight. A possibly false logic might yet encourage hopes here, that small steps must be taken in a slow and incremental advance toward world order and world government. Yet in economics we are familiar with something called "turnpike theory," whereby an indirect advance is required for progress toward the goal of industrial development in an underdeveloped country, an advance which first expands the agricultural sector. It is equally plausible that real peace would have been accomplished in the post-1945 world only in a military conquest based perhaps on someone's nuclear monopoly. The UN as an organization may grow in size and perhaps in stature and prestige, but there would seem to be some asymptotic limits which will hem it in long before it can decisively assure any absence of war either between great powers or between small.

Real peace for the time seems precluded by the obdurance of the great powers who will not go further in surrendering their sovereignty than they already have done. If this were surmountable, we today must face the prospect that other nations could quickly race to manufacture nuclear weapons once the great powers had destroyed their stockpiles; indeed, the enormous arsenals of the U.S. and Soviet Union may be important in currently dissuading further proliferation of nuclear weapons, since the "nth" country could do so little when compared with the "super-powers."

If the risk of some new nation reaching for super-power status could be overcome, a danger would still remain that the military and political apparatus of the new world government itself would not remain subordinate. Insubordination would undermine the substantive legitimacy of representative mandate for such an organization; more seriously it would threaten that some parts of the apparatus remained loyal while others disobeyed, with the result that "war" would again be very possible in the world, instead of "peace." As suggested earlier, it is possible that a monopoly of force in the world could be established which would remain internally integrated and subordinate. Yet it is not certain that this would happen, on the basis of the internal conflicts of many or most of the nations which are nonaligned members of the United Nations today.

To gauge the impact of the United Nations on world peace, one might be so perverse as to characterize it as just one more country in our international arena. The UN has its own budget, derived largely from "foreign aid" contributed by other nations. It has its own postage stamps, and most importantly, its own bureaucracy. The people who join this bureaucracy have their loyalties transformed enough so that they are almost as nationals or citizens of the new country that has been created; to be sure, it is unusual for all the citizens of a "country" to be employed by its government.

The UN has its own territory, in the area of the UN building in New York which is not subject to United States law. For a time, it exercised control over a far wider domain in West New Guinea, and a little more farfetched, it holds a claim on some remaining "trust territories" which have not achieved independence. The UN, quite significantly, has its own armed forces, hired as "mercenaries" from other nations. These armed forces are typically not kept at home in their own land, but rather are normally engaged in interventions in other nations' territory, albeit usually by invitation, and always in the interest of preserving peace.

In terms of "foreign policy" the UN is thus a most peace-loving state, trying to preserve the balance of power or whatever is required to keep wars from breaking out in the first place. Perhaps it functions thus as a modern England or Switzerland, making life and peaceful interaction easier for other states enmeshed in the same system.

The UN as a nation-state, of course, would have to be adjudged enormously susceptible to the views and influence of other states, and thus be rated as relatively less independent than the norm for foreign policy. Yet the internal workings of the bureaucracy allow the UN to generate many initiatives in independence, often by playing off the strength and advice of one foreign state against another, a trick known to all astute diplomats. In the end, such a state, despite its peculiar citizenship and financing, must be adjudged quite a useful member of the international system, but perhaps not as qualitatively different or "nobler" as first approximations would have predicted.

Some of the pessimism about the United Nations might thus simply reflect the cautions about world government that were voiced at the very outset. If the UN does not become a world government, but merely some kind of peculiar international organization which occasionally aspires to make a contribution to peace, what more could we have expected? Commentators sometimes also note with dismay that the UN has become relatively less useful, or less used, for even this more modest task in recent years. Yet this may simply show that the United States and the Soviet Union and the other influential powers have improved their national capabilities for conflict resolution, so that an international organization has been less needed.

International law and international organization thus remain short of being world law or world government, while they simultaneously remain enormously significant in channeling and stabilizing the uses of force in the international arena. If such law and organization could someday outmode reference and recourse to force, peace would be assured and the study of international relations terminated. Yet this is not yet to be.

FURTHER READINGS .

Claude, Inis L., Jr. *Swords into Plowshares: The Problems and Prospects of International Organization.* New York: Random House, 1964.
Goodrich, Leland M. "From League of Nations to United Nations," *International Organization*, February, 1947.

CHAPTER FOUR

*The Historical Development
of
International Politics*

A large portion of the international politics can thus be broken down into such basic components as the potential for violence, and the declarations states make about how they will use such violence. The latter declarations, it has been contended here, are what we think of as "law." If international law is the beginning of a process of coordination that leads on into international organization, this may in the end modify the potentials for violence upon which the entire system is premised.

If military force and international legal structure are thus so central, one must still enquire whether the forms of these components have all along been as we know them today. Can it be that our imagination on what is possible as an international structure would be artificially constrained if we focused only on contemporary events? Do we take for granted some forms of international politics that may not be so inevitable? Might there be a trend over time by which the international components of the international process are steadily evolving from stage to stage? It may thus be altogether appropriate for us now to consider some aspects of the historical development of the international system, as it sets the stage for the international politics of the 1970's.

Why should anyone study his history, and the history of international relations in particular? An historian might answer simply that history should be studied for the sheer enjoyment of knowing what has happened,

138

for its own sake. A political scientist might add that such knowledge can help us to predict the outcomes of alternative policies in the future. Yet how relevant will history be to predictions of the future? How much of history is relevant? How much of the environment of international politics must be the same from one century to another, if lessons from one are to be applied to the other? And what parts of this environment in particular must be the same? Is it necessary for us to hunt back infinitely into history to assure ourselves that we have missed no evidence relevant to the concrete problems we now confront? Or is there some convenient point at which "international politics" can be said to have started, a point beyond which we do not need to retrace our steps?

One kind of relationship of past to present can be phrased in macrostructural terms, in terms of what kind of international or world governmental arrangements existed or were missing on this globe. Perhaps this would suggest no need to go back much further than the last 1,000 years, since the world before that knew no real "nations" as we know them today, and no "international relations," but what was rather either a host of tiny duchies or world government. Yet if men pursued personal and often hostile purposes without organized states as the tools of pursuit, are there not still many lessons to be learned or confirmed from this experience relevant to the present? Some aspects of game theory or the theory of conflict, for example, are equally applicable to states or to individuals, simply showing how certain strategies produce better results in a context of disagreement. Yet a world with millions or thousands of significant actors will be very different from a world of one hundred or ten. Perhaps the crucial question of historical relevance here should be rephrased in terms of the number of actors in the system. Today we debate whether the world is "unipolar," "bipolar," or "multipolar." Yet "multi" might have to go from ten up to ten million to encompass the disorder of the medieval period of European history.

One can also consider the relevance of earlier history in terms of whether the same functional interrelationships bound together as much of the world as today. How much economic interchange was there in the 5th century, or in the 15th? Was the world, as history records it, more or less unified than today in terms of religious and cultural interaction? To put the question in very operational terms, we are very used to having precise boundaries to demarcate the sovereignties of the states of the international system, but were such boundaries always necessary? If there were fewer economic and social interactions, there may also have been far fewer political interactions, so that international boundaries were hardly required, so that not much of "international politics" existed.

As a halfway point between the extremes of nations crowding each other and nations totally oblivious of each other, we might note the presence or absence of "frontier" conditions, the existence of open spaces not yet claimed by any functioning member of the international system, into which nations might channel whatever lust for expansion struck them. The frontier might be open within the internationally recognized sovereignty of a nation, as in the American West in the 19th century, and the Russian development of Siberia in the same century. Alternatively, the frontier might be open to anyone who had the energy to enter it, as with Africa in the 19th century, or the "New World" of the Americas after Columbus. With the second-order exceptions of Antarctica and outer space, no such frontiers remain open for national expansion today. Yet the "closing of the frontier" is a very recent phenomenon, so that some of contemporary international relations might be explained by it; earlier historical periods may thus acquire some relevance when they illustrate similar conditions.

One might almost subdivide the presence of a frontier of the international system into types of frontier. The ones suggested above are inviting frontiers, frontiers offering opportunities which may divert nations within the system from their quarrels. If two race for the same opportunity, of course, new quarrels could emerge.

Whether or not the frontiers were inviting, in our swing through history we might wish to know when they were "fighting frontiers," frontiers requiring or suggesting relatively continuous military activity (with whatever implications this has for the militarization of home environments, or perhaps for catharsis of military urges). One would further wish to know whether the frontiers were threatening to the international system we are contemplating, threatening in the manner of the Huns or Mongols, and thus perhaps driving national actors to greater cooperation.

The relevance of an historical period will also obviously depend of the speed of political interactions at the time, relative to the possible speed of decision-making. How fast men could move from place to place, or communicate from place to place, can obviously change the course of events. One must only remember that the last battle of the War of 1812 between the United States and Britain was fought at New Orleans months after peace had been agreed upon at Ghent. Clearly the speed of electric communications would prevent such a futile expense of lives today, but it is not certain that human decision-making processes have been accelerated to match the speed of radio transmissions. The persistence of combat between Jordanian Army and Palestinian Commandos after truces are "declared," may reflect a phenomenon very similar to the Battle of New Orleans.

Attention will also have to be devoted to the nature of military hardware, specifically to whether the offensive or the defensive is more effective at a given stage of weapons technology, with important implications for whether wars may generate themselves in times of crisis. Since the atomic bomb is as powerful as it is, are there any earlier periods of military history with similar or comparable destruction threatening civilian populations? Was it ever the case that such destruction might befall a people even when its armies had "won the war," by sweeping the other army off the batt-lefield. How capital-intensive or labor-intensive have military technologies been? Some might force recruitment of entire populations for war, while others would leave the bulk of manpower behind.

In relation to all the above variables, we might want to examine the extent of diplomatic activity in any decade or century from which we wish to seek lessons, examining the amount of such activity, and the extent of international law codified on the subject. For example, if we compared British-Japanese interactions in 1955 with those in 1855, the expansion might seem so enormous as to cast doubt on generalizations based on the two periods. While Japan's isolation from the world until the mid-19th century was extraordinary, the general level of diplomatic interchange of that time was enormously less than what we are so accustomed to now.

Turning away from macroscopic evaluation of the entire globe, or of some entire "international system," a number of microcosmic consider-ations may also be of great importance in selecting whatever history is germane to our problems today. Important changes may have occurred in the relation of governments to subjects in the national units we are consid-ering. Were the governments of history as centralized and efficient as those of today, or were they not? Were they as stable, or perhaps even more stable, and how would this effect the ways foreign policies were blended into a form of international relations? Were these regimes "professional," in the rational sense we are accustomed to today?

Were the regimes essentially extortionary in their relations with subjects, or were they instead responsible to those governed, either by direct election processes, or through some recruitment and selection process which will impose ideological requirements that the ruler at least pretend to be in sympathy and identification with his subjects? If the regimes were more representative, did this emerge in a context of stable policy, or rather "riding a tiger" of increasingly insatiable public opinion, with consequent drives toward aggressive foreign policy and escalations of war?

We also might want to know something about the individual characters or philosophies of the peoples involved in the international relations we are comparing. Were they Christian or non-Christian, Catholic or Protestant? Were they educated or illiterate?

Was the legal system under which they lived basically a rational system, requiring some sort of ratification and consent by those governed under it, or rather an ascriptive system justified by derivation from a higher law which had gone unchallenged in more fearful ages? How developed were these smaller societies and individuals economically? Would they expect economic growth and progress, or were they resigned to stable and perma-nent economic existences?

Having once sorted out such similarities and differences in stages of historical development, a question remains on how we propose to apply similarities when they are found. Various kinds of analogy come to mind.

At a microcosmic level, we will be looking for simple examples involving small groups of men or individuals who often are so significant in determining the course of the entire world. This basically anecdotal approach presumes that men do not change much from century to century, nor does the way they react to the basic constraints and challenges of power politics. The truths we believe today are more convincing and memorable when they can be tied to illustrations from the behavior of memorable figures of the past. If Frederick the Great said the only reason to adhere to treaties was so that others would sign new treaties with his nation in the future, he was mouthing an insight which we still might endorse in general terms today. Yet it is still more revealing that someone of his importance found it apt so many years ago. Similarly when Rathenau dismissed last minute indications at Rapallo that the French might make concessions to head off a German-Russian agreement, his comment was "The wine is open, we must drink it." What a useful reminder that some situations can not be reversed once they have been initiated in a definite direction.

Yet the danger remains that we will attach too much importance to such lively insights, or to the implicitly accompanying proposition that great men account for most of the decisions of international relations. History tends to remember the interesting, the inspiring, and the memorable. Leaders who never phrased their policy decisions aptly or heroically tend to be forgotten. Yet the statistical inference we might draw from collections of such material may be unrepresentative of the performance of the international system as a whole. For example, the cold-blooded amorality of Frederick was unusual for a head of state in his time, since most of the rulers in the international balance of power sensed a great vested interest in international as well as domestic legitimacy. If Stalin was less quotable than Khrushchev, we must not jump to the conclusion that he was less important, or that our theories of Soviet foreign policy behavior can pay any less attention to his years of rule.

Turning to more macrocosmic models of how international politics work, there are at least three kinds of theory that can be presented here. The first simply would note that certain kinds of arrangement have existed from time to time (for example, Pax Romana, or the balance of power system), demonstrating that the elements of such a system have coexisted in reality at least once, and arguing that they can not therefore be incompatible. If the system really was a system, every part of it had some possible effects on every other part, and we look to history to tell us something about how these effects can synoptically settle into a pattern.

A second approach would seek some broader theory to explain or predict the patterns of international relations over time, in terms of grand cycles of history. Pax Romana thus presumably carried within it the seeds of the breakdown of Pax Romana; Pax Americana must therefore similarly bear the probability of its own demise.

As an alternative to a dynamic model in which history repeats itself in a tight cycle, some other "theories of history" might attempt to uncover a "political development" of the international system, a causal progression wherein the 16th century explains the 17th and the 17th the 18th, and so on, but wherein each century and decade develops different characteristics without repetition. The determinism here might be compared with theories explaining the political or economic development of various domestic societies. To predict the next stage does not require that it be a repetition of the past, since our imagination can go beyond what has already occurred in the past.

The stress on predictability here may raise some old issues of political science—whether writings in this area inevitably have to be in a form which advises a particular course of action. If one forsees that the 1980's will see some resumption of the balance of power system, does this necessarily make him an advocate of a particular course of action? A good case can be made that the two are not so much intertwined, in that good predictions of the future can be exploited by either side of an argument. In the example above, those whose ideals on the domestic shape of society would be advanced by an international balance of power system might wish to accelerate this historical development, while those who were opposed might be induced to find ways to delay or avert it.

Yet there is at least a certain danger that analyzing historical trends may make it impossible to realize one's predictions. Santayana is well remembered for having warned that those who do not study history will repeat it; the inverse suggests that studying history will have an opposite causal impact, preventing history from being repeated. Perhaps the effort to understand and avoid a repetition of World War I caused World War II; the UN is perhaps doomed to ineffectiveness because it is designed to prevent World War II. If the Anglo-French strategy of 1939 was designed to defeat a repetition of the Schlieffen Plan, it perhaps made it all the easier for the Germans to win a victory with their Ardennes offensive. Perhaps political science needs a humanistic version of the Heisenberg uncertainty principle, that to observe something is to alter it.

FURTHER READINGS

Butterfield, Hubert and Wight, Martin, eds. *Diplomatic Investigations: Essays in the Theory of International Politics.* Cambridge, Mass.: Harvard University Press, 1966.

Hinsley, F. H. "The Development of the European States System Since the Eighteenth Century." *Transactions of the Royal Historical Society.* 1961.

Where to Begin?

Establishing the beginnings of organized warfare in the history of mankind would be an enormous exercise in anthropology. Working from a concept of warfare, we might nonetheless be able to define and to trace at least part of whatever historical cycle there has been in international politics.

War is more than an armed brawl, for it reflects the violent power of organized groups of men, trained to cooperate with each other and to channel their killing and wounding capabilities exclusively against an opposing group of men. Even when the weapons of combat were nothing more than the spear and sword, therefore, a superior organization for such combat might decide victories and defeats.

The normal form of such organization involved some definite geometric prearrangement which would compensate for each man's blind spots and weak spots by relying on the strong points of the man next to him. Standing in place, it was possible for armies in the days of the Greek city-states to maintain such a formation and thus to impose a generally effective attrition ratio against any less organized horde of barbarians. Maintaining such a formation in movement would have been much more difficult, however, for the diligence and training required would be much greater. It was indeed normal in the Peloponnesian Wars for armies to move forward on their own right flank, the result of each soldier seeking the protection of the shield of his neighbor on the right. The predictability of angle of attack this offered made strategy less than the most interesting aspect of any battle.

If movement in formation was difficult, and the angle of attack predictable, the defense could be said to hold the advantage; by standing in place, it kept its ranks in better and more efficient order. The wars of the Greeks testify to the defensive advantage, if in no other way than by the large number of states that managed to assert and maintain their independence. Elementary fortifications of cities compounded the defensive advantage, and "offensive" campaigns typically involved only the burning of an enemy's crops. The latter would weaken the enemy, or perhaps force him to attack our prepared position in an effort to drive us away from his crops. Catching a smaller force where we could outnumber it, of course, always suggested prospects of victory, but a smaller force standing in place might still acquit itself well against the disorganization of a larger force moving against it.

The mere ability to shift the point at which contact was made, from the previously predictable right flank to a more randomized point, gave the Macedonian armies a tremendous advantage which they employed against Greece and then farther east. This innovation of personal discipline, even when in motion, was enormously enhanced by the armies of the Roman Empire, explaining why the empire in effect conquered all it had to deal with. Roman discipline had a psychological element of course, in that self-confidence bred resolution in hand-to-hand combat, with the result that panic was far more likely to break out in the enemy force. In practical terms, it meant that the most efficient patterns of sword use and shield handling could be maintained in combat. The element of mobility, however, is what is most crucial for the question of offense or defense. Roman armies could engage an enemy on either or both flanks. They could march substantial distances to catch an enemy by surprise; the same marching ability could be used to assemble numerical majorities on short notice, or to allow a single garrison to do double duty in attacking components of the enemy force separately, before the components could be brought together for an attack.

As the balance of offensive and defensive was the reverse under the Romans as compared with the Greeks, so the political result was the reverse, a unified empire rather than a system of many autonomous states. The discipline the Romans produced may be traceable to egalitarian standards of citizenship, or perhaps may simply have been an historical accident; if it was an accident, it became a self-perpetuating one.

Where then do we begin our historical search for insights relevant to international relations today? The years of the Greek city-states are a tempting place to begin, because extensive written accounts of the politics of the time have survived to the present, while no such documentation exists for earlier societies, and because the interactions of these states shows some interesting parallels to contemporary international relations. The Greek states illustrate philosophical tensions between idealism and what we often call realism, between emphasis on the more humane fields of human endeavor and more martial, between the foreign policy approaches of democratic and nondemocratic regimes. The period also demonstrates an early form of the balance of power mechanism, whereby the substance of any particular quarrel might only be crucial for the first two belligerent states, while others are drawn in, or stay neutral, on the basis of preserving their power position, by keeping likely winners from winning too much and becoming too powerful.

The conquest of the Greek states by the Roman Empire drastically alters the relevance of the historical pattern, indeed, perhaps suspending most of what is relevant to international politics today. By sheer military prowess, the Romans achieved absolute political domination over all the civilized and organized tribes, in effect sharing boundaries with no foreign *states* in any direction, but only *frontiers* along which disorganized tribes and peoples had occasionally to be beaten back or subdued. Yet the legacy of the Roman Empire is hardly a trivial consideration for the subsequent course of international events. Given that the bulk of "international politics" as we know it will occur in Europe, it is of great significance that Europe retained the myth of political union as a bequest from Rome. The myth in effect legitimated one attempt after another toward hegemony; it also dignified the general anarchy and lack of central authority which covers Europe immediately after the Empire had fallen apart. Long before Europe could bring itself to admit that it needed or possessed international law, it might refer to the common tradition of Roman law. The military superiority that had projected Rome was now to fade, in face of the mounted hordes that swept in upon the Empire from the east, but the Roman legal tradition was to be applied to a vastly different political reality.

The years from 750 to 1400 are sometimes described as the age of cavalry, but they might better be seen as the age of local and atomistic defense. A knight on horseback might indeed effectively combat a great number of ordinary soldiers on the ground, but he could do so effectively only within a short distance of his home base.

Heights and thickness of walls thus became dominant. The ideal place for a castle was on a hill overlooking some mountain pass or some narrow point on a river. The defensive advantages of the hill itself would be bolstered and enhanced by walls and turrets rising still higher. The man on horseback would be equipped with body armor which greatly reduced his vulnerability to the sword or spear, at the small price of reducing the ranges across which he could comfortably operate. His horse offered the same advantage of elevation as did the hill on which was perched his castle, and was fed by grains stored within that castle.

One may question how inevitable the rise of the castle defensive was, since it did not occur farther east. It may be a case of technological patterns falling to either side of an unstable equilibrium point. An empirial organization could have overcome local fortifications, even organizing the feeding of its cavalry mounts, if it had not been preempted by the erection of walls locally; perhaps feudalism, by thrusting Europe into an uneducated age, killed off the very talents that could have reunited Europe. Castles preempt roads, just as roads preempt castles. Knights in armor preempt disciplined armies, and vice versa. High castle turrets preempt the dissemination of siege technology, and vice versa. The sudden appearance of a force more mobile and offensively capable than the legions thus led to a system where no one was offensively capable.

The superiority of the knight over ordinary soldiers thus depended on his suit of armor and his superior fighting position on horseback; the horse, conversely, now was probably required to give him anything beyond the most rudimentary mobility, given the weight of his armor. The maintenance requirements of armor and horse tied the knight to the castle from which he operated; because the knight was so effective within the limited radius of operations this allowed, it definitely strengthened the defensive capability of these castles; knights attempting to attack such castles would have had to bring their retainers out into the open, in camps supporting the seige, in camps extremely vulnerable to attacks sallying out from the castle.

It is very possible that the military superiority of the armored horseman was artificially prolonged as a political result of feudalism once it was established. New weapons techniques which might have upset the superiority of the noble would obviously not receive encouragement from those who held authority under the old technology; military equipment and training for the common serf were thus to be repressed.

The offensive ability of the horse-mounted knight in Western Europe was thus very limited. Aside from the castle walls which stood in the way, the resulting atomistic independence of the political system precluded the military discipline and organization required for offensive campaigns far from one's home base. When such an effort as united offensive campaigns was made, as in the Crusades, the knights performed as a disorganized rabble, quite effective and heroic in individual combat, but lacking in discipline and coordination.

The fall of the Roman Empire saw Europe in fact resume the condition of multiple sovereignties, but in a context of declining economic activity, population, movement, and learning, a decline which thus saw far fewer system-wide interactions requiring any management or adjudication. While Rome solved the system-wide problems on a "national" rather than "international" basis, Europe after Rome did not have such problems to solve, and certainly did not organize in any profound way to confront such problems. Why indeed do we devote so much attention to Europe rather than to those other parts of the globe which did not undergo a similar decline? Could we not extract some more useful lessons from the "foreign policy methods" of the Mongols or the Arabs, or the Turks and Chinese, or even our own American Indians?

To a great extent we cite these outside examples less because we know these periods of history less well, and our biased example indeed produces distortions of factual and statistical accuracy. The detailed and written knowledge of the structure or political dealings of these systems is lacking, when compared with what we know of Rome and Greece, and even of the less literate times of Charlemagne. Yet another reason for our geographical selectivity here is that the western European tradition is the only one that is continuous with the practices of the present, and causally related through this continuity. If, for example, we wish to account for the foreign policy style today of Mexico, a country which pays serious attention to its Aztec cultural heritage, we still will find that Roman or Venetian practice is far more relevant than Aztec diplomacy. Europe conquered the world after 1500; and the world, agreeably or otherwise, has standardized on the evolving European diplomatic practice.

It may thus be difficult to recognize much in the way of *international* activity in the affairs of Europe following the decline of Rome, as the competing fragments of nobility locked in conflict with each other hardly had the characteristics of "nations." Only at last with the upswing of European culture and commerce in the 13th and 14th century is there a reappearance of some methodical and effective instruments of national interaction. The renewal of the balance of power system in the Italian city-states must thus have seemed extremely novel, as the first resumption of truly international relations since the conquest of Greece.

The basic questions of the role of power and morality in foreign dealings now were reopened for analysis and discussion, most memorably by Machiavelli. Yet Machiavelli's stress on the need for hardheaded amoral realism may have missed the greater political implications of the Renaissance. Machiavelli was properly concerned lest France in its earlier unity and effective governmental organization overpower the weaker Italian states. Yet his ideals of a state properly prepared for international action placed excessive stress on citizen instead of professional soldiers, on small states defending themselves, generally avoiding commitment to foreign adventures. Other analysts drew substantially different lessons from the Renaissance, that states needed now to be organized at the least on the scale of entire cultural groups or nations, and perhaps on the scale of Europe itself, as the legacy of Rome would once again be given some reality. International relations is thus given more meaning again in the Renaissance with the appearance of functional and effective national armies, together with national governments and national foreign ministries. Yet the international system now several times came close to terminating itself, if only because the nation that adopted the advantages of effective nationhood first might be able to overwhelm all who were slower to do so.

Generalization about any long period of technology or politics is dangerous, but one might now venture to sketch out a period of offensive advantage which began with the final demise of the armored knight and towering castle, and which ends with the consolidation of national units and emergence of the balance of power system after the Thirty Years War. The Wars of Religion from 1560 to 1648 are remembered as a period of great violence and human suffering, provoked and exacerbated by men's concern for each other's souls, therefore lacking the moderation of wars fought simply for material advantage. The intensity of the stakes between Protestant and Catholic supported, and was supported by, the offensive advantage which now in effect dominated the battlefield.

After 1500, high walls no longer could resist cannon, and mounted knights were vulnerable to the arrows or musket shot of the foot-soldier, as well as to the iron discipline and zeal of mercenary companies based on the Swiss pattern. It is only reasonable that this ferocious zeal in combat was reinforced and sustained by the religious questions underlying the war. For the mercenary groups not so motivated by religion, the intensity of the war allowed for gains in terms of booty that made comradely valour in battle worthwhile. The same religious intensity which sanctioned slaughters for religious grounds moreover allowed troops to live off the land in general without concern for the property rights or the suffering of innocent bystanders. An army that could live off the country without compunctions could travel greater distances in any particular day, thus reinforcing the mobility which might so greatly assist those who had taken the initiative in forcing battle.

If Catholicism wished to eliminate the Protestant heresy totally, or if Spain wished to control all of Europe, this could seem to explain the continual military initiatives and continual warfare of the period. Yet hopes of total conquest were importantly reinforced here by military assumptions that victory went to him who brought his forces forward to battle first.

Whichever state first got organized would thus be tempted to preempt others from doing so, by applying superior military skill, by flaunting the power and glory of a particular regime to suggest that imperial pretentions which might psychologically intimidate resistance, by laying claim to the legal heritage of the "empire" itself. Yet some other motives appeared to fortify these basic lusts for hegemony in the 16th century, for Spain in particular, motives which came close to facilitating such a conquest.

To begin, the sudden opening of the new world had opened new resources for commercial development and, more directly for Spain, had offered deposits of gold and silver which would be accepted as legal tender by all the commercial countries of Europe. Such a sudden increment of economic power could easily enough be converted to military strength in the hiring of mercenaries, the purchase of weapons, the distribution of bribes, and so on. Other nations might share or attempt to share in the exploitation of the new worlds discovered overseas in the Americas and the Far East, but as long as Spain held an advantage in this exploitation, it might convert that advantage in a drive for hegemony within Europe.

The second major impetus relevant to Spain was the breakup of religious unity in Europe as a result of the Protestant split from Rome. For a devoutly Roman Catholic nation such as Spain, Protestantism was heresy purely and simply, and military force was entirely appropriate to eradicating it—such force would thus have a higher and purer motive even than the heritage of the Roman Empire. The religious zeal and military prowess of the Spaniards was accentuated all the more by the recentness of the victory of Christianity over the Islamic forces which had long occupied Spain. Defeating the Muslims had required skill at sea and skill on land, skill which could now be brought to bear in other theaters.

In the 16th century, Spanish forces and influence merged the possessions of Spain on both sides of the Atlantic with the domains of the Holy Roman Empire. From these bases on the eastern and western fringes of Europe, penetrations were made of all the rest of Germany and Italy, and considerable influence came to be exercised in the internal affairs of France. With religious motivation as the source of zeal, wars were pursued against the Protestant Netherlands and United Kingdom. After a decisive rebuff with the defeat of the Spanish Armada in 1588, the push for hegemony was stalled for a time, only to be rekindled again in what became the Thirty

Years War (1618–1648), a war perhaps unrivalled even in the present for the sheer devastation of the territories over which it was fought.

The two "wars of religion," 1560 to 1590, and then 1618 to 1648, were made horrible by exactly the religious zeal which motivated them. With the very salvation and souls of men at issue, much less attention had to be devoted to the niceties of civilized warfare and respect for innocent civilians. The unifying influence of the Roman Church might have moderated an outburst of dynastic violence in earlier times, but no single source of authority on the morality of combat could now win recognition, for the very nature of such authority was an important issue in the war. The war was also made horrible by the uneven degrees of military competence and organization of the forces involved. At one extreme were the superbly trained and relatively disciplined forces of Catholic Spain and Lutheran Sweden. Yet the same religious zeal and lust for political hegemony that raised these forces sanctioned also the *ad hoc* recruitment of the most opportunistic of adventurers and brigands, epitomized in the end in the highest ranks by the personality of Wallenstein.

If religious considerations made the war horrible, decidedly nonreligious considerations made it possible, for resistance to the Spanish Hapsburg drive for political and religious unity was facilitated in the end by French support for the Protestant forces, a support which emerged after Spanish subversion had been contained in France itself and was, a paradoxically, guided and manipulated by a Prince of the Roman Church, Cardinal Richelieu.

The motive for the French actions is simply an illustration of what has come to be called the balance of power system, the understandable desire of France to keep Spain from winning control over all of Europe. Preventing a single power's hegemony, as in the days of the Greeks, required that weaker states come to the support of other weaker states, and this might require forgetting the religious affiliations of the various sides.

History had thus presented Spain with an irresistible temptation to strive to end international politics, and Spain almost succeeded. Had religious feelings not been as strong as they were, Spain might not have embarked on such an effort. Had they been stronger, France might have had to become an ally rather than enemy. As noted, the rest of Europe was hard pressed for almost a century to resist the Hapsburg expansion, and to keep the separate sovereignties of an "international system" alive. Yet some of the explanation of the final Spanish defeat is grounded in the very factors which originally spurred Spain forward. The religious zeal that led men to see the Armada as another crusade also produced the most severe intolerance at home, leading to expulsion or terrorization of Jews and Moslems, even of those who had converted to Catholicism and whose sincerity was now questioned. The horrors of the Inquisition were real enough, damaging the kind of critical thought and curiosity that keeps a nation in the forefront of such technology as can be applied to the battlefield. The shadow of the Inquisition could not help, moreover, but bolster the resistance of Dutch and English Protestants, who had more than their political independence to lose.

The Spanish reliance on direct acquisition of gold and silver, in lieu of genuinely productive industry, also would impose costs after a time, in that industrial and technological growth within Spain itself was artificially held back. The conquistadors brought home the liquid assets which could then purchase abroad the tools of Spanish power within Europe, but the dynamic impact on Spanish economic development was predominantly detrimental.

Yet the repulse of the Hapsburgs hardly determined that Europe would thereafter exhibit the characteristics of an international system, for the Spanish defeat in effect left a vacuum which another state would quite easily be able to fill. Because the Spanish outposts had surrounded France, in an effort to subdue and absorb France, it followed that these territories would be easy prey for France once Spanish power went into abrupt decline. Several other factors now contributed to making Paris a candidate for the "new Rome." France, of all the "nations" that were collecting themselves into effective units, had the largest natural population and economy. When this nation was now to be endowed with a superbly professional and rationalized state apparatus in the reign of Louis XIV, the rest of Europe would have to pay attention again to the hegemonic threat. One of the partners in resisting Spain was now to become the threat; Spain, the former threat, became little more than a potential ally in the resistance to French power, or a potential prize for French aggrandizement.

The wars which ensued from 1667 to 1715, were characterized by much less religious zeal, since the religious future of Europe in 1648 had been stabilized on the principle that rulers could essentially decide the religious futures of their subjects. The absence of religious zeal now combined with generally more professional (and smaller) national armies to reduce drastically the costs and horrors of war. Yet if wars were lessened in their intensity, they were not made impossible, for the real prevention of war might well have required that someone like Philip of Spain or Louis XIV of France succeed in unifying Europe under a single sovereign. The other states of the system, with Britain as a leader, but always with substantial allies, were not prepared to allow this unification. As before, Germany was a battlefield of the new balance of power game, while France, now as principal participant, escaped being fought over. If it followed that the battlefield would be fragmented politically, German political unification was thus again postponed, with long-term consequences for the course of international politics.

The War of the Spanish Succession from 1702 to 1713 represented the culmination of French efforts to dominate the international system of Europe, as Louis XIV attempted to arrange the ascension of his grandson to the throne of Spain, and the other powers of Europe intervened to prevent this. A successful absorption of the Spanish colonial empire might indeed have put France into a position from which hegemony was possible, but the alliance of other states now sufficed again to prevent such an accretion of power from taking place. As earlier with Spain, the temptations of such a world-dominating position would be difficult to ignore, as the international system had not yet reached a stage of multiple sovereign units of approximately equal strength, none of which could outweigh the rest.

The aftermath of the wars with Louis XIV saw this system at last reach a more "balanced" form, with France, Spain, and Britain as solid and independent members of the system, accompanied now by an Austria with a political unity beyond the holy Roman Empire and entirely separate dynastically from Spain, by a modernized Russia and a newly emergent Prussia. Each of these states would now be modern, in that feudal subunits no longer held a legal or de facto independence. Each would have a military force which could be deployed beyond its borders, being of sufficient size to generate the economies of scale required for such foreign adventures. None would any longer hold particular advantages in money reserves or political organization or religious zeal which might give it a special capability for threatening all the rest.

FURTHER READINGS

Ganshof, Francois L. *The Middle Ages: A History of International Relations.* New York: Harper and Row, 1970.
Mattingly, Garrett. *Renaissance Diplomacy.* London: Jonathon Cape, 1955.
Oman, C. W. C. *The Art of War in the Middle Ages.* Ithaca: Cornell University Press, 1953.

The Balance of Power

Most commentators on the historical evolution of international relations tend to describe the period now ensuing, from 1715 to 1789, as the purest example of the "balance of power" system in action. If "international politics" had only just begun in the previous two centuries, it had barely survived the French and Spanish efforts to terminate it. With the defeat of France, the world was now to see a system which reassured that international relations would survive, and that the number of states would not decline below a certain number.

Yet descriptions of the "balance of power" system must be made more precise and less intuitive, for the phraseology here is often used too loosely to have any precise meanings. The term "balance," for example, is sometimes used simply in the sense of "bank balance," a synonym simply for the "distribution of power." Authors can thus be using the label "balance of power" simply to refer to any distribution at any time, no matter what form it takes, no matter how it works. Sometimes the phrase is used instead to refer to the differences between the more powerful and the less, analogous to the "balance of payments." If Germany is stronger than France at any particular point in time, Germany "holds the balance" in this particular use of the phrase, the balance perhaps being Germany's power *minus* France's power. At other times, the term "balance of power" is applied to any distribution of strength which preserves peace or the existing distribution of territorial power. In effect, one is saying that power can be "in balance" or "out of balance," regardless of whether the mechanism is armed resistance, or retaliatory deterrence, or economic sanctions, or a simple lack of international grievances and enmity.

Yet a considerably more profound sense of the balance of power will apply to a particular system in which the various participating states are consciously watching any war erupting between two of them to be sure that neither aggregates too much power in the process. In the pure form of the system, the third, fourth, and fifth members of the system continually intervene on the side of the likely loser, not because they believe in the justice of his position, but because they fear the consequences of having his power potential absorbed by the imminent winner.

For the balance of power system to function in the manner described, some basic prerequisites had to be satisfied, however. To begin, most of the separate entities participating had to be "countries" rather than "nations." This means that the boundaries of these regimes were not yet closely related to ethnic or language considerations, since no dependence of government on popular opinion and consent had as yet appeared to require such a "nationalistic" approach. In effect, the balance of power system in its prime was a grand conspiracy among the ruling hierarchies of the international system, a conspiracy increasing each hierarchy's security or job tenure, at the costs of each reinsuring the job tenures of the others.

If the populations of the various countries had been enthusiastically behind their rulers, there might have been no need to seek a balance of power support from abroad to repulse possible aggressions. There would, moreover, have been less leeway for the rulers to play the same game in wars affecting two other powers, for the same popular backing might have produced a popular involvement with one of the sides. The predominance of "countries" over "nations" at this stage is exemplified and accentuated by the widespread use of imported mercenaries for essential purposes of state. As armies were small and tempers cool in the absence of serious religious warfare, hiring regiments from abroad would often be cheaper or more cost-effective than recruiting additional regiments at home, as wars were often fought largely with altogether reliable imported troops. The practice of hiring foreigners extended far beyond this, moreover, as important cabinet positions often were manned by experts recruited from abroad, as a certain kind of career specialist moved from country to country in the process of career advancement. Being professionals, the instantaneous loyalty of such bureaucrats was rarely in question, and it was hardly thought urgent or natural that these officials be recruited from the country they governed and served. Since so much of government business (especially international business) was conducted in French, language barriers were not serious. Once the populations of such countries had been mobilized into full and emotional participation in the process of foreign policy and international relations, the detached and professional tone of the system would have to change.

The balance of power system also depended on the condition of military technology. If the defense had been enormously effective, in the manner of the Swiss mountaineers, there would have been no need for such a system, since each nation could easily have defended its own territory whenever any two-state war broke out; outside parties would not have needed to intervene in the fear that the stronger of the two would defeat, conquer, and absorb the weaker. If the offense had been enormously effective, conversely, in the manner of the "Blitzkrieg" of Germany against Poland in 1939, there might never have been time for third parties to intervene effectively to bolster the weaker side. A military technology which did not guarantee success to the defensive side, but which at least allowed that side to prolong the struggle long enough to allow help to arrive, was the context of international relations in the 18th century, and was required to let the balance system work as it did.

For the system to work well, it is also generally assumed that the number of states in the system must exceed four. It also follows that no single state must grow so large that it can overwhelm the other members of the system. This therefore suggests some of the precariousness of the system. One or more of the countries might be inactivated over time by domestic revolution, or civil war, or industrial lethargy, or a declining population perhaps caused by famine and disease. Another country might experience a tremendous industrial boom, or expansion of population, or great success in its colonial endeavors. None of these threats to the system need to be the result of a war, a war in which other members might intervene, yet each would threaten the stability of the system, just as much as a war in which France simply invaded and conquered Spain.

It thus followed logically that the balance system was not thus primarily intended to prevent wars, albeit this was a very attractive by-product. The intent of the system's actors was to preserve their own job tenures. Knowing that the gallery would intervene against any winner in a war, to deny him the full fruits of victory, might indeed have discouraged any individual ruler from beginning a war he thought he might win. Yet in other cases, such as those suggested immediately above, the balance would not deter the outbreak of war, but require it. If country D were becoming too strong through the most natural workings of its economy and birth rate, countries A and E might legitimately attack to slice off some provinces from country D, and countries B and C would applaud, rather than intervene.

One can wonder whether the nations of Europe were ever as free of nationalistic (or more importantly, religious) emotion as the balance of power system seems to require. Wasn't it always true that these nations saw themselves as serving substantive causes, higher causes, than the mere policy of "divide and avoid being conquered." All of politics consists of a mixture of cooperation and counter-production. Sometimes counter-production takes the form of inducing counter-production among two or more other parties. If Austria and Prussia can be kept menacing each other, neither will be able to attack Russia. Yet beyond the intuitive sense that one can always exploit such effects, how realistically can we describe a particular period in history as elevating this ploy to the status of a logically closed system?

Some of the continental states were indeed often concerned with the substance of neighbor's quarrels as well as with the power implications. We are thus perhaps brought back to the system by the special role of Britain, a special role which allowed the British to be very faithful to power considerations, and openly and explicitly so. Behind a secure moat in the English Channel, Britain could afford to be more detached about particular quarrels; yet the security of this moat over time could become a fixation which always led to Britain's taking the long and fearful view, a view which became agitated at any suggestion that some European power was moving toward unifying the continent into a single political and military force.

Britain's boundaries presumably were settled by geography; while there might be some temptation to try to hold bits of the European continent, such temptations would pale because a defense on the Channel would be so much easier. The absence of English-speaking peoples on the mainland reduced any nationalistic drives to cross over. Yet even Britain might become too involved in a continental conflict once a decision had been taken to intervene on balance of power grounds. Coming to the aid of a probable loser might induce propaganda and rationalization on the moral superiority of the cause, at times based on the defense of Protestants against Catholicism, at times on other grounds. The country receiving British assistance might not only survive a neighbor's aggression, but might also take the field in reverse to inflict total defeat on the aggressor, thus in effect creating a Frankenstein from the British point of view. The writings of Jonathan Swift on the balance of power were precisely a call to Britain to forgo becoming excessively involved on the continent, to avoid losing sight of the original purpose and intent of the intervention. Even after the balance of power had ceased to be a true system for Western Europe as a whole, Britain would have to assess its obligations and opportunities in such a context. The questions as always were twofold, who to intervene against, and how deeply to intervene.

The fluidity and flexibility of the balance system at its best might be illustrated in the so-called diplomatic revolution of the middle 1700's, which saw Britain continually angling to contain French power. In the War of the Austrian Succession of 1740–1748, this pitted Britain and Austria against France and Prussia. In the following Seven Years War of 1756 to 1763, Britain now joined Prussia to confront Austria allied with France. We might today be ready to believe great evil about the nation we are fighting, but this can hardly have had any deep effect on decision-makers who displayed so much flexibility in the process of forming alliances.

The balance of power system, even if it only indirectly served the purposes of peace, might seem quite attractive today; wars were few, the temptations of hegemony and aggression seemed under a continual check and deterrent, nationalistic passions were moderated, wars were fought on a more civilized basis than in earlier or later centuries. Yet some limitations of the effectiveness of the balance must be acknowledged even within its own terms. No state could truly be certain that intervention would come in to spoil the exploitation of a victory. Intervention was likely, but it was always possible that a smashing victory based on very rapid offensives might allow one to collect his winnings without challenge. Conversely, weaker states might never be fully certain that they would be guaranteed assistance. The simple confusions of geography would be a factor. It would be easier for Britain to intervene in the Netherlands or Spain than in Bohemia, and the latter theater would seem less threatening to Britain also. The number of countries might seem higher than required for the maintenance of the system, as with Poland in the 18th century, so that no outside power would really feel driven to intervene to prevent its partition. At other times, as noted above, the number of effective states might become too low to check the natural increase of some particular nation's power.

If each national leadership were assumed primarily to be seeking power, with which to reinsure and expand its domestic preeminence, this did not perfectly coincide with preserving the "balance of power." Seeing one neighbor being overwhelmed by another, a nation might have been greatly tempted to join the aggressor, rather than coming to the victim's aid, assuming that 40 percent of the carcass would be better insurance against attacks from the winning neighbor than some futile and costly efforts to keep the weaker neighbor alive.

FURTHER READINGS

Haas, Ernst B. "The Balance of Power: Prescription, Concept, or Propaganda?" *World Politics*. July, 1953.

Kaplan, Morton A. "Balance of Power, Bipolarity, and Other Models of International Systems." *American Political Science Review.* September, 1957.
Seabury, Paul, ed. *Balance of Power.* San Francisco: Chandler Publishing, 1965.

Revolutionary Nationalism

The balance system of the years from 1648 to 1789 reflected and supported a basically nonrepresentative system of national units, governments which depended on traditional legitimacy rather than rational sanction, on ascription rather than description for the identification of rulers. Such a system could not hope to rally the peoples of any particular state to a last-ditch defense of their government, and did not wish to. The balance system supplied an alternative form of insurance for ruler tenure, therefore, and in the process kept wars rare and limited in scope. Since armies were intended to protect the position and prerogatives of monarch and aristocracy, rather than to save the souls of heretics, these armies had to be trained to spare the property they were defending. Civilian property, and civilians, were thus spared the worst rigors of wars when they were fought; quartermaster systems had been expanded as armies had decreased in size, and "living off the land" would be the exception rather than the rule.

It was perhaps inevitable that the domestic background of this form of international system would sooner or later be challenged by theories of political legitimacy questioning the validity of traditional custom, endorsing instead rule tailored to those ruled, perhaps even full democracy. The emergence of such a revolutionary approach in France after 1789 thus upset the entire international system, for the balance had served, and depended upon, a much less rationalist approach.

Could a revolutionary France and a traditional Austria have coexisted in peace, perhaps living by the rules of the old balance of power system? The answer almost certainly was no. To begin, the popular base of rule now allowed the raising of tremendous armies in France, armies which the Austrian or any other monarchy could have matched only at the expense of a tremendous surrender of prerogative. Since armies were no longer intended merely to guard property and privilege, they would once again be set loose to live off the country, freeing the revolutionary French armies of some of the constraints of the limitation of the quartermaster.

Raising such armies had indeed required that the government seem to be responsive to the wishes of the masses. In some ways, this had to put any French regime in a position of riding the tiger, for if French popular opinion now saw any grievances against a state like Austria, it could no longer be ignored. The very principle of democratic rule, moreover, seemed morally universal, and thus equally appropriate for the subjects of the Hapsburgs. Frenchmen could hardly revel in their own newfound liberties without sympathizing with persons lacking them across some border. Regimes across the border could hardly welcome a French regime into the community of nations, without accepting similar risks of revolutionary change within their own domains.

Hence the French revolution introduced the first major "ideological question" into European politics since the powers had agreed to forgo religious unity. Disagreement would previously have been absent on the domestic *forms* of government, arising only perhaps on *who* would govern in the aristocratic form over Silesia or Burgundy, or elsewhere. Disagreement on domestic legitimacy thus upset what had been a legitimacy on international method; one perhaps challenged the other state's army in combat, but one normally did not dispatch agitators to induce rebellion in the opposing state. Now propaganda and subversion would be a powerful tool which France was by no means willing to renounce. The introduction of political ideology was accompanied by the tremendous imbalance of force with the French *levee en masse* had facilitated. The ensuing result was that France, first under various more genuinely revolutionary regimes, then under Napoleon, threatened again to acquire a hegemony over all of Europe, and some 25 years elapsed before the threat was finally eliminated.

The wars that ensued now were of a substantially different character from those of the balance system, precisely because of their motivation and their scale. The powers that had to resist France were resisting hegemony, and in the same motion, were resisting threats to their own aristocratic tenure from simple force of example. Since France was so willing and able to deploy resources for war, the other states had to exert themselves much more to match this effort. Wars were thus much more demanding and expensive; although some of the worst horrors of the Thirty Years War could be avoided, the need to conscript so many young men and to live off the land nonetheless took a heavier toll than had the wars of the prerevolutionary years. The first fruits of popular rule were thus indeed more demanding wars; partisans of the traditional system could honestly claim to be opposed to wars, as well as to revolution and modernization.

After France fell under the rule of Napoleon, it obviously lost a great deal of the revolutionary purity of the years immediately following 1789, but much was also retained. Enough revolutionary elan was still present to induce larger numbers of young Frenchmen and other Europeans to risk their lives for the Emperor. Since Napoleon had no "legitimate" background on which to base his claim to rule as monarch, the implicit challenge to ascriptive authority in all other states similarly remained in effect. An attempt to acquire such legitimacy by marriage to an Austrian princess of the Hapsburg family came too late to decouple the challenge from Napoleon's person, or to soothe the fears and anxieties of the regimes which felt threatened here. Even if legitimacy could have been confirmed in such a marriage, the extent of French conquests and power by 1810 already posed so much of a threat in traditional balance of power terms, that

Britain, Prussia, Russia, and even Austria would have to be watching for opportunities to cut Napoleon's empire down to size. If Napoleon had come to resemble Louis XIV, this was desirable for the sake of legitimacy, but extremely menacing in terms of how much national military strength had again been aggregated under a single continental command.

Napoleon played the game well, in winning battles lesser generals would have lost, in exploiting the political weaknesses and needs of his opponents to come closer to satisfying his own cravings for political power. In 1814 the other states of Europe were indeed prepared to allow a retention of Napoleonic rule over France itself, a France even enlarged to include German, Belgian, and other territories west of the Rhine, as this might have been sufficient to restore the balance without prolonging a terribly costly war. Threats of revolutions induced by the very example of a Napoleonic France might still have posed problems for the other states of the system, but might have seemed manageable and preferable to the costs of pushing for a total defeat of the emperor. Yet Napoleon's rejection of a peace giving him only an enlarged kingdom forced the powers to pursue the costly war into France itself, with a final restoration of the Bourbons to the French throne.

Could the balance of power system now be restored as the form of international politics? Or would the new system be more than the balance? If the balance before had motivated participating nations primarily or solely by the fear of mergers which might become stepping stones to hegemony, other fears now would grip many of the regimes in the system, specifically a fear of new revolutions posing the new challenges France had raised in 1789. This fear of the subversion of political tenure at the least suggested tighter domestic controls on possible sources of revolution, more effective censorship and secret police, and so on. If revolution should nonetheless succeed in some state in the system, the others were now, moreover, prepared to launch an armed intervention to restore the legitimate rulers to power. The Holy Alliance as proposed by the czar may have been an easily ridiculed institutionalization of this. Yet most of the powers which previously might have stayed away from military interventions until a war between two neighbors had erupted would now consider preemption at a much earlier stage. Indeed, to legitimate such interventions, and to ensure that they would not be used for the power aggrandizement of a particular state, the Holy Alliance foresaw joint interventions orchestrating contingents from several legitimate regimes.

International relations prior to Napoleon had thus been a true balance model, in which member nations exploited competition amongst others as part of their own competition with all the others. In the aftermath of Napoleon, a more genuine cooperation was being espoused, to head off revolutions and moves toward rationalization and modernization in the domestic regimes of Europe. If Metternich's goals and accomplishments could be summarized at all fairly in his impact on the system, it was that he sought to use the system to postpone or defer indefinitely the political modernization of Europe.

The major exception to the shift from balance considerations to concern for suppression of revolution remained with Britain, which under Castlereagh now shifted again toward the role of detached holder of the balance, concerned again lest any particular states collect too much of Europe under a single control. Avoidance of British commitment to the methods and goals of the Holy Alliance was followed by occasional identifications of British opinion with the insurrectionary forces challenging "legitimacy" on the continent, for example, the Greeks seeking independence from Turkey. Britain was still a special case, able to exploit the moat of the English Channel to delay any threats from the continent, therefore more fixated than it might otherwise be on resisting any possible combination of forces sufficient to leap across that moat. As before, a sense now arose of excessive commitment to having defeated the last hegemonic threat, a concern that freedom of maneuver and detachment be recaptured.

It is interesting to note how closely the forces of political liberalism and ethnic nationalism were linked in the post-Napoleonic period. The regimes that had defeated Napoleon regarded either political movement with great suspicion. To say that boundaries should be based on language spoken was just as much a threat to traditional authority, in terms of functional and rational justification, as to say that government should derive authority from a legislature linked by a constitution to the people governed. Just as the regimes of postcolonial Africa today are very fearful of irredentist arguments based on ethnic factors, since all their boundaries are simply carry-overs from colonial regimes, so the regimes of 1820 had to be very resistant to ethnic self-determination. Similarly, the same liberal forces that were denied political reform would sense themselves frustrated in terms of cultural and ethnic fulfillment in Germany and elsewhere; for reactionaries as well as radicals, the issues seemed linked.

Some concessions to the national principle, of course, were inevitable, for it would have been impossible to restore the map of Europe exactly to what it had been before the French Revolution and Napoleon had changed it. In Germany, for example, Napoleon had reduced the number of separate political identities from more than 300 to approximately 30. Perhaps of equal importance, Napoleon had forced the final termination of claims to sovereignty of the Holy Roman Empire; now at last it was to be clear that nations of sovereign standing would be equal in stature within the international system, rather than structured according to some bequest from Rome. Ambassadors before 1815 had taken precedence by a status hierarchy prescribed by the Pope, and generally related to an imagined link with Rome; such precedence now would simply stem from the length of time anyone had served as ambassador, with the smallest country being able to claim preeminence if it only had left its envoy in place long enough.

The boundaries had been drawn by Napoleon on what at least purported to be ethnic lines; even as revised by the powers that had defeated him, these boundaries now suggested that the geographic limits of sovereignty would no longer be simply a matter of tradition, bequest, and ascription, but something more functional and rational. In the process of elevating units such as Bavaria and Saxony to the status of kingdoms, Napoleon had made some modifications which would never be undone. What was legitimate in 1788 at many points had been compromised by Britain to win the necessary allies with which to defeat Napoleon.

The German case was clearly the most significant, if only because earlier wars and the workings of the balance of power system had so long deferred German political unity. The restoration of 1815 hardly provided this unity, but it certainly set the stage for those Germans who aspired to ethnic unity together with responsible government. What might have seemed impossibly distant in the 18th century would now seem within reach, because Prussia was so much expanded as its reward for having defeated Napoleon and the rest of Germany was now assembled into more functional units.

Despite these concessions, the policy of the major powers now was to resist attempts at nationalistic unifications or revisions of territory, on the very correct fear that such accomplishments of ethnic unity would carry with them tremendous concessions to popular rule. Between 1815 and 1848, concessions to national sentiment were thus the exception rather than the rule. Belgium won its independence from the Netherlands in 1832, but with frontiers designed to assure the Netherlands (and Britain) that Belgium would never become a base for French expansion northeastward. Greece won its independence from Turkey, but the struggle of Christians against the Islamic Turkish regime was always likely to capture enough European sympathy so that the normal fear of revolution and reform might be suspended. The identification of British public opinion with the Greeks, under the prodding of Lord Byron, was strong enough to contribute substantially to the Greek success.

What the European establishment had more generally feared broke out all across Europe in 1848, as revolutions spread from one German state to another, demanding representative governments and constitutions, demanding the unification of all German-speaking peoples into a single state. Similar outbreaks occurred in France, in Italy and Hungary, in Bohemia, and in Ireland; the armies of Prussia and Austria-Hungary for a time seemed unable to cope with the extent of the insurrections, but in the end succeeded in suppressing them on a city-by-city basis, often ruthlessly with substantial loss of life. The German liberals meeting in Frankfurt at the height of their seeming success had offered the Imperial Crown of a united

Germany to the King of Prussia, who rejected it precisely because its source would mean a commitment to much less legitimate and ascriptive political authority than what he had held. Prussia thus paradoxically rejected an opportunity to expand, because expansion would bring more territory but less power for its regime. The same German liberals who demanded such sweeping and democratic reforms now also showed themselves most aggressively nationalistic in staking out their claims to an ethnic frontier, extremely reluctant to renounce any of the Polish-speaking districts of Prussia, or the Czech-speaking provinces of Austria, Bohemia, and Moravia.

After the defeat of Napoleon, the powers which had been allied against France thus were determined to prevent a recurrence of the kind of revolutionary national regime which had so gravely disrupted the old system. The example of any one country adopting such a political style could be infectious, causing domestic unrest in neighboring states. The power of such a national style would, moreover, allow the mobilization of far larger armies than before, overwhelming the military defenses of neighboring states. Suppressing such a tendency toward revolution thus seemed to call for preemptive intervention against any state undergoing internal unrest. While the old balance of power rule would have suggested an attitude of wait-and-see, the net offensive punch of a radicalized society seemingly made this less possible for the future.

Yet the nations intent on suppressing all moves toward revolution would have to be careful lest they succumb themselves in the process of preparing to suppress it. Larger armies, raised on a basis of broad national service, tended to force concessions from the traditional rulers of nations, to those who had traditionally lacked political and economic power. A small professional army conversely was far more likely to serve and protect aristocratic privilege. In the process of repulsing Napoleon, a number of nations had made commitments to engaging their entire populations in the common cause of restoring their national integrity, exactly as France had done. After the final exile of Napoleon, the same powers now moved to make a mere empty shell of their domestic military mobilization systems; the military needs of intervening against revolution elsewhere would be balanced against the revolutionizing tendency of excessive military preparation.

The question of offensive or defensive advantage thus became a curiously complicated problem after Napoleon. As long as revolution was still suppressed, as long as each of the nations limited itself for domestic reasons to a small professional army, the balance of power game might be played much as before, with the defensive fortifications of each state most probably sufficient to delay any foreign incursions until outside help arrived. If a state had its regime deposed by revolution, however, its professional army might thereby have been removed from the scene; fearing revolution, the outside states might moreover have been willing to sanction a total invasion to restore the legitimate regime, perhaps even an invasion mounted by all the outside states cooperatively.

Such a stable system might survive as long as no revolutionary regimes such as that of France in 1789 succeeded in establishing themselves. Yet if this threat were averted, the risk remained that one state or another would find a way to reconcile total mobilization of population with the maintenance of aristocratic privilege. If the mobilization systems were then restored to functional reality, a great offensive advantage might have arisen again to complicate the relations of any two states, even if they shared a reactionary attitude on the correct form of domestic society.

The ability to go from an army of 400,000 to an army of two million in any short time is destabilizing for the defense. The military advantage clearly accrues to whoever has given his mobilization signals first, to whoever strikes first in an ambiguous situation. The aggravation of offensive advantage in military instability was furthered by the great advances in general mobility resulting from the steam engine, with the extensive construction of railroads on land, and the development of the fast steamboat at sea. Not only could an opposing state suddenly outnumber another in terms of total force-strengths, but his army might be moved suddenly from other areas to a single crucial area of the front, there to win a decisive victory which would determine the entire remainder of the war.

FURTHER READINGS

Hinsley, F. H. *Power and the Pursuit of Peace.* Cambridge, England: Cambridge University Press, 1963.
Kissinger, Henry A. *A World Restored.* New York: Grosset and Dunlap, 1964.
Nicolson, Harold. *The Congress of Vienna.* New York: Viking, 1961.

Conservative Nationalism

The aftermath of the barely successful suppression of the revolutions of 1848 produced a substantial change of strategy for the conservative hierarchies of most European nation-states. If liberalization of the 1848 form was so closely linked to ethnic nationalism, the two could not be resisted forever. One option clearly was thus to harness national sentiments to the preexisting regimes.

Liberals might on reflection conclude that their most important goals were delayed or lost because they had allowed themselves to become misled by the superficial accomplishments of ethnic and national unity. A contrary view would concede, however, that national unity on a cultural basis was more than a superficial accomplishment, for even the poorest and politically most ignored citizens were to derive some substantial gratification from national unity, and from the respect this engendered for their culture. At the least, national unity for Germany and Italy could mean that these areas would less often be used as arenas and battlefields for the balance of power game in the future. Countries already unified, such as France or Russia, could offer their citizens similar returns in the form of expansions into Belgium or Savoy, into Poland or the Slavic Balkans; the serf or peasant who derived pleasure from this should also not so easily be characterized as foolish, or misled by superficialities.

The principal architect of the transformation of the European international system in this shift toward conservative nationalism was Otto Von Bismarck. As Chancellor, first of Prussia and then of a unified Germany, Bismarck succeeded in harnessing popular sentiment for a German ethnic reunification behind a regime which was determined to resist liberalizations of domestic political practice. Because of this emergence of German nationalism, or because the same device of coopting the nationalist drive had occurred to other conservative rulers, similar reconstellations now occurred in France and Russia, and to a lesser extent all across Europe.

As a practitioner, Bismarck was extremely able and astute in setting the diplomatic stage for the military campaigns which served his purposes. The war with Denmark in 1864 was provoked to mobilize German sentiment against a Danish regime which clearly seemed to be denying self-determination to the people of Schlewig and Holstein. In the war with Austria of 1866, the German sentiment was divided, but Bismarck persuaded the Prussian king to deal generously with Austria, while ruthlessly absorbing some of the smaller states which had only been led into combat by Austria. The King, still laboring under an older notion of right and wrong and legitimacy, could only be persuaded with difficulty that the chief enemy, Austria, should go unpunished, while its satellites completely lost their legitimate political tenure. But this tenure for Bismarck had lost its paramount legitimacy in international terms, for the interests of the Hohenzollerns and the Prussian upper class now would require that real service be given to a German reunification, a reunification for which Austrian acquiesence would be required.

In the 1871 war with France which at last produced German unity, Bismarck cleverly provoked the French Emperor Napoleon III into statements and positions alienating British opinion and ensuring Britain's neutrality. Similar maneuvers kept Austria out of the war, and assured the participation of all the other German states in what was at first an alliance against France, but with the "functionalist spinoff" of commitment to a political union.

Realpolitik, political realism, as practiced by Bismarck, was thus shocking precisely in that he was no longer rendering cooperative international support for traditional legitimacy, either as under the balance of power system, or in the cooperative suppression of revolution and radicalism which had been presided over by Metternich. If the power of a few of the traditional ruling houses was now to be furthered in a partnership with national sentiment, the relations with other ruling houses would be characterized by higher levels of potential violence, competition, dissimulation, and deceit.

Bismarck's wars were all cheap and short, implemented by a superior Prussian preorganization that disabled much of the opposing force at the very outset of the war. The gain for Germans was quite real, even for the common people whose drive for fuller democracy was thereby put off and delayed, for Germany as a cultural and economic unit was to experience a substantial boom in the aftermath of 1871. Yet the same victories that boosted German morale and satisfied German national aspirations bred a resentment among French and Slavic nationalists, a resentment that earlier regimes in these countries might have ignored, but now would be unable to ignore. While Metternich would not have wanted to support such national sentiments, and long might not have had to, Napoleon III had matched the Bismarckian example by encouraging hopes for French national expansionism, thus leaving behind a legacy of irredentism after the defeat of 1871. The later Russian czars were similarly capable of basing otherwise unpopular regimes on national feeling, with sympathy abroad for Serbs, and persecution at home for Jews. Bismarck's ingenuity thus had generated a new form of international system in which such ingenuity would continually be required, as the balance no longer managed itself, as the community of interest among governments was much less than it had been in the past.

In a perverse way, these changes in the international system can be seen as an unavoidable accommodation to popular will in the countries involved, with the unhappy result that the balance of power system could never function again as it had prior to 1789. In the days of the balance, the conservatives had generally succeeded in maintaining peace, without ever having any recourse to nationalism. In the years after 1848, the same establishments had become nationalists themselves to exploit and control the sentiments involved, with unhappy consequences for the likelihood of peace.

Having made a commitment to "nationalist" sentiments to reconfirm their hold on political power, the regimes of Europe were therefore much more bound than before to taking substantive issues seriously. In earlier times, accretions of power by transfer of territory or strategic position were much more interchangeable and liquid. Now the special attitudes of the people would drive the pursuer of power into very defined and narrow assertions of foreign policy goals.

Some of the earlier insecurity of political position in the face of outside attack was now eliminated. At an earlier time, it might almost have been conceivable for a victorious Prussia to absorb large portions of France; by contrast, in 1871, even the absorption of all of Alsace-Lorraine, of which much was indeed German-speaking, caused Bismarck some uneasiness. Since absorptions of this kind were less likely, the bystanders would be under less of a balance of power compulsion to intervene to protect themselves. Britain or Austria or Russia in 1871 would have to worry less about the Prussian victory upsetting the balance, and more about satisfying the national cravings of their own populations, populations whose appetites might be whetted by the German example.

FURTHER READINGS

Rosecrance, Richard. *Action and Reaction in World Politics.* Boston: Little, Brown, 1963.
Taylor, A. J. P. *Bismarck.* New York: Random House, 1955.

Imperialism

The late 19th century saw European politics spread out to affect the entire globe. This process of "imperialism" is an international interaction which itself requires an explanation. Without imperialism, great damage might not have been inflicted on the cultural traditions of various peoples in Africa and Asia, and many forms of exploitation might have been avoided. Without imperialism, some economic gains might also not have been achieved. Most relevant for the study of international relations, the same imperialism in effect standardized the world's traditions of international law, organization, and practical politics on the style of international politics evolving in Europe.

There had been expansions of European military power and political influence in several earlier spasms, as early as the 15th and 16th centuries. While Britain, the Netherlands, and Portugal staked out a network of immensely profitable trading posts, Spain conquered a large portion of South and North America, in quest of souls for the Roman Church, in quest of the gold and silver which facilitated the military power described earlier. In the 17th century, the British entry into North America shifted from simple trading posts to enormous colonies, colonies which by the end of the 18th century, of course, had broken free to become the independent United States, followed soon by similar independence for the Spanish colonies in America.

Whether or not the original flow of Spanish, French, and English settlers into the New World can be called imperialism may raise some semantic questions—questions all the more difficult to resolve since these colonies eventually won their independence. Until the latter part of the 19th century, there was no similar expansion of European presence into Africa, or the Far East. As the United States expanded westward, so presumably did Brazil, and the Russian Empire pushed eastward across Siberia. Because the countries involved are independent, because the territories absorbed were entirely contiguous to the home territory, these expansions are not so normally labeled as imperialism, although Chinese spokesmen today might question whether the Russian presence in Vladivostok is "nonimperialist."

Independence for Australia and Canada similarly serves to ward off indictments on the process by which these territories became such obvious extensions of Europe. The latter 19th century, however, saw Britain somewhat inadvertently complete its seizure of political control over India, and there followed then a race for territorial control and sovereignty over virtually all of Africa and Southeast Asia. Ethiopia, Iran, Thailand, and a few other states escaped domination simply by serving as buffer states between competing European interests, but had to make heavy concessions to European commercial presence. Japan almost uniquely Europeanized itself in terms of industry and military power, and thereby succeeded in heading off domination by foreign powers. China's escape from partition among the powers was much more of a near thing, in part due to the semibenevolent intervention of the United States, in part because various important European states checked and delayed each other's ambitions.

One can speculate interestingly and endlessly about the motives for such imperialism. At earlier times, the expansions outward from Europe might indeed have been intended to preserve the prerogatives of aristocratic and traditional power, as with the "proprietary" nature of some of the British colonies in North America, the Dutch patroon system in what became New York, and the Russian czarist colonies in Alaska and down the Pacific Coast as far as California. At other points, the argument of commercial exploitation was quite convincing, especially for the earlier trading posts which generated such enormous profit margins for the delivery of spices in Europe. Whether the same commercial motives can explain the "ink blot" process by which the territories in between these trading posts were then occupied and claimed is not so clear. An accurate reading of the commercial balance sheet for the imperialist experience will always be a very debated exercise. It is at least plausible that many of the individual colonial ventures of the latter 19th century cost their home countries more than they produced.

Given the popular nationalistic sentiments unleashed in the latter 1800's, it would be surprising if nationalism did not also account for much of the imperialistic drives which followed. If one, correctly or incorrectly, saw material benefits in increasing the number of persons speaking one's language, be it German, French, Italian or English, the idea of overseas colonies for a nation's emigrant population, rather than a melting-pot such as the U.S., could become quite attractive. Even seeing large portions of the map colored in pink or green might stir the national sense of accomplishment, however sparsely settled or valueless such space might have been at the onset. Who in Germany could know for certain that Southwest Africa

would always be a desert? If the boundaries were pinned down, any technological breakthrough for irrigation and industrialization would at least
benefit this territory as German "living-space" rather than non-German.

Related to the popular drives noted above are the real and presumed
demands of a changing military technology. While naval sailing ships might
have been able to sail from Britain to Australia without stopping for fuel,
modern steam-propelled warships, vastly more effective in combat, did not
have this range. The need for bases thus generated an interest in seizing
fueling points along the coasts which had not yet been seized by another
European state. Any naval base for another state, moreover, would seem
intended to interfere with these "life-line" bases, and coastal enclaves might
thus be seized as much to preempt their acquisition by a hostile naval
power as for their own value. China thus became pockmarked with such
naval bases as Tsingtao, Weihaiwei, Kwangchowan, and Port Arthur, in
part because various navies would need them, but also because other naval
powers feared such bases.

Because of this mixture of political nationalism and military preemption,
so much a reflection of the politics and military technology of Europe
itself, European governments indeed now sought economic excuses for
intervention, in effect bribing commercial firms to undertake ventures of
dubious economic return merely to give the government an excuse to
protect them.

It is interesting to note how little condemnation of imperialism one finds
in European opinion prior to 1920, the process being taken almost for
granted as natural and in the interests of civilization. The military technology of Europe was indeed enormously superior to that of most African or
Asian societies, making it possible for very small contingents of men to
defeat and conquer huge populations. The Europeans were also quite astute
politically, improvising solutions from one native society to another to
maintain their law and order with a low investment of resources. The
imperialist regimes differed in the extent to which the native culture was
to be left unspoiled, or to be assimilated with that of Paris or London. In
some cases, only the loosest of colonial regimes was imposed, as local
traditional rulers were allowed to retain authority so long as they served
the purposes of the colonial power. In other countries, enormous staffs of
bureaucrats were brought in from the home country to deny the indigenous people almost all career opportunities in government.

Depending on one's contemporary perspective, great disagreement is
possible on how much harm was done in the imperialist period. The forced
labor practices of the Congo, for example, were particularly and noticeably
barbaric, and were replicated at one time or another in many African and
Asian colonies. At a more subliminal level, African and Asian patriots will
argue that even greater damage was done by instilling alien cultural forms
in their societies, leaving many of the elites confused and rootless in their

cultural heritages. The purely arbitrary natures of the colonial boundaries, often splitting African ethnic groups, often lumping together groups with little of a common cultural heritage, may have burdened Africa, in particular, with political problems which will take centuries to solve.

Defenders of the imperial experience will be quick to respond by citing material benefits introduced by the European conquerers, the railroads which serve India so well, the sanitation and health systems which prevent disease and prolong life (in the process of greatly expanding the population), the introduction of modern industrial techniques which can expand the personal incomes and living standards of persons living in the former colonies. Since so much of the political style of newly independent nations is modeled on European bases, the imperialist might claim credit for these also. Even where regimes become Marxist, it might be contentiously argued that Marx was brought to Africa or Asia by European radicals working under, and against, the umbrella of the colonial regimes. The last argument hints that the superiority of the European political tradition is somehow proven in that almost all new nations model their regimes on some form of it; yet this argument may only be strong by default, because the colonial regimes were repressive and total enough to wipe out any local traditions that might have become relevant. The world's standardization on European forms, in domestic as well as international political practice, thus hardly supports an objective recognition of the superiority of such forms, but rather the realities of military and political power. It has been wryly suggested that anyone saying that ideas cannot be killed with a bullet should try reciting the Albigensian Creed; he might as easily try to recite particulars of the Zulu governmental structure.

Imperialism has indeed been rolled back, as one area after another has acquired the political and military means to expel colonial rulers and win national independence. The Portuguese colonies in Africa are the most glaring exception to this generalization, along with such enclaves as French Somaliland and Hong Kong, and various small islands lacking the population to qualify for separate foreign policies. For reasons suggested earlier, this view exempts the American hold over what were Indian lands in the Far West (as well as Canadian imperialism into similar longitudes), and the Russian control over peoples in Central Asia. Contiguity plays an important role, suggesting that geopolitics or political geography may still have a life of its own, in what people of the world see as reality, if not in reality itself. If the Siberian and American Indian territories were not fully adjacent to the rest of these two super-powers, a more telling charge of imperialism might be formulated. As it is, the United States occasionally confronts indictments of its sovereignty over Puerto Rico, the Virgin Islands, various trust territories in the western Pacific, and even in the time before statehood, Hawaii. (While statehood, that is incorporation into metropolitan United States, apparently eased any plausible criticisms here, this ploy might not always be as effective, as with the French attempt to treat Algeria as part of "Metropolitan France," or the Portuguese redefinition of Angola and Mozambique as "overseas provinces.") More important, for warding off the indictment of imperialism within the continents, is the fact that the USSR and United States have successfully carried on programs and processes of assimilation, whereby Russian and English come close to replacing whatever indigenous languages might have persisted as rivals. Such assimilation will require a mixture of forced education in the national language, plus intensive immigration of speakers of the language, to outnumber the original natives. A demand for American Indian sovereignty over, and independence in, New Mexico would thus confront the sheer numbers of non-Indians who have entered the state.

In what sense, therefore, is anyone "imperialist" today? Is it possible or probable that nations are fighting to expand their territorial domains, or their "spheres of influence," perhaps merely to find the markets which might offer full employment or prosperity? Radical critiques of American foreign policy tend to believe in such motives as an important explanation of wars that are otherwise totally irrational. Yet as will be argued, this explanation of foreign policy as a product of pathological aspects of the domestic economy is quite open to challenge.

What about cultural drives to imperialism? Within boundaries that for the moment are unchallenged, this is presumably what explains the drives for linguistic and cultural standardization in the U.S. and Soviet Union. Perhaps it also explains part of the Portuguese reluctance to surrender control over African territories, although critics contend that Portugal is indeed reaping substantial economic benefits from these territories, benefits reaped only because there are no compunctions about forced labor.

What about pursuit of political power generally, the desires of the United States to check and contain Russian or Chinese power, and the reciprocal moves of these powers? Isn't this also what one could describe as imperialism? In a broad sense, the term can be applied and is often thus applied to any nation's tendency to accrue power, or to be visibly in quest of influence over territory. Yet it must be remembered that there are substantial differences between the forms of political power which require explicit political control over the laws, tarriffs, and military forces of an area, and the mere quest for influence. Both the U.S. and the USSR today are of necessity prepared to be content with far less of explicit power and authority than were the European powers in Africa in 1895. The explanation must stem largely from how easily and economically such explicit trappings could be acquired then, and how much resistance to them would arise today.

The European commitment to imperialism in Africa and Asia was quickly accompanied by the entry of a significant non-European power into the arena of significant international politics, the United States. The

United States had prided itself on a policy of nonentanglement and isolation since the time of its first president, contenting itself with the assertion of a Monroe Doctrine which purportedly shielded the rest of the western hemisphere from European intervention. The actual significance of the Monroe Doctrine has been somewhat distorted as Americans have been taught their history, its initial formulation actually having arisen in the context of Russian moves down the western coast of North America from Alaska toward California, rather than the Latin American republics. The Doctrine indeed shortly did become a form of moral encouragement to the Latin American republics in their wars of independence against Spain, a moral encouragement however, not accompanied by any significant deployment of military or economic force. The fact that Spain and other continental powers did not more actively try to restore their hold on South and Central America was due more to the opposition of Great Britain and the strength of the British fleet. Britain for decades in effect was the crucial silent partner in the efficacy of the Doctrine. Yet the American enunciation of the Doctrine was nonetheless enormously important for the future of American foreign policy, for myth which seems to shape precedent can develop a reality of its own.

The earliest American "imperialism" as noted, came in the form of "manifest destiny" claims on all the lands west from the Mississippi to the Pacific Ocean. It was clear almost from the outset that the new nation wanted to challenge any European title to Louisiana or Oregon or Florida, and that the flow of English-speaking immigrants would produce claims in the end on Texas and California also. The wars fought in this context might functionally be compared more to the ways in which Germany was united under Prussia than to the European seizures of territory in Africa or Asia.

In terms of military power, the United States had already assembled a formidable force-in-being at the end of its Civil War in 1865, perhaps the largest and most effective army in the world to that time. Lack of a serious navy presumably would have made it difficult to deploy this strength overseas, but when parts of the Union army were moved to the border of Mexico in 1865, this was more than sufficient as a warning to the French government that its support for the Emperor Maximillian would not long be tolerated.

The first burst of explicit American imperialism, in the sense of expansions into noncontiguous areas, came some 30 years later in the Spanish-American War. As in the European cases, it is hard to prove any particular motive as determining in the territorial expansions now undertaken. Even when the statesmen involved have committed their supposed intentions to paper in memoirs or documents, these must be treated with some distrust because they oversimplify or because they self-consciously reflect what was thought noble and honorable at the time.

In a few cases, the ultimate motive may have been the same as with

California and Oregon—the desire of the United States to territory that could be called "American" on the map, an area sharing the same culture, values, and political system. Whether or not this was the original intention with regard to Hawaii, annexed in 1898 at the time of the Spanish-American War, the process clearly did succeed here, even despite the fact that the Islands have remained racially nonwhite in majority population. Culturally and politically, Hawaii became a state as American as any on the mainland, and there is almost no challenge to this today from either within the U.S. or without. Whether the same integration and assimilation process could be undertaken successfully in Puerto Rico is much more open to debate.

In some of the other territories seized from Spain in the 1898 war, any attempts at absorptive legal possession were foregone, as sheer population would have precluded the admission of the Philippines to statehood, and the size of Cuba similarly precluded assimilation. Many Americans felt at this time that political control without the promise of statehood and self-government would be incompatible with the constitutional style of the United States as a whole. Most Americans today would probably agree.

If at least some of the territories seized by the United States could thus never have been intended for absorption into the domestic political system, various other motives must be explored. The annexations could still have been intended simply to give the public the pleasure of seeing "American possessions" appear all across the map. Alternatively, if Europe was already embarked on collecting unclaimed territories as military bases, the American venture into imperialism could be defended simply on the basis of military preemption. The Hawaiian islands in Japanese, French, British, German, or Russian hands might have become coaling stations supporting a threat to the California coast, and a ready rationale for American seizure could thus be found.

Finally, some Americans stated that territorial acquisitions would open up opportunities for trade, just as American resistance to the colonial partitioning of China was explained in the terms of maintaining an "open door," an open door for missionaries perhaps, but more important for American merchants. American defense for imperialism and engagement in power politics in terms of trade opportunities may to some extent have reflected real intentions, but these also reflected an American popular attitude which frowned on the immoral European practices of seeking such irrational commodities as power and glory for their own sake. Freed of the trappings of royalty and nobility, Americans wanted to see themselves as practical and unassuming, the kind of people who would deploy a navy only to protect the rights of trade, trade which would benefit Chinese and Philippinos as much as Americans. If a Marxist critic today sees such arguments as the strongest possible self-indictment, they were not seen so at the time.

The costs of American participation in imperialism were not trivial, whatever the gains that were expected. In the Philippines and later interventions in Latin America, imperialism required the United States to cope with suppressing insurgency, which involves much time and effort as well as instances of cruelty, torture, and atrocity. The legacy of the image of American intervention may have been forgotten in much of the Philippines because of a generally beneficial administration which followed, but this legacy has hardly been forgotten in Latin America. The resentment of explicit political domination earlier is all too easily coupled with fears of economic intervention or domination, in the power of the great American business corporations which operate so extensively in Central and South America.

While the end of the Spanish-American war for the time terminated the moves toward explicit annexation of territory, the expansion of American military presence in the Caribbean continued thereafter, with a series of interventions under the "Roosevelt corollary" to the Monroe Doctrine, and the sale, under some duress, of the Virgin Islands (then the Danish West Indies) in 1917. World War I brought the final removal of the British Navy's Caribbean fleet, and the decision that the waters of the Western Hemisphere would now primarily be the domain of the U.S. Navy. The great expansion of this navy in World War I left the United States able thereafter to exercise a much more visible presence at the further reaches of both the Atlantic and the Pacific Oceans.

In retrospect one might see even greater costs for the United States here, beyond the simple resentment of local populations subjected to an occasional landing of the U.S. Marines. In committing the United States to the defense or domination of the entire "Western Hemisphere," the real military interests of the United States may have been warped to conform with misleading images derived from the Mercator Map projection. Chile, after all, is farther from most of the United States than is Belgium. Yet the American people in 1914 or 1940 would have thought just the opposite, perhaps not concerned enough about Europe, or concerned too much about "Latin America."

Similarly one may wonder whether the seizure of the Philippines was not a mistake, in committing the United States to activities and interests in the Western Pacific; these activities were certain to threaten Japan, or at least to increase the possibilities of war. The seizure of the Philippines exemplified the preemptive arguments that motivated so many other seizures of military bases and territorial enclaves at the end of the 19th century. While the people of the Philippines desired independence, the argument ran, there were no guarantees that some other military power would not have taken them over as soon as Spanish control had been terminated. For a time, American schoolchildren were taught to believe that Imperial Germany had desires on the Islands, that a German naval squadron in Manila Bay had verged on conflict with Admiral Dewey's ships. However exaggerated these tales, it is true that Germany hastened to purchase the Marshall Islands, the Marianas and Carolines, as Spain proved anxious to be rid of them. If there was a serious prospect of someone moving into the Philippines after 1898, however, it could just as plausibly have been Japan, which soon would be turning northward to challenge Russian presence in Korea and Manchuria.

Yet by seizing Manila Bay and the Philippines, the United States did not conclusively preempt an assertion of Japanese naval power; in effect it only postponed any Japanese expansion in this direction—postponed by American investment in the naval and ground forces that would be required to garrison the islands, postponed by the threat of war which was now to emerge regularly for the next four decades. Having once set foot on territory this far west, it would be difficult for the United States to waive its interests at any point in the future. There may be good substantive reasons for a country to take an interest in the military and political events of China or Hong Kong or the Philippines or Indo-China; yet one must remember that merely having shown an interest in the past can generate a new drive for action into the future, as the nation fears that its resolve otherwise will seem to be slipping.

FURTHER READINGS

Fieldhouse, D. K. *The Theory of Capitalist Imperialism.* New York: Barnes & Noble, 1967.
Hobson, John. *Imperialism.* Ann Arbor: University of Michigan Press, 1965.
Langer, William L. "Farewell to Empire." *Foreign Affairs.* October, 1962.

Technological Instability

Because "nationalist" sentiments had substantially undermined the simple balancing of power as the determinant of foreign policy, the statesmen of Germany and Europe were thus confronted with serious difficulties after 1871. If Bismarck could satisfy the new imperatives without wars, and without embarassing capitulations in terms of national honor or prestige, it would require such a virtuoso performance that it might not be duplicated by his successors.

Germany's position after unification was inevitably a little precarious in that each of its principal neighbors would wish to capture territory at its expense. On grounds of ethnic nationality and national pride, France might wish to recover Alsace-Lorraine, and Russia would have liked the Polish portions of Prussia. Any Austrian desires would have reflected the more traditional rivalry of competing dynasties in which the Hapsburgs had been decidedly worsted by the Hohenzollerns in the war of 1866. Over time, Vienna's power was to decline, as the increasing power of ethnic nationalism threatened to tear the Austro-Hungarian regime apart. Yet even if this were to eliminate any threat of revenge from Vienna, it might simply leave an already outnumbered Germany with a weak partner against Russia and France, if the alliances became crystallized that way. Germany in effect had to keep both Austria and Russia from building any firm alliances with France, for either combination might leave Germany exposed. Since Austria and Russia themselves were at odds over the territorial settlement in the Balkans, this would not be an easy task.

It might indeed thus have required the skill of a Bismarck to keep the possibilities of alliance sufficiently confused after 1890, so that no threats to Germany would ever materialize. His successors in Germany were not up to the task. The Kaiser's own lack of tact certainly helped to drive Britain into committing itself to France and Russia, and his decisions in favor of a navy and a colonial empire played an important role here too. Bismarck would have regarded such overseas accomplishments as quite expendable for Germany, as long as Britain could be kept in its traditionally detached role.

Yet the Kaiser's judgment may basically have been correct that one could not indefinitely convince both Vienna and St. Petersburg that they had an ally in Berlin. Whatever the British attitude, a Franco-Russian alliance had become very likely, an alliance which might steadily grow in power if Slavic nationalism could be counted upon to erode Austria-Hungary as a real military partner for Germany.

At an earlier point, the French and Russian governments might not so enthusiastically have contemplated imposing a total defeat on some other nation, for fear that it would upset the balance of power on which they each depended for security. Yet Germany had never been a country in those days, but rather a congeries of principalities serving as the battlefield whenever the balance-system required a war. With a national following based on Slavic or French nationalism, Germany's rivals could now scheme for a total defeat of the regime in Berlin. Perhaps the boundaries of Germany and France could have been redrawn through Alsace and Lorraine to do justice to the ethnic longings of German-speakers and French-speakers. Perhaps ethnic self-determination could similarly have been applied in the Balkans and eastern Europe. Yet this would have dismantled Austria and left a weakened Germany alone against a stronger France and Russia, with no guarantees that the Germans would not again be dominated by outside forces.

In explaining the outbreak of World War I, we thus often lament the hardening of alliances which occurred after the departure of Bismarck. Why was it so necessary for Russia to pledge once and for all that it would take part *ab initio* in any war between France and Germany, removing whatever flexibility might have resulted if both sides could have been left guessing as to whose side St. Petersburg would support? Why was it similarly necessary for Berlin to pledge its intervention on behalf of Austria against Russia? According to the rules of the balance of power system of an earlier day, each could have stood on the side for the first months or years of any war, waiting to see how the war was going, waiting to see whether any state's national existence was threatened by total defeat. Why in the end was it necessary even for Great Britain to plan in advance (albeit not to promise by treaty) to fight with France against Germany, if war should break out on the continent?

What drove the nations of Europe to surrender their freedom of action in reciprocal exchanges of alliance commitments was primarily the increasing speed of military action, a speed which became likely with the introduction of steam-powered transportation on land and on the sea. The rapid victories of Prussian armies over Austria in 1866, and the French in 1871, had suggested that the offensive would normally hold the advantage, if only it were organized properly, if mobilization schedules and railroad schedules were properly integrated for the attack. Wars thus promised to be short and cheap, compared with the enormous advantages which might accrue in victory, real advantages unless one does not care what language is taught to one's children in school or used in a civil service examination.

The outcomes of wars thus seemed to depend on who first realized that war was inevitable. The same nationalism that drove nations to take ethnic questions so seriously had also made it possible to carry out universal military service systems. Such systems at one point had been seen as a liberal safeguard against traditional oppression after 1815, and had typically been left unexecuted where regimes preferred small professional armies of unquestioned loyalty. Now even "national" armies could be loyal, where the enmity of neighbors was so obvious. And now any army could be expanded in short order from its peacetime core to perhaps ten times the size; whoever chose to mobilize first, just as whoever chose to attack first, might win all the battles, simply by having his enemy outnumbered.

The European powers might have amended some of their assumptions of a short, quick war after the experience of the American Civil War, in which the firepower of breech-loading rifles had time after time imposed sufficient casualties to stop armies on the offensive. Yet Europeans either ignored this experience, or wrote it off to the inferior organization of American armies for rapid offensives. In retrospect, the defensive firepower of 1914 (as now augmented by the machine gun) made it problematical whether the quick victories of 1866 or 1871 could be repeated on either side. Scheduling mobilizations and railroads properly and taking the initiative might lead to decisive victory, but missing such victory even by a little bit could then lead to the most horrible and prolonged stalemate.

In earlier days we might thus have deterred a neighbor's attack simply with the prospect that our resistance would prolong the war long enough to draw intervention, intervention by those other states having a natural interest in keeping us in the international system. Once wars could be much more rapidly executed through sudden mobilizations and movement of troops by railroad, or by sudden steamboat movements into some port, there might not be time for the "balance of power" interventions. Thus it strengthened all the parties to an alliance if each was pledged in advance to come immediately to the other's aid if war should ever break out. An alliance might be nothing more than a promise to act. The promise described a response which might not have followed naturally in and of itself, if no promise had ever been given. Yet promises are often kept just because they have been made, merely to renew the nation's reputation for keeping its word. When Italy failed to keep its promises to Austria and Germany in 1914, it failed at the expense of that nation's reputation in the future for reliability.

Two nations signing an alliance thus reinforced each other's ability to go to the brink in a crisis, to stand up to the risk that an opponent might be willing to fight a war over the political issues at stake. Each party to the alliance lost some of its ability to maneuver, and could no longer attach primary concern to keeping all hegemonic threats whittled down to size. Yet in exchange it won an indispensable reinforcement of its security, which otherwise was threatened by the new rapidity of military movement and strength of the military offensive.

Britain until the very outbreak of World War I did not grasp for the pledge of France or Russia that would have been proffered as part of an alliance, still remaining intent on keeping itself nominally free to stay out of a European war, or to intervene at the strategic moment on the side of whoever might need it. Britain had, of course, enjoyed a unique degree of military security for a long time based on naval power and existence of the English Channel, a security which had allowed Britain to dispense with large standing armies, but which had prevented entanglements on the continent itself.

Yet even with the special moat of the English Channel to reinforce its military position, Britain by the second decade of the 20th century was driven to make advance plans which definitely would limit its freedom of action. As always, it would be crucial that Europe not be united under a single hegemony which could then funnel its forces up to Belgium in preparation for a leap across the channel. Since the channel and naval force were so central to British security, it would, moreover, be particularly crucial that no European naval force be in a position to challenge the British Navy. Both these considerations now saw Britain forced to choose its enemy *before* the war had begun.

In 1910 it indeed seemed that whoever struck first on the continent might be able to win a war simply on the basis of the power of the offensive. After the poor Russian performance in the war against Japan, however, it might still have seemed the better bet that Germany and Austria would defeat France and Russia, if only because of the superior industry and easily mobilized population of the Central Powers. Britain to be sure would not like to have seen French and Russian armies meeting in Berlin. Yet the speed of modern war no longer would allow London to wait to be sure that this would not happen, and the greater risk of German troops racing into Paris thus required that London plan to intervene very early.

London also had to choose Berlin as the enemy because of a very much enhanced German naval construction program. Germany, in coming to national unification late, had been late in seeking out colonies, and had fewer possessions already abroad to use as stepping-stone bases for expansion. A naval presence, and a demanding tone, would thus be all the more required to achieve "a place in the sun." German calculations on the investment in a navy were originally premised simply on being one of a number of naval powers which could challenge Britain, thus in effect transposing the balance of power game to the oceans also. Britain had so long held an absolute dominance at sea that it had become compulsive in demanding it as basic to English security, and arrogant in using it to determine the course of events around the world. If a German navy now took a place alongside the Russian and French and other navies, Britain at the margin would have to be more accommodating from time to time.

What had been merely an entrant in a multinational field of navies after 1900 became a unitary challenge to Britain, however, as the new technology of naval power suddenly seemed to outmode most of the warships of the later 19th century, in the new Dreadnought type. Unless France and Russia and other nations had the industrial resources which Germany and Britain commanded, it would rapidly become a two-nation race for superiority in naval weaponry, with the result that British fixations on naval threats now would focus entirely on Berlin. Naval armament was a substantive issue from which Britain had never been detached, for its very detachment on other issues which troubled the continent was founded on the security of Britain's moat and the vessels that patrolled it.

The naval and colonial component of the German posture was signalled in two crises over the disposition of Morocco, each of which saw Germany demanding either a part of Morocco itself or compensation elsewhere in colonial possessions, each of which involved the dispatch of a German warship to show the flag. The Kaiser's personal style, in such gestures as dispatching a congratulatory telegram to President Kruger of the Transvaal after the Jameson raid, added to what was thus already becoming a basic conflict of interest between Berlin and London.

Britain, in its balance of power reasoning, had always been prepared to confront any potential rival that seemed to have gathered all the relevant units of European power together to attempt a move across the Channel. In the past, this had always allowed a policy of wait-and-see before Britain had to commit herself. The prospect of a possibly rapid German defeat of France, coupled to the inadvertently unique German naval challenge, thus now forced Britain to plan on Germany as its enemy if war were to come. Since Britain did not need reciprocal pledges, it was still reluctant to offer *pledges* of alliance to France or Russia, lest its last flexibility be lost. Yet where verbal pledges were missing, battle plans by 1910 began to serve the same purpose.

British accommodation of French interests was paradoxically furthered in an even more mechanical way by the German investment in a fleet. Fearing the sudden German strength in battleships, the British navy was forced to bring its own ships back from the Mediterranean where they otherwise patrolled the "lifeline" to India and Australia; guarding the coasts of England had to have the highest priority. The French government moved its ships in the opposite direction. Already exposed to invasion by land from Germany, it did not see the prevention of a German amphibious attack in the English Channel as any kind of primary threat to its security; France indeed could never have the security of the British with their moat, and hence could not be so compulsive about trying to maintain it.

It was likely that the British navy guarding against a German amphibious attack on England would also not tolerate any German entry into the English Channel with a force intended to storm ashore in northern France. French vessels were thus moved to the Mediterranean to protect colonial troops being brought to Marseilles from any interference by the Italian or Austrian navies "allied" with Germany. While this redistribution of naval power straightforwardly reflected British and French priorities with regard to possible threats from Germany and Austria, the net effect was to leave British movement through the Mediterranean to the protection and-/or mercy of the French navy. German investment in naval weapons had, as intended, forced Britain to be less self-reliant and imperious in the management of its colonial empire. Yet the new accommodation came first with France, and not with Germany.

Britain's role as a balancer could thus have dispelled only a little of the enthusiasm each of the continental powers showed for the taking of the offensive through rapid mobilizations leading to smashing and decisive victories. Such a role might still have survived if only the substantive issues had remained to maintain tension toward France or Russia as well as Germany. The Fashoda incident in 1898 had indeed seen Britain and France on the brink of war over the control over the upper Nile in the Sudan. British and Russian aspirations had long been in conflict in Persia and the lands north of India, and the British alliance with Japan during the Russo-Japanese war had hardly suggested close relations between London and St. Petersburg. Yet these colonial rivalries were substantially eased in a series of agreements establishing firm demarcation lines and buffer zones; paradoxically, therefore, the British reasonableness which assured peace in long-standing colonial conflicts outside Europe increased the chances of war within Europe, as British conflicts came more and more to focus on Germany.

Before leaping to the conclusion that Europe in 1914 was only primed for warfare, with no compensating factors to leave a hope for peace, one would also have to consider the political and cultural links that still drew the significant nations together. If the national elites were increasingly "riding the tiger" of their nationalistic popular opinions, they nonetheless knew each other quite well, sharing a set of well-understood standards of international conduct and interchange. Prior to 1914, for example, one typically did not need either passport or visas to cross from country to country within Europe, and the personal and intellectual interchange across such boundaries was considerably higher than it was to be in later decades. The monarchs of the principal national states, while far from holding absolute or predominant power, were in fact closely related, since Queen Victoria was the grandmother of the Kaiser, the Czar, and, of course, the King of England. If these first cousins did not love each other any more than most first cousins, they nonetheless had frequent contact with each other. The Kaiser may indeed have been Victoria's favorite grandson, and visited her often; it is rumored that the location of Mt. Kilimanjaro in Tanzania today rather than in Kenya is simply her response to his expressed preference for a Christmas present. Each of the monarchs of this time were commissioned generals, colonels, or admirals in each of the other's armed forces, and took pride in wearing the uniform of such regiments when they visited the capitals in which they were based.

It would be difficult to perceive any important ideological differences between the major European states prior to 1914, perhaps with the important exception of czarist Russia which had lagged so far behind in political and social modernization. Unless one defines each nation's stress on its own ethnic virtue as an ideology, it will be hard to characterize Germany or Austria or Britain or France as more or less radical, more or less liberal or socialist. If Russia lagged behind with its pogroms and systematic suppression of dissent, this also did not explain her alliance with France or her war with Austria and Germany.

What about the possibility of links uniting the various proletariates or poorer classes, similar to those among the aristocracies, as a possible barrier to, or moderation of, war? Here the links were weaker, despite the hopes of Marxists and other socialists that unity could be achieved. The ultimate cause of World War I might be traced to the popular enthusiasms of Europe, which had been channeled into pressing ethnic claims on each other's boundaries. With the single exception of Britain, even the socialist parties across Europe supported their national causes wholeheartedly at the outbreak of war, to the initial disbelief and colossal dismay of Lenin in his exile in Switzerland. Even the British Labour Party split on the war issue, with only part of it reverting to a more traditional advocacy of a wait-and-see, hold-the-balance policy.

The dominant classes, to be sure, also welcomed the war, but in large part because they felt it would be swiftly executed, and moderated along the lines of the gentlemen's agreements of the past. When the war descended into the prolonged barbaric contest of attrition which ensued, one still saw striking anachronisms in the way it was fought from one arena to another, anachronisms illustrating what a different war it was for different classes. Ordinary soldiers suffered through the prolonged agony of the trenches, occasionally punctuated by the most ghastly and deadly attempts to break the stalemate, a war in which prisoners were often murdered and chivalry had totally disappeared. Overhead, the first combats occurred between air forces manned largely by the aristocracies of each side, retaining the most painstaking courtesy and respect for human dignity, including elaborate receptions for distinguished and gallant prisoners after they had been shot down and captured, knightly challenges to combat, and the dropping of funeral wreathes for the fallen heros of the opposite side.

FURTHER READINGS

Albertini, Luigi. *The Origin of the War of 1914.* 3 vols. Oxford: Oxford University Press, 1952–57.
Schmitt, Bernadotte G. *Triple Alliance and Triple Entente.* New York: H. Holt and Co., 1934.
Taylor, A. J. P., *The Struggle for Mastery In Europe, 1848–1918,* Oxford: Oxford University Press, 1954.

World War I

As Europe went to war in 1914, therefore, it was unfair to charge the various regimes and populations with willingly and knowingly submitting to the tremendous carnage and destruction that would follow. Yet it also does not follow that nations never deliberately choose to accept some such death and destruction as the price of concrete gains. One can always claim that to fail to prepare for war is simply to invite wars in which many more of one's citizens will be killed. Yet nations prepare for war not only to avoid the killing of their citizens, but often to improve the material, political, or psychological lot of their citizens, and the ethnic conflicts of 1914 fell into this category for most of the nations involved. Rulers may simply have been offering the presumed gains of war to their peoples as a substitute for fuller economic or political democratization. Yet it presumes too much to say that the average German did not welcome the enhanced industrial,

educational, and psychological esteem he had gained after Bismarck's victories, gains which might be all the greater if he were allowed to possess a
big navy and to color in more of Africa in the German colors.

There are many examples in society of deliberate risking of death, in
pursuit of alternative returns. The construction of any tall building is likely
to cost the lives of two or three construction workers. More than 50,000
persons a year are killed on the highways of the United States, a price that
could be drastically lowered if the public were ready to accept laws forgoing speeds over 50 miles per hour. Human beings do not maximize their
future happiness with reference to any infinite horizon, but rather with an
implicit acceptance of the idea that death will occur sooner or later.

The very outbreak of World War I still is surrounded by questions of
specific fact upon which historians are not able to agree. Was Great Britain
foreordained to enter the war on the side of France and Russia? The
evidence of naval deployments by which the British navy had been concen-
trated in the North Sea, while that of France was moved into the Mediterranean suggested a degree of prearrangement. Yet British spokesmen would
always claim that the German invasion of Belgium as an avenue into France
was crucial, and that a wait-and-see policy might have applied had Belgian
neutrality not been violated. German planners may thus have decided to
throw away the possibility of keeping Britain out of the war in moving
through Belgium; but this only shows again how basically the new issues
of naval power had seemed to pit London and Berlin against each other,
and how the prospect of a quick and decisive war made British Army
intervention a less serious consideration one way or the other.

Another set of factual questions pertains to whether Germany "wanted
war" in 1914, and thus egged Austria-Hungary into making impossible
demands of Serbia. To begin, the dialogue between German and Austrian
statesmen was conducted at enough different channels (as often happens
when allies share a single language) so that it is difficult to prove any
coherent signal from Berlin, either to be moderate or to be demanding. If
a substantial humiliation and weakening of Serbia had been possible without war, this outcome would have been very acceptable to Berlin, for it
would have bolstered the viability of its only ally. What is unclear is
whether Germany preferred war to settling for only a partial humiliation
of the Serbs. Politically, the European situation in the summer of 1914 was
akin to a game of "chicken," where whoever gave up first would run the
risk of supplying important momentum for the opposing side's psychological position. Militarily, the confrontation verged on being a prisoners'
dilemma situation, in which whoever mobilized first and struck first might
win total victory, and such mobilization seemed the only sure way to
preclude a similar victory by the opposing side.

Hence any debate on whether Germany "wanted war" or "didn't want
war" must be phrased in terms of who or what one is talking about. Men

prefer war to a state of peace which they see as unacceptable, or they prefer one version of war over another, if the other would serve the purposes of their enemies much more. There are few cases in history of war being preferred to peace, and far more of one war being preferred to other forms of war. It thus is entirely plausible to contend that France and Russia in 1914 also "wanted war," in that their expectations after a certain point suggested that this would best suit their values. International politics in 1914, as in any other year, was a delicate problem of assessing the probabilities; only in 1914 it led to war. The probabilities as they seemed in the last days of peace suggested easy victory. In Berlin, as in the other capitals, troops marching off to do combat were cheered by crowds lining the sidewalks. In 1939, there were no comparable crowds in Berlin to cheer the departure of Hitler's armies.

Some of the condemnation of Germany as the principal source of World War I reasons cold-bloodedly that time was running against the German power position, and that this had to make Germans more anxious to get on with the battle than their opponents. Yet whatever the next decades might bring, every ground-force commander in 1914 thought victory could be his, if only he were the first to get his troops marching across the frontiers. French and Russian commanders were not any more in the mood to sit and wait, and their civilian political chiefs were not anxious to be so conciliatory as to buy time. Some trends indeed favored Germany for the future even if Austria-Hungary, its only ally, was in danger of falling apart. Farsighted observers could have foretold that czarist Russia also would soon suffer serious internal unrest, some of which had appeared quite markedly during the Russo-Japanese War. The trends of industrial production, research and technology, education, and development of military and naval weapons also favored the Germans, such that their aggregate strength in 1924 might have been much more impressive than in 1914.

The military conduct of World War I for the first weeks seemed to confirm those who had predicted great accomplishments in a rapid offensive. The German armies lunged across Belgium and northern France to come within sight of the Eiffel Tower in France, but then were repulsed in a spasm of confusion on the Marne River; after this the machine gun and the trench established a stalemate on a line from the English Channel to Switzerland, close to the points of furthest German advance. This stalemate on the western front was to persist for some four years, despite repeated efforts on each side to break through the defensive lines and recapture the momentum of the offense.

It is easy to conclude that the failures to break through the trench lines, failures costing horrendously large totals of lives, were due to simple incompetence of the generals and officers commanding the troops. Yet the hope of a breakthrough seemed always so close, if only the artillery barrage was orchestrated a little differently, if only the infantry advance was arranged in a slightly modified pattern. Offensives on either side did several times come close to breaking the lines, after which a rapid forward motion might have become possible again, and with it victory in 1915, or 1916, or 1917. German campaigns in Russia, and Italy and Rumania, indeed suggested that breakthroughs and decisive victories were still possible.

Since the costs of attempts at victory were so high, so much higher than anyone would have predicted, why then did not the powers of Europe negotiate some sort of peace or compromise? In part the unwillingness of the governments on all sides to compromise their demands is traceable to the degree of popular rule which already applied. To retain office in coming elections, each government would have to be able to claim that it had won a victory sufficient to redeem all that it had cost. Yet, as the costs rose from month to month, the victory that would have to be won would necessarily be all the more one-sided, all the more incompatible with any image of victory serving the symetrical purpose for the government on the opposing side.

The popular control over government which had been endorsed in the century from 1815 to 1914 thus paradoxically prolonged a war whose burdens fell most heavily on the masses of the people. Casualties, as noted, were enormously higher than anyone would have predicted, as machine guns and artillery took a heavier toll than in earlier engagements, as the war dragged on from engagement to engagement, from year to year. The introduction of the airplane and airship as weapons of war soon enough led to the bombardment of civilian residences, with damage and casualties which might seem trivial by World War II standards, but which caused enormous shock and indignation. The Allied decision to impose a blockade on shipping to Germany went beyond previous practice in declaring all civilian goods, food included, as contraband, even when carried by neutral shipping. The same blockade was imposed on shipping to neutral states which otherwise might trade with Germany, particularly the Netherlands and Scandinavian countries. While earlier blockades might have been imposed close to the mouths of the harbors affected, the improved accuracy of coastal artillery, and the innovations of mines, torpedo boats, and submarines, now forced the British and French navies to stand farther out to sea, causing numerous irritations by what neutral states such as the United States regarded as practices contrary to international law. The German response to the blockade came with a sudden investment in submarine warfare, not only against enemy warships, but also against merchant ships bringing supplies to Britain and France, at times including neutral ships also. Since submarines could hardly stay surfaced long enough to ensure the safety of the crew and passengers of the ship they were sinking, this produced a much greater loss of life, a violation of international law which more saliently irritated the sensibilities of neutral states than Allied practices.

The German commitment to submarine warfare increased and diminished in response to expectations of American response, but the decision in the end was taken to try to force defeat on Britain by these methods, even if it also brought American entry into the war. If unrestricted submarine warfare was the deciding factor in the American decision to enter the war, however, some other factors must be introduced to explain why American neutrality had become unlikely. "Freedom of the seas," to be sure, had long been a sensitive issue in the trade-minded United States, as it was in the smaller neutral countries. American indignation here would shift from side to side, as both navies interfered with American commerce, but the sudden loss of life which attended submarine attacks made a deeper impression. In the middle 1930's, the charge was made that American manufacturers had become a powerful lobby for intervention on behalf of the Allies, simply because so much war equipment and other produce had been sold on credit to these states, incurring debts which might go unpaid if Britain and France lost the war. The British control over the surface of the oceans inevitably produced very one-sided trade relationships, in which American prosperity depended on sales to one side alone.

The cultural links between Britain and the United States now also facilitated a great deal of American intellectual involvement, especially along the east coast of the country, with the supposed moral rightness of the British and French causes. On a more practical and military-power-oriented basis, any American government had to recognize that British dominance of the high seas was a known condition, to which the United States had been able to adjust quite amicably since 1815. If defeat of the Entente brought German naval dominance instead, it would take far longer to see how the new interaction would work. The United States in any event was to construct its own navy now, to challenge either the German or British Navy in the future. Yet if the Monroe Doctrine had depended on the quiet cooperation of the British Government and fleet, memories of this would tempt the U.S., merely in terms of Realpolitik, to be ready to maintain this situation.

After the defeat of Russia in 1917, in the aftermath of the Bolshevik seizure of power, it was possible for the Germans to move large forces to the western front for the 1918 campaign, perhaps to break the stalemate before large American forces arrived to augment the Allied forces. Using new skirmishing tactics developed by General Ludendorff, the German army indeed made major advances in the late spring and early summer of 1918, only to be stopped again before reaching Paris. Having left the prepared positions of its four-year trench lines, the German forces were no longer able to capitalize on the advantages of defensive positions, and the Allied forces now achieved a momentum which had eluded them throughout the war, pushing the enemy continuously back toward Germany until the November 11 Armistice. Ironically, it could be argued that only the prospect of victory had drawn the Germans out of their trench positions, positions which the Allies would have had difficulty in storming. Yet, sooner or later, some new tactical innovation might have broken the fortifications which had persevered so long, and each side was indeed in a hurry to terminate the war in its own favor.

In the aftermath, of course, it is easy to condemn the two sides for persevering so long in a bloody and fruitless stalemate. Given the costs in young men and material resources, it is often argued that victory was meaningless for Britain and France, as they emerged from the war weaker than before it had begun. At least the Allied leadership had the prospect of retaining power, while the Kaiser had to flee to the Netherlands, and the German establishment now saw its position decidedly challenged. Even Germany gained, however, from prolonging the war, rather than agreeing to Allied terms in 1916 or 1917. The entry of the United States brought the idealistic and somewhat moderating influence of Woodrow Wilson to bear. The rise of Bolshevism in Russia, moreover, frightened even Britain and France into some return to balance of power reasoning; there was also the fear that Germany itself might go Bolshevik if it were excessively humiliated and punished. Surrender by the Germans in 1916 might have had to be a more real surrender, while the outcome in 1918 could have seemed a split decision.

Conversely, if the Allies had not persevered, and the Germans had won a military victory, France, Belgium, and Britain indeed would have suffered far more than they did as victors. There was no threat of a Bolshevik republic in the Atlantic to force the Kaiser's government to moderate its territorial or military demands. Perhaps the emerging power of the United States might have led the Germans to welcome British and French power as a means to playing balance of power politics, but it was all too plausible that Germany would wish enormous colonial concessions in Africa and elsewhere and substantial territorial gains in Europe itself.

One can indeed compose compromise peace terms for 1915 or 1916 which will seem eminently sensible to an outside observer, which if accepted would have spared Europe years of ghastly slaughter. Yet for either side to concede the need for a negotiated peace would have tempted the other to make many of the excessive demands outlined above; for either to slack in its military effort would have tempted the other to have another try at the grand offensive which might bring total victory.

The prolongation of the war was thus more than a simple plot in each leadership to retain its tenure in office; for the peoples involved, it was the kind of contest where conceding a compromise becomes very difficult without conceding too much, where the hope continually appears that the other side will choose to surrender tomorrow, or will lose the grand battle tomorrow. It is not true that it made no difference who won World War

I. It is still also difficult to show that German or Allied offensives in any month of the war were bound to fail.

FURTHER READINGS

Falls, Cyril B. *The Great War*. New York: Putnam, 1959.
Liddell Hart, B. H. *The Real War*. Boston: Little, Brown, 1930.

The Versailles System

Many problems of the Versailles Treaty can be traced directly to the conflicting images of the postwar world held by the major powers which composed the treaty, the United States, Britain, and France. It is probably a fair charge that the American position was burdened by a serious naivete, traceable to a lack of much previous experience in international politics. Americans, including President Wilson, seemed determined to convince themselves that they, as a nation, had always been more moral and less warlike or power-mad, than the Europeans; this was perhaps a useful self-serving image, but one which would make it hard for other states to understand or predict American policy. In concrete terms, American plans for the League of Nations seemed to assume that effective communication and coordination among the nations would be a major preventive of war, and that morality in international dealings tended to be contagious, all the more so if the contagion were accelerated through something like the League. An important ingredient in the Wilsonian world-view was that ethnic self-determination was a legitimate issue to which national boundaries had to be adjusted if peace was to be maintained. Once all the boundaries of Europe had been redrawn on representative ethnic lines, any other legitimate issues could be settled without war in the procedures of an international organization like the League, an organization which would facilitate coordination and which would bring world opinion to bear.

The French view of the Versailles Treaty and the League of Nations was decidedly different, seeing the necessary fruits of World War I to be a major weakening of Germany, in territorial and military terms, accompanied within the League by a firm commitment of United States alliance and assistance in the event of any future German aggression. Peace and war were far less abstract problems for Clemenceau than for Wilson. War came in the past because France had revenge to be claimed for 1871. War might come in the future if Germany now sought revenge, and peace required that France be made strong enough vis-a-vis Germany to deter such revenge. The formal establishment and structure of the League of Nations, in the French view, was thus simply to be an alliance against Germany, as the USSR sometimes today purports to interpret the UN.

The British view of post-1918 Europe differed from both the American and the French. British statesmen did not share Wilson's naive optimism that wars in the future could be avoided simply if the world renounced "power politics." Yet it hardly saw its own interests as duplicating those of France keeping Germany in a position of relative suppression. The costs of World War I had indeed been shocking to the British people and government, so that the avoidance of such conflicts in the future would have a high priority. Excessively punitive treatment of the Germans might only increase the likelihood of such wars in the future as revenge could still stir nationalist emotions. Excessive military strength for France could, moreover, produce the kinds of conflict with the continent which Britain had always seen as threatening.

It would thus be an oversimplification to state that Britain shared all of French skepticism about Wilson's view of the League, or that it now relapsed wholly toward a standoffish balance of power pose. Yet the classic fear of supporting one side too much, so much that it became the dominator rather than the victim of domination, explains much of the rapid shift which now occured in British sentiment. The year 1923 saw British opinion in the end sympathizing with Germany on French occupation of the Rhur, and saw British air planners preparing their country for possible air raids from France, not Germany.

The mix of national viewpoints in the end may have allowed the Versailles settlement to fall between two stools, producing a peace neither punitive enough nor generous enough to guarantee peace. The combination of American and French attitudes supported a series of territorial changes which were quite likely to produce German grievances. While nominally the principle of self-determination was being applied, it was in fact applied unevenly and quite often selectively by ethnic standards. Poland and Rumania grew far too large after 1919, including substantial minorities speaking other languages. The same was true for Czechoslovakia. It was no secret that France welcomed such boundary settlements, since they weakened Germany and Hungary, and would force the new East European states to share France's fears of any German revanchism and thus to be natural allies of France. Hungary was rendered too small by the same standards, while German-speaking Austria was denied the option of merging with Germany. Danzig, a purely German-speaking city, was separated from Germany, while a "Polish corridor" was carved through East Prussia to give Poland an outlet on the sea.

It is easy to exaggerate how horrendous these boundary arrangements were, since Hitler afterward would indeed play on western guilt about the appropriateness of the 1919 boundaries by Wilsonian standards. Fairness would require a comparison of the Versailles boundaries with those of the treaty of Brest-Litovsk, which Germany had forced on the Bolshevik government of Russia, a treaty which had torn enormous territories away from

Russian rule and placed them under only very thinly disguised German control. If the Polish corridor seemed somehow an unnatural disruption of the territorial contiguity of Germany, leaving East Prussia off to dangle by itself, it should be remembered that such noncontiguous territorial arrangements were very common in Germany until the final unifications in 1866 and 1871; customs and other problems which Americans might find strange were an old story in central Europe. (Indeed, isn't Alaska north of the "Canadian corridor" to the Pacific, creating no earnest cravings as yet in the U.S. for the seizure of British Columbia?)

One had to be a little paranoid to become so upset about the Versailles frontiers, but it was nonetheless true that they displayed an Allied hypocrisy which would invite challenge and exploitation by any German statesmen, most effectively by Hitler. The issue of national culture was still real. If Czechs had chafed under the rule of German-speaking administrations from Vienna, the Sudeten Germans would chafe somewhat under Czech-speaking government from Prague.

Apart from the frontiers, other aspects of the Versailles Treaty were also likely to leave Germans in a mood for revenge. It would again have been an oversimplification to have concluded that only the Americans in 1919 were disposed to be self-righteous in comparing their own morality with that of others. Either for self-delusion, or to appease the sentiments of their electorates, the French and British governments were also intent, at least initially, on proclaiming Germans as guilty of having caused the war, and therefore as generally less honorable people than those who had defeated them. The War Guilt clause of the Treaty, Article 231, may have lacked any real practical impact; but the war had itself been fought to some extent as a contest over culture and what territories it would pertain to, and Germans were quite likely to prolong their resentment of the outcome when such a clause was inserted into the peace treaty. The moralistic opportunism of the British government was exemplified in Lloyd George's election campaign of 1919, wherein he had pledged to "hang the Kaiser." French election campaigns saw even more ominous pledges that Germans would be forced to pay enough reparations to cover the entire cost of the war.

The imposition of serious limitations on German rearmament, including a ceiling of 100,000 men on the standing army, would similarly prolong the memory of those Germans who sensed an injustice. While the League of Nations Covenant was to pledge all its member states to pursue a similar disarmament, no progress in this area was to be expected very quickly. The one-sidedness of the arms limitations under the Versailles Treaty thus again seemed related to the proposition that Germans were particularly criminal or untrustworthy members of the international system, a proposition that even the Social Democrats in Germany were unlikely to accept. The result of all such provisions of the 1919 peace was thus that the national and ethnic issue was hardly settled once and for all as a dispute possibly causing war, but rather left all the more unsettled as they were emphasized.

One could still have argued that peace might be assured if the Germans were kept militarily under check, regardless if they felt any need for revenge. The same disarmament provisions which were an irritant might prevent the irritation from leading to war, if it were accompanied by the maintenance of a strong alliance of the powers that had defeated Germany. Yet the United States and Britain did not stick by France militarily and politically after 1919, so that the strong united front required for the tough approach to maintaining peace was also not available. In a longing for the less complicated days of American noninvolvement in European politics, the American electorate explicitly endorsed a return to isolation, preventing ratification of the Versailles Treaty and American membership in the League of Nations, electing Warren Harding as president in 1920 to succeed Woodrow Wilson. As noted above, British interests now similarly reverted to an earlier attitude of balance of power detachment, not indifference or isolationism, but rather avoiding excessive commitment to a French power position that could also become too aggressive.

The logic of the French approach to controlling German military strength required the recruitment of allies, since Germany still greatly outweighed France in manpower and industrial potential. It required vehement opposition to any unification of Germany with the new republic of Austria and it led to encouragement for separatist movements in the Rhineland, or in Bavaria, that wished to fragment Germany even further into small national units. The high point of such a basically harsh approach to the German question came with the French and Belgian occupation of the Ruhr industrial areas in 1923, in an effort to force delivery of overdue German reparations payments. The occupation of the Ruhr led to a German policy of passive resistance, and forced the Weimar Republic to finance measures which produced a most horrendous inflation. Yet the French government did not extract any wealth from the Ruhr to substitute for the missing reparations, and the government in Paris thereafter also shifted toward a policy of detente with the Germans, for lack of anything more reliable or effective.

It would thus have been an exaggeration to claim that the popular attitudes even in France after 1919 were as single-mindedly attached to nationalistic goals as before the outbreak of World War I. The mere avoidance of war, after the casualties of that war, now held a substantial priority, although no one would wish to give up national status gratuitously if it could be preserved without risking war. The threat of Bolshevism in the east, or within Germany itself, had led France as well as Britain to sense some need to accommodate the more moderate elements in Germany. The absence of firm Allied support precluded pushing deep into Germany to win political assurances by simple force of arms.

By intention or default, France as well as Britain thus became parties to what could be called a collective security system, which was not so removed from some of the original assumptions of Woodrow Wilson, and might function well in a Wilsonian manner, at least until one of the powers began to lose its aversion to war. At an earlier time, participants in the balance of power system would have held as their primary goal the prevention of excessive aggregations of power. Wars could be tolerated until they threatened to allow a decisive victory on one side. Wars might even be initiated to cut someone down to size. In the aftermath of World War I, the British and French concensus might now have been that wars would be too costly to be tolerated in even this framework, and that active rather than detached diplomacy would be necessary to head off such wars. The declared intervention policy of a country like Britain (indeed in some sense of all members of the League) was thus now to be to attack the instigator of war, rather than to attack simply whoever seemed to be on the verge of victory. If the initiation of wars could be coupled to a firm prospect of punishment, wars might be prevented.

Much would thus depend on accurately determining the guilty party in cases of aggression, and it was desirable to have for this as large a jury of states in the League of Nations as possible. The ideal number of states in the balance-of-power system might thus perhaps have been five. In the League's mutual security system it might rather have been 100. In the later balance of terror system, the ideal number might have been two.

The most vivid exemplification of this new attitude appeared in the treaty of Locarno (1925), wherein France and Germany guaranteed their mutual boundaries, and Britain and Italy pledged themselves to intervene against whoever violated this guarantee. British military officers were to boggle at the idea of holding staff conversations with both sides to some future war, presumably to draw up contingency plans based on who had been the aggressor; but their political superiors regarded the changed political environment that might result as worth the confusion to which these officers might feel subjected. As part of the same spirit of detente with stress on war-avoidance, Germany was admitted to the League of Nations, and French troops were withdrawn in 1929 from the zone of occupation they had held in the Rhineland. Conversations on possible disarmament arrangements were assiduously pursued, although with little concrete results. From the point of view of the Weimar Republic, it was essential that the unequal arms limitation left over from Versailles now also disappear, if German grievances were not to fester on and on.

Substantial disarmament in Britain and France might have eased the image of inequality here, and might also have reduced some risks of war. Yet, as later, the problem of adequate monitoring of disarmament proved to be a serious obstacle, given a widespread impression that German subterfuge had managed to evade many of the restrictions of the Versailles agreement. Because of the control problem, or because France was not yet ready to move entirely away from reliance on military strength, it was impossible to achieve agreement on general disarmament across Europe prior to 1933. The economic depression which struck Europe at the beginning of the 1930's thus arrived when ethnic and national grievances within Europe had receded in importance, but had not disappeared. A transition from policies of restraining Germany to accommodating Germany had not been completed, and Allied policy may have failed precisely for not concentrating on one or the other.

FURTHER READINGS

Claude, Inis L., Jr. *Power and International Relations.* New York: Random House, 1962.
Luard, Evan. "Conciliation and Deterrence: A Comparison of Political Strategies in the Interwar and Postwar Periods." *World Politics.* January, 1967.
Mayer, Arno. *The Politics and Diplomacy of Peacemaking.* New York: Knopf, 1967.

The Failure of Appeasement

The Versailles/League of Nations formula might have succeeded in keeping the peace, if not for the most unlucky series of events in German domestic politics. It will always be impossible to determine exactly what would have been required to keep Hitler from coming to power, but it is clear that his seizure of control was by no means determined by the aggregate tendencies of the German people, for his electoral appeal was indeed on the wane in 1933, and had crested at less than 50 percent of the electorate. Slightly greater resolution or vision by several of his opponents, and less naivete on whether he could be controlled once in the government, might have left far more moderate nationalists in positions of power in Germany through the 1930's.

Having once seized power, Hitler's attitudes indeed set the stage for World War II, since his own aversion to any resumption of war was far less than that openly expressed by France and Britain. When this willingness to risk war was coupled with a citation of Allied failure to live up to the self-determination principles of 1919, a credible German irredentist feeling emerged which many in the west saw as legitimate, and would wish to try appeasing. On its face, a very satisfactory solution would see the 1919 norm simply brought to bear in the territories where it had been ignored, allowing those who earnestly wished to be Germans to have their territories absorbed into the Reich. Yet the simple making of amends by a standard of international justice may ignore the political momentum which may thereafter be difficult to control. If everyone who wished to be German was allowed to be, would this not aggregate a power unit that France or Britain thereafter would find it difficult to resist? If the German government and its people became used to the idea of making demands and having them granted each time after a suitable period of bombast, would this not encourage the making of more unreasonable demands, wildly out of conformance with the self-determination principles of 1919?

The English-speaking world may never cease debating whether a policy of appeasement was appropriate to dealing with Germany after, or even before, Hitler came to power. By the standards of 1919, a number of Germany's territorial acquisitions now seemed perfectly justified. The Saar actually voted to return to Germany in a plebiscite administered under League of Nations auspices, some 90 percent favoring this course over continued autonomy or merger with France, a far larger endorsement than Hitler had ever received in the free elections of the Weimar Republic. The movement of German troops into the Rhineland in 1936 was certainly a violation of the Versailles and Locarno treaties, but it could easily be viewed as Germany simply "occupying its own backyard." Unless Germany were to be a permanently inferior member of the international system, it could not be expected to leave part of its frontier demilitarized while its neighbor France in no way followed suit. The population of the Rhineland, as of the rest of Germany, was indeed enthusiastic about the return of the Wehrmacht to this part of German soil.

It is plausible on the basis of the documents captured since the end of World War II, that a French mobilization would have forced Hitler to call his troops back from the Rhineland territories. He indeed seems to have promised his military chiefs that this would be done, in face of the weakness and lack of preparation of the German military establishment. Yet the French government in the end was unprepared to act without an accompanying show of force by Britain, and the British government was enough persuaded of the moral inequity of the previous treaty arrangements to be unprepared to defend them by force. Whether an Allied show of force would have produced an ignominious withdrawal by Hitler must, moreover, remain a little debatable, regardless of whatever promises the dictator had given his generals. Contingency orders for withdrawal could always be countermanded at the last moment, with a resulting confrontation that might have produced war in 1936, but might instead have seen an ignominous backing down by the Allies.

If Allied mobilizations had indeed led to war with Germany in 1936, the war might also have produced a quick defeat of the German forces, with tremendous consequences for the future. Yet the world thereafter would always have to debate whether Hitler was as bad as he had pretended to be, whether he would really have killed Jews and invaded countries, whether the West had not overreacted and produced a needless war, aggressing into what was legitimately German territory.

The next territorial acquisition came with the Anschluss of Austria in

1938. Austrians would not have been given a fair plebiscite by the Schuschnigg government, and were not given a fair one by Hitler. Yet they did speak German, and Hitler would probably have won a plebiscite for merger with Germany, even if he had not used terror and intimidation to boost the totals over 90 percent. Hitler's attachment to Austria may indeed be traceable to this being his youthful home, but the Versailles formula could hardly have found that what was left of the Vienna dominions was any less German than other segments of Germany. Austria had been left out of the German unification in 1871 in a tactical decision by Bismarck, who had accommodated nationalist sentiment only so far as was necessary to bolster Hohenzollern power. If the Hohenzollern dominions thereafter needed the strength of the Hapsburg dominions there would be no irredentism expressed toward Austria. The German Liberal Nationalists of 1848 had indeed demanded the inclusion of the Austrian territories. Now Hitler would demand them also, either because he was the sincerely ethnic nationalist he claimed to be, or because Austria was an asset in power terms which could be seized because the Wilsonian morality had suggested it be seized. The incorporation of Austria added some eight million people to the German domain. In terms of strategic position, it gave Hitler a springboard southeastward into the Balkans, and a position of surrounding most of Czechoslovakia. Political and military realists had to be nervous about such an accretion of strength and position, but ethnic purists could hardly deny the enthusiasm of most of Vienna and Austria at being absorbed into a Hitlerian Germany which seemed very much of a going concern.

The next object of Hitler's attention was the Sudetenland, a strip of territory all along the frontier of Czechoslovakia and Germany inhabited by German-speaking people. Whether or not the Czech government in Prague had dealt fairly with the ethnic interests of this minority after 1919 can be endlessly debated. It seems clear that the leadership of this minority after 1933, and even before, hoped for transfer of the territory to Germany, and hoped that the Prague regime would not kill off nationalistic yearnings for secession by any effective compromises. Konrad Henlein, the proto-Nazi leader of the Sudeten movement at the end had described his policy vis-a-vis the government as "always asking for so much that we can not be satisfied," a bargaining approach which has an altogether familiar ring in more contemporary efforts to rule out moderate compromises.

Again, the desire of the inhabitants of these territories would, by 1938, have fairly definitely awarded them to Germany. Again, the practical effect would be to weaken Czechoslovakia as a military and political unit, for the ethnic frontiers were inside the mountain passes, and therefore less defensible. The loss to the Czech economy similarly suggested that Prague would find it very difficult to maintain a foreign policy independent of the dictates of Hitler.

German demands for the Sudetenland brought Europe to the brink of war in 1938, and it is sometimes argued that Hitler actually preferred a war at this point, feeling cheated when the Allies pressured Prague into surrendering all the disputed territories without a military resistance. Whether Hitler's spasms of rage were real or feigned may always be difficult to determine, but at the time they suggested an indifference to war that may have produced Allied concessions far in excess of what was necessary. In the end, it seems plausible that Hitler still must have preferred the surrender he received to any armed victory over his enemy, the Czechs, for virtually all the German-speakers of Europe were now under Berlin's unifying rule for the first time in modern history, in what Hitler assured Chamberlain was his last territorial claim in Europe. The ethnic principle allegedly underlying the Versailles settlement had as yet not really been violated in the German revisionist expansions.

Would British and French resistance to Hitler in 1938 have been more noble than the pressure exerted on Prague to surrender the disputed territories? The answer is most certainly yes. Would it have been wise for the Allies to make a stand here, with the Czech army still intact, still entrenched in its fortifications in the Sudeten mountains patterned after the Maginot Line? Here the answer must be a little less clear.

Since the war, it has been argued that the German Army, at the instigation of General Halder, was prepared to stage a coup and seize power from Hitler if Allied resistance suggested that the dictator's policies would lead to war. As with all events that were planned for a contingency, it is hard to tell whether the crucial generals and officers would have had the personal courage to carry through with the coup, and whether it would have succeeded. In a state with an effective secret police and the threat of instant punishment, such plots are undertaken only at the greatest personal risk. At a time when Hitler still enjoyed a relatively great personal popularity, how many officers could have been sure that their troops would execute orders to displace the Nazi party? Allied and Czech resistance might thus simply have led to war, with the destruction of Prague and perhaps of many other cities in Europe. As before at the time of the Rhineland invasion, the choice of either policy in a tense moment can destroy the data for evaluating the choice afterward. To succumb to Hitler's demands at Munich was to forgo the test of the German army and German people's loyalty to their dictator. However, it would generally seem risky to bet that a coup in the opposing capital will terminate any crisis in one's favor. To have fought a war in 1938, moreover, would have left untested Hitler's promise that he was only gathering in Germans wherever they might be located. Wouldn't Hitler have become more peace-loving and less bellicose once all his rightful demands were granted? Wouldn't a Thermidor have set in within Germany itself, when anti-Jewish, antiforeign, and antiliberal rhetoric became merely that, without serious meaning?

Less than a year later appeasement seemed to be proven a complete failure, as Hitler annexed even the non-German portions of Czechoslovakia, and invaded Poland, plunging Europe into World War II. It has thus been imperative for various factions within Britain and elsewhere to try to pin the blame for the appeasement policy on each other. Conservatives, to be sure, molded and executed the approach of trying to satisfy Hitler's seemingly legitimate claims, so that peace would be reinsured. Laborites, however, were continually opposed to most of the rearmament measures that were necessary to give Britain the means to oppose Hitler's demands. At Munich, for example, the threat of German air attack on London was a most important consideration in persuading Chamberlain and his advisers that war should be averted at almost any cost. A year later the Spitfire and the Hurricane fighters had come off the assembly line to make a defense of British airspace plausible; Hitler indeed interpreted Chamberlain's acceleration of aircraft production immediately after Munich as a double-cross from the British side.

Regardless of who was exactly to blame for British or French failure to resist Hitler, the failure could almost have been predicted on the basis of the momentum imparted by the granting of plausible and legitimate grievances. While all Hitler's claims prior to 1939 were quite valid, they imparted a sense of western weakness and German strength that seemingly made legitimacy much less important for any more territory that might be desired. What in later years would be called a "domino effect" clearly took hold in the aftermath of the concessions at Munich. Allied guarantees were less reassuring, as some states, for example Rumania, made haste to switch their allegiance from France to Germany. In Latin America one saw various national leaders imitating the surface style of Germany and Italy, seeing Fascism somehow as the "wave of the future."

It is also plausible that the publics of the countries making concessions to Hitler's Germany lost some confidence in their own ability ever to reestablish resistance, ever to deny further claims as they emerged. Every world crisis leads to some reassessment by each party of the determinations and weaknesses of all such political parties in the future.

Yet one must be careful not to exaggerate the determinacy of what has been called the failure of appeasement. It was, and is still, possible that concessions properly made can satisfy the power demanding them, so that the irredentist state would become content to live in peace in the future. Concessions can also turn around opinion in the state making the concessions; rather than destroying all remaining resolve, these can produce a sentiment of "this far, but no more." The British reaction to Munich was indeed not to prepare for an endless series of further concessions to the German dictator, but to bolster the Royal Air Force so that a tougher negotiating line would be possible in the future. While Britain bolstered its military strength, however, Czechoslovakia had been shorn of its frontier defenses and had been required at Munich to terminate its formal alliance with France. Prague thus lost all ability or will to resist, making it easy for Hitler to administer the final partition of the country in March of 1939.

Hence it was hard to see any real guarantee against war in the latter 1930's. To satisfy any legitimate aspirations of the irredentist states was to tempt them to make far more excessive demands. It was not likely, however, that the status quo powers would continue to purchase peace at any price. The preservation of peace thus depended on the most delicate judgements of Hitler and his adversaries. When he at last guessed wrongly that one more concession (on Poland) might be extracted, that Chamberlain would again shy away from hostilities, war was the result.

As before 1914, the need for advance preparation for what could be very rapid warfare had frozen the major states into alliances again. In retrospect one always sees such alliances as reflecting basic ideological or social similarities, between Fascist Italy and Nazi Germany on one hand, and democratic Britain and France on the other. Where non-Fascist, nondemocratic USSR fit in was, of course, harder to tell, at least until Germany's attack on the Soviet Union in 1941 finalized the array of alliances. Yet the link between Hitler and Mussolini was not always so determined, as only the somewhat moralistic reaction of London and Paris to Italy's invasion of Ethiopia had finally eliminated the possibility of a British-French-Italian coalition against Germany. Soviet Russia in 1939 was somewhat underrated as an actor in the international military and political environment, in part because of the 1936 purges which had removed so much of the Red Army's leadership. Since Poland did not trust the USSR in any event, the Russians were not the logical source of support to which Britain and France would turn against Hitler.

With 80 million Germans united under his rule after Munich, Hitler on legitimate ethnic lines had assembled an extremely powerful base for aggression. In March of 1939, the occupation of Bohemia-Moravia now proved once and for all that his aspirations included territory beyond that populated by persons speaking German. The return of the Memel territory from Lithuania could have been justified more plausibly on ethnic grounds, but was obviously again the fruits of a threat of military force. The German demands on Poland, for the return of Danzig and a plebiscite within the Polish Corridor, were similarly still intended to apply the ethnic self-determination argument; yet the Czech experience suggested that it would be difficult to obtain a plebiscite free of duress, and that German demands might not stop with this simple initial concession. With more of an air force to support resistance, and a sense of betrayal over Hitler's violation of Czechoslovakia, the British government now issued a guarantee to the Polish government, which made the latter quite ready to resist and reject the German demands.

When war thus broke out, did it in the end prove the futility of appeasement? Or was the British and French support for the oligarchic government of Poland mistaken, since some rectification of the German-Polish boundary was probably still in order by the standards of ethnic self-determination? Despite all the further German military moves into Poland and the Balkans and all the rest of Europe, appeasement might still find some partisans to argue that if this last demand of Hitler's had only been compromised, war and further conquest might still have been avoided.

It is easier to believe, judging from the internal documents of the Nazi regime uncovered after the war, that Hitler would not have been satisfied with minimal concessions such as these, and thus that a pure policy of appeasement could never have insured peace. Yet any earlier contrary policy of preemptive intervention would have left the Germans and others afterwards convinced that the Allies themselves were unreasonable and arbitrary in their application of international principle, prone to intervene in the internal affairs of Germany, prone to begin wars long before they had any reason to. Even a war in 1936 when Germany had not yet completed its rearmament would have had serious costs for Britain and France, costs which a public opinion with memories of World War I might not have tolerated.

Rather than advocating either consistent appeasement or consistent resistance, a case might be made, as outlined much more elaborately and sophisticatedly by A. J. P. Taylor, that the Allied mix of these stances was basically inept, too often signaling resistance and then not following through, in effect baiting Hitler at one time and falsely encouraging him at another. Appeasement at the wrong moments, plus resistance at the wrong moments, can thus lead any opponent to take risks of war when he could no longer fairly be expected to perceive the risk. If it is easy to condemn the Allied mixture of firmness and concession as inept, however, it is more difficult to prescribe the proper mixture, for the latitude of successful policy is very narrow when a basically aggressive state has some initial legitimacy on its side.

FURTHER READINGS

Bullock, Allan. *Hitler: A Study in Tyranny.* New York: Harper and Row, 1953.
Churchill, Winston. *The Gathering Storm.* Boston: Houghton-Mifflin, 1948.
Craig, Gordon, and Gilbert, Felix. *The Diplomats.* Princeton: Princeton University Press, 1953.
Taylor, A. J. P. *The Origins of the Second World War.* New York: Atheneum, 1961.

World War II

The first six months of World War II, the "Phony War," might have seemed to confirm Hitler's suspicions that the Allies would not really pursue active combat for the mere preservation of Poland. Allied inactivity was in part explained by the French investment in the Maginot Line, the enshrinement of the defensive advantage which had been remembered from World War I. Despite the rapid German advance into Poland, the Allied counter-move was not to be any drive into Germany itself, but rather to sit in the frontier fortifications, respecting the alleged strength of the German Siegfried Line fortifications symmetrically opposite. Allied policies on the use of airpower were similarly tailored to the formula of a limited war, with no bombings sanctioned of any targets at all close to residential areas. Searching for roundabout ways to strike at the Germans, the British and French came close to provoking a war with the USSR, as part of using the Finnish defense against Russia as an excuse to set up an anti-German front in Scandinavia.

The spell was broken when German Forces occupied Denmark and Norway, and then rolled through the Netherlands and Belgium into a successful conquest and defeat of France. After the invasion of the Netherlands, Neville Chamberlain was at last replaced by Winston Churchill as Prime Minister of Britain, setting to rest any lingering speculation that a peace between Germany and Britain could be based on some negotiated settlement appeasing most German desires. However ready Hitler would have been to terminate the war in 1940 with his forces controlling most of Europe, Britain under Churchill was quite unready to accept such an arrangement. One could interpret this as traditional balance of power vigilance which would never relax while any power controlled so much of Europe. One also had evidence, of course, that Hitler was a particularly brutal, aggressive, and deceitful leader, who might hardly be trusted to leave Britain alone. With the final military defeat of Hitler, Churchill would be congratulated for his determination and perseverance, but history often tends to reward and validate what was done, in blotting out and forgetting what could have been an alternative course of action.

Just as with the possible invasion of Germany in 1936, a possible negotiated peace with Germany in 1940 is dismissed because history, in moving on to other things, makes the alternative so difficult to assess. The unconditional surrender of Germany allows us to answer more questions, perhaps, than if the documents of the Third Reich had never become available. Yet Hitler's documents and "table talks" still leave many questions unanswered. It seems clear that for the time the German dictator respected the British Empire and regarded it as a stabilizing influence throughout the world which he would want to retain. Whether such thoughts would have proven transitory as his naval capacity for a cross-channel invasion grew is problematical. Yet one also does not know what would have become of Germany and Europe if it had not been freed of Nazi rule by Allied prosecution of the war to a successful invasion of the continent. Would the terror of Nazi rule have gotten worse and worse, or would some sort of Thermidorean reaction again have set it? Was it really in Britain's interest or Belgium's interest, for British forces to fight their way through to liberate Belgium?

The success of British perseverance in the war against Nazi Germany makes one wonder less at the absence of debate on such perseverance in 1940, but still we must remember that a policy of appeasement had attracted so much sympathy and support only a few years earlier. Some of the unanimity of 1940 is the product of Churchill's policies of repressing dissent on the question, of preventing the expression of opinion favoring a negotiated peace. Very few British leaders would have thought it tolerable to suspend hostilities with all the continent under German control. Yet more of them probably thought it tolerable than the record now indicates.

Parallel to the outward momentum of Nazi Germany was the expansion of Japanese power after 1931. The Japanese expansion could almost have been predicted, on a general rule that power vacuums get filled. Japan was unchecked within Asia as a military and industrial nation, so that any weakening of European power in the China area was very likely to induce a Japanese expansion. Russia and Germany had been pushed away from the scene in the aftermath of World War I, as Japanese forces had indeed played a prominent role in the Allied intervention in Siberia after the Bolshevik seizure of power. The economic depression had caused nations such as France and Britain to allocate fewer resources to military and naval equipment, and the new tensions of Europe after 1936 forced these powers to shunt manpower and weapons back toward Europe. Once again a sort of "domino effect" could be seen, as the image of Allied irresolution at Munich must have suggested to Tokyo that less resistance from this quarter also need be feared in China.

Power vacuums, of course, still do not get filled unless some power wishes to fill them, and we would have to ask why the Japanese government or people so much desired to assert themselves militarily. The European assumption that prosperity was linked to territorial expansion must have seemed equally relevant to a Japanese people that felt crowded and hemmed in by the narrow territorial confines of the Japanese Empire. The relatively untapped and underexploited resources of an area such as Manchuria seemed wasted when a modern industrial society such as Japan could put them to good use. If Germans could talk about "lebensraum," so also could Japanese.

The most consistent resistance to Japanese expansion came from a power which had again detached itself from European rivalries, the United States. The prospect of war between the two Pacific Ocean powers had indeed appeared and reappeared almost through the entire time after 1900. Yet a war in the Pacific between Japan and the United States did not necessarily have to be linked to a war in Europe between Germany and France. To produce another "world war," links of alliances would again have to be forged to permanize and predict the sides to a conflict, and to make certain that an outbreak of war in one theater would soon pull all the others in. As late as 1922, Japan still had been formally allied with Great Britain, and the more imaginative literature on wars of the future had speculated about naval engagements pitting the combined Anglo-Japanese fleet against that of the United States. Pressure from the "White Dominions" of Australia, New Zealand, and Canada had caused Britain to be glad to be free of this alliance in the aftermath of the Washington Naval Disarmament Conference. Yet, as late as 1931, Britain was much less in the mood to condemn the Japanese seizure of Manchuria than the United States.

Conversely, German support for China in the 1930's wars had remained quite strong until 1937 and 1938, including the supply of arms, and the services of a military mission commanded by General Von Seekt; German-trained troops handed minor setbacks to Japanese forces in several engagements, and it was only finally in 1938 that Hitler forced all the German officers involved to return home in compliance with pressure from Tokyo, as prerequisite to the formation of an alliance. The issue of Japanese alignment with Nazi Germany was thus not as inevitable or determined by the character of domestic regimes as intrawar propaganda often painted it. The formalization of the Italo-German-Japanese alliance in the Anti-Comintern Pact thus again removed the possibility of any of the major powers of the world serving as middlemen in conflicts which might arise halfway around the globe.

The domestic incentives for Japanese penetration into China have sometimes been compared with the United States involvement in Vietnam since 1960. Having made the commitment to establishing political and military control over an area, neither power could easily quit with the job only half done, for the precedent of conceding defeat might be exploited by rivals intent on pushing one even further back. Admitting defeat can mean the loss of power back home, as one is held accountable for an expensive project which produced no return. In the U.S., this was objectified by the prospect of electoral defeat for Lyndon Johnson. In Japan, it would have come with a reshuffling of the cabinet, reducing the influence of the army. Externally, a Japanese withdrawal might have seen the United States and the Soviet Union showing a greater presence in China, egging the Nationalist regime on to demand the return even of Manchuria. The underlying rationale for maintaining the military drive in the Japanese case was presumably economic, while the American commitment to Vietnam is more complicated. Tokyo's fears of China, the USSR, or the U.S. may have been distorted, but this sense of momentum or "dominos" might indeed still have had some reality in predicting that a Japanese failure would be seen thereafter as a sign of Japanese weakness.

As noted, some Europeans at earlier stages of the Japanese aggression had welcomed the intervention on the grounds that "China needed a policeman," the Japanese being seen as the functional equivalent of Europeans for this purpose. When Japanese political authorities tried to monopolize trade opportunities in the territories they had occupied, Americans and others reverted, however, to an almost doctrinaire espousal of free trade, reminiscent of the "open door" which the U.S. had purportedly been defending even in 1898. Whether the American commitment to economic openness is the real or the feigned explanation of interest in China can still be debated. American identification with China was bolstered by the presence of numerous missionaries in the area, and by their reports of the extreme brutality with which the Japanese army behaved in the areas it conquered.

As the Japanese campaign against China seemed to be entering a crucial stage in 1941, Japan encountered increasing pressure from the United States. This included the denial of strategic materials used in war industry, the ABCD (American-British-Dutch-Chinese) conversations presumably planning for war against Japan, the deployment of American bombers to the Philippines, and a stepped up construction program in naval vessels which might be dispatched to the Pacific. The American price for a normalization of relations now came to require Japanese withdrawal from the parts of French Indochina which had been occupied in the aftermath of the German defeat of France, and very probably a substantial withdrawal from China as well. In short, in Tokyo, it must have seemed that American resistance proposed not only to contain Japanese expansion but also to shrink the Japanese sphere in size once Tokyo had begun making concessions. As in some other crisis situations, politics led the leaderships to feel that they had only two choices now—to continue going forward or to go backward a great deal, once a lack of resolve had been demonstrated.

Yet the Japanese decision to attack Pearl Harbor and begin the Pacific phase of World War II shows more than a simple willingness to launch a war; the decision was in the nature of a daring gamble that the sneak attack on Hawaii would not be detected before it had succeeded, a gamble that Americans thereafter would not wish to persevere in the war to see it through to victory. No serious military analyst in the Japanese hierarchy really expected to be able to defeat the United States decisively by military means, that is, by invading California and dictating peace terms in St. Louis. Rather the hope was that enough short-run victories could be won in the first 18 months to push American forces out of sea and air range of the home islands, and then that the costs of returning to the western Pacific would prove more than Americans wished to pay. The Japanese decision-makers thus expected to win a permanent hegemony over the western Pacific or to lose everything, militarily and diplomatically.

Attacking Pearl Harbor may thus indeed have been a great political mistake from the Japanese viewpoint. To be sure, a number of American battleships were sunk, but the battleship would soon prove to be less than the decisive weapon in any event, as the dominant role passed to the aircraft carrier. No American carriers were at Pearl Harbor at the time of the

attack. By attacking with treachery, on what was clearly American territory, the Japanese most importantly mobilized the American people behind
a war which otherwise they might have supported only most lukewarmly.
The alternative operation for Japan might well have been to attack only
British and Dutch possessions in the Far East, allowing American forces to
become involved more gradually, in a manner for which many Americans
would condemn their own government rather than the Japanese.

It similarly would seem to have been a mistake for the German government, after Pearl Harbor, to declare war on the United States. To most
Americans this served only to prove that Germany had been privy to
Japanese treachery, although Hitler in truth had not been informed of the
Japanese intentions (in retaliation for his failure to advise Tokyo in advance
of his attack on the Soviet Union). In search of some clarity for the
international scene, Hitler may have felt forced to clear the decks by
declaring war to match Japan's action. Had he not done so, the U.S. might
only most gradually have been drawn into full hostilities with Germany,
again disunited on whether this was not a misguided diversion from the
main task of defeating the Japanese. Japan's failure to declare war on the
USSR is clearly the best example of how either the Allies or the Axis could
have left the polarization of all the world's power around a "World War
II" much less pronounced, perhaps in ways very helpful to the Axis side
because of the uncertain resolve of Americans in such a confused case.

One is thus tempted to pick and choose in extracting analogies from the
outbreak of World War II. Defenders of the American intervention in
Vietnam will see parallels with the British and French problem at Munich.
Failure to resist an expansionist political force, even a force with an initial
legitimacy based on the achievement of independence, presumably led to
further aggressions as the defending side's resolve has been disproven, with
consequent attacks to be anticipated perhaps on Cambodia, Laos, Thailand,
and beyond.

Critics such as Noam Chomsky would rather draw an American parallel
with the position of Japan in China in 1938, a badly conceived initial
investment of forces and resources, drawing behind it good money being
thrown after bad, as regimes become incapable of admitting defeat. It is,
of course, possible that both analogies would apply simultaneously. Vietnam is perhaps indeed being contested because the U.S. is unwilling to
admit defeat, but any admission of defeat might now indeed have "domino
effect" consequences in many parts of the world.

In 1940, Japan was thus being carried forward by dreams of economic
expansion and prosperity, unable to retreat for fear that any withdrawal
would lead Americans to demand even further withdrawals. The U.S. may
have been induced to intervene by competing economic interests, or by
naive notions that it was the patron and protector of China. A tug-of-war
situation nonetheless had been established, where either side risked giving

up far too much if it showed any willingness to compromise. The Japanese decision to launch a war with the U.S. was thus not a lighthearted incident of militarist adventure, but rather the outcome of a desperate survey of options seemingly left for the Japanese regime. The mere slimness of the expectation of victory shows how constrained the Tokyo regime felt. It also unfortunately shows that regimes are capable of undertaking the most desperate of gambles, a desperation that for the future may reduce our confidence that no one will ever venture a try to win a World War III.

What can one say about World War II in terms of the aims pursued by the winning side? It is normal to remember the Allies as being enormously more humane than their German and Japanese opponents, in their treatment of conquered populations and prisoners of war. Yet the Allied attitudes on the bombardment of civilian residential areas from the air was considerably more severe than that proposed by either the Japanese or Germans. If the Axis powers had more to fear in their vulnerability to Allied air attack, this example still does not by itself demonstrate that the Allies were trying to make war less horrible than the Axis.

Nazi Germany killed millions of Jews, and the Allied victory had the consequence of terminating such murders. Yet any suggestions were rejected while the war was in progress that something be offered to the Nazis in exchange for sparing these lives. One must achieve political power first in a general sense, if one wishes to affect the political future of the globe. Yet the Allies had some political power over Germany as early as 1944. A trade could have been suggested that German cities no longer be bombed if the inmates of German concentration camps were released. No such offer was made, on the assumption that total power and total defeat of Germany should be pursued ahead of such substantive considerations.

One could similarly ask again whether fewer Belgians might have died if the liberation of Belgium from German rule had not been carried out by military force, for it indeed seems true that fewer died during the entire Nazi occupation than during the campaign of liberation. Yet again liberation established definitively that Belgians would now govern rather than Nazi Germans, settling the power question in a way which was an assurance against later Belgian suffering. The desire to be humane in dealing with the world was surely an important element in the resistance to Hitler, and the implementation of a more humane approach was an important consequence of victory. It was not, however, the entire substance of why the Allies were determined to defeat Nazi Germany, and humane considerations in several important ways were thus postponed and put aside.

The Allies in 1943 defined their goal for World War II as the "unconditional surrender" of the Axis powers. It is possible that this phrase was chosen simply on the spur of the moment for the boost it might give to Allied morale. Yet the phrase, by close analysis, may indeed have been meaningless, since one never gets the other side to surrender without there being some "condition," some promise of exchange which persuades the enemy that he is better off laying down his arms. Italians got a number of conditions in exchange for their surrender, Japan retained its emperor and a great deal more, and Germans, in effect, won the right to choose to whom they would surrender. If the phrase had to be void of logical meaning, however, the propaganda agencies under the direction of Joseph Goebbels were quite adept in harnessing the phrase to steel Germans to more prolonged resistance.

Rather than debating whether the surrender of Germany and Japan was conditional or not, the significant aspect of the war's termination was that Allied armies were not content to drive the Axis back within their frontiers, but rather insisted on entering and occupying the entire home area of the Axis powers. One alternative would have been to offer a German regime the option of withdrawing back to the 1935 borders, an option which would have produced less German resistance and thus have shortened the war and cost fewer Allied soldiers' lives. A second option would have been to negotiate with and support German military officers who were trying to oust Hitler, including those who, on July 20, 1944, came close to assassinating the dictator.

It may be that Roosevelt and Churchill and Stalin had come to believe some of their own propaganda about the nature of German society, assuming that all Germans, Nazi or otherwise, were evil and bellicose, never to be trusted again with the military prerogatives of national statehood. The German army, dominated by the Junkers of the General Staff, might thus have been seen as the real launcher of aggression, only using Hitler as a means to mobilize popular support behind their wars. Whatever the picture the Allied leaders had of German society, the decision to occupy Germany completely, and similarly Japan, was clearly a luxury, for it gave up opportunities of shortening the war, and of restoring a "balance of power." Rather than maintaining two additional states as balancing elements of the world power scene, the two were in effect to be eliminated. Was the Allied leadership now oblivious to balance of power reasoning, or had the world changed enough to make such reasoning no longer relevant?

To begin, the American government seemingly had overestimated the ability of various European states to recover and play a role again. Germany might have to be eliminated as a power politics player, but France and Britain were expected to assert themselves again as great powers. It was not really until 1948 that the depth of the damage to Western Europe had been perceived, and with it the implication that Britain and France would be very weak and dependent on the United States.

If the defeat of the Axis had thus reduced the list of great powers to two, the U.S. and the Soviet Union, the U.S. might also have been quite confident now that its own enormous defense industry could allow it to prevent aggression even without the intervention of any floating powers. The U.S.

for a time even paid lip service to ideas of dismantling German industry, and of dividing Germany into a great number of separate states. The USSR, perhaps more acutely aware of the need for future allies, if it were to hold the U.S. colossus in check, paradoxically said little about the fractionation of Germany, giving early endorsement to German "national committees" recruited from its prisoners of war.

Some part of the American desire to inflict total defeat on Germany also had to stem from a short-term assumption that Moscow and Washington would get along, or at least that they would have less difficulty in dealing with each other than with any independent German government. "Unconditional surrender" thereby was intended to head off suspicions of doubledealing between the Allies, since each might otherwise suspect the other of negotiating an overly appeasing separate peace. At the least, peace might be possible if the cooperation of the powers which had defeated the Axis was not upset.

There was also an important development in technology to account for the decision to press on into Germany, in pursuit of total control of the geography. The American atomic bomb project had been launched in 1940 and 1941 on the expectation that Germany was racing to produce the bomb also. Any compromise peace with Hitler or with his generals would thus have run the risk that the Germans would become aggressive and demanding once again, just as soon as their atomic bombs were ready. Since the first American bomb was not tested until after the German surrender, the possibility had remained, until almost the last months of the war in Europe, that Germany might suddenly win the race for the A-bomb. This would have had dire consequences for London, Moscow, or New York, with the implication that many German demands might now again have to be satisfied.

Knowing that the German bomb was possible, the U.S. had raced to produce its own atomic bomb. Knowing that this was coming similarly might have reduced worry for the future about the "balance of power." Perhaps the bomb in 1945 was already seen as the absolute weapon or the absolute deterrent, a means of warding off attacks by any enemy. Just as German possession of the bomb might make the Allies reluctant to pay the price of reaching Berlin, American bombs might deter German invasions in the future, or Russian invasions, or the outbreak of war in general. If war was not to be enormously more horrible, this might make balance of power maneuvers morally unacceptable in the future, as well as unnecessary.

FURTHER READINGS

Feis, Herbert. *Churchill, Roosevelt and Stalin.* Princeton: Princeton University Press, 1957.
Snell, John L. *Illusion and Necessity.* Boston: Houghton-Mifflin, 1963.

The Emergence of the Cold War

It was one thing to assume that a total defeat of the Nazi leadership was worth pursuing, if peace was to be preserved in the future. It would have been naive to go beyond this to conclude that peace among the remaining powers would be assured once Germany and Japan had been defeated. Any traditional observer of the balance of power system would have noted that the elimination of a common enemy very typically raises the importance of issues which previously were deferred, issues which now can cause new conflicts between recent allies.

As the American and Russian armies advanced toward each other across Germany, such issues inevitably had to arise. Germany forces could surrender to either army, but might typically prefer to surrender to the British and American forces in the west, while maintaining a tough resistance to the Russians in the east. In some places entire German commands were prepared to negotiate local cease-fires, as in the Netherlands and northern Italy. Yet the net impact of tolerating such German behavior was that Russians suffered more casualties and the western Allies suffered fewer.

Of long-term significance would be who got to liberate various countries, for the immediate process of eliminating collaborators and reinitiating the political process could settle a country's future political system. Countries like Denmark or Czechoslovakia might remain in doubt as to their liberators until the very end; the suspicion could arise, on either side, that troops were being deployed more to settle such postwar political questions than to speed the final defeat of the Germans. Once the political reconstruction process was under way, either Russian or Western influence would predominate from country to country. Each side would be alert to whether it was being sufficiently included in this reconstruction process. Were non-Communists being systematically intimidated in Poland, and were Communists unfairly excluded from positions of authority in Belgium or France?

As part of the exercise of attributing blame for the outbreak of the Cold War between the U.S. and USSR, some retrospective analyses have focused on the American decision to employ the atomic bomb against two cities in Japan, Hiroshima and Nagasaki, at the very close of World War II. Portions of the American deliberations on the bombings suggest that they were at least in part intended as "demonstrations" for the USSR. Critics of American policy interpret this to mean a hostile demonstration, intended to intimidate Moscow for the postwar period, by an actual use of what would be a most horrendous and impressive weapon. The American destruction of two Japanese cities, in this view, showed how big and destructive the bomb could be, and also removed any doubts on whether the United States would be willing to use it against enemy cities.

Yet the American deliberations on "demonstration effect" vis-a-vis the

Russians are hardly as uniformly hostile and combative as this analysis presumes. While some attention was inevitably paid to whether the United States had enough military strength for the postwar world, any rush to use the A-bomb in World War II equally much reflected a desire to show Moscow that America had done its part in defeating the Axis. Criticism had often been forthcoming from Moscow and other Communist sources during the war that the western Allies were taking it too easy and letting the USSR do all the serious fighting. Showing the enormous effort and resources that had gone into the Oak Ridge project, with enormous results, might thus serve to reassure Stalin and his government that his allies had kept good faith during the war; the project after all had principally been carried forward for fear that Nazi Germany was working on a similar weapon.

It is also sometimes charged that the bomb was rushed into use in a last-ditch effort to keep Russia out of the war with Japan. Since Russia and Japan had not been at war with each other for the bulk of World War II, the American leaders presumably wished to keep Moscow from claiming any fruits of victory by declaring war at the last minute.

It is hardly disputable that the U.S. had lobbied long and hard to get Stalin to agree to enter the war against Japan, making substantial territorial concessions at the expense of China as well as Japan. Yet the knowledge that the atomic bomb was perfected and ready for use, in the revisionist view, now probably led President Truman's government to wish to terminate the war without going through with the bargains negotiated with Moscow.

Again this interpretation is open to some serious challenge. In retrospect it may seem certain now that Japan would have surrendered soon, even if the atomic bombs had never been brought into use, perhaps even if the Russians had not declared war on Japan. Yet what is far less demonstrable is that any American decision-makers in 1945 could have seen Japanese surrender as certain, without first launching an American invasion of the home islands which would have cost a great number of American (and Japanese) lives. If it was thought probable that the war would carry on into 1946 and 1947, the United States all the more would have wished for Russian entry into the war, since this would tie up Japanese army resources and make the American invasion easier, and would have tied up Russian resources as well, if Cold War considerations were really already so salient. Even with the use of the atomic bombs, it was not by any means certain that the Japanese government was on the verge of surrendering. American plans for the use of the next few atomic bombs to be produced called for their employment as tactical support for amphibious landings in Japan itself. If Hiroshima and Nagasaki did not succeed in bringing about a surrender, Russian intervention in the war would still have been welcome.

The moral argument against the bombings of Hiroshima and Nagasaki in any event begs the question somewhat. If it is argued that Japan would soon have surrendered in any event, one might still ask what was driving Tokyo to such a course. Two factors existed to make surrender a plausible option, the naval blockade which was severely crimping the Japanese war economy, and the regular bombings of Japanese cities by conventional means. Yet the latter raids themselves were inflicting a frightful toll of damage, killing more people in single fire-raid on Tokyo than were to perish in either Nagasaki or Hiroshima. If the case against the use of a nuclear explosive is simply that the same political effect would have emerged in a matter of months through the terrible use of conventional explosives, any gains in morality are hardly so evident.

The use of nuclear weapons in Japan, of course, set a precedent. If these weapons, which at 20 kilotons were only the precursor of far more menacing weapons going into the megaton range, had not been used, their existence and potential use might seem far less real and plausible today. It is significant that no nuclear weapon has been detonated in anger since the second bomb fell on Japan. Much would be different in international politics today if this tradition of nonuse had not been developed and maintained. But it is also terribly significant that the two bombs were used as they were. Would international politics really seem as menacing and as clearly dominated by the "nuclear threat," if we had not all seen photographs of the destruction and human suffering which occurred in 1945? Would it be plausible that the United States or anyone else would meaningfully threaten to initiate such nuclear war, if it had not been initiated once before?

We may come to believe that the existence of nuclear weapons, and the threat of their use, establishes a real deterrent which makes war very much less likely. If so, we might be grateful for the precedent of 1945. If we concluded instead that the decreased likelihood of war is outweighed by the enormous increase in its cost and horror if it comes, we would have to regret the precedent.

All such debate on the specifics of the Cold War's origins thus simply masks the reality that conflicts usually emerge between two powers as a third declines. The same dramatic and violent gesture can serve as a proof of alliance effort and as a proof of hostile strength. The U.S. desire to have Russia attack Japan may have depended crucially on fears and expectations of Japanese resistance. The atomic bomb that was developed to preempt a German bomb took on a very different meaning when Germany had been conquered and proven to be far from developing its own bomb. The German troops which were a threat to the world suddenly may have become an asset when they became refugees seeking to escape Communist rule for life in the "free world."

Before leaping to the conclusion that the Cold War was inevitable simply because conflict is inevitable, however, it is still necessary to touch on some remaining issues of fact, on specific Russian intentions and American intentions in the post-1945 world, on the extent to which either was limited in its geographic power goals, without having to be restrained by the other side.

Given a relatively cautious approach to the outside world prior to 1939, with "socialism in one country" coming ahead of revolution abroad, Stalin is sometimes seen as having held very limited expansionist goals in Europe. A buffer zone for protection against Germany, in the aftermath of the World War II experience, and perhaps some restoration of territories torn from Russia in 1917, these presumably would be the limits of Soviet expansionism, if only because Stalin had real doubts about his ability to control much more of the world. Russians sent west to govern Germany or France might be subverted by what they saw. Local Communists might become nationalists, as indeed Tito would soon demonstrate, and thus fractionate the unity of the Communist movement.

We may never know whether this picture of Stalin was correct, or whether his government alternatively would have wished to take over all of Western Europe if only the costs were low enough. To make the costs assuredly high enough to deter such a takeover, the United States after 1945 entered into a series of political, economic, and military commitments which in the end defined a defense line for the "free world" running through Western Germany and around West Berlin. As in earlier decisions on resistance or appeasement, the decision taken here blotted out some of the possibility of evaluating the alternative option. It is entirely possible that such defensive measures will alter the political outlook of the country being defended against. The mirror-image theory of the Cold War conflict can thus argue that premature fears of Soviet aggression led the United States to preparations which antagonized the USSR, thus seeming to confirm the initially pessimistic evaluation.

Realists may still argue that the evidence objectively showed Stalin's Russia willing to take all of Europe under its influence. It may indeed be plausible that every political regime will be willing to export itself where there are no political or military costs to doing so. It takes an extraordinarily particularist view to assume that the lessons of one's own political, economic, and social experience have no relevance for other peoples, peoples who may have to be artificially induced to see the wisdom of the advice being offered. On the governments to be restored in Poland and Czechoslovakia, and in Hungary, Bulgaria, and Rumania, and indeed in Lithuania or even Russia itself, would the United States not have been willing to exercise some leverage in favor of political democracy or economic free enterprise?

It may thus have been just as imperative for the USSR to take care to deter and "contain" the United States. Or Moscow's premature fears of

American intentions may have caused the USSR to stake out forward positions in Poland and the Balkans, thus stirring American fears. The Cold War might thus indeed have been somewhat of a prisoner's dilemma, in which neither side could perfectly trust the other, and each in being cautious alarmed the other. The common enemy in Nazi Germany had allowed such fears and suspicions to be put aside, but when the common enemy was defeated, the fears became dominant. As in earlier times, the presence of unaligned powers capable of intervening against either of the parties to a conflict could postpone that conflict; the military defeat of the potential balancer in Germany thus unbalanced the situation.

Much of this might have been predicted (and was predicted) as World War II ran its course. It is thus paradoxical that so much of the Cold War rhetoric has been couched in terms of betrayal and deceit, implicitly thereby leading into the debate on "who started the Cold War." The American stress on Russian deceit is intended to imply that no disagreement was expected after World War II, since Moscow had promised to support the same political arrangements favored by the West. To the extent that this feeling is exaggerated, it might be traced to the "Pearl Harbor Mentality" which emerged from the way Japan had so treacherously begun World War II. It also reflected the distrust of the domestic Communist parties in the United States and in Western Europe, which could reasonably be expected to serve the Soviet Union in the event of war, and thus to play the role of the fifth column. In later years, much of the Soviet-American rhetoric would hinge on proposals and counterproposals for disarmament. Since the Soviet Union typically could not accept inspection arrangements which would have brought outside control agencies on to its territory, the United States could fairly claim that its own adherence to any particular disarmament agreement would be more assured by the glare of normal publicity than any promised Soviet disarmament. Portraying itself as the victim of Russian duplicity and deceit after 1945 was thus a very practical reinforcement for American propaganda about the impracticality of disarmament without verification.

Interpreting the origins of the Cold War on the basis of the atomic bomb may, moreover, exaggerate the significance of the bomb as perceived by either the U.S. or the Russians in 1945. It must again be remembered that a number of conventional bombing raids of World War II on Germany and Japan inflicted more damage than in either Hiroshima or Nagasaki, and that Germany had not surrendered even in face of this continuous bomber onslaught. While the H-bomb assuredly supplied a deterrent that can not be ignored, military and political planners on either side in 1945 may have felt that the A-bomb might still be stood up to, if the gains of some sort of war were sufficiently large.

If asked to predict the nature of a World War III, American military planners of 1946 might thus have seen it as a long, slow war, very much on the pattern of the World War II which had just been terminated. Most battles would still be fought with conventional weapons, if only because nuclear weapons were expected to remain expensive and scarce. The Russian army would probably roll westward to conquer all of Europe, while the U.S. Air Force tried to erode its strength by bombing the industry that supported it. After extensive preparation, an amphibious assault similar to the landings in Normandy would be launched to liberate Europe once more.

Hopefully, the thoughts of such a war would prevent it, not because the mere use of the atomic bomb would make war unthinkable, but because the Russians would not expect to win the war once American resources were again mobilized to field the amphibious ground force that could defeat it. Since the mere threat of the atomic bomb could not deter such a war by itself, it also could not be used to intimidate Stalin's Russia into surrendering or into making wholesale political concessions. A World War III launched by the United States on the basis of hopes of a cheap nuclear victory would also be unlikely.

At least some part of American expectations on the post-1945 military balance assumed also that Western Europe would quickly be able to muster the economic and political power to take care of itself. France and Britain seemingly would play a role again in international politics, sparing the United States any substantial effort in defending them against Soviet aggressiveness.

Part of Cold War mobilization on the American side thus came with the sudden realization that Europe had suffered far more economic damage in the last war than had previously been supposed. The unfortunate circumstance of several severe winters amplified the delayed-action impact of the damage of the war itself, and the continued dismantling of German industry had done nothing to speed economic recovery. The prospect of European economic collapse did not merely postpone any hopes of French and British military recovery to stabilize the balance in Europe; it also threatened the kinds of domestic disorder and unhappiness which might support more direct Communist takeovers of power in France and Italy, and perhaps in Germany. The American economic assistance of the Marshall Plan, while carefully avoiding some of the anti-Communist phraseology of the earlier aid to Greece and Turkey, thus reflected an American realization that Europe could not yet be counted upon to stabilize itself against various prospects of Russian expansion.

Apart from being weak, Europe after 1945 was widely thought to have shed the nationalistic motives which had accounted for World Wars I and II. Germans, to begin, had to feel guilty about the mass murders and atrocities perpetrated by the Nazi regime. Yet other publics, in France and Italy and Belgium, also felt a tiredness with the national identifications which seemed to lead to wars. Some of this was a reaction to war and assertion in international politics in general. Some rather reflected a prescient sense that only a united Europe could have any impact by the rules of the traditional arena against super-powers such as the U.S. and Soviet Union. Yet between 1946 and 1948, it was questionable whether even a united Europe would have impact, rather than becoming a power vacuum.

In retrospect we must now express some doubts on whether nationalisms of less than continental scope were really terminated in the aftermath of World War II. The possible retention of various colonial possessions offered a symbolic object for nationalist sentiment in France, Belgium, and the Netherlands; Britain, with its Commonwealth, never showed much enthusiasm for the European spirit. While the European Coal and Steel Community, followed by the Common Market and Euratom in 1956, showed impressively how many economic advantages there were to European integration, the movements for a European political or national unification never reached the fulfillment expected in 1947. Young European students no longer feel intensely German or French or Belgian, but they also have not come to feel European in any sense that comes close to replacing the sense of nationalism that the smaller terms connote.

Anyone attending college today may take the Cold War alignment almost for granted, since it will seem that the NATO allies have always been arrayed on one side and the Warsaw Pact powers on the other, with a churning and growing mass of nonaligned states in between. Yet some of this alignment would have been in doubt for the first years after 1945, as were the relative strengths and intentions of the two great powers.

Since it was unclear whether Western Europe would recover economically, Communist victories at the polls were possible which could have drastically altered the political map. It was similarly unclear whether the economic recovery of the USSR would take a longer or shorter time. At least some observers feared that the Russian military drive westward was only being delayed by the process of such recovery. Perhaps by 1949, when the damage of the German invasion had been repaired, the Red Army would move toward Paris, undeterred by the atomic bomb. The economic capabilities of the Untied States itself were also the subject of some debate. Democrats as well as Republicans feared that any prolonged effort at military defense might cause great difficulties for the United States economy, ranging from inflation to unemployment, or at least a crimping of domestic consumption and investment.

The local political strengths of Communist and anti-Communist parties, to some extent dependent on these economic developments, were also in some doubt. Stalin would have to move cautiously in some instances, where local political opposition was strongly based. Yugoslavia thus slipped out of Moscow's orbit by June of 1948, because Tito would not submit to the standardization and control Stalin required. Prague had not been subjected to the outright Communist control until February of the same year, because the electoral strength of the non-Communist parties could not so easily be bypassed or ignored.

It is often remarked that American postwar foreign policy first received definition with the 1947 "Sources of Soviet Conduct" article by George Kennan, known more familiarly for its "containment" thesis. Yet while the definition provided here was valuable to both observers and participants, the substance of containment was not entirely new to American policy in 1947. The doctrine essentially noted that American interests would pertain more intensely to territory not yet under the control of a foreign power than to territory already under its control. While one might in the abstract identify equally with the freedom and well-being of all peoples, one in fact identified more strongly where there was an ongoing attachment, and where liberty could more easily be defended, not having first to be restored. The territorial status quo could also serve as a psychological bench mark or guarantee that progress was indeed possible as defined by American values, for only a loss of territory would offset the gains otherwise expected from economic recovery and expansion, and from political modernization and reform.

On the spectrum of American interests, the current division of territory thus defined a substantial discontinuity; defending the last piece of one's territory might seem rational even if no liberation of Communist-held territory could be under consideration. As part of this satisficing point, there might additionally have to be an absence of military operations, for the suffering of human casualties touched on another discontinuity in the American value scheme. A stable status quo without physical hostilities thus represented the most natural plateau. Kennan's argument suggested that containment would be a natural cutoff, moreover, in that it would induce a softening of Russian attitudes toward the world as visions of world conquest progressively became more clearly unrealistic, as fears of external attack faded.

A question remains on whether containment therefore represented anything new for American policy in 1947. For much of its history the United States had been a status quo power, in that it preferred to develop the territory it controlled rather than to expand it. If one focused on one's own territory, this was labeled self-defense; if one focused on likely threats to one's territory, it could be labeled containment. If there were but a single threat, then the containment side of the coin was most likely to be in view; when there were several threatening powers, these might conflict with and cancel each other out, in a "balance of power" obviating the need for great American defensive vigilance. Clearly the postwar situation thus was peculiar for the United States, in that the threat to the American-influenced land area was single and identifiable, in that American effort had to be expended to defend the perimeters, in default of any power rivalries on the other side to sap the aggressor's strength.

Yet the United States might have preferred to expand its influence rather than settling for the status quo, as when in 1945 it had gone on into Germany in quest of unconditional surrender, rather than contenting itself with pushing the Nazi regime back within its own boundaries. The end of World War II may or may not have illustrated a transcendent American desire to "liberate" Germany from the Nazi regime, but it at least demonstrated a preemptive fear that the future military attacks by such a regime could not be deterred or easily warded off. The 1947 American containment statement thus expressed and formalized the most significant conclusion of 1945: that Russia was not yet so obnoxious or so aggressive that preemptive operations would again be required.

The exact commitment of the United States to the defense of various parts of the world might have remained in question even as late as 1950. Commitments indeed sometimes get made only in the process of initially being fulfilled, establishing a precedent from which neither side wishes to back down. The American commitment to West Berlin therefore emerged from the successful but costly operation of the airlift from 1948 to 1949, where a counter-policy of giving in to Russian demands with regard to Berlin might have allowed the enclave to slide into Communist control quietly. Once the airlift had been carried through, however, it would thereafter always have seemed a major erosion of American and Western resolve for any other demands on the enclave to be accepted.

Similarly the American defense of South Korea in 1950 might have come as a surprise to the Communist leadership, given various statements of Secretary of State Dean Acheson and General Douglas MacArthur seemingly placing Korea beyond the perimeter of territories the U.S. wished to defend. Perhaps the American commitment of aid was simply President Truman's instinctive reaction, given memories of the unsuccessful appeasement of Hitler, but the effect would be to define an American commitment to the defense of Korea thereafter. For a time, it even seemed that the United States, under "United Nations" auspices, was intent on unifying all of Korea under a non-Communist government, by completely conquering the territory from which the original North Korean attack had been launched. When the intervention of Communist Chinese forces drove American and South Korean forces south again, the United States ultimately showed itself content to push north once more to a line comparable to the original 38th parallel demarcation line.

The American commitment to the defense of Yugoslavia by contrast never became so pronounced, in part because it was not established by the process of being tested and carried through. In the immediate aftermath of Tito's defiance of Stalin, a certain risk existed that the Russians and their remaining satellite armies might attempt to invade Yugoslavia to oust Tito from power. U.S. supply of military equipment, with an implicit promise of defensive assistance thus materialized after 1950. When Khrushchev in the middle 1950's for a time abandoned the anti-Tito policies of Stalin, however, the Yugoslav regime seized the opportunity to reclaim a more nonaligned status for itself. As a nominally "Communist" regime in terms of ideology, it would have been difficult in any event for the world to come to see Yugoslavia as settled into the American "orbit."

The more serious consequence of the Korean War may indeed not have been the commitment to the defense of South Korea itself, but the impetus the war supplied for an expansion of American military procurement and defense preparation in general, as the defense budget rose to a new plateau which was thereafter to characterize Soviet-American relations for at least 20 years.

The military strategy accepted by either of the two super-powers for the Cold War also had an uncertain and somewhat unstable beginning. As part of the general response to the Russian blockade of Berlin, the United States moved B-29 bombers forward to bases in Britain, from which they might presumably threaten the USSR with nuclear attack. Proposals for any expansion of ground forces to challenge the strength of the Red Army were not given any support.

After the North Korean invasion of South Korea, however, the response was rather to augment conventional ground forces, and to attempt to repulse Communist forces in a ground campaign comparable to those of World War II. At the same time, this augmentation of American forces in the wake of Korea also saw a substantial augmentation of the U.S. Air Force and its nuclear component, the Strategic Air Command. Some of the difference in this case might be related to much more pessimistic estimates of the future course of Soviet-American relations, estimates which at the time of the Berlin crisis had not yet seen conflict in an armed variety to be quite as likely. The change from 1948 to 1950 reflected also two developments in the field of weapons—the Soviet detonation of an atomic bomb detected in 1949, and the discovery that an H-bomb was theoretically possible, a bomb which could inflict far more damage than the atomic bombs used in World War II.

In the early 1950's, therefore, the Cold War as we have since known it finally took shape. There were increasingly firm commitments to military action along much of the frontier, by each side in defense of the territory it controlled. There was an increasing sense that the horror of the newer atomic weapons would be enormous and mutually deterring, such that each side would have to think long and hard before attacking territory to which the opposing side had committed itself. This new "Balance of Terror" may indeed have placed us all in much more imminent danger of losing our lives than ever applied in the days before airplanes and giant explosives. But it also made possible a peace which previously might have seemed difficult or impossible, a peace between two sides greatly in disagreement on values and ideology, with no significant uninvolved states to maintain the balance. The stabilization of the European political situation since 1950 has not gone without question, however. Abstractly, it has depended on a simple threat, that any crossing of the demarcation line would bring nuclear warheads down on Moscow, even if no attack as yet had been launched on New York. Critics have long noted that this threat is basically not rational, for to carry it out would be to sacrifice far more, from the viewpoint of an American President, than could possibly be gained. (Implicitly, such retaliation is taken to be rational if it followed a Russian attack on the cities of the United States, although one could as well ask what any American President would gain by retaliating here.)

Regardless of whether all forms of retaliation are equally "irrational," the more serious charge has simply been that such a response would not be credible for a Soviet seizure merely of Berlin or Hamburg. If the Russians thus applied "salami tactics," continually stripping off small pieces of territory which never seemed worth a World War III from an American standpoint, won't the policy of massive retaliation thus fail to stabilize European frontiers as intended?

Yet there are various ways for an American President to couple such a nuclear strategic response convincingly to minor Soviet aggressions, to make such responses indeed credible, or at least plausible and probable enough so that the Soviet Union never really elected to test them. As noted, the U.S. can simply have its President commit himself in terms of honor, so that to fail to prepare for World War III in such circumstances would always suggest that American word could not be trusted. To reinforce such verbal commitments, the deployment of American soldiers to such front-line positions as West Berlin and West Germany has further ensured that the American government and public could not easily ignore even minor Soviet aggressions. Finally, the deployment of "tactical" nuclear weapons to forward areas made it quite probable that such weapons would come into use in any war, with the ensuing risks of step-by-step escalation into all-out war.

If an American hold on Western Europe and other positions around the globe might thus be reinforced simply through the risk of nuclear war, one can in retrospect still question why the need was felt for such a hold. In other times the American interest in Europe would have been much more limited. Other great powers in the past had often allowed some power vacuums to exist, without rushing to fill and divide them.

Some areas, of course, were worth defending simply because Americans regarded it as right and desirable that these not be under Russian occupation. American identification with France and Britain during and after World War II would not with any equanimity have allowed these countries to fall under hostile rule. Other countries at first might not have drawn as much intrinsic identification, but seemed instrumentally valuable for their resources or for their strategic position. In 1945, for example, the U.S. hardly identified with Germans so much as to grieve at their mistreatment by a Communist regime. Yet it always had to be obvious that German industry and manpower under Communist control would greatly augment the strength of Stalin's Russia. A Russian army in West Germany, moreover, would be a far more direct threat to Paris than one still on the Elbe.

Finally, as noted, some areas had to be defended simply because the precedent of surrendering them might seem to encourage aggression elsewhere, as the people we intend to defend lose confidence in our resolve. The West Berliners thus initially were not the subject of great American affection, nor were they an enormous resource contributing to defense of other areas elsewhere. Yet the surrender of territory to which the U.S., Britain, and France had a legal claim might have seemed to suggest further Allied surrenders elsewhere, and Berlin therefore has been defended.

If territory in Europe was important to both Moscow and Washington, this could have caused war between the two super-powers. It could cause continual tension, also undesirable, accompanied by continuously inflated defense expenditures. A long series of proposals for disarmament have thus emerged for the confrontation across the European Central Front, proposals which have, however, not overcome some inherent difficulties for any such disarmament.

The suspected size of the Soviet conventional ground force has itself been a continuing obstacle, as NATO estimates continually assumed that the USSR had not divested itself of its World War II ground force potential as had the U.S. and its allies. Even if a man-for-man or battalion for battalion comparision along the front did not prove such an asymmetry, Moscow was rated with an inherently more massive and rapid reinforcement capability, based on large reserves and easy railroad access from bases within the USSR. Any matching reinforcement of the American forces commited to NATO in a crisis would have to come a longer distance across the barrier of the Atlantic Ocean.

With these background assumptions about force levels, the United States generally concluded that it would be impossible ever to erect a conventional defense sufficient against Soviet military attack. The prospect of nuclear retaliation was thus presumably essential to deterring such an attack. It might, therefore, have been concluded that the United States very naturally desired conventional disarmament in the postwar years, to chip away at the Soviet advantage, while the USSR just as naturally would wish disarmament in, or a ban on the use of, nuclear weapons.

Yet the cleverness of authorship in disarmament proposals hardly constrains the opposing sides to such simple and straightforward positions. When the object of such proposals is to place the opposite side in an embarrassing position, each side managed to compose plans which seemed addressed to the other's grievances. The American Baruch Plan, for example, was seemingly addressed only to the nuclear weapons over which the United States still held a monopoly in 1946, magnanimously surrendering this military advantage. Skeptics might, however, have contended that the plan would have frozen American superiority in the nuclear weapons field; Americans might always have retained their experience and expertise in already having produced such weapons, and thus might always have won any race to rearm with A-bombs, if a political crisis had driven the powers to tear up the agreement.

At later stages, the USSR came forward with detailed proposals for reductions in conventional force levels in Europe and throughout the world, at one point seizing on the levels proposed by the West some years earlier. Yet again such plans called for reduced force levels proportional to the levels at which armies had stood prior to disarmament. This might have left the remaining Soviet force all the more able to push past token NATO forces, whenever it had crossed the Elbe and Rhine. If accepted, the proposals in each case would have burdened the opposite side; when rejected, the opposite side was subjected to some embarassment in terms of the propaganda impression made on neutral powers.

Given the nature of the balance in the Eisenhower years, it is indeed plausible that the United States had privately desired no disarmament at all. Nuclear disarmament was to be avoided lest this cast doubt on the willingness of the U.S. to escalate to all-out war on behalf of West Germany. Conventional disarmament might be inappropriate because Western ground forces were already only large enough to serve the token "tripwire" function required for a plausible nuclear escalation threat.

The deterring threat of escalation to nuclear war may thus have worked exactly as it was intended, for the protection of NATO territory against salamic tactics or more serious Soviet military offensives in the 1950's and in the 1960's. Yet there was at least one small piece of territory for which the efficacy of this deterrent would remain in some doubt, specifically West Berlin.

Everywhere else, the Russians would have had to initiate hostilities themselves to try to change the territorial status quo; around West Berlin they could try to change it simply by denying passage to supply services crossing East Germany, closing rail, canal, and Autobahn highway links, and perhaps somehow clogging the airspace so that the airlift of 1948–49 could not be repeated. In such cases, it had to be the United States and NATO which initiated hostilities by any effort to reopen supply connections with the enclave; the risk that this might lead to nuclear war could thus deter the West instead of the USSR, causing the loss of the enclave simply by default.

As always, the United States could not gracefully withdraw from the exposed and abnormal geographic holding because of the momentum this might seem to generate for Communist claims on the rest of Germany or elsewhere, because earlier American persistence had encouraged the West Berliners to commit themselves in ways which had produced a genuine American identification with their lot. Yet it is also not difficult to understand why the USSR and the East German regime were anxious to absorb Berlin, even on defensive grounds. The crossing of its territory by Western trucks and Western airplanes inevitably left the image of sovereignty in the German Democratic Republic somewhat marred and imperfect. More seriously, the ability of East Germans to move in and out of West Berlin, and to leave East Germany by this escape hatch, was enormously destabilizing for the economic and political future of the Communist regime.

If the youngest and most productive Germans could continually move over into the Federal Republic, attracted by its political freedom and higher wages, the risk of collapse in the GDR would always seem close. East Germany was hardly a mere issue of precedent for the Soviet Union, moreover, having the highest per capita GNP in the Communist bloc, and the tenth largest absolute product in the world. If the Soviet Union feared the revanchist inclinations of a reunified Germany, holding the East German portion was a most valuable and reassuring check, in terms of military and industrial potential, in terms of strategic geographic position.

FURTHER READINGS

Kolko, Gabriel. *The Roots of American Foreign Policy.* Boston: Beacon Press, 1967.
Schlesinger, Arthur. "Origins of the Cold War." *Foreign Affairs.* October, 1967.
Westerfield, H. Bradford. *Foreign Policy and Party Politics: Pearl Harbor to Korea.* New Haven: Yale University Press, 1955.

A Receding of the Cold War?

It is possible that the erection of a wall through Berlin in 1961 thus definitively settled that impasse, guaranteeing that East Germany could now have an orderly economic development without absorbing West Berlin. The Communist leadership may not yet have been assured of this in 1961, and might still have been happy to take over Berlin in the process; cartographically, West Berlin still seems an ugly and anomolous foreign space in the middle of the East German territory. Yet American resistance to any pressures for more than a wall dissuaded the Communists from going beyond the control on exit that was now achieved.

Not nearly as much can be at stake for the East German regime today. If the costs of blockading Berlin remain high, such a maneuver no longer can offer appropriate returns. In part this will hold true because the West has always held some nonmilitary retaliatory options, for example a counter-blockade of all Western trade relations with East Germany, or with the countries of Eastern Europe in general. Since the Communist countries each year, despite their best efforts, become more rather than less dependent on crucial industrial components from the West, a blockade would not be an empty threat.

Does it therefore follow that military balances and arrangements are losing their importance and relevance for the international politics of America, Europe, and the world as we move into the 1970's, to be supplanted by other considerations? It may be somewhat misleading to measure the importance of inputs simply by whether our attention is called to them in the course of events. If the balance of terror is working very well, there will be little news of threats of Russian aggression in Europe, and this may allow German, Frenchmen, and Americans to disagree all the more openly on subsidiary questions of economics. Yet this hardly will suggest that these three national groups have ceased to be functionally allied for military resistance to the Soviet bloc, or that such resistance makes no difference for politics. As long as the Soviet Union, and the countries it dominates in Eastern Europe, remain equipped for large-scale military operations, the question of what prevents such operations will have to be answered.

Economic considerations, as noted above, play a role in balancing the East-West confrontation, as well as dividing the ranks of the West. If a blockade of Berlin is not likely today, it is partly because the countries of the Socialist camp need industrial imports from West Germany and Western Europe. Any military tension between the two blocs is likely to hamper trade. Any increase in arms will moreover require higher expenditures, and greater sacrifices or postponements in these other areas of economic activity.

Some of the world's political future may thus be stabilized by the needs of economic development; in other cases, the balance continues to be maintained by threats on either side of escalation to all-out war. Yet, if the commitment of one of the super-powers is in doubt, the other may still try challenging for control of some marginal area. Where the current political complexion of an area is already in doubt, there may be no clear line of aggression to which threats of massive retaliation can be coupled.

For example, it is generally understood that each of the two major powers attach enough significance to their portion of Germany to be willing to wage nuclear war in its defense. The same is hardly true for the defense of Iran or Yugoslavia or Finland. At times in the past it might have seemed that the Russian commitment to and hold on various East European countries made an American challenge unthinkable. Yet such a hold can erode, as in Hungary in 1956 or Czechoslovakia in 1968. If Moscow's leadership in these areas had been left in doubt for a longer time, the United States might have felt it had the leeway to try its own hand at political influence, even with accompanying military commitments. The Russian interventions of 1956 and 1968 thus came quickly, in part because it was important for Moscow to prove that its commitment to these areas had not been diminished. Sending in tanks was necessary to put persons loyal to the USSR back into power. Sending in tanks was also necessary to suggest that Moscow would have used rockets and bombers also if a challenge from Washington had made this appropriate. Yet the need remains to maintain this kind of commitment where political ambiguity of any sort appears. While the United States had in effect promised its nonintervention in Czechoslovakia in 1968, it stated thereafter that it might not stand by if similar intervention were launched into Rumania or Yugoslavia. Secretary of State Rusk's statement also contemplated extension of a NATO commitment to Austria. President Nixon's visit to Bucharest early in his administration similarly was intended to widen the ambiguity on whether Rumania fell entirely within an unchallenged Soviet sphere of influence.

Despite the efforts to paint the NATO alliance as a uniform field of commitment and agreement, some doubts must remain here also on whether the U.S. would really go to World War III in defense of some area. Greece, Turkey, and Portugal all have regimes of uncertain democratic legitimacy, and all are of relatively lower industrial value. The possibility of a war between Greece and Turkey, possibly over the Cyprus issue, compounds the difficulties of an absolute defensive commitment from the U.S. Within the decade it is also not inconceivable that guerrilla compaigns would materialize in such areas, accompanied by harsh campaigns of government retaliation and repression. The loss of any of these countries, if it wished to leave the alliance, would also not threaten the American strategic position as much as a defection on the central front.

If massive retaliation therefore explains the defense of Hamburg and Paris, other factors must explain the stability of the dividing lines between Communist and non-Communist areas around the globe. It is always entirely possible, of course, that the military forces of Greece could do well in repulsing an attack from Bulgaria, at least well enough to make any territorial gains very costly for the opposing side. There have been no explicit Communist ground movements across a border since the invasion of South Korea in 1950. The American response then was indeed not to start World War III by bombing Moscow, but rather to fight out the defense of the area only with conventional weapons in a campaign which was nonetheless very costly to the Chinese and North Korean regimes. If the Communist bloc saw opportunities for a successful guerrilla insurrection in Greece, of course, this might be a much more attractive prospect. American retaliatory commitments, as noted above, can be based on real identification, or strategic value of the territory in question, or because the precedent of aggression must be resisted. It is not certain that the last can be coupled to the massive retaliation of a World War III.

Since the commitments of the two super-powers to the defense of various territories can always be questioned, they must continually be deployed forward to prove that commitment. Such deployments of forces can themselves cause tensions and fears of attack, however, aside from being expensive, and obtrusive to the local populations. At various times the proposal has thus been advanced that the two major powers "disengage," that is, leave a zone between themselves into which neither would deploy forces or attempt to negotiate alliances or maintain political control. A chain of neutral states, in this view, would reassure each side's control over the territory behind the chain of buffers, while eliminating the need for large and threatening standing armies.

On a somewhat de facto basis, some such buffers for disengagement have emerged as the Cold War ran its course. As noted earlier, Finland and Sweden together probably amount to such a buffer. The Soviet Union abstained from imposing a Communist regime on Finland, although it could easily have done so by military force, or even by a coup carried through as in Czechoslovakia in 1948 with a mere shadow of the threat of military intervention. The abstention here was hardly due to oversight, or to some flagging of Marxist revolutionary fervor, but rather was a quid-pro-quo for Sweden's remaining outside the NATO alliance when Norway and Denmark joined. Either side overstepping the balance would cause the other to respond. If Sweden abandoned its neutrality to align itself with the West, it would probably have led to Finland being taken over completely by Moscow. Conversely, a Russian invasion of or coup in Finland would probably lead to a severe realignment of Swedish defense and foreign policy.

As this example suggests, more is needed for a successful disengaged zone than mere disengagement. Sweden's leverage in the "Nordic balance" depends on its own military strength, which has been considerable ever since World War II, and on the political strength of its government. The strong domestic support for the Finnish government also is necessary, requiring that any political takeover involve an explicit Russian move, rather than merely a more subtle seizure of power.

In 1956, as part of the agreement by which the Allied occupation of Austria was at last terminated, Austria was pledged to a neutral foreign policy, and thus in effect extended the Yugoslav zone of disengagement north to the border between West Germany and Czechoslovakia. The Austrian government was allowed to maintain a small army and air force, again presumably sufficient to protect its neutrality without any invocation of outside help at the first instance. A number of commentators regarded the Austrian example as a hopeful sign of what the Soviet Union might agree to for Germany: reunification of what had been separate occupation zones in a neutralization with the military forces of each side withdrawing a discreet distance.

The differences between the Austrian and German cases, however, were serious enough to make Russian acceptance of the disengagement proposals unlikely. Austria was not a large enough state to be a military, political, or industrial threat on its own. A single government for the entire country had been tolerated by the Russians all through the occupation. It was clear that the government of the unified country after 1955 would be democratically chosen in a regular process of contested elections, and that the foreign policy of the country, while scrupulously neutral within the constraints of the treaty, would be psychologically pro-Western. Free elections for a unified Germany would probably produce very similar results, but in a country with enough power potential to shake off most foreign policy restraints that a treaty might try to impose. If a unified and "neutral" Germany were left no armed forces, it might have become a power vacuum vulnerable to coups by paramilitary formations of either the right or the left. If allowed armed forces comparable in per capita terms to those of Austria, a unified Germany would have had options for choosing a de facto alignment with the West, or choosing to embark on an independent military and foreign policy of its own. With the recent memories of World War II, the latter at least would have been disquieting for all the powers, while the former prospect was intolerable for the USSR.

The Soviet Union had indeed already established its own political administration in the Eastern zone, not tolerating the unified administration created in Austria. Having a sure grip on the geographic position and economic and military resources of this zone, it would have been very risky for Moscow to surrender this merely in the interests of easing tension, or satisfying German cravings for national reunification. If German revanchism was seriously the main Russian fear, being able to turn a part of Germany against the rest was a substantial form of reinsurance against this. If the advancement of Communism in Europe was rather the major fixation, East Germany's resources were simply too valuable to be thrown away.

One could, of course, conceive of unification schemes, and "disengagement" schemes, which could have been more attractive to the USSR at this time. If the political arrangements of the reunification were molded along certain lines, a Communist takeover of all of Germany might have seemed practicable—as the "workers militia" of the Eastern Zone played the same role as similar paramilitary forces had played in Prague, as the secret police that had now been well established in the East was allowed to terrorize and intimidate opposition party representatives in the unified government now presumably gathered within easy striking distance in the national capital at Berlin. Most of the unification proposals advanced on the Soviet side indeed called for the retention of existing zonal political structures, through some intermediate phase, which might produce exactly the above results, as long as some forms of government are more suited to totalitarian expansion than others. Western proposals conversely called for internationally supervised free national elections at the outset, which could indeed have produced exactly the reverse kind of expansion, that of a pro-Western political style taking over the Eastern zone.

As noted earlier, Yugoslavia is similarly not aligned with either of the military blocs, the result of its peculiar history of being Marxist in ideology, but anti-Stalinist in the late 1940's. Yet the position of Yugoslavia can illustrate how a disengaged zone could produce wars rather than easing tensions. In the early 1950's, and then again for a brief time in the aftermath of the Russian intervention in Czechoslovakia, it was not totally implausible that the forces of the Soviet bloc would invade Yugoslavia. Since the commitment of the United States to the defense of Yugoslavia could not be firm, for reasons of ideology and Tito's desire for nonalignment, it was altogether possible that wars would inadvertently arise as Moscow invaded, not expecting the American response that would come. If Tito's forces were able to prolong their resistance at all, either in conventional ground warfare or by recourse to partisan tactics, the temptation for the United States to offer military and logistical support would have been great.

It is thus important that middle areas have political regimes which do not seem to threaten either of the major powers politically or otherwise, and that these middle areas have enough indigenous strength to generate part of their own defense and deterrent to outside attack. Because the Swedish military forces and the Yugoslav military forces are strong enough to keep their areas from becoming a vacuum, the buffer zones along these stretches of the "iron curtain" have served some very useful purposes in keeping American and Soviet forces apart.

None of this discussion argues that disengagement is not a very sensible approach to alleviating international tensions wherever circumstances make it applicable. Wars are threatened by close contests over bits of territory which seem immensely important for their own sake, or for their instrumental resources, or for the precedents which seem involved. Wherever such close contests can be avoided by good fortune or careful planning, wars and tensions become much less likely.

In cases when war can very well escalate to the most horrendous forms of nuclear exchanges, it requires special circumstances to produce tensions great enough to merit taking this risk. The value of the two Germanies presents such an entanglement in the heart of Europe; the entanglement has been all the more complicated by the peculiar existence of the enclave of West Berlin deep within East Germany.

Outside Europe, relatively few such direct confrontations exist. Japan is an enormously valuable country, but the waters around it preclude any direct Russian, Chinese, or Korean challenge to its alignment with the United States. A more serious long-term issue is raised by the legal status of Taiwan as part of China, such that any continued American defense of the Nationalist regime automatically implies a disrespect for the territorial integrity of China as a whole, and thus has delayed assuredly peaceful relations with the Communist regime based in Peking.

The uncertain future of Vietnam has suggested that momentum might be generated for further expansions if the Communists captured control of the south; what begins as an issue of precedent becomes a test of resolve which in a "domino effect" fashion is seen as influencing far more than the immediate territory in question. Yet it may well be that ideologists and theorists on both sides have exaggerated how much one can generalize about the processes of insurgency and counter-insurgency. Whether or not Vietnam is ripe to fall to Communism may prove little about any other country; when local conditions predominate, precedents may make less difference. The realization of this may be an important part of the explanation of the detente which occurred between China and the United States with the Kissinger and Nixon visits to Peking in 1971 and 1972.

Apart from genuinely "Cold War" issues pitting Communist factions against non-Communist, since 1950 there has also been some danger that the major powers would be drawn into war situations related to local nationalistic conflicts with relatively little ideological tone, most specifically the contests between Israel and the Arab states, and between Pakistan and India. While these have brought several outbreaks of full-scale conventional war between the local parties, and several symbolic confrontations between the U.S. and the USSR, the two super-powers have each thus far shown some prudence and caution in face of their lack of control over the local regimes.

A Chinese-American detente might also be traced to the general breakdown of alliances in the 1960's (which will be discussed below). Chinese hostility to the Soviet Union has now perhaps blossomed into a serious fear of Russian invasion, so that Nixon's visit to the Chinese capital may have been intended to make this less likely, in the same manner as his earlier visit to Bucharest placed the prestige of his office and his country on the line.

Apart from fear of Russia, or loss of faith in guerrilla insurgency, there may yet be other reasons why China has elected to warm its relations with the U.S. in the 1970's, becoming slightly more flexible on the Taiwan question, and ceasing to give its moral support to potential anti-American guerrilla movements all around the globe. Economics again can rear its head as a peace-supporting factor, as the Chinese regime may simply have desired to terminate the domestic economic sacrifices that were a part of a posture of challenge to the outside world, or more specifically to reap some of the benefits of trade with the United States. A posture of mobilized hostility can have its domestic costs on either side, and the Chinese seemed to recognize this in 1970 as much as President Nixon.

Since 1945, the United States has not only affirmed its determination to defend Western Europe against attack from the East, but also has continually been in favor of the economic and political unification of this area of Europe, at times far more enthusiastically than Europeans themselves. A part of such enthusiasm for unification obviously has assumed that a unified Europe would more readily contribute to its own defense against Soviet encroachments, but this has only been a part of the total American motivation.

Another important ingredient in the American attitude was the reaction to the nationalisms of the prewar period, nationalisms which had presumably caused World War II. If such unification was initially seen as a means to controlling German politics or German industry (or a little later, German armed forces) it could easily enough be transformed into a European structure which subdued and controlled all nationalisms. An obvious, perhaps very misleading, analogy could be drawn with the United States and its unification of the 13 colonies. In effect the U.S. was endorsing the very opposite of the balance of power reasoning. Western Europe should not be kept fractionated against itself to protect America from invasion, as might have been the earlier British approach. Europe rather should be united so that various ethnic and national groups could control and check each other within what had become a domestic political process. Parliamentary struggles at the European level, rather than wars, would serve the purpose of keeping any particular ethnic unit from embarking on aggression.

As noted earlier, such sentiment for European unification was not missing within Europe itself in the immediate aftermath of World War II. While American commitment to unification has remained steady, if somewhat shallow, the more crucial input of European interest has had pronounced ups and downs which can be traced in the history of various specific integration proposals.

The formation of the European Coal and Steel Community in 1951 was the earliest and most encouraging of the efforts at unification, pooling the resources and policy choices of Italy, West Germany, France, and the Benelux countries. The European Defense Community (EDC), which would have been followed by a European Political Community (EPC), was intended to facilitate the rearmament of West Germany by pooling the armed forces of the Six into a single force. When the EDC treaty was in the end rejected by the French parliament, it seemed that European solutions had been pushed too hard, or had been exploited overly much to compensate for the unpopularity of German rearmament. West German military forces emerged nonetheless, in a separate national army for the German Federal Republic under NATO command, but Europeanization had thus been dealt a serious setback.

The formation of the European Economic Community (EEC) and of Euratom, an agency for the development of nuclear energy, followed in 1956, occasioning the second great wave of optimism on unification. Euratom, after the closing of the Suez Canal in 1956, was premised on fears that

Europe would be short of fuel, thus requiring production of electricity by nuclear energy to make the difference. Events would prove such dire forecasts untrue, with the result that Euratom's positive activities never amounted to as much as had been hoped. Within the six nations, however, it has supplied valuable assurances that materials allocated to peaceful uses will not be clandestinely diverted instead to the production of nuclear weapons.

The EEC, by contrast, has been tremendously busy and successful, credited with much of the responsibility for the economic prosperity of the six nations since 1956. It is possible that trade within the six would have boomed even without an agency to set common policies on agricultural prices, tariffs, subsidies, and so on. As it was, however, the establishment of a central governing agency was accompanied by a great boom in commerce for all the countries involved, and the causal connection seemed to support those who hoped for further political integration of the countries involved.

While the EEC has been a functional success, the hope has not been fulfilled that it would quietly foster a European rather than national sort of patriotism, and lead to full political integration. Part of the blame for this must be laid to the personality of General De Gaulle, who attained power in France in 1958 and expressed a continuing aversion to any subordination of French image and authority to that of agencies based in Brussels. But part simply denies the functionalist assumption that national loyalties would shift naturally to a higher plane as political reality required integrated decision-making. Europeans today are assuredly less jingoistic and chauvinistic than their grandfathers, and war between the nations of western Europe is indeed most unlikely for the present. But this has neither required nor produced the kind of nationalistic identification of Europeans with Europe that Frenchmen felt for France in 1873, or even feel today.

American hopes for full European unification have thus not been fulfilled. As noted, the hopes have always been implicitly accompanied by an expectation that a united Europe would side with the United States militarily and politically, as conflicts with the Soviet Union arise. Yet if such conflicts are kept under control, disagreements can arise on economic questions, and here it has hardly been certain that a unified Europe would be aligned with, rather than against, the United States. In the commercial area, Americans will fear exclusion from a unified Europe, as customs barriers which are lowered within the system are kept in place around the outside of it. Europeans conversely fear the superiority of American technology or business management practices, which may allow United States firms to penetrate and dominate their own home markets, while siphoning off the most competent European personnel.

After World War II, there was clearly a change in the nature and function of alliances. As noted, the later 19th century mechanism of the treaty of alliance was a mutual exchange by which each party increased its relative power, as each was pledged on its honor to intervene on behalf of the other at the very outset of a war, rather than playing a balance of power waiting game. Parties combining their potentials in such treaties were typically of comparable strengths, neither being sure enough of his own military power to dispense with the other. Signing such a treaty meant forgoing a flexibility and independence which was desirable in its own right, because the commitment of the opposite party was more necessary, and therefore worth the sacrifice.

After 1945, it was obvious for a time that only two major powers were now to have significant military influence over the course of international politics. Neither of such powers really needed the pledges of military support of its allies, and when such support was invoked, as in Korea or the Dominican Republic or the Russian intervention in Czechoslovakia, it was mainly to put a multinational light on the affair, rather than to augment the military capability of the major power in some functional way. Why then have the United States and the USSR indulged in negotiating treaties of alliance such as NATO and the Warsaw Pact, the Sino-Soviet Pact and SEATO and CENTO? When Secretary of State Dulles was accused of being misled by a certain "pactomania," the criticism was implicit that such treaties were inappropriate to the postwar world, either in focusing overly much on military power, or in linking a strong nation with a series of weak clients from which it could hardly expect to draw much strength and resource support in return.

It is clear that in NATO as well as SEATO the United States has been more of a producer than consumer of security. It was once proposed that European NATO countries would detail some of their air defense personnel to participate in the protection of North America, but nothing came of this. The United States (and Canada) thus are agreeable to seeing NATO functionally deployed for the defense of Western Europe itself. Yet it is hardly so silly or irrational for either of the super-powers to have committed itself to such a one-way mutual defense alliance.

The United States assuredly does surrender its legal right to be indifferent in a war between the USSR and France, and the return assurance that France will assist the U.S. in a war with Moscow hardly explains American interest in the trade. For it is precisely because the United States wanted to surrender or shed its options of indifference that the NATO alliance and similar alliances were negotiated. In a nuclear world in which the prospect of all-out war might otherwise have cast doubt on American willingness to intervene in defense of Paris, the classic formula of an alliance reduces such doubts, for any country which attaches the least significance to its treaty commitments. A more explicit statement of the treaty relationship would thus have omitted any French obligation to defend Maine or Alaska. Since all nations of the world are reluctant to admit or stress the gross inequalities of power that characterize the nuclear world, it was only politic for the United States to draw up alliances in the seemingly dated classical format.

Some important consequences flow from this changed reasoning for entry into an "alliance." Previously one's own commitment was mainly the price one paid for a commitment in return. The national interest thus might typically have suggested whittling down this commitment whenever the occasion presented itself. In the world where one wants to give an impression of commitment, however, the major powers will lobby in just the opposite direction, trying to reinforce and renew their sense of commitment to an "ally" in dubious cases. Very different reasoning applies where the commitment is given more grudgingly, merely in exchange for some concession in return. A postwar example of this emerges in American pledges to Israel after 1956, pledges given in exchange for the Israeli withdrawal from the Sinai desert. Critics of American policy in the spring of 1967 could argue that the United States was quite inconsistently backing out of such defense commitments to Israel, while it had been deliberately exaggerating (or expanding in the process of defining) its treaty commitments to South Vietnam. Yet the difference here is readily understandable, in that the American government has not wanted to appear committed in the Middle East, but has wanted to be committed in Southeast Asia. Commitments in the Middle East were embarassing for U.S. relations with the Arab states, and would be eroded as soon as was decently possible after the Israelis had complied with American demands. Commitments in Southeast Asia hopefully would deter Communist forces from trying to win power in various countries, and would reassure friendly regimes in the area that such forces would be resisted.

If the function of alliances has changed, some of the mechanism by which it plays a role in polarizing international politics remains the same as in earlier times. Presumably, the alliance is launched on the basis of some degree of community of interest, which for the moment overrides whatever issues of disagreement remain between the two countries. Pledges of mutual support in the event of war are exchanged, as noted, and perhaps a certain infrastructure is then induced of military staff conversations and government-to-government interaction. The building of such infrastructure can then induce a further improvement of relations in at least two ways. Frequent interaction may presumably lead individuals to be influenced by the values and outlooks of their opposite numbers, so that each set of national elite preferences is changed in a way which diminishes remaining disagreement, and increases consensus. The same interaction gives each side an assurance that compromise agreements will be adhered to even if disagreements persist. Much of the negative interaction of normal international exchanges is simply the result of each side being unsure that the other will not double-cross it. The "prisioner's dilemma" situation is relieved here when regular visits back and forth generally eliminate the possibility of either side catching the other by surprise.

The narrowing of relations between partners in an alliance will come as no surprise, on the basis of the alliances we have known. It occurred between France and Russia before World War I, and then between Britain and France, albeit their alliance was not formalized. It occurred for a time between the USSR and Communist China, and has existed between Britain and the United States ever since 1940. Yet two contrary possibilities exist, that substantive relations might actually worsen after an alliance has come into effect, and that the self-reinforcing process by which an alliance grows can also be reversed so that the alliance falls apart.

An obvious illustration of the first case might appear in the emergence of a series of disputes between China and Russia after 1956. The mutual defense treaty between the two countries as yet has not been allowed to lapse (in fact the treaty is directed only against Japan and "any nation allied with Japan"). Yet the extent of disagreement between the two powers has widened considerably. These are ideological issues on the ideal form of socialist society and the proper tactical approach to the advancement of socialism against American resistance. There are questions of prestige priority, on who shall have primacy within the Communist group of nations. There are disputes about the exact location of the border between the USSR and China.

As a result of the initial opening of such issues, the infrastructure of the Sino-Soviet alliance was allowed to erode, as students were called home from Russia, as technical assistants were called back from China. A diminished diplomatic presence in each capital, and the removal of military advisers and coordinators, further decreased the possibility that familiarity between the two bureaucracies would breed greater concensus and understanding or at least greater trust that alliance cooperation would not be only for one nation's benefit or the other.

A similar receding of alliance ties has occurred in the case of the French membership in NATO. Here again various differences of interest led France to limit foreign military personnel on French soil, and to reduce French participation in the decision processes of the NATO command, in the end expelling NATO headquarters from Paris. In the NATO case, however, the widening of conflict appeared to reach an outer limit; since the election of President Nixon there has indeed been a certain American rapprochement again with Presidents De Gaulle and Pompidou.

The weakening of the NATO alliance may have reflected the very success of the alliance in the first place. Because American commitments to the defense of the NATO area had become so plausible, it was no longer necessary for France to play at the process of alliance agreement and coordination to maintain the image of this commitment. As the prospect of a Russian invasion of Western Europe diminished, it was possible for Frenchmen and other Europeans to turn to other questions, questions on which the adversary might not anymore be the USSR, but rather the United States.

The procedural workings of an on-going alliance may thus tend to induce still further agreement, perhaps at the extreme leading some day to full political and national integration; but the substantive success of such an alliance may either further this or undo it. As with the successful American-British-Russian campaign against Nazi Germany in World War II, success in international politics can defeat a common enemy and therefore turn an ally into a new enemy. Since the Russian menace to Western Europe has not been as decisively eliminated as the menace of Nazi Germany in 1945, the success of NATO and the American commitment can only be partial and relative. For this reason the induced alienation of various NATO partners from each other may also only be partial. More serious and deep-seated divergences of outlook would have had to appear, as in the Sino-Soviet case, to produce a wider rift.

If the Cold War could be said to be receding in the 1970's, it must be explained in two ways. First, some of the "prisoner's dilemma" issues which plagued the world after 1945 have indeed been settled, as each side is more secure in what it holds. West Berlin is secure, but so is East Germany. Marxist Cuba is more secure, but so is non-Marxist Venezuela, as guerrilla war may not be the wave of the future. Economic interdependence may make it more difficult for either side to start wars or crises or blockades. If Vietnam seems to disprove this, China and Russia and the United States seemed in the mood to get on with business even while the Vietnam struggle had still not totally played itself out.

Second, only in part for the above reasons, alliances have cracked enough so that a multipolar conflict structure is replacing the bipolar Cold War. The U.S. and Communist China in effect can cooperate against the USSR or Japan. At other points, France or Western Europe find themselves opposing the U.S., and drawing de facto support from Japan or the USSR.

All this may simply be the product of the essential military stabilization that the Cold War in its early form so successfully produced. It is thus, as always, difficult to say whether military factors have lost their significance, or simply done their job so well that we for a time cease to notice them. Wars may yet break out, perhaps between Israel and Egypt, or China and the USSR, or India and Pakistan, seemingly disproving any real relaxation of tensions; yet in such conflicts, the world alignment would at least no longer be simply that of the "Cold War."

FURTHER READINGS

Dinerstein, Herbert. "The Transformation of Alliance Systems." *American Political Science Review*. September, 1965.
Stoessinger, John G. *Nations in Darkness*. New York: Random House, 1971.

CHAPTER FIVE

*Alternative Approaches
to the Explanation of
International Politics*

International politics, all in all, is not a happy subject. If the field still must be defined by the possibility of war, war is something we could all do without. A survey of history may help us understand how we arrived at our world of the 1970's, and what some alternative worlds might look like. Yet we are where we are, burdened or blessed by a nonmonopolistic array of military force, and without any overarching legal structure to make up for the lack of monopoly.

If the threat of war remains real, of course, this may only be an appropriate price to pay for the national autonomy and independence cited at the outset as part of the explanation for resistance to world government. Yet this threat of war at least will drive political scientists and others to search for deeper explanations of international events, explanations which might just possibly allow us to avoid war at some point and to generate an extra decade or two of peace. An eclectic approach, reaching out to other disciplines, thus seems entirely in order. Such an approach will uncover theories based on individual human behavior or on group behavior, on psychology, economics, or geography, or on theories of bureaucratic politics. Often enough it will be based on extrapolations from the domestic politics of some states involved in the world arena, considering such variables as the presence or absence of nationalism, or ideology, or political or economic democracy. None of these sources of supplementary analysis may produce a satisfying "general theory" of foreign policy or international politics to replace what has already been said, but even partial improvements in our understanding of the causes of war and peace would be most welcome.

How systematic and theoretical should an analysis of international politics therefore seek to be? Such an apparently straightforward question has also generated a great deal of heated and sometimes fruitless debate among scholars and practitioners of the foreign policy process. What indeed does one mean by a "theory," or by "models" of the "system?" How much is threatened in being "too theoretical," or "not theoretical enough?"

Presumably "theory" refers to propositions about causality in international relations, propositions that go beyond saying that X is the case and Y is the case, but rather that X happened because Y happened, so that a similar X in the future would cause a similar Y. A "system" in international relations, or presumably anywhere else, is a causally interlocked series of variables, such that changing any one is very likely to change all the rest. A "model" of such a system represents an effort to identify only those causal relationships which are particularly strong, ignoring those which are of little importance, as well as those where no causal relationship exists.

Why are we thus concerned to collect theory which can give us models of the system? As students of the foreign policy process, we may simply wish to know causal relationships to satisfy our intellectual curiosity. This is a slightly higher form of curiosity at least than that which motivates the collection of mere factual data with which one can do well in trivia contests (for example, who was the Portuguese Foreign Minister in 1924?). It is also possible that a knowledge of theory conditions the mind to be more retentive of simple factual data.

As practitioners of foreign policy, we would also wish to know whether certain inputs produce the effects we desire, or the opposite effects. Do Voice of America Broadcasts in some particular language increase the electoral support for our friends, or do they lose such support? Well-founded theory can help us to skip over most of the vast amounts of available factual data on the outside world, as culled through the press, the community of scholars, and the intelligence services at the State Department's disposal. Theory tells us which input facts are important, so that we can then skip the rest, when what we want to do is predict some key outcome. There will still also be times when our problem is not having too much information, but too little, when we can not get the key input data we want for our predictions. Well-founded theories can then tell us what else to substitute for the data we lack, data on C which will tell us the condition of A, so that we can indeed foretell the reactions of B.

A great deal of such causal theory already exists, for one could not get through the dealings of everyday life very well without it. Yet a methodical review of the conventional wisdom in such theories is often appropriate, for the theories may be wrong, leading us continually to policies which produce disappointing results opposite to what we desired. It can be shown, for example, that much of the conventional wisdom is tautological, or sometimes flatly contradictory. Bits of evidence will thus seem to support "laws" of political process, when they do so only because of the way we have defined our variables; directly opposite bits of evidence emerge without seeming to upset our presuppositions, as just another part of our basic understanding is very misleadingly "confirmed."

Such failings indeed support those who distrust the qualitative or subjective impressions under which we have been working. Perhaps the study of international relations must instead be based on disciplined data, which is sorted by objective categories before any consideration of what it will be assumed to prove, and collected in quantities large enough to apply rigorous and meaningful statistical tests, from which causal inference might then be extracted. With so much data available on the politics of this world, the argument goes, we should be less quick to settle on theories as to what can be forgotten and what must be monitored. Statistical calculations can harness the capacity of computers to measure, from a neutral start, what the significance and impact of all the known variables can be for the variable we are trying to predict.

If objective data is to be applied to eliminate subjective biases or semantic obfuscations which otherwise mislead us, what kinds of data will be available, and what kinds will be significant? We have large amounts of data on concrete and cardinal values for important variables, the amount of steel produced from country to country, the number of men under arms, the number of missiles deployed, the numbers of television sets and college graduates. In some cases, attempts to produce quantitatively exact measurements will be highly suspect, but ordinal rankings will still be plausible even when cardinal values can not be agreed upon. It is clear, for example, that the gross national product of the United States is larger than that of the Soviet Union. But the exact relationship between the two is less clear since the exchange rate between dollars and rubles is set very arbitrarily and even a more market-oriented exchange rate might not reflect the real value of the two GNP's.

We are thus often concerned with absolute figures such as those suggested above. For other political needs, we may be more interested in such relative figures as the GNP per capita, the ratio of armed men to territory defended, the percentage of GNP that goes into defense spending or into education. Plausible theories can be constructed by which important political questions may depend on such relative variables. Having the data, statistical tests might be done to test such theories; for example, is war more likely as a greater percentage of GNP is devoted to defense spending? If the statistical correlations prove to be weak here, they may prove unexpectedly strong in other places, in which cases new theories may have to be constructed to account for the facts as more sophisticated statistical methods have uncovered them.

Yet some difficulties may plague our efforts to improve the quality of international relations analysis by recourse to statistical methods. To begin, the number of logically comparable crises, or other discrete instances, may be too small to allow mathematically meaningful tests to be conducted. The number of nations until recently was itself relatively small, and even the more than 130 independent nations of the world today may not constitute enough meaningful actors to produce the kinds of data we need. Statistical studies of voting in legislatures of the United States have demonstrated some important hidden truths about what really explains the trends of American politics. Similar studies of the UN General Assembly voting may not have enough important voters or important issues to reach such meaningful conclusions.

As noted earlier, it is far from certain that all military history is made meaningless by the introduction of the atomic bomb, for some very useful lessons can be extracted from past experience. Yet to attempt to lump together 50 or 100 crises, including Cuba in 1962 and Munich in 1938 and Agadir in 1911 may be to miss some obvious categorical differences, differences which the more traditionalist analysts of international politics will regard as crucial.

Even when larger amounts of data are available, other pitfalls will remain. A statistical correlation does not prove that two phenomena are causally related. To take an illustrative example, universal military training may simultaneously democratize a society and make it more belligerent towards the outside world. Yet the more it makes a society democratic, the less perhaps it becomes belligerent, and vice versa. Two effects are competing for the momentum imparted by a single input. The single input produces both outputs, but the outputs are still antithetical in that more of one will mean less of the other. Statistical tests might suggest the opposite, that democracy and belligerency rise and fall together.

Even if enough data exists in the quantifiable categories, there may be some crucial inputs for the political process that will never lend themselves to quantifications: the personalities of the leaders, or even their mood, the internal political considerations of this leadership as it jockeys for power and status, the "existential choice" of such a leadership when difficult decisions present themselves with risks on either side. Can we ever hope to collect enough data on similar cases to explain retrospectively the Japanese decision to attack Pearl Harbor?

Deliberately or otherwise, the drift of analysis by objective mathematical methods has been toward nonrational background variables as the explanation of events, an "essentialist" approach. The more traditional foreign policy analyst implicitly placed much more stress on the rational decision pattern of countries and men; "Because Russia wants warm-water ports, it can be expected to take an interest in Iran."

Perhaps this earlier approach leads to falsely anthropomorphic views of nations having a single set of values, a single centralized decision-maker. Perhaps we will never be able to get the necessary information on what goals are agreed upon within the Politburo. Perhaps the formulations on "searches for warm-water ports" are unconsciously designed to verify themselves, no matter what policies have been adopted, thus giving traditional political science a false sense of prowess and accomplishment.

Yet to ignore or downgrade rational models of political behavior may be to throw the baby out with the bathwater, for a great deal of international as well as domestic political behavior can be explained only by the conscious and astute pursuit of goals. Statistically collected background factors do not explain American or Russian behavior during the Cuban missile crisis nearly as well as the deliberate desires and calculations of Kennedy and Khrushchev. When the methods of data aggregation are applied to collecting information relevant to such desires, the two approaches thus can be brought together. For example, it is useful to know public opinion in India or Japan on the production of nuclear weapons, for such opinion will obviously constrain government decisions on the question.

Attempts have also been made to predict and account for political events by content analysis; the volume of phrases in the speeches, messages, and pronouncements of international politics would surely seem large enough to allow for aggregation and statistical correlation. Yet here the studies sometimes seem to accept the words at face value, as unmanipulated indicators of some basic trends toward or away from decisive action. A more traditional critic could argue that words can easily be manipulated to indicate trends counter to reality, that as weapons deployments were moving out of hand, the tendency might be all the greater to cool down the verbal rhetoric. If differing societies have differing degrees of control over their verbal outputs, and differing biases in terms of which words are used where, a large amount of evaluative correction would have to be introduced before it was decided that any new explanation for war and peace had been found.

The statistical approach can also underrate the significance of political structure, a variable which does not lend itself to quantification and mathematical analysis. An important explanation of U.S. foreign policy, for example, may hinge on the relative power and influence of the State Department as contrasted with the advisers to the president in the White House. Close analysts of Washington happenings can predict shifts in power here, based on the relative interest devoted to one area of the world or another by key persons, by the workings of the bureaucratic process.

On a grander scale, as noted earlier, much may depend on whether the country in question has a presidential or parliamentary system, on how much public opinion will be allowed to effect policy, on whether or not terror can be harnessed to stifle opposition. The interrelationships of such variables may have to be extremely complicated to account for foreign policy as it emerges, not too complicated for an observer to grasp in his personal intuition, but too complicated to be readily translatable into the outside check of an independent and objective statistical model.

There are those analysts of international politics who would recommend that we shift our attention away from the anarchic international arena *per se*, to concentrate instead on the particular human behavior patterns that explain various foreign policies, and the "international relations" that result. Yet even here we have a choice of paradigms or models of foreign policy behavior.

Should we assume that most policy is "rational," in that goals are consciously pursued, while ends are logically related to means? Or should we assume that much of policy is inadvertent? An economic approach would tend to stress the first kind of model, seeing most moves and decisions as basically goal-oriented. A more sociological approach would tend rather to stress the unanticipated and accidental aspects of all human interactions.

If policy is largely irrational, we might moreover have to decide whether this reflects the limitations of particular individuals who are burdened with neuroses and warped views of reality, or rather distortions at the multiperson level which result from any "standard operating procedure," or "organizational process." If policy is more rational, we would have to determine whether the goals so consciously furthered were really those of the "national interest," or instead the interests of particular bureaus or individuals.

This last distinction might sometimes be cast as between "selfish" goals and the pursuit of the public good. Yet that formulation has some serious problems, since the person who truly seeks to serve the "public good" in formulating foreign policy may also be extracting a considerable amount of "personal satisfaction" out of this. Men who pursue a goal in a "selfless" sense of the national or public interest can still be "a small group of willfull men," if they disagree with much or most of the public on that interest. A more real distinction thus pertains between those who selfishly or otherwise seek certain substantive policies, and those who seek after a procedural sense of political power or priviness for its own sake.

FURTHER READINGS

Allison, Graham T. "Conceptual Models and the Cuban Missile Crisis." *American Political Science Review.* September, 1969.
Kaplan, Morton A. *System and Process in International Politics.* New York: Wiley, 1964.

Mueller, John E., ed. *Approaches to Measurement in International Relations: A Non-Evangelical Survey*. Chicago: Appleton-Century-Crofts, 1969.
Rosenau, James N. *The Scientific Study of Foreign Policy*. (Glencoe, Ill.: Free Press, 1970.

Pursuit of Personal Power

As noted earlier, the political scientist often envies the central assumptions that so much benefit economic analysis. To be sure, the economist knows that entrepreneurs do not always single-mindedly pursue profit; sometimes they hire their nephews, or members of underprivileged minority groups. Yet when he assumes that love of profit will dictate decisions on levels of production and prices asked, he very often predicts what could not otherwise be predicted, explains what could not otherwise be explained. If power is not the universal goal of entire nations, isn't there still some general goal of maximization or normal pursuit that can give us a similar lead in predicting and explaining politicians' behavior?

As an alternative to monetary profit or the public interest, perhaps we might do well then to assume that politicians are peculiarly guided by a love of "power," a love which explains legislation, bureaucratic infighting, and party platforms. It certainly is plausible that a number of able persons in any society will enjoy directing the lives of other people, for the very pleasure of it. Since some such direction is necessary and inevitable under all circumstances, there will never be a total absence of such jobs to be filled, but never either a shortage of persons anxious to fill them.

The "pursuit of power" model has been moderately well developed for explaining some areas of domestic politics, as, for example, by Anthony Downs in showing why two-party election systems tend to produce "tweedle-dee, tweedle-dum" platforms for the parties, or in explaining why bureaucracies tend to seek greater expansion when they are recently founded than when they are "old." In the making of foreign policy as well, it is entirely possible that we have typically been exaggerating the substantive appeal of particular national policies for the decision-makers involved in formulating them, and forgetting how much the participants shape their recommendations in order to rise to higher positions of power within the hierarchy. For example, in accounts of the American policy process on the Cuban missile crisis, can not most of the participants in the ExCom be accused of basically enjoying the process, and of hoping that they will be invited again to any similar sessions in the future?

If we are thus persuaded that "power" is a discrete and non-tautological goal that determines how bureaucrats and politicians behave, there will still be some problems of refinement in definition. Is it simply the total impact one can have on future policy? If so, a cabinet officer who was disillusioned with American policy in Southeast Asia might have exercised a maximum of power by assassinating the president. To be sure, this would impose a penalty of death or life imprisonment, which even a power-hungry person such as a cabinet official might consider too high a price. Yet the same official might exercise his greatest total impact on policy by dramatically resigning. If Secretary McNamara had resigned in 1966, for example, would this not have focused dramatic attention and pressure on President Johnson's handling of the Vietnam War, thus exercising more power in this crucial arena than all of the insider-influence the secretary could deploy by staying at his post?

Individual public servants will often defend their own behavior in substantive terms, that by "swimming with the tide" they at least can channel it somewhat. Detailed case-by-case examinations would be required to tell how accurate and honest such self-appraisals are. The cabinet member who openly forces a congress or prime minister to overrule him may often have more substantive impact than those who content themselves with adjusting minor details in ways which will not be overruled. Those who are less open in their opposition will conversely hold office for longer tenures, and have great chances of promotion.

Since the time of Hobbes, men have argued or rationalized that one must first have power to exercise it; this is either a tautology or an often erroneous empirical observation. If one already has power, one can choose to use it or conserve it, to consume only the interest from one's stock of power, or to eat into the principal also. Love of power for its own sake may thus deter bureaucrats and others from eating into this principal, with the result that substantive policy preferences are tailored to "higher authority," perhaps happily for the electorate at large, but perhaps not.

Albert Hirschman makes a convincing case that economists will tend to exaggerate the power of leaving or ceasing to deal with an organization ("exit") and underrate the power of working within it ("voice"). Political scientists and sociologists conversely underrate the power of the "exit" mechanism. However powerful "voice" may be, it has seemingly been repeatedly overestimated by government officials who stay at their posts when they disagree with policy. Either we have widespread error on the part of government officials in evaluating their own options for influencing public policy, or these officials are quite astutely choosing the personal returns of staying in a *position of power.*

Perhaps it is thus the *sense of power* that bureaucrats are more consistently pursuing. To have tremendous impact, but all in the course of a single day, would thus be less satisfying then to have less aggregate impact, but spread out on a day-by-day series of digestible and perceivable doses. The *sensation* that one is having impact will thus be spread out over time, and the bureaucrat stays at his post, rationalizing to himself that he could not have had more net influence anyway by dramatically resigning.

The sense of power leads to a slightly modified goal which may in the end account for even more of political behavior as we know it, and in the process dignify the politician as the truest of "political scientists." The goal that explains party platforms, bureaucratic plans, advice given to the president in an international crisis, and so on, may simply be *priviness*, the sense of knowing in full detail what actually explained a government decision, even if one's control or impact over that decision was not great. To read an account of a policy decision in the *New York Times* the following morning, and to note where the *Times* has the story wrong, must be one of life's great pleasures, a pleasure which can explain much of the behavior of the people involved.

In effect, this argument is that the behavior of participants in President Kennedy's ExCom during the Cuban missile crisis was primarily and importantly determined by a desire to be "invited again," to be in on any similar sessions in the future. Being invited again, being made privy in the future, may of course require that one makes himself useful this time, but it may also require that one not defend too strongly whatever substantive points he believes in, that he not seem tiresome or disloyal to the President, and so on. The lust for priviness may thus explain the rush to be in on governmental decisions big and small, whether to escalate the war in Vietnam, whether to make Tioga Street in Ithaca one-way northbound or southbound. What is crucial is that the press always gets some part of the story wrong, so that only by being in the decisions-process can one have a full sense of how it went. Some of us call ourselves political scientists and are fascinated and content to watch government from a distance. Others, those with real curiosity, drive in to get a closer look.

If we thus concluded that all policy-makers were attracted to the process by the sensation of power, we might thus reach the depressing conclusion that the same kinds of people show up in government regardless of country, in the United States and in Communist China, in Stalin's Russia and in the Fourth Republic of France, in Great Britain and in Nazi Germany. Yet the similarity of motivational form could obscure important differences in substantive form the "power issues" of a country can take. One can enjoy allocating foreign aid in the United States, and at the same time not enjoy listing persons to be purged in Russia, or vice versa. In the case of economics, it may be true that all entrepreneurs can be usefully assumed, on the first approximation, to be seeking to maximize monetary profit. If this is true of the watchmaker as well as the wheat farmer, however, it hardly follows that the watchmaker and wheat farmer could enjoy each other's professions, or easily switch. Similarly, the kinds of things a government typically has to decide and do considerably affects which citizens will seek the enjoyment of making these decisions.

Some political systems, moreover, expect people to wait in orderly lines for the achievement of high authority, while others tolerate a very disorderly scramble of power at the end. Personality types attracted to one style will be repulsed by the other. The parliamentary systems of Britain and Canada more typically produce the former effect, while the presidential nominating conventions of the United States suggest the latter.

Some political systems will attract those amenable to violence, while others will be totally removed from even the threat of violence. It is unfortunately still true that one can not be in the upper echelons of the political leadership of the USSR without having graduated from the purge atmosphere of the 1930's, when staying alive could easily have required acquiescing in someone else's loss of life. The Chinese party leadership, by contrast, was relatively free of this experience, with fewer purges and less severe penalties normally imposed on those purged from party leadership or membership.

Japanese politics in the 1930's selected out participants who were prepared to run the risk of violence, since assassination was a threat to cabinet after cabinet. The United States, by contrast, until recently has not been burdened by this kind of adventurism in political careers; it would be unfortunate if the change in the tools used in political contests now drastically changed the personality types attracted to the quest for public office.

There are political systems, moreover, which encourage and attract moral purism or "extremism," while others discourage this and reward rather those parties which succeed in merging with the consensus. Much of this can be traced to election laws, as some kinds of laws encourage two-party electoral choice systems, while others encourage multiparty systems, perhaps by giving legislative seats to parties even when they never collect a majority vote in any particular district. For all persons interested in public office, a relevant question will be thus whether one gets ahead by standing firm on principle, or by attempting to duplicate the feelings and stands of a consensus of the majority. Young persons may thus be warped toward one style or another on moral questions. Different kinds of people may also be recruited in the first place to run the electoral races. Society may gain something if citizens are encouraged to defend their principles, but this can also produce a far greater degree of conflict and polarization in society.

Political systems can screen out personalities on another dimension— their aversion to, or fondness for, uncertainty and gambling. Unstable parliamentary systems, such as Fourth Republic France and Weimar Germany, may bring to the fore the gambler who enjoys upsetting coalitions and provoking votes of no-confidence, on the bet that this will result in a promotion for him and his party in the next cabinet to be assembled after a period of crisis. By contrast, we might consider the calm and stability that pertains in the assignment of committee chairmanships in the U.S. Senate. The man who would find a career in one parliament attractive might clearly dislike the other. Yet in either case, some significant impact on foreign policy might result from the personalities recruited to it.

One must also speculate on the role of inheritance in motivating government officials to do their duty. Unlike private business corporations which can be willed to sons and daughters, a successful government operation does not remain the property of the individual who built it up. We all tend to disapprove of class structure, nepotism, links of personal friendship, in the execution of duty on anything as public as foreign policy. To appoint a college roommate as an ambassador seems far less than optimal performance of duty by a president or secretary of state. Yet it is natural for parents to wish to take care of their children, or for friends to wish to help friends. If we wish public officials to perform well, we may have to tacitly allow an accommodation of some of these private goals. Yet the manner in which public officials thus "bequeath" their "firms" obviously affects who will be admitted and recruited to policy-making positions in the future. Different societies tolerate nepotism in different ways, with differing results for the kinds of personality which appear in office.

Political power can indeed be transmitted by monetary wealth, if individuals leave the government to accumulate private fortunes as lawyers or businessmen, and then endow their children with enough financial independence to let them become significant public figures. The Kennedy family is an obvious example of this. A society which precludes the passing of fortunes by inheritance, or which limits the abilities of wealthy "in-and-outers" to enter and leave the public service, makes this considerably less possible.

One can transmit political power to one's children instead by training, something which even the most confiscatory inheritance taxes can not preclude. Astute Russian foreign ministry officials see to it that their children learn foreign languages, since to be fluent in English, German, Arabic, or Chinese guarantees a more interesting and materially rewarding career. The use of standardized literary examinations always favors the children of those who have already passed them and this is true of candidates for the U.S. foreign service as well as of the Chinese who wished to be Mandarins. If political power is importantly transmitted by the specialized kinds of knowledge that parents can inevitably but "unfairly" channel to their children, it can condition the making of policy also, perhaps bringing out the formalistic and cautious, stressing standard operating procedure and professional competence ahead of innovation or the blending of different disciplines.

Political power can also be passed from parent to child simply by ascription, by a class system in which heredity is assumed to reflect genetic superiorities to which all of society must accord recognition. It is a fair criticism that the British Foreign Office has not recruited personnel independent of class considerations; this is so even when the educational system of Britain sees to it that more "objective" parameters can be cited on crucial decisions than simply the parentage of the candidate for a post. Such a system obviously can miss a large portion of the talented persons in a country, and can also leave those endowed with office too secure to be motivated to work at highest capacity.

Finally, political power can be transmitted by bureaucratic direction, such that sons are promoted within a bureaucracy at the direct behest of their fathers, or indirectly through the intervention of friends of their fathers, and so on. Such a pattern of recruitment appears to apply in the military forces of many countries, including those of the United States and Soviet Union. At various stages of its history, the U.S. Navy in particular has been accused of favoring sons of officers in terms of entry through Annapolis. Some of the statistics in all such cases can be explained by special advantages vis-a-vis the examination system, as noted above, but some part is indeed simply due to what is known as "pull."

Practices on inheritance of political influence thus effect how jobholders perform their tasks. Ins-and-outers will advocate "fresh ideas" for their own sake, while those wedded to the examination system will stress professional competence. In Communist countries, parallel debates will rage on whether national policy and foreign policy should be made by those who are "Red" or those who are "expert." The inheritance question also determines who will be making policy in the next round. Even if the sense of power attracts most of those who wish to hold political office, different kinds of personalities can be attracted to "power," and will handle it in turn in different ways.

FURTHER READINGS

Halperin, Morton. "Games Bureaucrats Play." *Foreign Policy*. Spring, 1971.
Neustadt, Richard E. *Presidential Power*. New York: John Wiley, 1960.

Decisions With Limited Information

Returning to the distinctions spelled out earlier, there is also much to be said for "organizational process" as the explanation of policy, regardless of whether individuals pursue power or substance when they are behaving at all deliberately. Organizational process can be interpreted in various ways, but it may simply refer to the inevitable shortages of information that will occur in any organization as large as those entrusted with foreign policy. How to adjust to such shortages, however, will be subject to much disagreement.

Apart from the debates noted earlier on "idealism" versus "realism," or between "isolation" and "foreign policy," another "great debate" on American foreign policy has thus emerged, confronting "incremental" or pragmatic policy approaches with "long-term analytical overview." The incremental position "plays it by ear," moving from one ad hoc solution to another, assuming that perfect analysis in advance is impossible in any event, or at least so difficult that it would hardly be cost-effective to expend much time and effort on it. The analytical view instead stresses the totality of long-range as well as short-range results, hoping that with more careful study no major foreign policy alternatives can be missed, no opportunities overlooked.

The incremental position must itself be sorted into several variations, which are not always consistent with one another. Such variations might be illustrated by a hypothetical problem of moving an army to the top of a mountain. One version of "incrementalism" would simply suggest that a good working rule is "always move uphill." Even in the densest fog, one will sense which direction leads upward, and upward movement will assuredly lead one toward a peak. The "analytic" critique of this approach would note that an overall look at a map can often suggest a shorter and more direct route, or one with more manageable grades. There will even be times when surveying the landscape can spare us climbing the wrong, lesser peaks in regions where the ground rises to several summits. The incrementalist would counter that this is all well and good when accurate maps are available, or when the air is clear. When maps are lacking, and the climb has to penetrate thick brush and dense cloud, however, the incremental rule may still be the best.

A very different approach, which often carries the "incremental" title, is "Everyone meet at the top." Here overall analysis has not been foregone as much as overall coordination. It will sometimes work quite well to leave each individual component of our governmental unit to make its own decisions. Yet if there is a hostile army to be confronted at the summit of this mountain, it will hardly do for our forces to arrive one man at a time. There will even be a risk of us shooting at each other in the dark and fog.

In reality, all decision-making in government must be at least a little fragmented and "incremental" in this sense, although the extent of this fragmentation must vary from one institutional arrangement to another. The "independent actor" image may fairly describe many aspects of American domestic policy, in fact more so than U.S. foreign policy, where the President is legally Commander-in-Chief and relatively unchallenged. Foreign policy in Britain has perhaps shown more signs of divided authority, where the Prime Minister, the Colonial Office and the Home Office, as well as the ministries related to armed forces, each have had some independent legitimacy.

A third notion of incrementalism takes yet another form, embodying an assumption that all commentators on a problem will have some wisdom to offer, that each will have a little bit of right on his side. The recommended solution for scaling the mountain in this case would perhaps be to "appoint a committee," a committee which somehow would coordinate a compromise on a route. The route in the end might be far less than ideal, however, simply because the process seemed to stress compromise instead of accuracy or objective value. Also, the style encouraged in such sessions might place the nation's representatives at a severe disadvantage when confronted in negotiations by a less compromise-prone country.

In response to all such pragmatic or incremental approaches to foreign policy, the partisans of the "analytic overview" commend to us various attributes which we all might be quick to praise. One such desirable quality might be labeled as "courage," defined here as the ability to suppress momentary adverse considerations in seeking the longer-term good. All of us are perhaps overly frightened by short-term costs and dangers. Perhaps it is only reasonable, therefore, to train ourselves to ignore the immediate future, and thus to compensate for such tendencies toward miscalculation. At the extreme, courage might go beyond such marginal compensation, producing drastic emphasis on the future as balanced against present risk, an emphasis that perhaps might lead individuals to take great risks in quest of very uncertain gain. Some of the courage of the military hero who survives to wear his medals might seem foolhardy to the prime minister, but it may also not be totally out of place.

We often allude to "leadership," which again confronts the incremental positions, if we define leadership as the ability to demonstrate the longer-term to others who have not already seen it. One must not only be far-sighted to be a leader in this sense, but also able to communicate and convince on the priorities one has adopted. A third desirable quality might be "initiative," again if defined as a capability for innovation in defiance of the simple incremental inertia and standard operating procedures which grip most governmental structures.

The incrementalist would have defended momentum; "You won't go far wrong if you keep on with what you've been doing." Yet the world may indeed produce some disaster in foreign policy for those who do not adopt drastic changes of course from time to time to head them off.

The arguments for courage, leadership, and initiative, and for long-term overall vision can be tellingly presented; yet the partisans of the sloppier, ad hoc approaches are not left without any counters of their own. Not all of international affairs will lend itself to the broad view, to prediction and to theory. If theory is indeed impossible in some cases, it can be dangerous if it instills false confidence or false doctrinairity. Critics of the war in Vietnam, for example, might find targets in either decision-making camp. Some of American participation in the war can indeed be seen as the "more-of-the-same" approach which seemed the height of pragmatism. Other aspects of the American commitment might be causally traced to excessively elaborate theories on the nature of guerilla warfare, which seemed to compare the Viet Cong to insurrectionaries everywhere, possibly ignoring local differences which might have made Vietnam seem less than a "domino."

It may thus be dangerous to conclude that sound policy must always be based on careful and conscious predictions of the future; this could drive us to adopt prematurely firm estimates about future possibilities which should have been taken to be random. We sometimes, therefore, see predictions shaped by the decisions which are supposed to depend on them, more than by any objective data. Meteorologists typically forswear making predictions more than 30 days ahead, but some military contingency plans have been written depending on considerably longer-range forecasts. In such cases, artificially exact weather predictions were only being offered because an institutionalized structure had come to demand it. Incrementalists charge that this is a problem beyond meteorology.

It may thus be natural and inevitable that "the left hand does not know what the right hand is doing," so that policy results as much from ignorance and imperfect information as anything else. There is correct or incorrect information implicit in many practices of any organization, information which may need implicit acceptance because it cannot be contradicted by any hard data, or because the routine of the conjecture-formation process is never clearly or explicitly confronted. Whatever the nature of efforts to scan the entire horizon for "all possible alternatives," it is close to impossible for any responsible public official to achieve this kind of synoptic comprehension of foreign policy. If some questions are thus declared to be more important than others, the impact is to bias all the answers.

If standard operating procedures thus bias us toward accepting the premises of the status quo, even the most tangible evidence contradicting such biases may not win acceptance. The most pessimistic version of this caution would be that no impact is possible even in very successful intelligence coups, since the government receiving such data will not be able to use it. One could note, for example, Stalin's failure to prepare for the invasion by Hitler's forces, despite warnings from British intelligence and the inside information from his own intelligence network as garnered by Victor Sorge in Tokyo.

American policy before Pearl Harbor would seem similarly unresponsive to warnings. Despite the fact that retrospective readings of the evidence make it seem very clear that the Japanese would attack the bases in Hawaii, Roberta Wohlstetter's analysis shows how the presumptions of intelligence analysts in 1941 precluded them from seeing what the decoded Japanese messages suggested. As the Soviet Union was deploying medium-range missiles to Cuba in 1962, various kinds of intelligence might have seemed to expose what was happening, but it was not noticed until the deployment was well along.

Yet such an assessment of the exploitation of clear data about enemy intentions would be entirely too pessimistic. The breaking of Japanese codes, for example, had been accomplished as early as the Washington Naval Conference, when the American delegation had advance information of concessions the Japanese would be prepared to make. In cases as concrete as this, American foreign policy-makers had no difficulty in adjusting their assumptions and predictions. The paramountcy of inertia and the implicit premises of the status quo of policy are a serious problem for any decision-making body, but not always an insuperable problem.

FURTHER READINGS

Kissinger, Henry A. "The Policy Maker and The Intellectual." *The Reporter.* March 5, 1959.
Lindblom, Charles E. "The Science of Muddling Through." *Public Administration Review.* PS–169 (1959): 79–88.
Wohlstetter, Roberta. *Pearl Harbor: Warning or Decision.* Stanford, Cal.: Stanford University Press, 1962.

"Great Men" and "Insubordinate Bureaucracies"

To get at the heart of how policy decisions are actually made, one school of analysis stresses the identification of the particular human beings who are the decision-makers, those people whose judgment and preferences causally determine foreign policy as it emerges. Presumably this will reduce substantially the number of people we have to consider in analyzing the policies of any particular country, and would help us guard against any false reification in talking about countries as if they were people. Instead of talking about "Germany desired, wanted, attacked," we would thus rather discuss "Bismarck," or "Hitler."

Before accepting the premises of this approach, one might have to ask how possible the technique will be. After the total defeat of some country, we may have access to its archives and to the minutes of its strategy sessions; captured leaders may help us with their memoires and testimony. Yet before the defeat of a country like Nazi Germany, it would have been far more difficult to determine the distinct attitudes or preferences of leaders like Goebbels, Ribbentrop, or Hitler. Contemporaneously, it is hardly easy to determine the real conflicts of interest among Soviet leaders and functionaries. It is, moreover, difficult to tell who has the most influence on decisions as they emerge, even if we can tell who would have preferred to go in one direction or the other.

Second, one may be skeptical on the need for the "decision-maker's focus" in the analysis of foreign policy. For many practical purposes, we can predict the aggregate policy outcome with greater accuracy than the leanings of the particular components. If Israeli foreign policy decisions were settled by cabinet vote, one might correctly guess that a certain measure will win the support of more than half, without necessarily being so correct on who was in that majority. A phrase such as "Israel will wish to negotiate" is thus quite accurate and meaningful even if there is no individual holding that name. The sentence merely indicates that whoever is necessary to approve negotiations on behalf of Israel will do so.

Focusing on particular decision-makers may, moreover, exaggerate the capabilities of specific individuals, or the stability of their hold on power from issue to issue, or even from moment to moment on the same issue. In the Cuban missile crisis, for example, who can really be said to have "made the decisions," as proposals were formulated and reformulated with the participation of so many people? This indeed broaches a more general question on the role of heroes or genius in history, in particular in the history of international relations. We do pay particular respect and attention to Metternich and Bismarck, to Churchill in World War II, and to Monnet in the moves toward European unification. Doesn't the salience of such men lend support to the "decision-making" approach, once again urging us to forget the morass of interacting bureaucrats and bureaucracy, and instead to single out the particular individuals whose impact has mattered?

History as we read and remember it may mislead us here, however. History is biased toward seeking out the remarkable and memorable, the great as opposed to the ordinary. History indeed tends to seek the more anthropomorphic representations of countries as they have acted, Frederick the Great instead of Prussia, Napoleon instead of France. If history is so biased, it does not prove that Napoleon or Frederick were any less powerful or significant than we normally assume. It does suggest that episodes such as that of Napoleon are less typical and more unusual then we tend to suppose. Much of foreign policy and history is more humdrum and routine than Napoleon's exploits, and the decision-making involved is far more collective and diffuse.

Great men thus come along from time to time, to enliven the international arena we are studying. If great men are more exciting and interesting, however, this does not mean they are necessarily to be admired. By and large, we see "greatness" in men who accomplish "triumphs of the will," who get much of the world to move as they would have it move; alternatively, we refer to men who have made their own talents indispensible to the wills and desires of much of the rest of the world.

When the first condition holds true, then a reckoning is likely to come when our hero passes from the scene and the outside world regains the power to determine its own destiny. If Metternich is impressive for having slowed progress toward liberalism in Europe for some 20 years, because he wanted to, he also is to be held accountable for the violence by which his influence was undone in the end, in 1848 and after.

Where the second condition holds true, the indispensible public servant also creates serious problems for the time when he will pass from power. To be very effective is to discourage replacements, since one only trains people in "decision-making" power by sharing some of it with them. Bismarck is our best example of a man who for many years manipulated Europe to his own interest, but also to Europe's collective advantage. The system he created was not able to function with similarly peaceful results after he left office, however, in part because it was too complicated and tailored to his own personal style, in part because he had not really trained competent apprentices.

"Theories of history" often turn out to be theories of the "political development of international relations," since their scale has to be so macroscopic in terms of geography as well as time. Such theories generally have difficulty in taking "great men" into account. Whether a theory of history is Marxist or non-Marxist, it will have to adjust any determinism to explaining the personal impacts of Lenin, Stalin, and Mao, as well as the apparent influence of Hitler and Bismarck and Napoleon. If such men could so easily have been assassinated or lost to the world in childhood illness, how can we argue that the events in which they were involved were preordained by any higher laws of history?

Deterministic theories have taken various approaches to the supposed importance of the individual. One approach might simply be to question the factual imputations involved, to deny that any individual was as causally significant as the records seemed to suggest. Was Hindenburg or Ludendorff really as crucial to the defeat of the Russians at Tannenberg as German personal propagandists later claimed? The answer is no, since staff officers really accomplished much of the successful military operation for which they later were denied the credit. So it might be with most great battles, as the contribution of the field marshals is always overrated in the "fog of war." So it must be on other questions of foreign policy or national policy.

A second approach would concede that certain individuals indeed played the key roles that history assigned them, but would respond that this is in no way inconsistent with the possibility of an overall determinism. If the class struggle determined that there would be a battle, it can just as easily have determined that Trotsky would be leading one army, and that ordinary proletarians would be on the barricades under his command. A modified version of this approach would concede that sheer accident could have kept Trotsky from becoming the general, but the class struggle would then have dictated that someone else take his place, to make almost the same choices. If Harry S. Truman was not preordained to be President of the United States, in this view, he was nonetheless preordained to rise to the challenge of the job once he had it, and so he did.

A belief in grander laws of history therefore does not force us to reject the possibility of heroic personal exploits by key "decision-makers" in the system. Yet there may still be something to be said for debunking the power and impact of the individuals whom history and the press condemn to excessive publicity. In Harry Truman's own words, orders are often given with little or no impact on the rest of the government, as the President may have far less power on a particular issue than the desk officer of the State Department who is charged with applying national policy in detail.

Power inevitably must be shared, because of the limits on a single person's attention span, because most governments and countries impose formal or informal checks and balances on their leaders. Even if a constitution should specifically assign the making of policy to higher ranking officials, the delegation of authority for interpretation and implementation inevitably brings a delegation of some policy-making authority with it. The constitution may allow the chief executive or head of government to appoint his subordinates and to remove them at will. Yet any leader who tries to use his removal power in more than a small percentage of cases will soon be seen as a very poor judge of men; "Why did he appoint all these people in the first place if he now must remove them all?"

Any veteran of governmental bureaucracy can indeed recount numerous examples of policy formulated from below, against the inclinations and intentions of the national leader. The instance might be as seemingly trivial as the quiet insertion of a phrase into the text of a presidential address, so that it can later be cited by its actual composer as authority to move ahead with some program. It might be as profound as the failure of an army to carry out legal orders.

Since military power in many ways provides the very essence of sovereignty or state power, subordination of the military might be the prior question relevant to each and every area of politics. The military bureaucracy can use all the normal ploys of constricting choices for its superior; in extremes, however, it can also overthrow its superiors by force, or at least alter policy by the threats of such coups. We are all too familiar with the recurrent military coups of Latin America, and now of the independent African countries. Yet it is easy to assume that some other countries are almost immune to such activity, for example, the "western democracies," and perhaps even the "Communist countries;" this assumption may also be incorrect.

Even in countries of great internal cohesion, virtual insubordination by the military high command has occurred: in Britain in 1914 (with regard to the Ulster separatism in Ireland, just prior to the outbreak of World War I), and in Switzerland in 1941 (with regard to demands from Nazi Germany about which the army felt the Swiss government was being too accommodating).

At the extreme, the army not only coerces or replaces the legal government, but assumes control over the country itself. At times, this assumption of control may almost seem beneficient, if it brings to bear a functional bureaucracy where no other was available. There are countries where only the army can issue an order in the capital and have it carried out throughout the country. Yet if the armed forces are typically effective at "output" functions, the execution of orders, they are notoriously bad at "input" functions, the assessment of public opinion to determine which needs are felt to be most urgent. Military government has thus almost universally seemed the most temporary and ad hoc of solutions for a nation's problems.

It has been suggested that the problem of military insubordination will hang over every country that has neighbors, indeed, over any country that must participate, however unwillingly, in the game we call international politics. If the insubordination is nothing more than the bureaucratic sluggishness we observe also in civilian sectors, perhaps there is nothing very pathological here. We might even be ambivalent on whether we really prefer central power to "shared authority" and "checks and balances." If the German army had only been a little more insubordinate to the "civilian" Hitler, for example, we might all have gained. Because the military carries weapons, however, we will perhaps find obnoxious even that level of sluggishness in obedience that we would welcome in the State Department or Department of the Interior. Clearly the most central of our fears pertain to the risk of an actual military insurrection or coup, in which the threat of violence and civil war is used to overrule all legal authority.

One approach to guarding against this would thus be total disarmament, with whatever risks of conquest by a foreign power. Another approach goes to the opposite extreme with universal military training, perhaps running the risk of totally "militarizing" society, but also bringing the hope of "socializing" the military. If everyone is a soldier for most of his adult life, the argument goes, there is far less chance of a confrontation of interests between army and society, between army and legal government. Interesting examples of universal military training emerge in Sweden, Switzerland, and Israel, all countries in which democratic rule has rarely been threatened. It may be that the particular cultural patterns in these countries more directly explain the rarity of threats of armed coups, so that universal military training would not work in the same way in other countries. Universal military training, moreover, has military value only for some very special circumstances of international posture. It might indeed be prohibitively wasteful of resources in a country like the United States.

FURTHER READINGS

Clark, Keith C., and Legere, Laurence J. *The President and the Management of National Security.* New York: Praeger, 1969.
Hilsman, Roger. *The Politics of Policy Making in Defense and Foreign Affairs.* New York: Harper and Row, 1971.

Public Opinion

Much has been said, and hoped for, on the role of public opinion in influencing the course of international affairs. Most people in the world will want peace; it follows that if their opinion is given a medium of expression (such as the United Nations) this may be conducive to peace.

Yet skeptics will be quick to call our attention to vast discrepancies between elite and mass opinion, and the latter's general lack of policy impact in most cases. The great majority of citizens of India, for example, do not follow international events with any diligence at all. If most are still illiterate, how much can be communicated verbally? It is thus very unusual for a foreign policy issue to become salient in an Indian election campaign. Local issues will predominate, and the Congress party will not directly win or lose office on the events of the international arena.

India may thus illustrate one of the greatest tensions between a higher degree of popular participation in elections, and a low quantity of knowledge about the outside world. Americans are hardly exempt from citicism on similar counts. Public opinion polls for a time showed that only some 40 percent of Americans in 1965 knew that there were still "two Chinas," two governments claiming authority over all of that great country, posing one of the most enduring and serious issues for American policy in Asia.

Among more well informed citizens, there is even still a need to distinguish between the general elite and the elite oriented to foreign policy. Most educated Americans, indeed the majority of American political scientists, have, for example, not yet become aware of India's ability to produce nuclear weapons any time it chooses to do so. It is sad but true that an Indian detonation of a bomb would probably be required to capture the attention of even this elite.

To the extent that there is a public opinion on world affairs, it has some peculiar and unreliable characteristics, moreover; at points it may even be indeterminate. Opinion polls on domestic as well as foreign affairs often have illustrated a "bandwagon" phenomenon, by which voters seemingly make their choice by how they assume the majority of other voters are making their choice. This might occur because we all have a secret craving for consensus or agreement, or because we credit the majority of our neighbors with greater insight into the substantive issues involved. Yet if many or most voters are susceptible to this influence, the consensus can swing wildly from side to side without any changes in the real foreign policy problem to explain such swings.

The opposite impact also appears from time to time, a "snob appeal" by which some voters just as directly seem to make choices so as to disagree or spite the assumed majority. This may also encompass a "sympathy for the underdog," whereby voters do not like to see any candidate win by too big a margin, lest excessive popularity go to his head.

A dominant characteristic of many voters is thus concern for what all other voters feel and desire on the issues of national and foreign policy. Yet voters typically are far from perfectly informed about what their compatriots are thinking. A form of pluralistic ignorance thus emerges here which may find individuals supporting a policy on the assumption that everyone else wants it, when indeed everyone is privately dissatisfied with it. Some political systems are almost designed to foster such ignorance. The two-party system, for example, typically makes it hard for persons on the extreme right or left to tell how many sympathizers they have. If such information were available, the ranks that could be recruited would seem much larger, and persons of extreme philosophy would be encouraged to stick with their principles rather than compromising with the "mainstream."

Aside from pursuing consensus, the public whose "opinion" we are considering typically tends to be pro-status quo in its orientation. When fighting a war, it approves of the government sticking with it. After that government has nonetheless negotiated a truce, the public shifts to endorse this heartily. One might conclude that hypothetical alternatives thus often do not receive the opinion support they might draw once implemented. Public opinion also tends to rally to the administration in office in a crisis, perhaps because bad fortune draws the nation together against outside threat, perhaps because a crisis seems a bad time even to consider changing the government which is in charge of events.

Perhaps the most skeptical inference one could draw from these insubstantial aspects of public opinion is that governments can do almost as they wish on foreign policy, since the public is so inarticulate in its preferences, so undemanding about particular policy. Lyndon Johnson could have terminated the war in Vietnam in 1965 instead of enlarging it as he did, and would have found a public tolerance for such disengagement that no opinion poll would have predicted. Perhaps this is demonstrated by Eisenhower's termination of the Korean War in 1953, or by President Nixon's Vietnamization of the Vietnam war since 1968. Yet the public's aversion to the monetary costs and human casualties of the Vietnam War between 1965 and 1968 suggests that there are still some limits to the public's vacuity about foreign policy, or its tolerance of policy as it is, whatever it is. If the domestic costs of an unsuccessful foreign policy become as apparent as they typically become in war time, "public opinion" may indeed impose restraints on such policy.

If a public opinion does not really exist on a particular foreign policy issue, moreover, opinion of some sort may still play a role. We may capture the bulk of our electoral backing on local or domestic issues, but we can not capture this unless we have the loyalty of party cadres, financial backers, and local campaign workers. If the masses, as in India, do not care so much about questions of nuclear weapons policy, the elite of the party workers and backers may indeed have an "opinion," which is not as fluid or malleable as suggested above. Elite opinions are important for foreign policy in India precisely because India has real electoral democracy, and one can *indirectly* lose an election on foreign policy issues. Similar linkages might be found in the United States, as the percentage that cares enough to know of "two Chinas" also can lead the remaining population into attitudes of satisfaction or dissatisfaction with policy.

When mass opinion is itself aroused, it of course merits more direct attention in an electoral democracy, as in the case of American policy in Southeast Asia. Yet even less democratic or "totalitarian" regimes will encounter limits on their ability to disregard public opinion on policy. At the extreme of what we remember as totalitarian we find Stalin's USSR, with concern for individual or mass opinion hardly being evident in the policy outcomes of the system. Yet the "deStalinization" of the USSR after the dictator's death was in large part due to the tensions and costs imposed by such autocratic rule. Stalin's successors realized that a totally unresponsive system could not hope to extract enough creative individual effort to make the USSR a full competitor of the Western powers in the international arena. In the Russian case, it may be that elite opinion was thus the hardest to ignore, since expert scientists could more easily withhold their best efforts from the state if the state affronted their opinion too much. Liberalization for the masses might thus have been the by-product of liberalization for the elites, but it occurred nonetheless.

Even in Nazi Germany, Goebbels' propaganda organization had to devote considerable effort to monitoring the opinion of the German public, rather than simply telling it what to believe. One can not use normal polling techniques in a totalitarian regime, since persons would, of course, be afraid to report their true feelings for fear of punishment. Yet Goebbels applied sound statistical methods, indeed learned from American opinion-gathering services, in stationing listeners on trolley cars to overhear the current grumblings of riders, to collect the opinion thus sampled rather than to arrest the dissidents.

Every regime must in the end thus be a little responsive to its public; but all regimes, no matter how democratically elected, can also get away with ignoring public opinion for extended periods of time. "History is the judge," and success can be rewarded in the end even when the public would have vetoed one's decisions through the period when victory was not yet assured. Winston Churchill certainly enjoyed enormous popular support during the most trying years of World War II, but anyone bent on openly advocating a negotiated peace in those years would have risked imprisonment for the duration. Elections were postponed for administrative reasons with the consent of all parties, but if they had been held, no pro-peace party would have been allowed to campaign or run.

In retrospect, we reward success, and punish failure, even if success or failure might have been determined by objective situations beyond the control of any particular office-holder. We tend to credit those officials who bring us good or bad news with indeed being responsible for the news. The temptation will thus be great for a leader to prosecute a war in which he has become entangled, for fear of otherwise not being able to redeem the costs already invested. Public opinion can thus certainly effect policy, but in ways which neither the public nor the government would have desired.

Democratic as well as nondemocratic states have an additional choice, beyond submitting to public opinion and ignoring it, for they can try to change it. For example, one can attempt to intimidate potential critics by the threat of midnight arrests or of destruction of printing presses. In a politically democratic country, such leverage may have to be administered instead via threats of political ostracism, exploiting the above-cited band-wagon effect. A clear example of mass pressures toward conformity, as exploited by a government, emerged during the First World War in the United States; a newspaper editor who questioned American involvement would not have had to fear arrest by the authorities, but would have been subjected to a great host of indignities encouraged by the governmental authorities.

Turning to positive levers over public opinion, one can bribe opinion-makers to take a favorable attitude towards the government and its policies. As in Germany and France before World War I, it can even be in the form of a direct monetary subsidy. More subtly today, it can be offered in the form of inside news stories and special access to political figures, perhaps to the president himself, who generate the most interesting news copy. Within the academic world, the prospect of being consulted by the government (with or without pay) on the making of policy might similarly have been a subtle encouragement for academics to endorse government policy as it was.

A state can manipulate, or at least contain the influence of, public opinion by making full use of the poll data that is now regularly collected. In countries where elections are scheduled on an ad hoc basis, such as in Britain, poll data may tell the incumbent government when the time will be ripe for it to be reelected with a handsome majority (although the defeat of the Labour government in 1970 on the basis of inaccurate poll predictions suggests caution here).

Effective polling can also tell any government, as well as candidates for the opposition, the best time to release various kinds of news. Perhaps a bit of unpleasantness can be forgotten quickly if released in a certain proximity to other news of a less negative nature. Perhaps good news should be released at a certain interval of time before any election, not too late, but not too early either. People do not only have opinions, but also intensities of opinion. A majority of Americans may not favor Israel, but may not have very strong opinions one way or the other on the Middle East. The minority that strongly supports Israel, on the other hand, allocates its support with an intensity far above average. A government will in general wish to know who it can appease most easily, and conversely, who is most dissatisfied.

Policy proposals can be broken to the public gently, through equivocal statements or "trial balloons" by which the government broaches the possibility of a new policy, but does not commit itself when the policy's acceptability is still unclear. Startling foreign events may, as suggested earlier, terminate dissidence and debate at home, if the country as a whole now seems threatened by a foreign antagonist who has exceeded all reasonable limits. If many Americans thought that Roosevelt's policy was too provocative vis-a-vis Japan and Germany in 1941, few felt this way after Pearl Harbor. Even if some might have felt retrospectively that American policy had baited the Japanese into attacking, history made such retrospection seem irrelevant, as the war now could allow little dissent on policy. The magnitude of the North Korean success in the first weeks of the Korean War similarly ruled out speculation on whether this really amounted to foreign aggression for which an American response would be appropriate. Nothing similar has happened in the Vietnamese conflict, with the result that public opinion has been generally freer to examine American policy from a critical standpoint.

One may finally speculate on whether the ability of states to ignore their "public opinions" is increasing or decreasing. A few tendencies toward greater influence by the public might be noted. Foreign policy is more expensive today than in the past, given the higher costs of weapons systems and the greater volumes of economic assistance now delivered by all the great powers in competition with one another. Where monetary appropriations have always merited close scrutiny by the legislature of a country, as in the United States, this would seem to give the public and its representatives considerably more influence and control over foreign policy.

The same technological complexity that requires missiles and technical assistance for underdeveloped countries also requires that powers draw on the specialized talents of all their citizens. The kinds of terror regimes which might have sufficed in more primitive economies will thus be ineffective where missile guidance systems and new strains of wheat are concerned; regimes such as that of Stalin are therefore less likely to recur in any nation aspiring to play a full role in international power politics.

Yet there are many contrary pieces of evidence to suggest that public opinion may be growing weaker in its controls over foreign policy. As noted above, states today have far better techniques at their disposal for identifying public opinion, and heading off dissidence before it can grow to any critical level of effective resistance. If the secret police can not be openly brutal in extracting performance from individuals and the masses, it has more imaginative technology at its disposal today for collecting information and neutralizing opposition. As life is becoming ever richer in consumer goods, moreover, the state may be more able to buy itself a free hand on foreign policy, as the masses in effect accept a bribe for forgoing their opposition.

If we welcome an increase in the power of public opinion, we might thus be hard pressed to find ways of accomplishing this. A certain amount of research has been done on the techniques of civil disobedience, often by scholars with a personal moral aversion to all forms of violence. As demonstrated by the Indian independence movement's success against the British, techniques of this sort can enable a public opinion to impose serious pressures even on a force which has a monopoly on military power. Yet one must wonder whether similar techniques would be as effective against regimes which were not under a parliamentary control back home, whether they would have a chance of success against someone like Hitler or Stalin, or even a contemporary Communist regime. Would it not be all too easy for the totalitarian dictator to be quite unscrupulous in arresting and executing the leaders of such movements? In the case of a sit-down by a mob insisting that everyone be punished together, would it not be too simple for the regime to adopt a policy of arresting only those in the front ranks? Since no mob can be effective without a front rank, would this not upset the collective disobedience tactic? Even democratic regimes have had to consider the counter-tactics to be brought to bear when a large portion of the population *in some particular district* is intent on violating the laws and regulations of the central government. Civil disobedience may have been the Indian national tactic against British rule, but it is hardly a tactic that the Indian central government would tolerate against itself, if it threatened to dissolve the Indian Union.

In the United States after World War I, serious proposals were advanced that the Constitution be amended to require a national plebiscite on any declaration of War. Yet a consideration of international politics as we know it will show that the definition of "war" is a very difficult proposition. Indeed, the United States has not been actively engaged in any declared "wars" since 1945. If American soldiers must ride international airliners to protect them against one Palestinian Commando front or another, we surely would not desire a declaration of war to normalize this situation. Yet the increase in levels of violence could be very gradual, thereafter, so gradual that no clear and obvious point of discontinuity would emerge to suggest a legal distinction.

The question of plebiscites raises the more general issue of the impact of democracy on international relations. Do democracies tend to become involved in fewer wars? On the basis of what might seem to be a few "controlled experiments," we might conclude quite the opposite. As the

states of the Arab world have replaced feudal regimes with more representative and modern governments, they have in virtually every case become
more bellicose vis-a-vis Israel. Similarly between India and Pakistan, it
clearly seems that peace would be easier to achieve if the two governments
did not have to take as much account of their public opinions on the
Moslem-Hindu issue. If American isolationist congressmen in the 1930's
believed that a plebiscite system would have kept the United States out of
World War I, or out of world wars to come, this hardly seems to accord
with American public sentiment as it stood in 1917.

If citizens can not be counted upon to resist their government's foreign
adventures and foreign wars, perhaps we could turn to the poor soldier
who must bear the brunt of the costs by risking his life, in the time taken
away from his normal career and his family. Perhaps soldiers should be
allowed to vote on whether wars are worth fighting before such wars are
begun, and perhaps then there would be fewer of them. Yet the bandwagon
psychology is nowhere so strong as within any armed force, since the very
effectiveness of any army typically depends on cooperation and coordination and a sense of unity and togetherness. If doubts are expressed on the
rightness of a war while it is being fought, it will still probably be fought
well by the army entrusted with it, and expressions of doubt within the
armed forces will be deferred until hostilities have been terminated. The
U.S. Army thus fought resolutely in World War II, albeit the population
from which it was drawn prior to Pearl Harbor had severe doubts about
its merits. The U.S. Army has fought well in Vietnam. As in various "We
Want to Go Home" rallies in occupied Germany in 1946, discipline may
suffer after military operations have ceased, but one could hardly count on
the rank-and-file of an armed force to veto inappropriate wars while they
were in progress.

Related solutions might include an end to all involuntary military service,
so that governments must depend entirely on volunteers for any warlike
operations they wish to undertake. A modified form, sometimes adopted,
allows for compulsory military service, but provides that such draftees may
not be required to serve outside the national boundaries. It is possible that
such a system could limit a state's foreign adventures when public opinion
disapproved of the foreign policy being pursued. Yet enough volunteers
are typically available to man a nation's military force, for pay, or for the
military life. A totally volunteer force presumably would mean that the
military is dominated by those persons and groups who like military life
the best, who therefore are quite unrepresentative of the nation as a whole.
Their awareness that they have volunteered, when others have chosen not
to serve, can, moreover, cause an alienation between the military forces and
the rest of society, with an increase in the danger of a military coup
overturning the legal government. What was intended to be a check on the

state's foreign military operations could thus become a check on all of the civilian government by those who are delegated the task of performing such military operations.

Some generalizations can be offered on the cultural developments which may be relevant to public opinion and its impact on international politics. If peace were at all furthered by any kinds of standardization on a single language and common cultural and material experience, a great deal of optimism might seem appropriate. In terms of language, for example, English is rapidly approaching an unchallenged position as the lingua franca of the world. Despite strenuous efforts emanating from Paris to win an equal or superior status for French as a world language, the trend, even in former French colonial possessions, is slowly but inexorably shifting toward the study of English. German still retains a vestigial hold on central and eastern Europe and the study of Russian in the Communist countries has been virtually compulsory for the last 25 years for any persons participating in politics and public life. Yet even in the "socialist camp," English is the foreign language studied after Russian, and Soviet dealings with countries such as Egypt or India are most typically channeled, ironically enough, into English. When having to choose between disseminating Marxist propaganda and spreading the Russian language, Soviet embassy information agencies abroad have repeatedly had to face a need for choice, thus dispensing English pamphlets for fear that no one would read the Russian.

Apart from such trends in language, the world also sees an increasing standardization in material consumer goods and brand-names, what one Russian analyst disparagingly described as the "Coca-colonization of the world." As most of the world comes to purchase its soft drinks from American companies, and its television sets from Japan, we might come to hope that such standardization will breed some mutual understanding and sympathy in the "opinions" that matter. Even in Moscow, automobiles will be purchased soon from Fiat, and rented from Hertz.

The same technology that seemingly standardizes much of opinion also seems to mobilize more individuals than ever before into what we would call "opinion." The per capita circulation of newspapers from country to country is growing slowly, while the distribution of radios is expanding rapidly, with television growing even more swiftly. In the near future, it will be technologically feasible for television programs to be transmitted directly to individual sets from satellites orbiting the earth, thus allowing states to "invade" each other's airspace in this most effective of mediums.

For the moment, most states have a monopoly of access to their own television audiences. The medium seems so powerful an influence that it would be very daring to allow political programming by another political entity to be seen; the basic technology of television transmissions restricts audiences to 50–70 miles of the transmitter, so that international propaganda of the short-wave radio bands as yet has no equivalent in the television spectrum. There are a few important exceptions. Viewers in East and West Germany can receive each other's television sendings, of course, and Israeli viewers have long been fans of American and other programs shown on Arab stations. Americans and Canadians along the borders can sample each other's programs, without any particularly obvious political opinion-making contest in progress, however.

It is already clear that the attractiveness of American entertainment products tends to dominate those national television-programming administrations that seek to please their viewers, very possibly with subtle and subliminal propaganda impacts supporting or upsetting the American government's appeal abroad. Such desires for entertainment thus presumably favor the countries with large and effective entertainment industries, with similar trends in the cinema. Just as with the move toward English as a standard language, there are great advantages to beginning with a large size, since the economies of scale that can thus be realized make for great efficiency.

There may be real doubt, however, about the propaganda impact of the kinds of cultural salience noted above. Implicit propaganda may be more effective than crude and explicit appeals, but it may also be far less manageable and predictable in its direction. If Hong Kong audiences love American detective movies, this may breed admiration, or rejection, of things American. Cambodian purchases of Coca-Cola may rise with an increasing aversion to the rest of American culture. English may be used as a language of communication among people very antagonistic to the United States or to Britain.

It is thus hard to demonstrate that the nation producing the most television entertainment programs for the world has any additional control over that world's opinion. It is similarly difficult to show that real "understanding" between nations or peoples is furthered by shared cultural or material experiences. It has classically been noted that relations between the United States and Japan grew progressively worse exactly as Japan's life style became more and more similar and comparable to that of the United States. It may be that shared material experiences simply produce more intense (and probably competitive) interactions. Learning to value the same material aspects of life may lead us directly to contesting possession of the inputs necessary to such material enjoyment.

Judging the impacts here is very tricky in any event, with numerous possibilities of false causal inference. It may well be that shared cultures and values *per se* do contribute to peace, for example, but that they normally are preceded by physically intense rivalries which have a greater impact in the opposite direction. If one could share culture without sharing disputed borders, for example, one might thus be channeling world opinion into paths which produce very happy results. Artificially induced "cultural-exchange" programs might thus be required, for the "cultural-exchange" which occurs normally may always be accompanied by confrontations of interest.

The effectiveness of cultural exchange programs is itself difficult to measure, with similar statistical fallacies. In any group of Indian students who study in America, a higher percentage is thereafter sympathetic to U.S. policy than the average for Indian students. Similarly, in any group that studies in the Soviet Union, a higher percentage is then sympathetic to Soviet policies than in the Indian educated population as a whole. Yet it is extremely dangerous to attribute the post-education opinion causally to the education itself. It may be that persons naturally inclined to sympathize with America are motivated to apply to study there, and similarly with regard to an education in the USSR. If so, it would be prior attitudes that explain later opinion, and not the process of cultural exchange itself. It could even be that visitors to the two super-powers were generally disillusioned by what they saw in each case, so that they would be less pro-American or less pro-Soviet than if they had remained in India. Given the difficulties each society experiences in preparing its people to be hospitable toward foreign visitors of differing racial backgrounds, it might well be argued that the American government should subsidize student trips to Moscow, and that the USSR should subsidize study in the United States. Prince Sihanouk is reported as commenting that all his students who went to Paris came home communist, and those that went to Moscow came home anti-communist.

However, propaganda and opinion-formulation should certainly not be dismissed as a hopeless task. Skillful and effective use of international exchange programs, of radio, cinema and television, are indeed possible; the net impact of propaganda may thus typically serve the interests of the states launching it, even if a minority of the individuals at whom it is directed reacts in an adverse manner.

One might, of course, assume that propaganda should typically be more effective at home, where the state holds a preponderance or monopoly of the message channels under its control. Hitler's use of radio prior and after assuming power was rated as enormously innovative and potent at the time, and more recently we have seen the president of the United States apply television presentations extremely effectively, in reducing tensions between government policy and public opinion.

Yet the aftermath of novel effectiveness in a medium is often a second-order skepticism. Immediately after the printing press was invented, books may indeed have been taken as the literal truth; since most books published were the Holy Bible, this was understandable. In a more sophisticated age, few readers will assume that something is true merely because it has been set in type. By 1941, few German listeners tended to trust radio broadcasts anymore; Goebbel's reports, and the reports of the BBC, were greeted with an equal skepticism, as a population once misled no longer trusted the medium at all. In election campaigns in the United States, voters by 1970 had apparently begun to distrust and reject candidates with whom they had only become acquainted through well orchestrated television commercials.

Hence the significance of information and cultural communication for foreign policy and international understanding is difficult to define. There is indeed a greater closeness of sorts within nations, and from nation to nation. Watching the war in Vietnam on television each evening creates a familiarity with "faraway lands" that would not have been possible in 1914 or 1938. Yet greater closeness is clearly not producing greater trust or greater understanding between nations or within nations. Public opinion can indeed be a force for peace if it is coordinated to support peace, but if public opinions remain hostile to one another, they become a force for something else.

The creation of the United Nations was expected to have quite beneficial impacts on the contribution of world public opinion to peace. The UN, especially the General Assembly, would provide a register for opinion, thus making salient and effective what otherwise might have been ignored. By allowing delegates of various nations to compare opinions on political disputes as they emerge, the Assembly presumptively breeds understanding between nations, and allows like-minded nations to compare and coordinate their disapproval of aggressive or arrogant behavior by any single state. A simple pluralistic ignorance whereby each of 80 states did not realize that the other 79 shared its anger on the course of events might have left such individual national "opinions" impotent. The aggregation and coordination of such individual reactions, conversely, could collect a power that had not existed before.

An opinion forum thus makes it seem more worthwhile to have an opinion, and few members of the UN neglect to send a delegate to New York. Yet the opinions sometimes will be ready-made for the occasion, rather than reflecting deeply felt and long held grievances of the country in question. When the issue is as complicated as the problems of access to West Berlin, the "opinions" of many member nations in the UN will be dilletantish and superficial at best. Since no deeply held "opinion" existed prior to a crisis on such subjects, this opinion will then not sway larger and more powerful states nearly as much as had been hoped. On such questions, moreover, many of the delegations feel no need to stay in touch with their governments and public opinions at home, especially considering the costs of rapid or continuous communication. As noted earlier, therefore, the danger remains that the delegates to the General Assembly have become a new constituency of their own, "talking only to themselves," susceptible to all the "bandwagon" effects that color other mass opinion phenomena, but not demonstrating very much about how the world at large is reacting to events in the Congo or to the plight of refugees in Palestine.

There are, to be sure, issues on which world public opinion knows what it wants and what it condemns, issues on which UN delegates have a real domestic opinion to relay to the world forum. Yet one can also express skepticism about the depth and staying-power of such indignation here, since this kind of "opinion" is still hardly a major deterrent to "crimes" of the great powers. If the world has a very short memory, a compulsive urge to forgive and forget, condemnations by juries of opinion contribute very little to peace. As great powers develop reputations for being arrogant and unreasonable, it is all too possible that, like the prodigal son, they will be forgiven and welcomed back into the "world community" at the first sign of the most trivial repentence of their arrogant position.

Aside from those who suffered most directly, is West Germany really under any moral handicaps in the aftermath of World War II? Even more so, what handicaps would one discover relative to Japan? Having lost World War II led to an enforced disarmament of these two countries to be sure, a disarmament which they have not yet undone, a disarmament which has contributed to their great prosperity since the war. Yet if there is any permanent political weakening of Bonn's or Tokyo's claim to be a great power, it is the result of the military and material events of 1945, not of the persistence of a condemning world opinion since then.

The world disapproved of U.S. intervention in Guatemala in 1954, but does the United States suffer seriously as a result of that disapproval? Perhaps Latin American nations subliminally regard it as confirmation of deeper fears that they have always held vis-a-vis the United States, but Guatemala did not first create those fears. How much does the USSR really suffer today because of its intervention in Hungary in 1956, or even for its actions in Czechoslovakia in 1968? The United States underwent much international criticism during the active phases of its Vietnam intervention, but the permanence of this is also suspect. Once Americans are out of Vietnam, will the world not rush to forgive them? Has the forgiveness not already begun with President Nixon's Vietnamization policy?

If UN Delegates represented their homeland opinions more faithfully, therefore, it is hardly certain that such "opinion" could be used to influence local issues. Asian publics are no more or less parochial than European or American publics. When a nation can exercise power, it tends to take slightly more interest in the world over which it has so much influence. When one's material power is more constricted, public opinion turns to domestic considerations, and shrugs off much of the outside world.

It is thus much more difficult than might have been thought to bring Afro-Asian opinion to bear on issues within Europe, for Asians and Africans in truth have a great disinterest in the legal status of West Berlin, or the proximity of West Germany to nuclear weapons. A former Indian delegate to the Eighteen Nation Disarmament Conference once noted that "Germany was not a Frankenstein" to India. Memories of World War II which might seem real and tangible in Western and Eastern Europe and in North America, have little impact in countries whose history books sometimes describe that event as "the second great European civil war." Even Chairman Mao allowed himself some offhand remarks to Japanese reporters suggesting support for German claims to territories east of the Oder-Neisse line, remarks which showed an indifference to, or unawareness of, the sore points such German claims can raise.

If the issue concerns long-standing principles of international law, a similar disparity of experience can produce relatively disappointing responses from the "jury" of the UN. Asian and African countries use and subscribe to basically European principles of international law, but only as a legacy of the imperialist past. If such international law supplies practical conventions, it hardly evokes deep moral indignation and response.

FURTHER READINGS

Rosenau, James N. ed. *Linkage Politics.* Glencoe, Ill.: Free Press, 1969.
Rosenau, James. *Public Opinion and Foreign Policy.* New York: Random House, 1965.
Steele, A. T. *The American People and China.* New York: McGraw-Hill, 1966.

National Character

Perhaps too much has already been said about the role of "national character" in international politics, with more bias than justification. Nations have often attributed the blame for wars to alleged character deficiencies of their opponent's culture, and simple prejudice has often enough become speculative generalization about the peculiar characteristics of one people or another. Germans, for example, have thus been characterized as efficient and as brutal, as docile followers of any national leadership whatsoever, and as clumsy and lacking of sense of humor, and so on. Japanese have similarly been seen as cruel and as fanatic, as clever and as businesslike. One can dredge up parallel prejudices and predictions about Frenchmen and Britons, Chinese and Americans. A most interesting transformation has appeared in American public opinion on the Turk, who in the wake of the Armenian massacres of the 1920's was almost universally regarded as "cruel," but who in the context of Russian Cold War threats in the middle 1950's had become "brave."

The Cold War confrontation between the U.S. and Soviet Union has been happily restrained in such ethnic generalization, in large part because the conflict is so often defined in terms of ideology. Since the "Russian people" are assumed to loathe Communist rule as much as the American people, questions of national culture play less of a role. Conversely, the leadership of the USSR portrays itself in full identification with the American proletariat and people, who someday will be liberated from the bonds of an irrational economic system. There has nonetheless still been some analysis of the international contest purportedly based on character traits of the two nations involved. French and other European commentators might be much more prone to view the contest as between nations rather than ideologies, as De Tocqueville long ago predicted that America and Russia would be the giants of the future. The Russian history of vulnerability to invasion from abroad is assumed to suggest certain psychological patterns for the future. Importance has also been attached to the fact that so many Russians play chess, a very careful and cautious game, while Americans more typically play poker, which encourages gambling, bluff, and deception.

The liberal American view has always been to debunk such generalizations about ethnic or national proclivities; the generalizations are viewed as inaccurate, and themselves causes of international mistrust and hostility. Yet it would hardly correspond with reality to assert that no differences whatsoever occur between nation and nation, or people and people, no differences which might really affect the political tone of foreign policy and international relations. It is not an unfair generalization to claim that Scandinavians are less exuberant people by and large than Latin Americans, or that stylistic considerations will require greater attention to decorum and sobriety in one area of political activity than in another.

If there is thus any reality to differences in "national character," one might attempt to find and account for these differences in various ways. We obviously have differences in domestic political structure, such as those discussed earlier, which can bend the "character" of nations in one direction or another. At a more psychological level, real differences of national culture and style can vary the output in terms of foreign policy. Finally, the historical experience of nations in international affairs will itself be varied, as some nations have won wars when others have lost, when still others have remained neutral. Such important disparities of experience can seriously color the way a nation sees the international arena and behaves within it.

From such factors, several interesting generalizations have been advanced about the United States. Due to the relatively smooth workings of our domestic governmental system, we have been disposed to accord excessive importance to law and lawyers, to indulge in a certain legalism about the ways in which international issues can be settled. Americans, it is alleged, have also been inclined to excessive pragmatism, to basically unideological approaches, as the product of a two-party domestic election system which discourages anything but tweedle-dum, tweedle-dee platforms. As a product of the domestic success of the system, an unconscious imperialism is thus instilled which sees Americans offering and thrusting their "system" upon others, an imperialism based on a belief not in racial superiority, but in political superiority.

APPROACHES TO EXPLANATION

Americans are also accused of having an illusory sense of how much power their country can exert in the world. The sense might be based on the basic solubility of all problems "at home," or on the novelty, after 1945, of being a people whose influence had to be taken into account. Perhaps such delusions can be traced back even further, to the experience of the frontier, with its continual conquests and progress, a frontier which was replaced in the 20th century by new "frontiers" of technological conquest.

The sense of American omnipotence is fortified by a tradition of "no surrender," a memory that the United States fights war reluctantly, but has never lost a war. The War of 1812, to be sure, required a little reinterpretation to have it come out a victory. The Peace of Utrecht was a compromise if anything, but the battle of New Orleans, fought tragically after the peace agreement because of the slowness of communications, gave the United States a "victory" on the battlefield that had already been "negotiated away" at the conference table. The South, to be sure, has its own remembrance of defeat and surrender, in the final demise of the Confederacy at Appomattox. It has sometimes thus been argued that southerners such as Senators Fulbright and Gore were uniquely qualified to lead the nation to admit defeat in the Vietnam War, but a cross-section of southern congressmen hardly shows a greater psychological reconciliation to defeat than in the rest of the country. The Secretary of State at the most significant part of the American intervention, indeed, was a southerner, Dean Rusk.

Due to the relative rareness of American participation in and preparation for war, there has been an "all or nothing" totalism about American attitudes, with demands for "total war" and "unconditional surrender." It has seemed patently immoral to fight a war under constricting ground rules, and even the "limited wars" in Korea and Vietnam have drawn much domestic criticism on these grounds, criticism arguing that escalation was in order whenever it would contribute to speedier battlefield victory and the termination of combat involving American young men.

Some of these defects in the American psychological preparation for foreign policy have been imputed even more directly to the style and composition of the U.S. State Department. Representing a nation of latecomers to international politics, the rank and file of the Foreign Service is often portrayed as being naive and pedestrian, self-consciously trying to emulate their more experienced opposite numbers in the British and European services, couching every dispatch in terms of geopolitical jargon and power political aphorisms, as if continually to remind one and all that the Foreign Service is more worldly and sophisticated than the isolationists of Indiana. In the years when many present senior personnel were recruited, it was indeed unusual for an American to care much about the outside world. To be an expert on Germany or Russia in the later 1920's was thus consciously to set one's self off from the rank-and-file of Americans; this bureaucratic defensiveness might not be shed so easily, even at a later time when many more Americans have taken an interest in the power politics of the world.

As additional contributing factors to a certain basic lack of confidence within the U.S. State Department, one might trace a pattern of recruitment from the middle class which did not compare with the secure upper-class nature, for example, of the British Foreign Ministry. The personnel thus assembled would lack the youthful financial and career security of their opposite numbers. They also lack security in confronting the "ins-and-outers" who by presidential authority continually intrude into the making of American foreign policy, persons who enter and leave government from financially rich private law and business practices, or from a base of inherited wealth, thus able to risk loss of political office and job tenure with much more equanimity than the careerists.

The foreign policy style of the British Foreign Ministry, by contrast, has shown a self-confidence which sometimes has extracted extra mileage for the government's position, but at other times has produced excessive assurance and serious disappointment. Part of such assurance, as noted above, stems from personnel recruitment practices which favor persons who have been affluent for most of their lives. Part also stems from Britain's long tradition of participation in world affairs. No one really expects Englishmen to be naive or inexperienced in the practices of international politics, and English diplomats, therefore, rarely have to play or overplay their roles to show others how professional they are.

Yet this is certainly not to spare the British national character and foreign policy establishment all possible handicaps in the handling of foreign policy problems. The recruitment process that encourages personal security also tends to be independent of personal merit, as the very biases of British education and recruitment pass over many a gifted human being, and give tenure to some who are wellborn but less gifted. The tradition of being a world power may breed confidence in general, but may breed bitterness and disappointment now that Britain is not really a first-rate power any more. In the drafting of the Nuclear Test-Ban treaty, for example, it was difficult for British diplomats to adjust their pretense to their real power and ability to contribute. There are thus "psychological" difficulties for a nation, or for its foreign representatives, in adjusting to a decrease in power and influence, just as, in the American case, there have been difficulties in adjusting to a perceived great increase of influence.

Far more significant from an American point of view today are whatever generalizations can be offered on Russian personality as it effects the course of Soviet foreign policy and international politics. Unhappily, the data available here is considerably more sparse, given the closed nature of Russian society ever since the Bolshevik revolution. In analyzing the tendencies of London, Paris, or Bonn, considerably more insight could be garnered from the numerous personal interactions which occur continuously on the public and private level. In these cases, it is not even necessary for an American analyst to read and peruse every document issued by the government under study. In the case of the USSR, however, so little is available that a Kremlinologist can hardly spare himself the effort of reading virtually all the documents, indeed reading "between the lines" to extract the subtle nuances that first betray a change in attitude toward the Chinese, or a change in relative power within a collective leadership. Noting the order in which men stand atop Lenin's tomb to review a May Day parade may seem almost a farcical approach to predicting Soviet attitudes and behavior; yet such orders of precedence are taken seriously enough in Soviet society to be worth analyzing, and we do not have any surfeit of material to replace it.

It used to be easy to contrast the recruitment and promotion policies of the Soviet Union with those of Western democracies. Under Stalin, as indeed under the Czar, fear and intrigue played crucial roles in determining who held power and who was attracted to seeking it. The Stalinist purges meant that rising to power on domestic or foreign policy required an agility at surviving purges, and ability to arrange the executions of others rather than having one's own execution arranged. Accompanying the pervasive fear of betrayal and death were pressures for the most rigorous orthodoxy and ideological compliance, where any nonstandard statement could be misinterpreted to one's detriment.

The disadvantages of the worst of the Stalinist system seem clear. The continual suspicion involved made it difficult if not impossible for officials to play the "devil's advocate," or even to report the views of opposing statesmen and negotiations. Opportunities for real cooperation with a foreign state might thus be lost as no one had the courage to describe them openly. In terms of the product in international policy, the Stalinist style tended to produce a clumsy diplomacy making the most brazen demands, demands which under test often turned out to be bluffs. This absence of subtlety caused the Russians to miss opportunities to exploit or subvert the Marshall Plan, or to win the early friendship of neutralist leaders such as Nehru in India. Some advantages, as always, might be found in partial compensation for this; Soviet foreign policy under this kind of management at least would not be plagued by insubordinate leaks of information from those opposing policy; in a clumsy fashion, policy could be said to be coordinated.

Much of this has, of course, changed drastically since the death of Stalin, albeit the current Soviet leadership is still composed of graduates of the Stalinist years. Persons who lose power struggles in the USSR are no longer executed, but rather retired to comfortable, if boring, existences, for example, an embassy in Mongolia. If the change of hazards is now clearly established, it presumably has lead to a somewhat different kind of person being recruited to the foreign policy-making process.

Where previously only the more adventurous or murderous might have had a taste for governmental power, the prospect of becoming a foreign policy-maker in Russia now may also attract those who relish the creature comforts and cosmopolitan prerogatives of contact with the outside world. As long as the USSR remains a relatively drab place, the prospect of representing it in dealings with foreigners may entice a great number of competent persons to learn foreign languages, to take the necessary examinations, to establish the professional credential to win the job security accorded to expertise. Persons inclined to job security and professional recognition might previously have gravitated toward one of the scientific professions, leaving the hazards of politics to the nonprofessionals of the *Aparat*. In the aftermath of Stalin, foreign policy, as well as other areas of "politics," has itself become more expert and professional.

Soviet policy-making today is thus obviously characterized by a greater flexibility, with many of the open internal disagreements on policy that we are accustomed to in other states. "Leaks" of one sort or another even occur from time to time, by which one faction complains about policies being implemented by another; some caution is in order, however, about whether such "leaks" are genuine, or stage-managed by a government which understands how such leaks occur and are reported in Western societies. Russian government spokesmen dispatched to Washington or to New York, for example, are extremely well-trained in responding to American feelings and prejudices, ready to assure Americans "privately" that they share the fears of Peking's irrationality, or even the irritation at Afro-Asian slowness in buckling down to economic growth and development. As with many other areas of information manipulation, a state which understands how information flows work can begin to harness such flows to its own benefit. Hence one sees what was formerly the most monolithic of Soviet institutions, the secret police, engaged in projects as imaginative as releasing the text of Stalin's daughter's memoirs, in an effort to preempt and confuse the public attention that would have been directed at her own release of these memoirs in New York.

FURTHER READINGS

George, Alexander L. "The 'Operational Code': A Neglected Approach to the Study of Political Leaders and Decision-Making." *International Studies Quarterly*. June, 1969.
Hoffmann, Stanley. *Gulliver's Troubles*. Englewood Cliffs, N.J.: Prentice-Hall, 1969.
Osgood, Robert. *Limited War*. Chicago: University of Chicago Press, 1957.

Rosenau, James N., ed. *Domestic Sources of Foreign Policy*. Glencoe, Ill.: Free Press, 1967.
Waltz, Kenneth. *Foreign Policy and Democratic Politics*. Boston: Little, Brown, 1967.

Communist National Styles

A basic question on Russian character pertains to the impact ideology is assumed to have. Does ideology really change the ends that individuals within the foreign policy apparatus will be pursuing, or does it merely serve as an after-the-fact rationalization for goals which would always have come into effect, under the czar, under Kerensky, under the Communist party? Does ideology, apart from changing the goals and ends of man, alter the way they see the possibilities, the relationships of means and ends; are distortions thereby increased or decreased?

Whether the ideology has produced a larger change in the preexisting national interest, or the national interest a larger change in the preexisting ideology, is a most challenging question, and this is, perhaps, what the real issue between "national interest" and ideology" has been about. Yet it might be difficult precisely to identify the ideology of the party as it was before it came to power, and the "normal" notion of national interest (all nations pursue power, and so on) may also be a poor approximation of the national interest of the particular country before the party took over. A country like Switzerland might, for example, behave more like a typical nation-state after it was dominated by Communist ideology than before it was so dominated.

As noted earlier, the concept of "national interest" has been used overly much in writings on international politics in both procedural and substantive contexts. In the procedural sense, every nation has an "interest," specifically whatever it happens to want in the world. By this definition no nation ever departs from its national interests anymore than an individual departs from his preferences, for nations choose what they want to choose. Substantively, the term has been used rather to refer to interests which nations normally have, for example, for national independence, for influence over neighbors, for economic well-being, and so on. To depart from such normal goals to seek something else (for example, improvement of the workers' lot in some distant country) thus would be a deviation from the "national interest."

What role does ideology play in all this? Ideology has also been variously defined, but subject to some challenge, it will be treated here as a set of beliefs on the rightness of certain actions and goals, accompanied normally, but not necessarily, by a set of beliefs on some other subjects. If an ideology is thus accepted by a national leadership, one will not be surprised to find at least some of the preferences of this leadership (at least some of the "national interest") changed, to conform with the rights and wrongs of this ideology.

Nations engaged in international politics of course must have more than interests (the indifferences curves of economics). They must also develop a set of perceptions on the opportunities world politics offer to serve these interests (the opportunity curve of economics). In the interaction between national interests and apparent national opportunities, foreign policy is formed. The effect of ideology will thus not be limited to changes in a nation's preference or value pattern, if it also includes or induces assumptions about the facts of the world. The factual assumptions induced by ideology will replace, or have to be reconciled with, the factual assumptions derived simply from empirical observations. Propositions so induced, of course, will vary directly from one ideology to another, but two special propositions, perhaps made more implicitly, will arise in most or all ideologies.

The first assumption induced is that the individual or the nation is indeed serving the ends which the ideology has defined as correct. It is difficult for me to believe that a course of action is correct and right, and simultaneously to believe that I am generally not following it. Either the picture of rightness, or of one's own behavior, must be changed, and this syndrome of "rationalization" is quite common. The second induced assumption is that all right ends are ultimately compatible, that one will not permanently have to defer the achievement of one in order to achieve another. This might be called the optimism syndrome.

The two syndromes of rationalization and ultimate optimism thus may more directly force individuals to choose between the implications of their ideology and the empirical impressions of their senses. Inconsistencies may result which in time force a revision of the internalized ideology. If one's natural behavior seems incompatible with a prescribed end, the prescription of ends may have to be revised. If prescribed ends do not seem to be compatible with each other, some end may have to be discarded as an illusory or false good.

Should we, therefore, expect that a nation's ideology will honestly and accurately express the personal or national goals of the actors involved? The answer most assuredly would have to be negative. Ideology will at best be a simplifying abstraction of the goals to which a movement or a nation has committed itself, glossing over a host of subsidiary motives which might complicate the picture. Apart from the simplifications of ideology, there are also strategic arguments why a nation should deliberately conceal some of its real goals in the ideological descriptions it circulates. By and large, one should pretend that there is a greater compatibility and overlap of interest between other nations' interests and one's own; if this propaganda is believed abroad, it will presumably lead to cooperation even when it opposes the foreign power's real interests.

It does not follow, however, that the ideology which oversimplifies national purposes and serves the intentions of the propaganda ministry is thereby silly and meaningless. Even an abstraction may come to have real meaning of its own if enough relevant citizens pay attention to it and thereby come to be motivated in accordance with the ideology. Even deliberately misleading propaganda over time may convince the propagandist as much as the intended object. If Russians in the later 1940's pretended to be unimpressed by the atomic bomb, for example, they may indeed have become genuinely unimpressed.

There may thus be some differences in stress in the public promulgation of ideology, as the pure and undiluted tenets continued to receive primary stress, while the adjustments are held in reserve to answer the skeptics or to satisfy internal doubts. Yet it is entirely to be expected that the preferences of the national interest will be kept consistent with each other, that the nations's ideology will be internally consistent, and that the ideology as revised will be kept consistent with the preferences of the national interest. For example, if Chinese Communist support is given to an obviously non-Communist regime merely because it strengthens China's national strength vis-a-vis that of the Soviet Union, this should not lead us to expect any great moment of truth in Peking by which the Chinese suddenly see themselves to be crass hypocrites deviating from their ideology and thus disproving it. Rather Peking may simply have discovered a new proposition that China alone realizes the importance of encouraging truly orthodox Communist regimes around the world, and thus must temporarily encourage other regimes to strengthen herself to perpetuate this insight.

Not all the ideology will thus be made over as it comes under stress. Some tenets will not conflict with the facts, but in other cases the facts will be suppressed. Some perceptions of reality will thus have to be distorted: Communists may indeed remain too optimistic. As the ideology is thus adjusted to face some realities, other portions of it are kept alive, and the whole seems to retain its consistency.

There may thus be some definite advantages to having an ideology on which to base domestic and foreign political policy. A "scientific" assumption of some grand determinism that shapes world history may breed confidence, the kind of confidence that lets men and nations persevere even when the momentary empirical evidence would suggest defeat and despair. Yet if predictions are repeatedly disproven, the same apparent determinism may breed disillusionment. Too great a confidence in the inevitable process of history might foster a certain apathy also, as individual heroism and effort no longer seemed as crucial as in a less determined universe.

Some of the unsettling impact of a deterministic ideology can also be passed over to the opposing nations and foreign ministries that did not originally hold to it. Marxism purports to explain why non-Marxists persist in their error, why nations of the "Free World" insist on resisting and opposing the "Socialist Camp." The comparison has sometimes thus been drawn between the basically ad hominem approaches of Marxism and of contemporary psychological analysis. If the American middle class expresses an aversion to the drug culture, the psychologist may fail to address whether the drug culture is really objectively threatening, confining himself to explaining why the middle class is driven to such excitement. If Americans complain that the Russians have cheated in allowing Egyptian missiles to be moved up to the Suez Canal area, the Russian response typically will not deny the charge, but explain why basic failings of the American system drove the government to make such charges.

By taking the long-term view implied in a theory of history, a Marxist ideology may at least raise the right questions, even in the process of positing the wrong answers. If American policy-making, for example, is excessively pragmatic, too easily swayed by momentary results which may be statistically insignificant as signs of the ultimate outcome, such a long-run focus could be a powerful antidote in countries which have been driven to adopt it.

Apart from the demise of Stalinist orthodoxy, Russian ideology has undergone refinement, revision, and moderation for several reasons. The dispute with Communist China, which purports to be wearing the mantle of fidelity and orthodoxy, has driven Moscow to adopt some more moderate stands as its part of the contrast. Perhaps more significantly, the prospects of winning friendship and support in the nonaligned nations has forced Moscow toward more flexible and reasonable propositions on the shape of the world and the causes of war and peace.

The USSR itself is no longer as much of an ideological or political monolith. Yet one must also avoid jumping now to simple bipolar models of Soviet interests and decision-making which pit "liberals" against "conservatives," or "doves" against "hawks." It seems more probable that the Soviet decision-makers who matter are distributed more evenly between these poles, or indeed that competing particular interests make for a very multipolar decision arena. Party leaders have one interest in international politics, military leaders another. The former, for example, may resent Egypt's suppression of the local Communist party, since Soviet support for such a regime seems to compromise important principles. The army may resent military aid that leads to defeats, and insults about the effectiveness of its training and technology. Treaty-negotiating teams have a vested interest in seeing their treaties accepted and ratified. Propagandists who have made a career of attacking West German revanchism may resent shifts toward detente. Administrators of agricultural or consumer goods programs may relish detente and disarmament for the resources and manpower this might release; scientists, conversely, can welcome the arms race for the research support it generates.

In short, the demise of terror and ideology makes it plausible that we find some of the same bureaucratic politics in the Russian case as in American or British explanations of decisions. Some terror remains, to be sure. One can not criticize national policy in Moscow as openly as Senator Fulbright and escape imprisonment. Some ideology remains also, taken seriously enough so that it can not be forgotten.

When analyzing the other major Communist power, China, we face much of the same dilemma on how seriously to take the ideology. Which determines Peking's foreign policy, ideology or classical "central kingdom" national interest? Has ideology really only been shaped as a window dressing for the raw pursuit of power inherent in the national interest? Or do Chinese international operations rather prove the honesty and accuracy of the goals endorsed in the ideological statements?

A correct analysis will probably accept elements of each kind of motivation in explaining Chinese policy. Maoist ideology is, of course, an abstraction which cannot account for all Chinese policy, an abstraction somewhat disingenuously designed for domestic or foreign motivation. The ideology is chosen for its memorability, and for its appeal. It shifts as the practical needs of the Peking regime shift. Ye this hardly makes the ideology an artifact, or suggests that Peking will pursue exactly the same foreign policy goals and policies that would have applied under the KMT or the Empire. Chinese Communist ideology does reflect and breed a greater identification with various classes of people abroad, and a desire that they be offered the option of a certain emancipated life-style. As elsewhere, it is wrong to assume that every regime is equally in quest of international power, power merely for the sake of power. Regimes with philosophies which they intend to export will be more concerned about power than other regimes.

From an American perspective, two imputations on Chinese Communist foreign policy have been especially disturbing since 1949. The first of these relates to the monolithic image of Communism which seemed so continually confirmed in the days of Stalin. Not only the Chinese party, but Communist organizations everywhere seemed loyal to orders from Moscow in the most obedient and mindless way. On the day before Hitler's attack on the Soviet Union, for example, American Communists were vehemently opposed to American involvement in World War II, arguing that Hitler was not any more evil that the capitalist forces opposing him. On the day after the attack, needless to say, virtually every American Communist had discovered that the American interest now called for full and early participation in the war. Coordination of this sort is rare in politics, and threatens to be quite powerful. It is thus understandable that persons and states outside such an efficient conspiracy came to feel menaced by it, which accounts for at least part of the early American apprehension on Peking's style—apprehension precisely that Chinese policy would be dictated as completely from Moscow as the foreign policy of Sofia or Warsaw, but now with 600 million or more people pooled with the 200 million of the USSR.

By the later 1950's, it seemed quite probable that this coordination could not persist, or in the case of China could not have existed in the first place. Unhappily for American understanding of the Chinese position, the first clear evidence of a rift in Moscow-Peking coordination raised a new kind of fear. The rift appeared to come with regard to Russian moves toward detente with the United States, which Peking now openly criticized and opposed. In the ensuing years, Peking was to adopt an almost "zero-sum" style of address vis-a-vis the United States, verbally denying virtually all community of interest, in a fashion which even Stalin had never adopted. If Americans were thus somewhat relieved of the fear of an all-encompassing conspiracy of the monolithic Communist bloc, this fear was thus replaced by a fear of "madmen" in Peking who would be intent on destroying the United States even if it meant the destruction of China also.

Happily, the latter image of China pertained much more to verbal than to real behavior, so that tacit signs of cooperation and coexistence were more regularly perceived by the United States government in the later 1960's. If the Chinese attack was only verbal, less agitated American responses would certainly be in order. Yet one can not either totally discount the verbal, since verbal activity has a reality of its own. American pressures might thus have been intended simply to force the Chinese regime to begin to admit that it was not engaged in an all-out struggle against the United States, lest some other nations take this kind of inflammatory rhetoric too seriously.

As Moscow's control over Peking has been disproven, the real and apparent style of other Communist foreign policies have also undergone change since 1953. Whatever the commitment of Communist party regimes from state to state to the general advancement of socialism and the proletariat, it seems clear that nonideological considerations of national priority have had some serious impact on their evolving domestic and foreign policies. Other things being equal, the Hungarian Communist party would prefer to see more rapid economic growth and prosperity in Hungary than in Rumania or East Germany, and each of the other leaderships would reverse these priorities to suit itself. It is not easy to incorporate such selfish nationalism into Marxist ideology, and this can only be done by nuance at the margin. Yet if one recognizes that ideology is never a perfect reflection of policy goals, even after it is redefined, we can see that Hungarian Communists will continue to be Hungarian as well as Communist. An ideological governmental leadership cannot tolerate enormous gaps between ideological prescription and real policy, but it continually tolerates small gaps.

One means of adapting the ideology is to stress national independence and sovereign autonomy, within the bonds of the socialist camp. To argue that Poles should make decisions for Poland can thus be a euphemism for saying that Poles should not share their resources with poorer nations in the socialist camp. Whether or not this kind of autonomy is really consistent with the spirit of Marxism, it has enough of a foothold in Marxist writings and rhetoric to allow various national leaderships to invoke it, because they are greedy, or because they simply identify with their own working class more than with the one across the border. Marx's writings, and Lenin's also, can even be invoked on age-old border disputes between nations of what is now the Communist bloc, as when Marx was cited as having concluded that Bessarabia was rightfully Rumanian instead of Russian.

It would thus be foolish to assume that Communists have been reeducated to think on nonnationalistic lines. Perhaps other leaderships could have been forced and terrorized under Stalin into slavish subordination to the interests of the whole, as defined from Moscow. Since 1953, less than total subordination or coordination or cooperation has been evident. It is equally foolish, of course, to assume that Communist ideology makes no difference, that the leaderships of Eastern Europe will now behave as any governments of their country would have behaved, pursuing national and parochial interests to the exclusion of any grander, unified purpose.

FURTHER READINGS

Brzezinski, Zbigniew and Huntington, Samuel. *Political Power: USA/USSR*. New York: Viking, 1964.
Lowenthal, Richard. *World Communism: The Disintegration of a Secular Faith.* Oxford: Oxford University Press, 1966.
Zagoria, Donald S. *The Sino-Soviet Conflict 1956–61*. Princeton: Princeton University Press, 1962.

Ethnic Nationalism

Ideologies acquire some reality in being enunciated. A nationalist ideology may produce more fervent ethnic nationalism than might have existed otherwise. A Communist Marxist-Leninist ideology, conversely, dampens out some parochial and national interests. This leads to generalizations about what we remember as the Fascist regimes and their foreign policies. It is only a little more than 25 years, after all, since Nazi Germany was defeated at the end of World War II, and the relevance of these ideologies and styles may not be totally behind us.

Fascism made explicit some beliefs that liberal democracies or Marxist regimes would not have endorsed. It stressed the special national virtues of the ethnic group to which it was appealing, and the supposed national defects of other ethnic groups. As a result, it sometimes presented an open and candid statement of hostility. Whereas liberal as well as Communist regimes would endorse the compatibility of the Russian and American peoples' interests, a Nazi statement might well have stated that what was good and necessary for Germans was necessarily bad for Poles or Czechs.

As part of assuming basic hostility in international politics, the Fascist and Nazi interpretation attributed a great hostility in reverse from all neighbors, interpreting history as a long series of foreign moves to Germany or Italy's detriment. Paranoia can be self-confirming, if one's fears drive others into defensive actions which then become good cause for real fears. The Hitlerian appeal might thus have entirely fabricated the hostility of British and French and other governments, but there may have been a real hostility remaining in the aftermath of World War I. The justification for Italian suspicions of foreign hostility might be a little harder to pin down. In any event, each regime launched its country on expansionist campaigns which then indeed generated foreign fear and hostility.

The stress on real and biological conflict could be transferred to minorities within the State, minorities which could serve as scapegoats for past failures and present defects of the society. The Nazi treatment of Jewish Germans is clearly the most horrendous example of this technique under an ethnically based ideology, but Mussolini's imposition of Italian culture on Germans living in southern Tyrol served similar purposes.

One could then argue endlessly about whether the Fascist ideology and style was particularly well suited to Germany or Italy, such that Hitler's assumption of power was naturally determined for Germans while Frenchmen were immune. Perhaps the basic psychological weaknesses and cravings of the German made the Fascist outlook very predictably congenial. Yet the possibility always existed until the last minute that Hitler would not come to power, or that he would not be able to consolidate it, and some conservatively oriented continuation of the Weimar regime was far from impossible. Even if Hitler's rise to power was very probable, one could as easily impute this to peculiarities in the German history of international relations rather than to defects of society or national character. Was it neurosis, or losing a war, that led Germans to accept Nazism? If losing a war leads to neurosis, it could have been both which served as causes.

It is somewhat misleading, of course, to think of Nazism or Facism as exemplifying "nationalism," for much more respectable domestic and international ideologies can also claim the title. Yet the aftermath of World War II was still widely interpreted as demonstrating the costs, dangers, and follies of "nationalism" in general, which indeed was blamed for causing the war. In the aftermath of World War I, conversely, nationalism was much more respectable, as ethnic self-determination was stressed, as irredentisms were dignified whether or not they were immediately satisfied. The Wilsonian philosophy at the founding of the League of Nations was indeed that neglect of nationalism had played an important role in inducing World

War I, as creations as artificial as Austria-Hungary had suppressed the legitimate cultural and political aspirations of Poles, Czechs, Rumanians, Slovenes, and Croats.

Perhaps the most interesting parallel with the anti-ethnic outlook of the Austria-Hungary establishment would be found today in the attitudes of governments in new nations of Africa, most of which had totally artificial boundaries handed to them by the colonial regimes of one of the European countries. For anyone to propose now that boundaries be redrawn on a linguistic or ethnic basis would be to open a Pandora's box of disputes and conflicts, and the Organization of African Unity is rarely as unified as on the idea that boundary disputes should be deemphasized. The 1919 tradition would have recommended plebiscites and boundary revisions on the way to justice and peace. The 1945 spirit suggests just the opposite.

If ethnic nationalism is thus more feared and disapproved of than in the past, it has hardly disappeared. In Africa, we have Somalia laying claims to the portions of Ethiopia and Kenya populated by ethnic Somalis. The Rumanian leadership has twitted the Soviet Union about its occupation of Bessarabia. Despite the intensely ideological nature of the conflict in Southeast Asia, it still seems at times that Cambodians distrust all Vietnamese, whether they are Communist or anti-Communist.

One could hardly explain the conflicts in the Middle East, moreover, without a heavy stress on the ethnic nature of the conflict between Arabs and Jewish Zionists. The "nationalist" character of this last dispute troubles both sides' supporters from without. Russian and other left support for the Arab side has had to stress the class differences which allegedly underlie the dispute over ownership of Palestine, pitting rich, advanced, capital-endowed Europeans against poor, tenant-farmer Arabs. Americans and other supporters of Israel have conversely had to stress that the Israeli form of government was democratic, while free elections are lacking in most of the Arab states, or that Israel is only defending the status quo, while Arab states are threatening peace by posing military threats to this status quo. While such issues have a certain reality of their own, they hardly explain the basic motivation that drives Israelis and Arabs to risk death in wars over claims to Palestine. The conflict is much more explicitly cultural, of one man's meat being another man's poison (or, more precisely, one nation's Palestine being another nation's lack of Palestine) than a conflict of ideology or political system; in part therefore it is an anachronism, a throwback to the conflicts of 1938 and 1914.

Some Israeli spokesmen claim that Arab Palestinian nationalists are totally misguided, and that the real interests of such Arabs are perfectly compatible with the interests and needs of Israelis; but others have in effect dignified the rationality of the Palestinian guerrilla by conceding that the conflict of interests is more real, as for example, General Dayan in his observation that he also would join Al Fatah if he were an Arab. Such concessions of opponent rationality may suggest greater sympathy and understanding for their point of view, but it may instead reflect a more resigned acceptance of uncompromisable differences and conflicts of interest.

FURTHER READINGS

Deutsch, Karl. *Nationalism and Social Communication*. Cambridge, Mass.: MIT Press, 1953.
Hayes, Carlton, H. H. *The Historical Evolution of Modern Nationalism*. New York: Macmillan, 1931.

The Nationalism of Newly Emerging Nations

Can a nation experience a nationalism not based on ethnic factors, not based on the assumption that culture A is superior to, and needs to be defended against, culture B? As noted, a great number of African states have no choice but to keep national feeling divorced from questions of race and language, since their boundaries were so capriciously imposed by the European colonial powers. Switzerland of course would be an example from within Europe itself, whereby French, German, and Italian speakers are united in their love of country (and in their distrust of the neighboring countries which on each frontier share a language).

Nationalism thus may be elevated above the invidious comparisons of ethnicity, perhaps extolling such positive accomplishments as love of one's fellow citizens, devotion to civic duty, conscientious payment of taxes, or performance of military service. Yet it is unlikely that we will come to use the "nationalism" phrase to refer only to civic zeal or to the elementary mobilization of populations that first gets them literate and reading common newspapers, voting in elections, expressing opinions, and so on. When the term is applied, even today in nations only very recently freed and sliced away from some colonial empire, we are almost always referring to the extolling of the particular nation-state in comparison and confrontation with other states. To teach children to love and serve the Congo is not quite the same as to teach them to love their neighbors, for the Congo has boundaries, armies, and a role in international politics.

New states may thus simply be emulating the older nations which have asserted sovereign prerogatives and fought wars so often in the past, the wars sometimes fought on an ethnic basis and sometimes not. If the new states cannot find any ethnic basis on which to challenge each other, this may be their good fortune in keeping international conflict from reaching its maximum of hate. The disadvantages of governing ethnically mixed populations of course amount to an enormous cost in domestic terms.

Some interesting generalizations can be advanced on the foreign-policy style of these so-called underdeveloped countries, nations which have only recently won their independence, and/or have lagged in the development of their industry and economic resources. If the West has tended toward bureaucratic pragmatism, and the East towards a mixture of ideology and terror-enforced conformity, the third world may yet have a very different foreign policy style.

Like the "socialist camp," these nations will be basically dissatisfied with the state of the world, and thus cannot fit into the category of "status quo" powers. Their struggle for independence, by definition, had to be anti-status quo, and the momentum thus induced makes them more skeptical of established practices and institutions on the international scene as well. Similarly the problems of poverty, of deficient education and health standards, again must make such nations impatient with their current lot.

Yet unlike the "socialist" nations, the "third world" has not accepted and internalized an ideology which generates a deterministic confidence that all such problems will be solved in the dialectic of historical conflict. Rather these nations and regimes will be more "pragmatically" seeking ways to solve their problems, or even assurances that their problems can indeed be solved.

The problem-solving approaches will, moreover, be derivative in many instances, since the example of one or another of the already developed nations will seem so attractive. The United States, after all, was the "first new nation," and might thus attract a great deal of emulative attention from states which have won their own independence and seek after political stability and/or economic prosperity. Lest historical experience seem too powerful, however, it should be noted that the "second new nation" was Haiti. The first socialist state was the Soviet Union, but other socialist states have now emerged, some of which have challenged the purity or relevance of the Moscow model.

When confronted with serious and immediate problems, and no ideological structure to develop assurance in approaching them, the states of the "third world" have thus tended to rely on charismatic personalities in their leadership as confidence-building substitutes. Such charisma is often first developed in the struggle for independence, perhaps conveyed by imprisonment at the hands of the colonial power which still was attempting to suppress independence movements. At later stages, if offers a symbol for the government and public at large, a symbol which promises new successes now that the struggle against colonialism has been won.

The international consequence of this dependence on charisma may thus be that such nations have to pursue policies which reinforce image and charisma, which stress the superficial and obvious over the subtle and more complicated in international processes. Leaders will indulge themselves in elaborate conferences of the nonaligned world, or will rush to New York to represent their nation personally at sessions of the General Assembly.

CONTINUING PROBLEMS IN INTERNATIONAL POLITICS

The diletantish nature of such policy is compounded by the fact that most of such "new nations" will be small in size compared with the more established powers of the East or West, India and Indonesia being conspicuous exceptions. It will thus be all the more difficult to maintain a large and full-time foreign policy establishment to give serious consideration to issues such as Berlin or nuclear testing, to Vietnam or the Middle East.

There is thus a general superficiality about such nations' foreign policy contribution which makes them unpredictable and unreliable as to which policies they are likely to endorse or support. There will be regular endorsement of the principles of self-determination and territorial integrity, amounting almost to a fetish. The trappings of sovereignty will be insisted upon in the most extreme fashion. The policy of "nonalignment" or neutralism will be endorsed again and again, but any neutrality will probably not be defined by classical standards of international law, but rather by substantive policy which seems to split the difference between demands of East and West.

Discussions of national character can thus include a folk wisdom which is often self-serving and can itself be a cause of international hostility and war. It can, also, however, produce macrocosmic analyses of varying political and social systems, so that foreign policy is explained that might otherwise seem random or undetermined. The latter more intellectual and profound kind of generalization thus attempts to trace the impact of the national system as a whole on the particular actors within it. In part this becomes psychological explanation, but psychological explanation does not have to be limited to comparisons of alleged national character, for much might conceivably be done by analyses which lay no stress at all on particular national attributes.

FURTHER READINGS

Black, C. E. *The Dynamics of Modernization: A Study in Comparative History.* New York: Harper and Row, 1966.
Kissinger, Henry A. *"Domestic Structure and Foreign Policy."* Daedulus. Spring, 1966.
Sigmund, Paul E., Jr., ed. *The Ideologies of the Developing Nations.* New York: Praeger, 1967.

Psychology and International Politics

At first glance psychology might seem to have many insights relevant to our difficulties in international relations. Since much international activity is destructive and counter-productive, it often seems that no rational explanation can account for it. Since psychology deals with deep and often unperceived motives, perhaps it can explain, and help us to avert, what otherwise perplexes and disrupts our lives.

Decision-making statesmen, or entire masses of the public, may thus be totally unaware of why they wish to "liberate" some province, or why they are fighting a war to vindicate some point of honor. Perhaps we know we are seeking "security," but do not know why we are seeking it, or what exactly security must include. Perhaps we adopt domestic positions on international events because it seems to accord with the particular status we are after as individuals. Perhaps we are satisfying even deeper needs and grievances in our role-playing in international arenas, making up for real or fancied mistreatments in our childhoods.

Apart from alerting us to the goals which really guide our behavior, but of which we are unaware, psychology can also identify persistent misperceptions of the opportunities we face. Are we, as human beings or as Americans in particular, addicted to wishful thinking, to assuming that whatever we prefer is likely to happen, more likely than objective reality would have it? Are we inclined to discover what we expect to discover in any confusing array of evidence, while discounting evidence which does not accord with and confirm our predictions? Do we tend to wish to confirm our hypotheses by bending all evidence in a single direction? If eight out of ten arguments seem to call for a military deployment, do we feel driven to reassess the last two variables until they too support the policy as decided?

If psychologists have basic advantages in a training and methodology which alerts them to nonrational phenomena here, there may be matching disadvantages, however, which severely limit the ability of the psychologist to make useful contributions to the political analysis of the international process.

Psychology by its very nature has an ad hominem approach, with focuses less on the substance of any argument, political or otherwise, and more on the supposed motives and drives that have driven the individual to make the argument. Since all men are fallible and less than rational, given the accidents of their psychological upbringing, it is temptingly easy to explain all statements of position in terms of these accidents. If Senator Keating thus seems alarmed about missiles in Cuba, it seems all too appropriate to discuss the drives for his alarm, rather than whether or not he is correct about the presence of weapons on the Cuban Island.

Since psychologists normally treat and discuss the ailments of their own countrymen, moreover, the drift of their analysis will suggest doubts about the validity of most substantive foreign policy positions as taken. We are likely to be wrong, and the psychological approach can tell us why. Since it can explain the "why" to us, there is no need to discuss whether we specifically will be wrong on predictions of Soviet attitudes toward Egyptian missiles in the Suez area, or Soviet submarine tenders in a Cuban port. When we cite the "facts" that disturb us, the psychologist often will not cite counter-facts about Cuba or Egypt, but facts about our tendency to misperception.

There is indeed a pluralistic ignorance in the community of educated men, which may have led political scientists to neglect such insights as psychology can offer on the analysis of foreign policy. Yet the pluralistic ignorance may work in both directions, as professionals in the field of psychology and psychiatry do not have the time or incentive to read extensively on political happenings and public affairs; when such people are asked to present their views on the origins of the Cold War, an embarassing indifference to particular events is sometimes revealed.

Aside from there being too few applications of psychological knowledge to international politics, there is also a risk of some premature misapplications; the public's interest in the private lives and personalities of its leaders may be exploited in studies which impute interesting but unprovable complexes, syndromes, and executive defects, in books which then sell a great number of copies. By the very nature of the science and the difficulty of collecting the candid evidence that may be required, much of what psychology might say about the motives and perceptions of leaders or followers will thus remain subject to dispute. The deterrent to withholding sensationalist analysis, or analysis tailored to the support of particular political positions, may thus not be very reliable.

What has been attempted in the application of psychological insights to international politics, and what could we hope to see done? One straightforward approach might involve examining the mental dispositions of particular individuals who rise to crucial positions of power, the premiers and presidents, the foreign ministers and secretaries of state, of the world we live in. This basically microcosmic approach would attempt to identify such individual neuroses or psychoses as are detected in everyday psychiatric practice, in the hope of noting the particular miscalculations to which various leaders will be prone, perhaps in the hope of detecting a psychotic leader before he can do too much damage.

Unlike the typical clinical practitioner, however, the international politics psychologist may have to rely on much more second-hand or third-hand evidence. Any study of Nikita Khrushchev, for example, had to use such evidence as his speeches, his biography to the extent that it was known, his visible behavior on film and on visits to the United States and United Nations. Psychologists will differ among themselves on how definitive any appraisal can be on the basis of such limited evidence. A similar study of Chairman Mao's psychology might seem even more tempting to those with a Freudian bent, for we know that in his youth he hated his father and was very attached to his mother.

Clearly the most psychologically salient international figure of recent history was Adolf Hitler, and the common sense on the Nazi leader today is indeed that he was deeply neurotic or psychotic, that he lacked "rationality," and could not be bargained or dealt with. Yet this raises a very basic definitional question on what we mean by the "rationality" of a statesman or of any human being, and whether Hitler was meaningfully "irrational."

The concept of rationality is often presented as a paradox in the social sciences; we are faced with the psychologist's verdict that man is "not rational," but we are also told that successful prediction requires some reliance on the rationality of man. Virtually every proposal of deterrent military strategy, of arms control, or of international negotiation tactics is offered with the proviso that it depends on the "rationality" of the opposing state; this proviso is then usually seized upon by the opposition as proving its lack of value. But rationality for the psychologist may not specify the same criteria as rationality for the economist, or for the analyst of foreign policy, and neither of these may jibe with the definitions of the game theorist or the specialist in public administration.

For most of the instances of foreign or military policy we will be analyzing, the concept of rationality simply involves having important parts of some person's actions caused by his anticipations of consequences. Hitler in this sense was decidedly rational, for he typically had very clear ideas of how his policies might lead to what he wanted. Hitler was not as indifferent to war as his opponents made him out to be, and was quite averse to seeing any suffering imposed on the German people. He therefore was reluctant to see unlimited recourse to the bombing of cities in World War II, and was slow to mobilize the German people and economy generally for maximum involvement in the war effort. He clearly showed signs of being willing to negotiate an exchange of concessions, where this would have made the war easier for Germans, an exchange which the Allies were quite reluctant to undertake. At the strategic level, Hitler also showed himself very perceptive in gauging the weaknesses and strengths of his diplomatic adversaries prior to 1939, again hardly suggesting any inability to relate ends to means.

If Hitler cannot be dismissed as totally irrational, therefore, he nonetheless displayed symptoms of some serious neuroses which handicapped him as a political and military leader after events began to turn against Germany. The temper tantrums to which he occasionally gave vent may indeed have been acts to frighten adversaries and colleagues, as several accounts suggest. Yet almost all witnesses agree that Hitler displayed a great inability to accept and confront bad news, with the result that his operational judgments after a time came to be extremely weighted with misplaced optimism. This may be nothing more, after all, than a general neurotic tendency in most human beings, even in positions of high power, as bad news is so politically unsettling as to cause leaders to evade acknowledging it. In retrospect we can ascertain that Hitler seemed more given to this fallibility than the average leader we have known. Yet it remains unclear whether such a diagnosis could have been rendered from afar during World War II, before we captured the records of Hitler's own entourage.

Hitler also displayed an extreme cruelty and indifference toward the welfare of various non-German groups. Can this not be presented as prima facie evidence that he was psychologically ill and "irrational?" Such cruelty may indeed reflect deep psychological troubles and handicaps, yet it might cause serious analytical confusions to show our disapproval of a person's or movement's ends by using the term "irrational." At the very least, it is a different kind of irrationality to want to kill other human beings, different from being unable to understand how to negotiate or how to make the best of defeat. One can negotiate with a Hitler or a Stalin who would like to be homicidal, as long as he understands that he would have to forgo other advantages as the price of indulging his perversion. One can not negotiate with a "madman" if his "madness" makes him unable to receive the signals of the bargaining table.

Attempts have been made at psychological analyses of various American presidents, most notably Woodrow Wilson, and then more recently Richard Nixon. Partisans of such men will resent the imputation that there are any psychological peculiarities whatsoever to be identified. Opponents may seize more gleefully on the implication that such men were handicapped in ways which make them unfit for the presidency. Given the world's continuing bias that only persons with psychological problems require close study, all statesmen will therefore have a continued vested interest in frustrating any efforts to perform close and regular studies of their personalities, even in some effort to advance peace through individual psychological analysis.

Proposals have thus been seriously proposed that the super-powers, or all the nations of the world, ensure themselves against any World War III induced by madmen by subjecting potential candidates to a battery of personality tests, such tests to be regulated and standardized by international treaty. Few proposals could be more doomed to failure from the outset. Even if we do not assume that the very desire to enter politics illustrates some basic psychological craving or flaw in the individuals recruited (and what of the cravings of those of us who like to watch and study politics?), the politician will resent the implication that he requires examination more than other men.

A very different sort of psychological approach to international relations falls somewhere between a macrocosmic and microcosmic approach. Rather than attributing war or international tension to the aberrations of any particular leader, it rather seeks to identify any mass psychological drives within a single nation which might give it a basically bellicose foreign policy outlook. War is thus assumed to have hidden purposes for the nation as a whole, purposes of which the individual citizens of the nation are perhaps not even aware.

At the very worst, war may still at least have some redeeming features, to which society perhaps unwittingly grows accustomed and dependent. War has thus been interpreted as liberating very noble as well as ignoble sentiments in men. Aside from the war profiteer and war criminal, it produces the hero, and finds the man who places his society and fellow citizens ahead of all petty personal considerations. Suicide rates classically tend to fall in nations immediately after wars are declared, as men discover a "purpose" in life again. Youth typically will feel less alienated from society as a whole, as will other minority groups. Perhaps some deep-seated needs for violence exist, which normally would produce murders, but now may be satisfied in wartime heroism. In many ways such theories are strikingly parallel to economic theories of the "military-industrial complex." Societies are seen to be basically deficient or vulnerable in ways which specifically cannot be remedied by any peacetime processes. Military expenditure or military operations are required to remedy the deficiency. War is thus not always a lamentable accident to be explained by simple stupidity or prisoner's dilemma; it sometimes is required to maintain the internal stability and happiness of the countries fighting it.

Yet there are limits to how seriously one can take such imputations about the actual desirability of war. Perhaps the psychological by-products of war tend to explain why men are no more averse to war than we know them to be. Perhaps the rapidly executed wars of the later 19th century offered psychic pleasures which actually made them thinkable or even enjoyable experiences; a certain amount of theorizing (for example, William James' "The Moral Equivalent of War") indeed was produced when it was still thought that all wars would be short and to the point. Germans were enthusiastic about the outbreak of World War I, as their troops marched through Berlin. In 1939, in sharp contrast, they were decidedly unenthusiastic. Theories of the psychological functionalism of war can, of course, argue that only the conscious desirability of war has been lost, but that military activity still satisfies deep and basic needs in ways which we no longer dare admit to ourselves in the nuclear age.

It is an easy step then from such general theories that states as a whole need to be warlike, to "national character" theories which again attribute particularly warlike qualities to one specific nation or another. Perhaps one could trace particular psychological syndromes prevalent in one culture more than another, and aggregate such findings into predictions on whether such a country will be more aggressive than the average. Perhaps the strict, father-dominated style of German homes engenders a submissiveness to authority, or a paranoia, which in the net made Nazism entirely to be expected, and with it wars such as World Wars I and II. Perhaps infants are toilet-trained too early in Japan, or perhaps Japanese and Chinese children have to devote too much of their youth to the rote learning of the many characters of their language. Yet there are serious quarrels to be had with any such findings. Swiss family life is not saliently different from that of Germany, yet Switzerland has maintained political democracy and the most nonobtrusive foreign policy imaginable. If Chinese today are bent toward authority by the cultural authority of their language, where was this political uniformity in the 1920's when disunity left China open to Japanese aggression?

The final possibility of an application of psychological insight to foreign policy analysis might shift to what could be called the macrocosmic level, whereby the interactions of entire nations with each other are reinterpreted in terms of bilateral syndromes or worldwide neuroses. A typical example of this has emerged since 1945 in analyses of the supposed conflict between the USSR and United States, analyses which argue that there is in truth no real occasion for conflict; each side is simply making preliminary misinterpretations of the other, misinterpretations which then become self-confirming as each side is driven and stampeded into precautionary responses. The writings of Charles Osgood, Erich Fromm, and Amitai Etzioni might fairly be included within this school, although they will differ on some finer points of interpretation.

The notion that the entire Cold War has been one grand illusion of mirror images (whereby each side imputes nonexistent hostility to the other and then each regards the other's imputation as proof of such hostility) is indeed an interesting alternative to our more conventional assumptions about the Cold War. Yet we must question whether the specific facts of 1944 or 1949 on the origins of the Soviet-American conflict truly suggest that real conflict never existed. Veterans of foreign policy-making on either side would argue that conflict was indeed real, that the Russian installation of Communist regimes in eastern Europe, or the American use of the atomic bomb against Japan, were Cold War moves beyond any simple precautionary fears of opponent's intentions.

A second challenge is also in order. Even if it could plausibly be argued that all of the Cold War has stemmed from mutual fears which become self-validating, the assumption of the psychologists has been that this is pathological, that is, avoidable, to be lamented and condemned. Yet our elementary analysis of the "prisoners' dilemma" model earlier would suggest that such "unnecessary conflict" may indeed be unavoidable in much of political life. The psychologist does not really tell us how to avoid the physical ground structure that produced the prisoners' dilemma between Moscow and Washington; yet it is not enough for us merely to know that prisoners' dilemma might be in effect. An American who really believes that all Soviet-American conflict has been originally caused by mutually erroneous fears might still have to conclude that the tension will continue. We may have to fear Russians just as much because they fear us as because they are basically hostile.

Such arguments have more often been applied of late to the relationship between Communist China and the United States. Again the analysis suggests that Peking menaced us unwittingly and that we menaced China without realizing it. We have had bases all around China, missiles aimed at Chinese cities, and a "fleet" in the Formosa Straits. When the United States discussed an ABM program, it insisted on describing it as aimed at China, as protecting American cities against the missiles that the Chinese would soon develop. Again the insight emerges that there was no real cause for basic hostility between the two countries, since each was simply overreacting to the activities of the other. Yet again, the question would be whether such a sad international interaction could indeed be avoided at the time, or quickly remedied.

There is obviously a great deal of truth in this "multiplier" model of international reactions, whereby anticipated hostility on one side breeds hostility on the other, and then breeds real hostility again in the first. The psychological approach implies that this multiplier can easily be reversed, by having one side or the other simply take "the first step," in "graduated reductions in tension" (GRIT), with a positive response then following from the other side, with another step then becoming appropriate on our side, ad infinitum. Yet skeptics may wonder whether every first step that might be taken would so surely lead to a very low level of hostility at the end.

It is also interesting to note some contemporary international conflicts to which the psychological mutual misperception model has not been so enthusiastically applied. For example, the conflict between Moscow and Peking might also stem only from mutual expectations of truly nonexistent hostility. Yet this same conflict has been extensively cited by liberal commentators as evidence that the U.S. does not really have to fear a Communist monolith, that we can count on internal differences within the "Communist bloc" to allow us to negotiate with either power, or to play one off against the other. At least this suggests a certain bias by a few of the psychologists who have entered the political fray, prescribing their mirror-image model only wherever the practical consequence would be greater American willingness to make concessions to one of the Communist powers. Since the same model when applied to the Moscow-Peking rift would suggest enhanced American vigilance, if the "Communist bloc" can be restored into an alliance at any moment, the argument does not get delivered in this form.

Obviously the mutual fear multiplier plays a role in the Sino-Soviet dispute too. Each side fears that the other will try to undermine its influence within various countries and various Communist parties. Each distrusts the other's dealings with the United States. Just as obviously, some of such mutual erroneous distrust is beyond practical remedy, as in all international conflicts. But just as obviously, some of the conflict may be basically real, rather than simply a psychological delusion.

The mutual misperception model has also not seen as extensive application to the conflict between Washington and Hanoi. Perhaps this is because of the sheer violence of the Vietnam War, which makes it less and less believable that it is some silly misunderstanding. Perhaps it is also because of the statements of the Hanoi regime itself, statements echoed by the American radical opposition to the war, which claims that the American government knows exactly what it is doing in trying to suppress insurgencies and revolutionary forces in underdeveloped countries around the world; it is trying to make the world safe for capitalism. Moderate Americans might have concluded by now that America had perhaps irrationally exaggerated the desire, or the ability, of Communist guerrilla movements to threaten the domestic life-style of the United States itself. Yet the most vehement and vocal portion of the antiwar movement has adopted a very different, basically nonpsychological model, that of a very conscious and deliberate reactionary policy on the part of the United States government.

The popularity of mutual-misperception models might thus be charged with having been overly coordinated with particular political drives from year to year. If it helped put across the nuclear test-ban, it was stressed. If it conflicted with the mobilizing of resistance to the war in Vietnam, it received less emphasis.

As with other human failings, however, the delusions of the self-confirming hypothesis might be attributed by the right to the left, as well as vice versa. Conservatives in western societies could hardly deny that such a syndrome is possible, although they would deny that it explained any significant part of the Cold War. Russian expansionism has been an objective fact in their view. If western defensive precautions at all exacerbated postwar relations, this might not alter the fact that the alternative to such precautions would have been Russian domination of much more territory. If pressed to find a real-life example of the illusions engendered by self-confirming hypotheses, such conservatives might instead cite the alienation of radicals from their governments and societies. The contention would be that such radicals feel alienated because they expect to feel this way, and act in ways which confirm the expectation. If there is anything unrepresentative about the U.S. Navy, in this view, it is because radicals have chosen not to enlist in it.

The self-confirming error is not the only risk one can encounter as propositions alter reality as they are advanced. One can also find examples of the self-denying proposition on international matters. The classic example, of course, emerges from the field of international economics, when a government tries to avert a monetary balance of payments panic by announcing "There will be no devaluation of the dollar." If the statement is mistimed, the financial public will read it more as evidence of the government's concern than of fiscal truth, and the panic to unload the dollar will be aggravated with the exact result that devaluation will have to be accepted after all. Outside the economic realm, one can find similar examples of "confidence-building" statements which backfire and thereby in effect disprove themselves.

In more general terms, it is thus entirely plausible that the analysis of politics in the international arena is confronted by a certain "Heisenberg uncertainty principle" of its own, whereby it is difficult to have a belief about the system without in the process changing the system. One most important property of all forms of politics is what the human actors involved believe about such politics. If the USSR and the United States indeed believe there is a Cold War, they will have to be correct in their beliefs, if only because the beliefs launched the "war."

Is this problem of self-confirming "feedback" becoming more or less serious as an impediment to understanding the international system? One clear trend of the 20th century is for greater speed in communication and transportation, and in the operation of weapons systems. Computerization of some sorts of calculation make certain kinds of analysis and decision-making possible in reasonable lengths of time, where previously these would have been impossible or prohibitively delayed. Yet this latter acceleration in "decision-making" processes hardly compensates for the accelerated needs for decision, and the human by himself does not seem equipped to make more rapid decisions or judgments than in the past.

Speed in communications can assuredly alleviate some problems. The last battle of the War of 1812 after all was tragically fought at New Orleans months after peace had been concluded between Britain and the United States, only because the news had not arrived. Yet today the fear of a successful preemptive missile strike might still seem to pose such urgent needs for decision that both sides would fire off their strategic arsenal simply in fear that the other was about to do so. Urgency in decision-making tends to exaggerate the pathologically self-confirming patterns that one would hope to avoid. Arms control, if it does nothing else, can thus hope to steer nations toward the kinds of weapons which minimize urgency and give greater leeway for analysis and contemplation of alternatives.

There are epistemological traps, of course, in every area of politics, and not just on international problems. How can we get interested in a problem without caring about the issues involved? But if we care, do we not tend to distort the facts as we see them? Above all, by acting on the "facts," don't we deploy forces and resources that change the facts? Yet, if a need for speed compounds these quandaries, what has compounded them all the more is the open and legitimate and uncontrolled conflict that is peculiar to the international slice of politics. There may well be an "enemy" out there, from whom military secrets and other secrets must be hidden, lest he use such information against us. But if the secrets are hidden from the enemy, are they not always also partially hidden from us too?

Self-fulfilling and self-denying propositions might seem pathological and remediable for neurotic individuals, but may be much less easily avoided in the particularly "neurotic" and anarchic process we know as international politics. What is crucial to the avoidance of mutual misperception can not be supplied simply by identifying the syndrome as it occurs. What must be supplied is a restructuring of communications opportunities, and of objective monitoring capabilities, such that individuals on each side can reassure themselves, to dispel any fears before they have time to act on such fears. Satellite reconnaisance devices, or close alliance ties, or reductions in the stakes of international interaction, can supply this, but mere analysis from a semidetached point of view may not.

The most serious pitfall to be avoided in an application of psychology may thus in the end be any assumption that errors identified are always errors that can be avoided. If we note, for example, that a certain psychologic binds most of us as decision-makers, in that we rule out evidence which contradicts assumptions we have already made, is this avoidable, or is it the inevitable price that must be paid for living with less-than-perfect perceptive abilities? Is paranoia really as avoidable as psychology sometimes makes it seem, especially in environments that seem to approximate the fear and hostility of Hobbes' state of nature? Or is it inevitable, in ways which engender real hostilities in others, which make paranoid fears accurate fears? Is prejudice about a foreigner bad, or simply less-than-the-best, in terms of guessing how some person will behave when nothing more is known about him besides his nationality?

There is also a danger of attributing faults most directly to those we know best. Perhaps we can be sure that our side of an international conflict is indeed neurotic, while we must still only guess that the opposing side is burdened by any similar problems. Since psychology is at heart a fault-finding exercise, unlike economics or political science, the entire tendency may thus be to condemn faults in whom and what one is treating. One normally treats one's own countrymen, and an indictment is thus most likely, if misleadingly, to fall on them.

There is a further danger here of "personalizing" nations, precisely in the way political scientists have classically been accused of misinterpreting or oversimplifying the political entities they discuss. Governments are not perfectly coordinated or cohesive, and it is only to be expected that the right hand will often not know what the left hand is doing. The need for speed in modern international decisions, the complexity of bureaucracies and governments, the degree of international and domestic conflict, all tend to make natural and understandable what the psychologist often purports to condemn and dissapprove of. When the psychologist, conversely, learns and interprets what we all know about these complexities in the workings of politics, he might be able to provide very useful services and predictions —predictions of perceptions and misperceptions, predictions of unusual and obnoxious motives.

Bramson, Leon and Goethals, George, eds. *War*. New York: Basic Books, 1964.
George, Alexander and George, Juliette. *Woodrow Wilson and Colonel House*. New York: John Day, 1956.
Jervis, Robert. "Hypothesis on Misperception." *World Politics*. April, 1968.
Kelman, Herbert C., ed. *International Behavior: A Social-Psychological Analysis*. New York: Holt, Rinehart & Winston, 1965.
Rivera, Joseph H., de. *The Psychological Dimension of Foreign Policy*. Columbus, Ohio: Merrill, 1968.
White, Ralph K. *Nobody Wanted War: Misperceptions in Vietnam and Other Wars*. Garden City, N.Y.: Doubleday, 1970.

The Rational Use of Psychological Image

A desire to be respected or loved may illustrate some basic psychological quirks either in the statesmen who influence international politics or in the countries they represent. Such respect or "prestige" is also an important means of getting one's way in the material decisions of the world, however, so even the most psychologically adjusted statesman must be concerned with maintaining his prestige and that of his country.

We thus begin a transition here back to more "rational" models of foreign policy behavior. What seems "neurotic" in a society governed by law may make perfect sense in the violent anarchy of international relations. If it would have been foolhardy for Hitler to throw a tantrum while negotiating a speeding ticket, the same tantrum may have been wise and astute in dealings with Chamberlain at Munich.

Expressions of admiration may similarly be genuine and spontaneous or, in the international political arena, controlled and manipulated. What the psychologist saw as spontaneously beneficial or pathological behavior in international politics might thus be generally much more calculated. Advocates of graduated reductions in tension thus point to various periods of detente between the United States and the Soviet Union, or indeed between other nations which have alternately hostile and friendly interactions.

We often speak of periods of good or bad relations, of moves toward and away from detente, in our chronicles of international politics, but there is a danger here that such terminology may be used in vague and misleading ways. When is a detente a detente? Have we really been in a state of detente with the Soviet Union, and far away from one with Communist China? If we were, could it still be that a greater portion of American resources in the 1960's was diverted from the civilian sector by Russian behavior than by Chinese?

Before reaching too many conclusions on the substantive issues, we should devote a little more attention to the very nature of the evidence we have been working with in the analysis of international politics, and some of the problems created by such evidence. Classically, as with domestic politics, one has had documents to work with; yet one clear result of nuclear stalemate, and the stability of the Cold War, is that archives are no longer to be captured and looted for the benefit of historians and political scientists.

Even before these documents became unavailable, moreover, difficulties existed with regard to accepting such paperwork at face value. As in the United States today, such records may have been written as much with a view to history as to practical policy, perhaps to prove to future generations that various decisions were elaborately rational when they indeed were much more implicit or ad hoc. When we see the possibly more "relaxed" accounts of decision-makers' thoughts, as with Hitler's "table-talks," or Albert Speer's recollections of the Nazi leader's conversations, one can again hardly know whether these comments were representative, or merely the offhand comments of an atmosphere quite different from the one in which decisions were made. A similar puzzle occurs with occasional personal interviews which have emerged with Mao Tse-tung, or Chou En-lai, interviews much livelier and forth-coming than the typically stilted lines of official Chinese Communist publications.

If one limits himself to more serious public speeches and documents, one insures himself against being misled by more whimsical utterances, but we must always remember that all such statements are hardly prepared in quest of candor, but rather to achieve some particular political purpose. Even in the United States one indeed can not be sure where responsibility for any particularly important phrase should lie, or what the true author intended to accomplish by it. The phrases in U.S. presidential speeches which seemed to validate various bureaucratic moves on behalf of the Multi-Lateral Forces (MLF) were inserted by the very State Department officers who afterward quoted them as authority, although it was hardly clear that the president delivering such addresses had intended such an interpretation.

We might indeed discover similar problems with regard to Soviet documents. Can we really tell what the Brezhnev doctrine was intended to convey to Rumania, or Albania, or China, with its implicit threats of intervention throughout the "socialist" area irrespective of national sovereignties? Can we really tell who inserted the crucial phrases here, or why? Analyses of Soviet foreign policy focus heavy attention on documents, striving to achieve a total coverage and monitoring of all such statements; nothing similarly intensive is undertaken in analysis of West German foreign policy. In part this reflects the great shortage of alternative material for analysis in the case of the Communist countries; but it also suggests a perhaps mistaken impression that statements from Communist countries are much more carefully orchestrated than in the West, so much so that each one must be taken seriously and fitted into the master jigsaw puzzle.

Perhaps it will therefore be necessary for us to supplement documents and other verbal indicators with some alternative measures of the condition of the international system at any particular time. For example, one can use international trade as an index of mutual cooperation in international relations, and expenditures on weapons systems as a negative index of mutually counter-productive activity. International telephone calls and mail flows can be measured, as well as travel among countries, or exchanges of literature.

Using a few of such indexes, however, one encounters some apparently paradoxical results in that periods of verbal tension seem sometimes to concur with times of lower military weapons expenditures, while verbal detentes sometimes seem to accompany escalations in the material activities by which one state damages the standing and positions of the other. How can one explain such apparent inconsistencies? Mere chance would probably not suffice, nor would any kind of iron rule by which nature had dictated that verbal and real tensions should be inversely related.

Part of the explanation for such paradoxes might simply note that the Soviet Union is a highly manipulatable society, in which Khrushchev could direct public statements to be more or less friendly to the United States as he chose. If this is correct, the Soviet leadership may have had a conscious policy of compensating for the ups and downs of the more material side of Soviet-American relations by casting the verbal side in the opposite direction. Thus, when the arms race or real tensions over Berlin were at a low level, Moscow would issue its most bitter diatribes against the West; when real conflict had been aggravated, conversely, the USSR would issue more conciliatory appraisals of the United States.

Yet it would hardly be fair to charge only the Communist powers with putting a verbal tone on the international arena at variance with the physical drift of things. It is often noted that the Eisenhower administration rarely acknowledged any community of interest with the Russians, but that defense budgets in the United States were also kept low, so low that the Democratic party in opposition made this a major issue between 1957 and 1960. The Kennedy administration conversely gave verbal endorsement to coexistence, while substantially augmenting the conventional and strategic nuclear forces of the United States. The tone of governmental statements and national verbal style may thus be as manipulatable in Western democracies as in the Socialist bloc; in any event, it would be a mistake for a student to identify periods of "tension" and "detente" through the Cold War simply on the basis of documents and public pronouncements. Some sort of credibility gap may thus be appropriate for any and all countries participating in international politics, simply since the ability to channel and harness communications is one attribute of the modern state.

The manipulability of communications can thus cause some easy confusions on any survey of current international alliances and confrontations. A casual observer might conclude that Communist China and the United

States had been the most bitter enemies in the last ten years on the basis of vehement verbal denounciations by each regime of the other. Yet the negative interaction in real terms has been small; few bullets have been fired, few weapons procured in ways which forced matching weapons procurements on the opposite party. Indeed, if we were to believe some charges advanced by the Soviet Union, the Americans and Chinese had actually been in tacit collusion on several matters related to the war in Vietnam, as in Chinese delay of Russian shipments of air defense equipment to Hanoi.

We might have had similar difficulty in establishing the alliance character of Pakistan, both before and after the coup which ousted President Ayub. Pakistan has been a nominal member of SEATO, a military alliance with the United States. It has been receiving arms from Communist China, whose press has generally avoided criticism of the Pakistani regimes, albeit their status as military dictatorships. Some American press reports have gone so far as to describe Pakistan as a de facto ally of China. Yet the number of Pakistani students in the United States still far exceeded the number in China. Was Pakistan, therefore, a "firm ally" or a "potential enemy" of the United States? In truth, it has been neither, and our picture of Pakistan's role must take us along more complicated paths of analysis.

The alignment of the Arab states presents similar problems. We think of the United Arab Republic as being increasingly dependent on the Soviet Union for arms aid, and therefore as becoming a satellite of the USSR. Yet the cultural dependence of Egypt on the West is as strong as ever. Far more people are learning English than Russian, and American programs provide a large share of the television schedule of Cairo. (Indeed, to complete the irony and to demonstrate how indecisive some such objective indicators can be, we have already noted that Israelis often watch their favorite American television programs on Cairo TV.)

FURTHER READINGS

Jervis, Robert. *The Logic of Images in International Relations.* Princeton: Princeton University Press, 1969.
Osgood, Charles E. *An Alternative to War or Surrender.* Urbana: University of Illinois Press, 1962.

Economic Interpretations of International Politics

There is obviously something to be said for more "rational" models of foreign policy behavior. What seems "immature" in domestic society may make much more sense in international politics. Simple economic greed may incline men to kill other men when this can be described as "war" rather than "murder," and especially when it does not bring the punishments which are attached to murder. We earlier discussed "rational" models of the policy process wherein diplomats and generals were motivated by a love of power. Economic models would tend rather to focus on a love of wealth.

The world has already seen many distinct approaches to interpreting international politics in terms of economic factors. What is involved here is not a theory of international economics per se, but rather whether economic variables do not play a crucial role in explaining international politics, or even in guiding the foreign policy-maker to correct policy decisions.

One such school of thought here appears with the mercantilism of the 17th and 18th centuries, perhaps most vividly exemplified in the policies of Colbert in France. The assumptions here were quite straightforward, and perhaps true to life for the period, that gold and other acceptable forms of money are immediately convertible into political power, since relatively purchasable or rentable factors such as manpower and grain are the major ingredients to military success. Since gold can be accumulated, preserved, and stored, any rise in monetary holdings thus signals a rise in the potential military power of the state in question. Since the supply of gold for the world as a whole is relatively fixed at any particular time, the trade relationship becomes essentially competitive. A desirable balance of payments for one side becomes an undesirable imbalance for the other, and the trade relationship becomes just one more arena for maintaining the balance of power. Much of the reasoning of the balance of power is implicit in the value assigned to ready cash; there must be enough neutral bystanders who are ready to sell their goods or their young mercenary soldiers to the highest bidder.

The policy recommendations thus include discouraging imports and stimulating exports, with a view to accumulating as much of liquid currency and wealth as possible. Tariffs, trade regulations, subsidies, state monopolies, all will be used to achieve this "favorable balance of payment." The criticisms that might be made of such an approach are numerous. To begin, it tends to ignore the economic welfare of the people governed by one's regime, in its straightforward emphasis on military power.

Even if the stress on military-diplomatic power seems appropriate, given all we know about the anarchic international arena, the stress on liquid wealth overrates the short-term aspects of military power. Gold assuredly will allow one to hire mercenaries, but less of a fixation on gold might have allowed more of a domestic industrial expansion, producing tools, techniques, and material product which over time might make mercenaries far less relevant, or which would produce national and professional armies which could easily defeat the more cash-oriented mercenary forces. The rapid decline of Spain from world influence after 1648 can largely be traced to the overstress on searches for gold and silver, and the insufficient attention devoted to technology and real material progress. As nations coalesced in resistance to the threats of Spanish and the French hegemony, moreover, the number of free-floating resources and units of armed manpower diminished, as balance of power reasoning dictated coming to the aid of the losing rather than the wealthier side. This is, of course, not to argue that cash holdings ever would become totally valueless in political power and influence.

An alternative school of economic reasoning emerged as a rational and enlightened answer to mercantilism, at first primarily in Britain with such advocates of free trade as Adam Smith, Jeremy E. Bentham, and Richard Cobden. This school systematically developed economic theory on the great and enormous benefits which might emerge if different nations were able to specialize in the products wherein they held a comparative advantage, and then exchanged such products in the process of trade. Compared to such benefits, it was argued, even the loot and material benefits captured in outright conquest of foreign territories were secondary.

Aggression in general is an economic waste of time, since the conquered population will still have to be fed and allowed to share in the national well-being, since the costs of military adventures are inescapable. State interference in the economy is generally counter-productive, all the more so when such interference comes in the deployment of armies in efforts to move the boundary outward. The policy recommendations of such a position are thus clear. All the artificial barriers to imports of the mercantilist period should be dismantled, and the principles of laissez-faire should be allowed to exercise their effect. If the state nonetheless accumulated a "favorable" balance of payments, this should be eliminated by altering the currency exchange rates if necessary, for this balance merely proves that the country is charging too little for its exports and paying too much for its imports, needlessly forgoing an additional increment in its standard of living.

There are at least two major criticisms that must be directed at this liberal, classic economic picture of the international system. From a political point of view, it can be charged with greatly underrating the value and applicability of political power. If one nation could conquer the entire globe, it is hardly certain that it would be materially unwise for it to do so, even if we omit the psychological and cultural purposes that might be served in such aggressions. Foreign populations can be mistreated and robbed and enslaved, and the difficulties in doing so may be more moral than economic.

Second, even in economic terms, to settle for the best in terms of specialization for the present may ignore the dynamic tendencies for economic and industrial development over the longer run, as some nations acquire the economic roles which lead to rapid growth and others do not, as some states accumulate economic characteristics which can be converted to military power, while others do not. The "national economic" school of analysis, as exemplified in the 19th century already by persons such as Freidrich List and Henry Clay, thus noted that divisions of the total world economy on national lines were perhaps inevitable, if only because of such noneconomic factors as cultural and political tradition. Since manpower and resources would not be able to move freely across boundaries, the benefits of a simple free trade economy would not be shared as evenly as the nonpolitical analysis would have suggested. Since the defense of national sovereignty is important in terms of politics, it therefore becomes important also in terms of economics, and trade policies comparable to those of the mercantilist era will have to be considered, including tariffs, absolute barriers to some imports, subsidies for exports and for "infant industries," and even state involvement in industrial management.

Yet the object of such policies could not any more be the accumulation of gold or currency, for this could only be converted to military or political power for the very short-term future; such gold moreover does little to benefit the economic living standards on one's population. Rather the objective in interfering with free trade will be to accelerate the development and accumulation of capital, since machines will now be more significant for the outcome of military campaigns than any companies of soldiers who might have been available for hire.

Therefore the policy recommendations of this third school of thought might include some attention toward autarchy, especially on items relevant to military production, since wars in the 19th and 20th century might see all trade curtailed, even trade with neutrals. More generally, the policy would stress economic development, avoiding the pitfall in accepting the temporary offerings of states which had industrialized earlier, to induce industrialization whereby the nation could supply this market itself. In ways the policy thus amounts to a state decision in favor of deferred gratification, in favor of increased capitalization, forgoing the affluence that immediate exploitation of trade with foreign producers would bring, but in the long run bringing a higher standard for all.

A fourth major interpretation of the international system in economic terms emerges, of course, from the Marxist analysis already discussed. As Marx gave the Hegelian dialectic a material framework, he in effect conjured up an economic deterministic theory of the system as a whole, a theory which can be regarded as one of several "socialist" theories of international relations. The Marxist analysis, as elaborated and considerably expanded by Lenin, sees imperialism simply as a subcase of the general internal contradictions of the capitalist system; one is that capitalists must bitterly contest their markets with other capitalists. To reduce the damage to continuing corporate profits, attempts are made to find new investment

and sales opportunities abroad, to carve out colonial empires in which sales
by other capitalist economies with similar problems will be excluded, while
ours are permitted.

As capitalist societies thus seek to postpone their own collapse by carving
out new monopolistic markets abroad, there will not long be enough such
virgin territory into which production can be dumped, and wars will thus
result in the wake of imperialism. In the end, these wars will be accompanied by revolution and the final stage of the Marxist dialectic.

The policy recommendations which appear in this analysis thus vary
from class to class. In terms of its own narrow and distorted class view, the
governments of the various regimes will have to race to capture markets,
and to try to win the wars that such races induce. For the proletariat which
truly sees the determined course of the future, such wars should be welcome as setting the stage for the final seizures of political power.

Yet at least some of the assumptions of the Marxist-Leninist analysis need
to be challenged for their correspondence with the facts. To begin, the real
exploitation of European colonial empires in terms of economics is very
hard to measure, and it can be argued that little or nothing of this kind of
value was extracted in the net. Trade outside one's "empire" in many cases
exceeded trade within the "empire." Even if one finds various governments
using economic or trade arguments as excuses for colonial interventions or
expansions, this often was a simple window-dressing, in an age when economic arguments were seen as more legitimate and less antagonistic than
they are today. French expansion into North Africa thus more often saw
the government in Paris asking French business men to enter the area, to
give a pretext for a political imperialism that would follow. The drive to
"color the map" thus is related to many noneconomic factors, to fears that
ethnic brothers will otherwise be lost to the English-speaking world, or that
opposing naval bases might otherwise be established if such moves were not
preempted. World War I, to be sure, seemed to prove that competitive
imperialisms would lead to a major war, a war which would enable the
proletariat to seize power. Yet the exact linkage of imperialism to the war
is as debatable as the linkage of the economic system to imperialism, and
Lenin himself was surprised and disappointed at the initial reactions of the
working class in most of the countries party to the war.

Not all of the socialist movement has stayed faithful to the Marxist
analysis, and a revisionist Democratic-Socialist tradition had emerged by
the latter 19th century which would present a substantially different interpretation of imperialism and international conflict. As objectified perhaps
best in the writings of John A. Hobson, this school of analysis agreed with
Marx that international conflict was indeed largely or exclusively the result
of domestic special interests, pursuing their own welfare at the expense of
the rest of society. Yet such imperialist conflict was indeed mistaken, for
countries as a whole and for most of their business interests; as liberal

economists had argued earlier, one could bring home all the world offered in material wealth by trade alone. If unemployment and maldistribution of wealth were the problems, they could be resolved by domestic reforms produced in an evolutionary exploitation of the parliamentary process.

Since the democratic socialist favored substantial government interference in the economy, he was clearly not an advocate of free trade; but government interference when it came to the international sphere could be every bit as cooperative as the trade relationships of classical liberal economics had been assumed to be. So far as policy recommendations were concerned, the antagonisms of a dialectic were to be avoided. Wars were neither necessary nor beneficial for either class, just as violent revolution was not required as the means to reform.

A criticism of democratic-socialist assumptions would refer again to the world of military power and political power by which wars can indeed make sense; international dealings with unreformed societies may thus force even social-democracies to prepare for war, to defend their political systems, or even perhaps to defend access to some markets which an opposing regime, however foolishly, was seeking to close. Perhaps Germans and Czechs ideally will have no conflicts of interest, economic or otherwise, once social-democratic parties have come to power on each side of the boundary. Yet cultural differences can lead to jealousies which can motivate men as hostilely as purely class issues, and social-democratic theory has as much difficulty in acknowledging this as do the Marxists.

The last decade has seen the evolution of still another major form of economic determinist theory of international relations, cast somewhat as a response to the Marxist predictions which so many individuals had come to believe and take seriously. As articulated most sharply by W. W. Rostow in his "Stages of Growth," this view stresses some of the same factors as the earlier "national economist" school, concentrating on discontinuities of aggregate national figures for GNP, savings, investment, consumption, and rates of growth. The major divergence from the 19th century aggregate analysis, of course, arises because the liberation of colonial areas and the long experience of European states since the mid-19th century has supplied us with so much more interesting factual data to digest.

The underlying assumption of relevance is broader, moreover. Economic development is not only a key to economic affluence in the future, or to military security, but also to political development and stability, indeed to forecasting whether Marx's predictions will be believed or institutionalized from country to country.

Rostow's analysis identified a definite chain of development from "traditional society" to a stage of high consumption, a pattern that countries such as the United Kingdom, the United States, and more recently, Japan, had passed through, a pattern that saw a relatively sudden period of economic growth and high capitalization which completely transformed the political and social as well as economic nature of the society in question. Prior to this period of self-sustaining growth to which all nations presumably aspire, came a preliminary stage in which certain preconditions for growth were satisfied, for example, the provision of human capital in the form of education, the accumulation of more general capital either indigenously or on loan from abroad, the achievement of subsistence levels in agriculture, the provision of social overhead, and perhaps as important as anything else, a change in the basic values of society.

The picture here of an economic development inexorably leading to political development was almost purposefully an optimistic one, suggesting that the problems of economic development could be solved, and that with development would come the alleviation or easing of various political problems, problems that might otherwise have caused tensions, insurrections, and wars. When Marx saw the economic process inevitably leading to revolution and war, the counterview saw a determinism which almost as clearly would produce happiness and peace.

Yet many and varied criticisms could be put forward about this optimistic view of domestic economic development as a balm for international troubles. To begin, at least some of the crucial input variables in Rostow's second stage, just prior to "take-off," defined economically, might really be seen as political variables. For example, the extent of education, the reform of the banking system, the provision of social overhead capital, are basically political inputs. If law and order can once be established, perhaps the economic privation that causes disorder can be eliminated, but the entire problem may seem like more of a vicious cycle than a basically deterministic evolution. A "change in the values" of society with regard to growth most assuredly seems to be a political or social variable, rather than simply economic.

At least some doubt must also be expressed on whether economic growth per se can be stimulated from the outside. The policy advice of the school of economic determinism here was that crucial inputs of aid should be administered to get self-sustaining growth underway in societies which seemed ripe for it, on the theory that this would create healthy and pluralistic societies which in the end would be welcome partners for a country like the United States. Yet the imputation of great leverage for foreign aid may be unwarrantedly derived from the peculiarly successful American experience in the Marshall Plan aiding Western Europe to recover from World War II. In that case, the human capital and industrial experience of the populations affected suggested that enormous material progress would occur with only a small input of outside assistance.

Whether other areas are as tractable to economic stimulation remains a source of nagging uncertainty. The mere increase in population produced by improved health standards may cause per capita gross national product to decline, even as absolute national product is increased. The essentially inappropriate character of capital-intensive modern Western technology may help underdeveloped areas with a labor surplus far less than would the technology which the more advanced countries abandoned decades ago, technology which they can no longer resurrect.

While it is assumed that increases of affluence will be accompanied almost automatically by improvements in the distribution of such income, social and economic processes may function so as to preserve or worsen inequalities of well-being in a society, with whatever unrest ensues.

When shifting from the economic tractability of the states in question to the assumed political fruits of economic progress, some additional questions must seem in order, in reflecting what has been said before. It is by no means certain that richer societies will be more democratic or representative politically than those that are poor. It is by no means certain that an increase in a nation's disposable wealth will make it more peaceful in its approaches to the outside world. To be sure, a new affluence will give a nation a greater vested interest in peace, and incentive to avoid World War III. Yet increasing affluence can also make more resources available for military expenditures, in the hopes of righting old wrongs, or avenging old defeats. As noted earlier, there is not even such a clear relationship between peace and democratic political systems, regardless of whether economic progress could cause either one.

To be sure, none of this is to deny the objective desirability of economic expansion per se. Americans and others will normally prefer that all people have enough to eat, and that all share in the richer material rewards of life, other things being equal. What rather is to be challenged are assumptions that an enhanced likelihood for peace is automatically to be expected as the very pleasant and natural by-product of this. If we care for economic growth for its own sake, this simply becomes a component of our foreign policy goals, but it hardly defines an economic theory of how the history and the course of international politics is determined.

Economic growth of underdeveloped nations may thus simply stand up as one of the values to be served in foreign policy, in accordance with most developed nations' value schemes. A few might dissent in that the aggregate figures normally used to measure growth produce a certain unreality and naivete, that at least a certain deduction should be made from such gains to account for material pollution and societal disruption.

Leaving aside general economic "theories of history," discussing the inducement of economic growth in underdeveloped nations can lead us to consider the growth also of nations already quite extensively developed. If Japan has maintained a far greater rate of growth than the United States, this often causes Americans to agonize about their own process. Americans seem agreed that U.S. growth should be closer to 10 percent if this can at all be managed. Why so much emphasis on growth, when some growth is indeed almost inevitable, when our grandchildren will be far wealthier than we are, no matter what government policy we elect to follow? Isn't this the relatively poor divesting themselves of assets for the clear future benefit of the relatively rich? And what of the costs in terms of ecological damage and pollution?

A large part of such an "economic" argument can again be explained in terms of the naked political power calculations made in the context of an anarchic international system. The argument is simply that political power will be a function of relative economic strength; even if we are rich, we dare not accumulate additional riches at slower rates than those of other rich nations. Perhaps these relative considerations have a basis within economics itself, as to allow some other country to grow more rapidly might let it corner certain areas of industry in ways which eliminated sales possibilities and ultimately reduced our own affluence absolutely. Perhaps the real significance of economic well-being is relative anyway, so that we would be less happy if we were twice as rich as today, but behind Japan, than we are now when we are ahead of Japan in per capita affluence. Finally, of course, there is always the prospect of military defeat, the prospect that some adaptation of economic resources might yet allow some other nation to attempt the great campaign of military conquest.

The ugly head of international military power considerations raises its head even more ambivalently in national policy on population control. Despite a general sense that the world is producing far too many children for economic progress or political stability, many countries are indeed lukewarm in pressing ahead with campaigns to discourage population growth, and some indeed have a policy of encouraging births. Perhaps Scandinavia presents a clue on the long-term future of the world, that once a generally affluent standard has been reached, families will lose the taste for many children, so that a real possibility will have to be found of normal population decline. Most of the world has unhappily not reached standards of living comparable to those of Sweden, and religious and other complications might make us less sure that any poor nation becoming rich will become less productive of children. Yet if Sweden has a conscious policy of encouraging its citizens to produce more children, as do France and Rumania, it is at least subliminally related to the fear that the burgeoning populations of other nations might ultimately threaten a Swedish territory which seemed to be empty.

Population is therefore still seen as a military or political power asset, even where it may not be an asset anymore for the quality of civilian life. To be sure, in military terms alone, it is conceivable that increases in population might someday become a liability rather than an asset, as additional mouths to be fed tied up more and more able-bodied persons in agriculture, imposing perhaps a net decrease in able-bodied manpower available for the armed forces. If China or the UAR thus were to pursue a population control policy, it would hardly reflect any conscious renunciation of power in the international arena, since shortages of manpower in neither case have been the constraint limiting military influence.

What forms of international political power can thus be pursued by means of economic tools? Nations have always reserved to themselves the right to forbid or restrict trade with foreign nations of which they disapproved. Yet some crucial questions must govern policy here, a series of questions which are often answered only implicitly rather than explicitly.

To begin, would the trade forgone really have stimulated the opposing camp's (the USSR or Communist China) industrial and economic development more than that of the United States? The normal assumption has been that this was so, perhaps because the free world was a larger economic unit than the areas being boycotted and embargoed, or because it was also much more efficient economically, since it has retained market mechanisms. Given the inherent inefficiencies of the command economy methods of the socialist camp, it is sometimes even argued that the USSR needs foreign trade if only to establish the price levels which must govern domestic sales and purchases. The enormous sophistication and variety of goods produced in the free world moreover is a strong inducement for the Communist powers to seek trade.

By contrast, the amount of likely trade with the Soviet bloc will be a relatively trivial percentage of the United States or free world total, and thus hardly crucial to the material affluence or economic growth of the market economies. To be sure, certain particular sectors will benefit from the economic opportunities of trade, and it comes as no surprise that the San Francisco Chamber of Commerce has long favored trade with mainland China. At the margin, certain kinds of qualitative goods will always be available from the USSR or China that would be unobtainable elsewhere, but these are truly less central commodities than those which might be needed by the other side.

Becoming a little more political, one will, however, not automatically want the economic growth of the Soviet Union to be circumscribed, for various assumptions must first be questioned in one direction or another here also. Would not higher Russian or Chinese industrial production stimulate demands for consumer goods, and perhaps be pulled into the satisfaction of such appetites once they have been whetted? This obviously mixes economic analysis with a good deal of Kremlinology, and it might seem quite paradoxical if an increase in Russian or Chinese GNP saw a decrease in the resources available for military spending, or for capitalization for the future; yet the possibility cannot be ignored that affluence will become a pandora's box for the austere regimes of the Communist world. At a broader level, it is argued that success in industrialization or in the accumulation of affluence would over time make such regimes more at peace with the status quo, and less ready to risk small wars or big wars in pursuit of something better.

Will trade make the communist world more dependent on continued trade, or vice versa? Will it make the western world more dependent on such trade relationships? Who will be more credible in threatening an abrupt economic rupture in some crisis?

As elsewhere, one would have to distinguish between short-term and long-term relationships. The damage done to Poland's Five-Year Plan by a quick termination of trade might be remediable in two or three years, even if its impact in first few months seemed devastating. Yet before concluding that the leverage here is only of secondary importance, one must note that many of the crises to which such leverage would be applied are themselves of quite short-term duration. What really deters Moscow or East Germany from imposing a blockade on West Berlin, to round out the territorial integrity of the lands east of the Elbe? To a great extent, the most effective deterrent is that trade from West Germany to Eastern Europe would almost certainly be cut off in retaliation for such a blockade, and that such a cut-off would upset the economic plans of every regime in the Socialist camp. While such regimes continually and regularly attempt to make themselves economically independent of Bonn and the rest of Western Europe, the inability of the Marxist economy to produce the required quantity and quality of goods continually undoes all these efforts, in fact increasing the dependency of regimes even as powerful as the Soviet Union on such trade. In the net, therefore, for much of what matters on the NATO central front, economic leverage is enormously powerful and substantially in favor of the West.

Will increased trade foster friendship for the West behind the Iron Curtain, or conversely would it breed sympathy or weakness toward the Communist regimes among Western businessmen? This clearly has been an important fear on both sides of the line, and the first Polish statements on cooperation with West German firms such as Krupp went out of their way to deny that political friendship would follow in the wake of economic convenience. Yet as elsewhere in politics, the denial of impact here precisely seemed to confirm its existence.

For either side to maintain an embargo will also require constraining multiple relationships between individual states on either side of the line. Previously the Communist bloc might have seemed to be more monolithically coordinated, but the breaks in Marxist solidarity are now obviously comparable to those in the always more pluralistic free world. Each individual state may thus be enormously tempted to rationalize that no great harm was being done to the alliance whenever enormous short-term trade advantages could be garnered in some trade deal. If trade is never really crucial for the West as a whole, it may still be enormously tempting for particular firms or particular nations. Fears of relative economic growth or domination within alliances will also be influential—French fears of the United States, Rumanian fears of Moscow, American fears of Japan.

Embargoes have generally not been very effective as a tool of political punishment; this is shown most recently in the pressures supposedly concerted against Rhodesia after its "unilateral declaration of independence" from Great Britain. Japanese businessmen have only been the more numerous of the entrepreneurs who have made themselves available for the purchases from, and sales to, Rhodesia, and the blockade has clearly not forced the white regime to give in. Agitation for similar economic pressures on the Republic of South Africa have not even won the nominal endorsement of the Republic's major trading partners. The argument is even made that a trade embargo in these cases would only hurt the suppressed Black majority that was intended to be helped, although a definitive economic analysis of how the damage of an embargo is allocated within a society under seige still perhaps remains to be done.

Similar problems will arise for restraints on the sale of complicated nuclear equipment to any nation which refuses to sign the Nuclear Non-Proliferation Treaty (NPT). The text of the treaty in effect requires suppliers to withhold such sales, where safeguards are not accepted to insure that materials are not diverted to the production of weapons. Yet arguments will occur on what is permitted and what is forbidden under the treaty, and a nonsignatory country such as India may yet find itself able to exploit what in effect has become a buyer's market rather than a tightly regulated ologopoly.

Yet there are other means besides trade of converting economic interaction into international political influence. It has been argued, for example, that the world's acceptance of the dollar as the international liquid currency has given the United States a free increment of influence, in that the U.S. can run additional balance of payments "deficits" in the process of deploying additional military forces overseas, and has an unusually large voice in the allocation of foreign aid monies for the encouragement of economic development abroad. If gold were the international standard, it might be argued, this one-sided accretion of influence would not occur, because various countries would be mining gold and thereby expanding liquidity, because there is at least some serious material effort involved in extracting gold. Since the United States now expands the world's liquid reserve all by itself, simply by running its printing presses, the world is spared the basically useless effort involved in mining gold, but the saving is converted into enhanced political power for the United States alone.

Yet another form of economic leverage has been assumed to exist in the superior management talents and techniques which have been developed in the United States, to a great extent because the American economy is large enough to support and tolerate the innovations that produce such techniques. The result presumably is that American firms are able to purchase and acquire control over European and other business entities, in the end creating multinational corporations whose national base and loyalty is very difficult to determine, but whose parent firm is very typically American. This may simply reflect economies of scale in management, or perhaps illustrates that "nothing succeeds like success," that the United States, having once moved ahead with superior management techniques, can now attract and co-opt the best management talent of Europe and Asia to its ranks. Related to this phenomenon is the "brain drain" by which talented and educated foreign nationals are induced to move physically to the United States, thereby augmenting the human resources all the more of the richest nation in the world, and holding back the development of poorer nations.

One response to the "brain drain" simply endorses a laissez-faire attitude, assuming that the world's economy in toto is served best if all human resources are free to move to where they are most needed. For the United States to rewrite its immigration laws to discourage this, in this view, would be a disservice to economic rationality in the large. Similarly, it would be counter-productive for other countries to attempt to hold back their nationals, as for example East Germany and Communist countries presently do.

Yet a counter-argument is that the scientists coming to America bring not only their native talent with them, but also the education and training which their home states have supplied as a free gift; the educational capital thus being accepted by the United States may actually more than counteract the diminishing amounts of foreign aid dispensed. The "brain drain" problem affects not only underdeveloped nations around the world, but also such advanced nations as Great Britain, and in the net clearly augments the political power of the United States when scientists settle permanently as American citizens.

The case of the multinational corporation might seem less directly insidious, in that the Argentinian branch of an American corporation continues to serve Argentinian customers, and even is largely staffed by Argentinian nationals. Yet these latter local businessmen are increasingly likely to have studied at American business schools, and the exact locus of decision-making for the multinational corporation as a whole may seem now to rest in North America.

Yet some of the radical critique may begin to become unclear here. Is it primarily that American corporations abroad serve the purposes of U.S. foreign policy, or is it that American foreign policy abroad rather serves the interests of American corporations? Perhaps the more serious charge against the multinational corporation is not that it serves the United States, but that it rather has produced a breed of "stateless persons" which really knows no national loyalties anymore. If U.S. corporations hire Canadians to staff their Canadian branches, and Latin Americans to staff their Latin American offices, this may thus make little or no difference, except as window-dressing and as an equalization of employment opportunities. Perhaps the multinational corporation thus produces no noticeable changes in the distribution of power among nations, but rather merely exacerbates an already unequal distribution of rewards, between the rich around the world who manage corporations, and the rest of the world's population.

The institution of multinational corporations in various ways allows escape from national political and economic regulation. If a state were striving to improve its balance of payments position by restricting imports and remittances to foreign accounts, the corporation can circumvent this within its own bookkeeping by accounting procedures which will be very difficult to detect. Attempts by one state to impose rules on such a corporation may be undone in the courts of another state, as with efforts to apply American antitrust law to the operations of an American firm in Canada. The mere attachment of independent states to their particular sovereignties will stand in the way of easy cooperation in the economic regulation of such institutions. In the long run, international regulatory agencies may be required to bring multinational firms under the same political control now already imposed on firms wholly within a particular country.

It is clearly true that most multinational firms have their home base in the United States. What is debatable, as suggested above, is whether this really affects the particular loyalties of the managements involved. Perhaps the only effect of this skewed distribution is that the United States public has been the slowest to realize the need for regulation on the international level. If the issue is a comparison of benefits for Britain or the United States, one cannot clearly see the corporations serving as the vehicle for the U.S. side. Perhaps the political leaning of the corporation as a whole will be more pronounced when the issue confronts the "free world" with the "Communist world," where a Communist take-over of some area might seriously crimp the ability of corporations to participate within it.

This leads us back to the more basic question of whether American foreign policy is significantly shaped by considerations of protecting the American business interest, whether the concurrence of business and government serves the interest of the former rather than the latter. Theories of business influence have been propounded for many years now, ranging from extremely microcosmic examples to studies of the American position in foreign policy as a macrocosmic whole.

As a microscopic example, one might cite the attitudes and influence of the oil industry, which has a clear interest in maintaining its access to oil in the Middle East, and therefore favors a foreign policy which would leave the United States less in support of Israel and more sympathetic to the Arab states. The forms of such influence can be several; grants of assistance can be made to universities which wish to establish centers for the study of the Middle East, on the simple but correct theory that academics tend to love those whom they study. More direct would be grants to political forces within the United States which are favorable to the Arab cause, including even some New-Left radical groups which have begun to criticize Israel along with other condemnable forms of "imperialism." Still more direct is lobbying in Washington itself, going as high as direct pleas to the Secretary of State to bend American policy toward the Arab view.

Yet it is hardly clear that American foreign policy on this subject has been skewed away from its proper representation of the whole public by the existence of a business community. Other businessmen exist who presumably are pro-Israel, either because they are Zionist and Jewish, or also because they share more general sympathies with the Israeli state. It is thus at least plausible that Zionist businessmen and oil executives have balanced each other on policy toward the Middle East, so that policy reflects broader American desires.

At earlier times, it was contended that American firms supplying arms to the British and French during the first years of World War I had deliberately lobbied to induce the U.S. to join the war, for fear that their bills otherwise would not be paid by the Allied governments involved. The Nye committee's "Merchants of Death" investigation convinced many Americans in an isolationist period of the 1930's that U.S. policy as a whole had thus been shaped by a very small particular interest. Yet events of the latter 1930's led most to conclude that this had indeed been an oversimplified explanation of the issues of 1917.

At a considerably more macroscopic level, a theory of the "military industrial complex" has been elaborated with regard to current United States arms procurement processes, a theory that weapons are purchased and developed to serve the needs of the large complex of firms that supply them, and the bureaus that use them, rather than the public as a whole. The nexus presumably is held together by those military officers approaching retirement who will join the management of the firms with which they have been dealing. It shows up in the promotion of weapons in the public press by advertisements paid for by the manufacturer, but facilitated by the military service which aspires to obtain the weapon.

A counter-argument would claim that this problem is overstated, since the interests of various firms such as Boeing and General Dynamics run counter to each other, as the interests of army, navy, and air force similarly conflict. Yet mere "checks and balances" are not always automatically effective in politics or economics. One must inquire about the relative size and power of different units of competition, and the likely compromises they will reach among themselves.

Power in such matters will tend to be a function of the size of the particular partnerships of industrial supplier-governmental user involved, and it is hardly clear that any such nexus exists which can successfully resist large expenditures for weapons. To be sure, one can imagine linkages between the Weather Bureau and the suppliers of meteorological equipment, or the Department of Health, Education and Welfare and the publishers of schoolbooks, nexuses similarly interested in channeling as much as possible of the government budget in their own direction. Yet these will always be smaller in size and power than the military-industrial combinations with which they are contending; the fact that military officers retire earlier, and can therefore seek employment in the private sector while still in their productive years, moreover tightens the coordination between supplier and user.

Some distinctions should be drawn within the military establishment about where this kind of military-industrial complex impact is most likely to appear. The large size of corporation required shows up primarily in the fields of aircraft, electronics, and missilery, fields which are expensive enough in themselves, but do not always dominate the defense budget even in normal times, and much less so during such an active "conventional war" as Vietnam. The producers of artillery ammunition, for example, are much less combined and coordinated by any natural economies of scale in the market, and it is difficult to prove that their lobbying has encouraged participation in a war such as Vietnam. Indeed, since the costs of Vietnam have somewhat held back expenditures on strategic weapons, it could have been argued that the military-industrial complex should be lukewarm about such a counter-insurgency operation, and be lobbying against it.

A still more macroscopic view of business influence on foreign policy would skip past the military-industrial complex, to assert that the entire business community of the United States, or of any other capitalist country, is dependent on investments abroad, and must thus deploy military power to protect such investment opportunities.

Investments abroad may be important simply as property rights purchased long ago at bargain prices. Without the threat of military intervention, the local government might now try to confiscate such assets, with little or no reimbursement for their rightful American owners. Access to markets also allows our manufacturers to sell at higher prices than if these markets were denied, thus pulling in the "producers' surplus" involved in a desirable trade. Similarly the ability to buy bananas and other "foreign" items nets Americans a certain "consumers' surplus," since we would have been willing to pay even more for some of the goods thus obtained.

Perhaps investment abroad thus nets much higher returns than would accrue from similar investments within the United States; the simple greed of the American in general, or the corporate profit-seeker in particular, thus might drive the U.S. to send in the marines to maintain access to investment areas. Yet there may be a more basic need for the capitalist economy to seek investment opportunities, for an unjust distribution of wealth at home may produce a lack of aggregate demand, such that unemployment and recession will occur, unemployment which if chronic would threaten the American distribution of political power and economic well-being as it stands. When wealthier persons collect so much of a nation's income that it far exceeds their propensity to consume, the nation's economy will stay in balance only if investment opportunities materialize to soak up all such savings, but such opportunities within the nation may become exhausted, so that opportunities abroad must be found.

Trading rights are thus highly dependent on political power. As noted, the mere question of who holds title to some particular capital property is a political question, as military pressure may have to be exerted to prevent some nation from abruptly changing this title. Political regimes may restrict or forbid foreign investment, or foreign sales. Conversely, they may encourage such investment, and even favor sales from one state to the exclusion of some competitors. Military threats can thus also bend policy in one direction or another here.

Yet some doubts must be expressed on whether this macroscopic picture of the entire American economic community dictating political interference abroad is at all true to life. American investment abroad is indeed extensive, but it is shifting increasingly away from the "underdeveloped" areas in which the threat of Communist insurgency is perceived, toward developed areas such as Western Europe. Keynsian economics has presented ways of preventing unemployment even when no overseas investment opportunities are discovered. If high investment returns sometimes seem to accrue in specific parts of the underdeveloped world, this often reflects a "risk premium" which covers the danger of one of the unilateral confiscations or nationalizations suggested above, nationalizations which the U.S. government will do little or nothing to prevent.

If insurgency in Vietnam in particular is to be related to this model, it has to be noted that there is almost no American business investment at all in Vietnam. If a Communist takeover were to close this door to "free world" investment, it would involve companies which at present are predominantly French, and which in the future would be largely Japanese.

If there is no specific American economic involvement in Vietnam, this may not yet exhaust the possibilities of a radical theory of business implication here, for it can be argued that the war has been fought to maintain the principle and precedent that such underdeveloped areas in general should be held open for American investment. If Vietnam fell to Communist control, so presumably would areas of Latin America or Africa or other regions of southeast Asia. Yet it is not normal to find American or other businessmen so far-sighted or community-spirited as this implies, for business firms rarely make any significant decisions on a time-horizon of more than five years. If domino theory on guerrilla warfare is inaccurate for the political contest between Western pluralism and various forms of Communism, it presumably would have been found to be overly deterministic by the business community also.

Persons denying that American foreign policy is business-dominated would note that Japan and West Germany also have very powerful business communities, but have not pursued interventionist foreign policies at all since 1945. Trade opportunities at substantial profit have even appeared in regions under Russian or other Communist control, and South Vietnam under Hanoi's rule might someday be inviting French or American firms to undertake particular development projects.

Power is always unevenly divided in a pluralist society, such that those who are economically more successful will typically have greater political influence that those who are not; but the business interest as a whole may not be excessively powerful in the formulation of American foreign policy, in part because different business groups disagree among themselves on what policy should be. The stock market has seemed to rise whenever an end to the war in Vietnam is in sight, and to dip when this prospect recedes.

Yet a final radical counter to this defense of pluralism would shift focus almost to the basic psychology of the nation, arguing that the mere tolerance of such unequal distributions of influence illustrates the psychological dominance of the economic system. The economic pathology of a society which is unjust in allocation of benefits, and prone to instability and unemployment, is thus mirrored sociologically in attitudes which take economic and social inequality for granted.

The basic weakness of the system thus forces a certain suppression of dissent, a dissent which many of its victims suppress within themselves. The vehicles for such suppression are a militant foreign policy abroad, coupled with a continuous and unquestioning endorsement of the system as it stands, in face of the challenge of foreign systems constituted on other principles. Foreign adventures in this view are based on nothing quite so rational or cold-blooded as markets needed for particular industrial enterprise, but rather on the need to suppress the criticism of the capitalist system implicit in any revolutionary force in any foreign country which seeks to oust such a system.

The net result of such an adjustment to capitalist economics might thus be a continuous tendency toward premature and erroneous imputations of hostility in foreign powers. Vietnamese insurgents are seen to be hostile to the United States long before they become so, and they become so only because American overreaction forces them into these paths in self defense. Similarly, missiles are procured to confront the Russians, in the end forcing the Russians to procure their own, thus seemingly confirming the erroneous forecasts that the Communist powers intended to attack the United States militarily. Even worse, when this syndrome is explained to the person driven forward by a supposed need to defend capitalist economics, he is allegedly driven also to deny that the syndrome exists.

The above discussion of economic models of international politics and of supposed economic constraints on foreign policy can lead us in the end to several bits of the public's conventional wisdom on what a nation's economy requires or will tolerate in such policy.

Far beyond Marxist or radical circles of analysis, the proposition has been widely accepted that large-scale military spending is somehow required for prosperity or full employment. Few serious economists would agree with this proposition as presented, since Keynsian analysis suggests that compensatory spending by the government can produce employment and prosperity regardless of the *form* of such spending. Perhaps political insensitivity to such macroeconomic needs may mean that presidents and congresses fail to generate the necessary fiscal remedies when they are required; perhaps a military program would then be necessary, only to supply the correct economic antidote for the wrong reason, perhaps in the wrong form from a political perspective. Yet Keynsian economics can be taught to citizens and their representatives, and it is hardly true that an international crisis must be generated to avert recessions at every low point of the economy. When military spending seemed due to be reduced, as at the end of World War II, the U.S. government indeed was prepared to reduce it even in the face of predictions that this would cause unemployment. Such unemployment did not materialize in 1946, but the behavior of the government suggested that unemployment would have been tolerated, ahead of continued military spending, when the functional need for such spending seemed to have passed. To suggest therefore that Roosevelt's rearmaments of 1939 and 1940 had the specific intention of alleviating unemployment, rather than responding to an objective threat from the Axis camp, is to ignore most of the evidence we have on American priorities and values.

A contrary piece of wisdom is that there is a tight limit to a nation's capacity to engage in military ventures, and if the economy is strained past this point, some sort of breakdown will occur. To be sure, every nation is under some constraints on its ability to deploy resources for military purposes—constraints based on absolute GNP, the needs of the civilian sector, the needs to maintain economic capital and to induce some growth for the future. Yet an examination of the World War II performance of various nations suggests that some tremendous margins exist for further shifts of resources to military purposes, and that the post-1945 period has been much less of an "arms race" than we often assume. The United States in World War II did not mobilize itself to even approximately the same degree of austerity of Great Britain or the USSR; both of these paradoxically were more mobilized than Nazi Germany, at least until 1944 when the war had begun to go very badly for the Axis. Yet the United States in 1944 expended a military budget of what would have been almost $200 billion in 1973 dollar equivalents, amounting to 42 percent of its gross national product. The foreign policy budget of the United States has thus been growing less rapidly than the GNP, but it would seem that it could grow as fast, or even more rapidly, without imposing any unbearable hardships by earlier standards.

Yet a dollar spent on defense or foreign aid is still presumptively a dollar which could have been spent on other functions; a third standard approach to the defense dollar is thus not to suggest imminent collapse of the economy as a whole, but rather to assemble the schools, the slum clearance, the hospitals or mass transit systems that might have been purchased for similar amounts in the budget. But a more basic question that would have to be raised here concerns the likelihood that dollars saved in defense cuts or arms controls agreements would actually have gone for these purposes, rather than into the space program, or the supersonic transport, or into tax cuts which will be diverted into cosmetics and luxury automobiles.

FURTHER READINGS

Hirschman, Albert O. *National Power and the Structure of Foreign Trade.* Berkeley: University of California Press, 1945.
Lenin V. I. *Imperialism, The Highest Stage of Capitalism.* New York: International Publishers, 1939.
Lens, Sidney. *The Military-Industrial Complex.* Philadelphia: Pilgrim Press, 1970.
Melman, Seymour. *Pentagon Capitalism.* New York: McGraw-Hill, 1970.
Rostow, W. W. *Stages of Economic Growth.* London and New York: Cambridge University Press, 1960.
Schumpeter, Joseph A. *Imperialism and Social Classes.* New York: August M. Kelley, Inc., 1951.
Vernon, Raymond, "The Role of U.S. Enterprise Abroad." *Daedalus.* Winter, 1969.

Geopolitics and Geography

From 1890 to 1940 it was widely held that important predictions and policy judgments on international politics could be based on a deep analysis of geography, the general subject being known as "geopolitics." If the specific teachings of Mahan, Haushofer, or MacKinder have not retained their appeal into the post-World War II years, much of such reasoning may yet be generally accepted on a more implicit basis, having penetrated the common sense of earlier discussions of international politics.

It is easy to find earlier theorists who found geographic factors significant to analyzing the political future of a region, for example, the works of Montequieu. Assumptions have been offered on the impact of geographical environments on the comparative characters of nations, as well as on their relative strength for purposes of military and political power. The climate of a country aspiring to serious influence presumably should not be too hot or too cold; proper composition of soil, or population density, may determine whether the agricultural problem could be solved early enough to generate a surplus of energy for industrial or military purposes. The shape of the terrain will also be of consequence, as mountainous land naturally favored the military defense, while flat land was conducive to commerce or to military mobility. Attention would have to be devoted also to the configurations of river basins and systems, and the needs for coordination in any irrigation projects. Economies of scale in the latter might condition a region to accepting centralized and even authoritarian rule.

At the least it will be important to bring such working assumptions to the surface, even if they in the end prove limited for predicting or explaining international events as they have evolved.

Moving ahead to the policies of nations, rather than their simple character or net strength, there is again much lore that needs to be brought out into the open, lest we accept it too intuitively and therefore uncritically. Some nations are assumed "naturally" always to be seeking "access to the sea," as, for example, the Russian Empire and then the Soviet Union. Any interest in Iran whatsoever shown by any Moscow regime will be rated as proving this historical and geographical determinism once again. Other nations are assumed to be seeking "natural boundaries," as with France moving eastward toward the Rhine River, natural here meaning some sort of "natural feature," as a river or mountain range. This theory, of course, does not explain why France is content with Strasbourg and without Mainz (Mayence), or without Belgium.

Still other nations are seen at all times to be seeking controls over commerce, presumably because they are island states dependent on seaborne imports. England and Japan, if they send a naval vessel to patrol any sea whatsoever, immediately prove this rule. Germany for a time seemed intent on "living space" (lebensraum), as was Japan in its seizure of Manchuria. Islands are moreover credited with a compulsive interest in the nearest landfall, the bases from which any invasion of their secure bastions would have to come. Thus Britain could never lose interest in the independence of Belgium, and Japan had to seek control of Korea, the "dagger aimed at Japan's heart."

These bits of geographical folklore all have a certain redeeming conformance with reality, albeit that the conformance is often demonstrated by definitional exercises that threaten to become tautological. Yet some more serious efforts at geopolitical analysis were to emerge at the end of the 19th century.

The first of the most memorable three analysts of geopolitics was an American naval officer, Captain Alfred Thayer Mahan. Mahan's analyses of the history of naval warfare won a wide and enthusiastic audience in Britain and in Germany before World War I, for he argued that naval power offered enormous political results; the outside 9/12 of the world that was covered with water could be brought to dominate the inside 2/12 (Eurasia with Africa) and the other 1/12 (the remaining continents and land masses). Since victory at sea was the key to political control over the entire globe, a direct effort should be made toward securing such a victory, by concentrating one's naval power for maximum battle impact, by aiming to destroy the enemy's fleet as directly as possible, by winning, as Britain time and time again had won, effective control over the sea.

The second major geopolitician, the Englishman Halford MacKinder, was quite concerned over what he foresaw as the imminent decline of British political strength, for his conclusions were almost directly the opposite of Mahan's on the basic determinant of geopolitical power. MacKinder saw the Eurasian 2/12 of the world effectively outweighing and dominating the oceanic 9/12 and the American continents' 1/12, as eastern Europe dominated the heartland, and the heartland dominated the world island, and the world island dominated the globe.

MacKinder saw eastern Europe as historically possessing the geographical attributes necessary to make it a cradle of power, being flat, with rivers flowing through to provide effective means of communication and interaction, and with grasslands to provide the fodder for the cavalry which so often had been the decisive military arm in the past. As this area transformed itself into an industrial region in the 20th century, it would still be able to exploit its central position and interior lines of communication, to threaten any seapower such as Britain. MacKinder attached a particularly menacing significance to the Trans-Siberian railroad, which could move troops from and to the Far East far more rapidly that the ship-borne forces of the British Empire could follow. Since land transportation was the more efficient, as well as offering the advantages of interior lines, sea power might not be able to intervene effectively any more along the edges of the Eurasian land mass. In MacKinder's view, moreover, this land mass might achieve industrial production sufficient to challenge Britain even on the seas, producing a navy which in the end would outclass the Royal Navy.

The geopolitical problem for Britain was thus to prevent any single power from dominating or controlling the German-Slavic axis, to prevent the all important heartland from being harnessed behind a single political leadership which might challenge British power. The creation of a large number of intervening states at the Versailles Treaty in 1919, a "cordon sanitaire" running from Estonia to Yugoslavia, might have been thought an application of MacKinder's reasoning and advice; yet the causal impact of his theories might be hard to prove here, as other considerations, for example Wilson's stress on ethnic self-determination, were probably more important. The creation of this belt splitting the heartland in any event failed, as the small states lost the assurance of French and British support, and then fell victim to German and Russian pressures and aggression.

MacKinder's reasoning on the industrial and therefore military importance of this region was somewhat mistaken. Whether or not it might have been possible to integrate economically the area from Germany to the Ukraine in the days of agriculture, the industrial interaction would be less than that between France and Germany. If steel production in the end was to be the threat to the British navy, the heartland for this had to lie further west. There was no inherent reason why the geography of interior line military movements would have to coincide with the location of raw materials satisfying the needs of steel and other heavy industry. As the geopolitician sensed that the two locations might coincide, the illusion of some higher political laws or science based on geography became convincing.

The theories of the third major geopolitician, the German Karl Haushofer, are basically similar to those of MacKinder, with the major psychological difference, of course, that what was England's danger seemed Germany's opportunity. There has long been talk of a German "Drang nach Osten," perhaps dating back to the Teutonic knights who had taken it upon themselves to Christianize and conquer Prussia and the lands further east. In the Nazi period of German history, this drive toward the east was related to a notion of "lebensraum," that nature somehow dictated that a population the size of Germany's must have more ground space than the borders of 1920 would have allowed it.

Even with the naked aggressions of Hitler's Germany, one must express some doubt, however, on whether geopolitical theories really explain the quest after territory, or on whether such theories were taken seriously by someone like Hitler in the process of making his decisions. To be sure, there is a superficial appeal to the idea that more real estate will mean greater prosperity, and Germans in 1935 might have found this as convincing as did Japanese with regard to their government's seizure of Manchuria. Yet the experience of decades since the war, as well as periods of industrial expansion and growth before, suggest many other roads to prosperity, roads which may seem far preferable, since contests for real estate are likely to provoke wars and thus inflict enormous financial costs on the nations involved.

Hitler at least paid lip service to Haushofer's theories, but his decisions to seek expansion, and the directions in which it was sought, may as easily be explained by the opportunities which presented themselves. Perhaps the lip service to geopolitical theory conditioned Hitler toward seeing the Ukraine as the promised land, or the key to domination of the entire world. But the pattern of German expansion is hardly single-mindedly toward the east, or toward the heartland. Hitler's Germany absorbed territory where local weakness, or the ethnic arguments of Wilson in 1919, seemed to facilitate it.

In more recent times, spokesmen for the USSR and Communist China have occasionally formulated statements of strategy which at least seemed to be geopolitical in style. Lenin is quoted as having said that "the road to Paris runs through Peking," but this was hardly a theory that geography dictated a road to political power apart from the workings of the class struggle; the phrase must rather be seen as a shorthand to describe the tactical situation as developed by the class struggle. Even Marxists will tire of hearing the battle plan fully and painstakingly described in terms of the working of the dialectic. As a summation of what has been detected by scientific analysis, Lenin's statement thus served its function. Yet it was all too easy then for non-Marxist interpreters in the outside world to see such a statement as geopolitical, perhaps demonstrating that Lenin's Russia had to perceive its goals just as the Russia of the Czars, as the immutable natural laws of political geography required this.

Even more recently, we have seen Lin Piao's statement of Maoist foreign policy strategy in 1965, that the "countryside of the world would defeat the cities." Since the cities were the developed countries such as the U.S. and USSR, while the countryside was the underdeveloped world as headed by China, the formulation seemed to analogize with the guerrilla tactics by which the Communists had seized power within China itself, working from a rural base against the urban centers which fell into their hands only at the end. Again, the analogy and the shorthand refer more to class structure than to truly geographical characteristics; it helped to explain and justify the Chinese deviation from the Marxist prediction that revolution would spring out from the industrialized cities, it served as a call to arms when the Chinese leadership saw itself confronting the U.S. and the Soviet Union simultaneously.

What, if anything, should one then take seriously about "geopolitical" styles of reasoning in international politics? The notion of "living space" presumably holds very true for the human race as a whole today, for if population is not somehow limited, the world's aggregate food supplies will indeed be exhausted; yet the nations most able to expand militarily are not those most burdened by shortages of food or consumer goods. Unless the most ruthless policy of murder or deportation is adopted, most seizures of territory will require some toleration of the population previously resident in them. One should not be doctrinaire in assuming that all seizures of land or property will be counter-productive in the end, that "crime never pays." Yet one must also realize that mere territorial control is a most imperfect index to how much wealth one has accrued, or how best to accrue it. Germans today are far more prosperous, with far less territory, than they were in 1935. Perhaps there are ways in which Germans could be still more prosperous, holding the territories of 1941, but the gains here are hardly so attractive as to outweigh the obvious costs occasioned by the resistance of Germany's neighbors.

A few bits of conventional wisdom on the impact of climate should not be totally dismissed. In assessing the difficulty of countries such as India or Burma in making economic progress, the continual heat and humidity of the climates of such countries are easily overlooked in statistical analysis. Qualities of soil and the impact on agriculture can surely effect the economic and political life-style of a nation, as will terrain, whether the land be mountainous or swampy. There are still periodic references in the press to "natural boundaries," in mountains such as the Alps, or rivers such as the Rhine, and such boundaries may indeed be relevant for effective military defense. Most paradoxically, this analysis has even been applied in the Israeli advance to that most "unnatural" of waterways, the Suez Canal. A pronouncedly visible boundary may reduce confusions and disputes. A moat or a mountain pass is most assuredly easier for either side to defend than a line drawn across a field. Yet the proponents of "natural boundaries" must remember that such military defense possibilities can become irrelevant to two nations neighboring each other (for example, Canada and the U.S.) or that the requirements of tactical military defense may change as technology changes.

Classically there has also been a conventional wisdom on "avenues of attack," the routes by which an enemy force would most effectively approach its target. It is still true today that a Russian armored force rolling westward against Paris would do better on the German plain than in the Alps, and the military and political calculations of NATO defense must take this into account. Yet some of the traditional passable and impassable points may have become enshrined by a folklore past the point of actual relevance. The tank may be able to move where trucks or trains could not. The advent of amphibious forces, and especially air forces, may have drastically altered this particular bit of "geographic" determinant for international politics.

This, of course, is not to suggest that no aspects of geography are really important for international politics even as we practice it in the 1970's. A knowledge of national boundaries is almost indispensible for any understanding of crises and political interactions as they emerge. A debate has been underway since 1945 about whether we are not overly accustomed to using the Mercator projection rather than polar projections, in flat wall maps of the world. Greenland, to be sure, is not really larger than South America. Greenland, rather than the Azores as a Mercator projection might suggest, is just as surely on the air route from Stockholm to New York. Jet airliners now regularly cross the Arctic on flights from California to Europe, and oil tankers have even explored the sea passage from the eastern coast of the United States to the northern shore of Alaska.

If the intent of a map projection were to show the normal pattern and volume of commercial and social interaction, however, the Mercator projection would still be more representative than any other, since most of the world's trade, and troop movements, will still have to pursue the warm-water courses open to sea transportation. The most active lobby for citizen attention to polar projection maps in the United States since 1945 has rather been partisans of the U.S. Air Force. The polar map was, and is, obviously relevant to the course that Russian Air Force bombers would use in attacking cities of the United States. For Americans accustomed to thinking of the Atlantic and Pacific coastal defenses as their sure guarantee against attack, the vision of bombers striking at St. Louis from the north can trigger a sense of alarm that we were not protected "in that direction," that we must invest therefore in air defenses, or in a retaliatory bomber force which could use the same polar route "short-cuts" to strike at the Soviet Union.

There are some other very important, albeit macabre, implications of the globe's contours which will not be obvious on a Mercator map, or even a polar projection of a flat map. Since missiles, unlike bombers, are basically inertial after they have been launched against an enemy target, they offer fewer choices on routing. It may be obvious that the Soviet Union cannot fire on the United States without violating the airspace of Canada in the process, unless it exploits its fractional orbit (FOBS) ballistic system to strike from the south by having first gone around the globe in the opposite direction (whereupon it would have violated the airspaces of several Latin American states). More seriously, perhaps, if there were ever to have been a U.S. limited war with Communist China, leaving the USSR neutral, it would have been impossible to fire missiles from the U.S. mainland at targets in China without crossing the Soviet Union in the process. Perhaps Polaris submarines in the Pacific could solve this dilemma, but the inertial path from the Pacific toward China inferentially continues on toward Soviet Siberia, so that doubts would remain on whether Russian radar observation stations would be at all reassured.

Turning away from missile trajectories, some other forms of geographical data are clearly relevant to international political and military problems, again data on which a map by itself might be very misleading. Physical geography by itself will suggest, for example, that Southeast Asia is enormously closer to China than to the United States, with all kinds of implications on whose "sphere of influence" it will join. Yet such assumptions on "nearness" and "farness" must also consider the relative cheapness of sea transportation, and the comparative resources available in each country for investment in transportation. When these are taken into account, Vietnam is indeed "closer" to the U.S. than to China in terms of how much material and how many men could be deployed in a given length of time. If the U.S. had to "lose" in Vietnam, distance from home cannot be the central explanation, anymore than would it explain the outcomes of a similar campaign in Cuba.

Technology is, moreover, altering the transportation comparison from year to year. The C-5A, however much it has exceeded its cost estimates, represents a tremendous expansion in the carrying capacity of air transport; one can note that as few as 20 of such aircraft could have flown the entire Berlin airlift of 1948–49. The advent of the SST supersonic transport promises to shorten the durations of intercontinental flights again in a drastic manner. Yet the sonic boom noise effects anticipated from this kind of aircraft may necessitate that they be flown only over water; the paradoxical result in the end might find flights from New York to Los Angeles utilizing over-water routes through the Gulf of Mexico and Pacific Oceans, slowing down only over the narrowest waist of Mexico, in effect reviving the routes used by goldminers in 1849, now as then avoiding the land routes in the interest of maximum speed.

The development of containers for shipment has again enhanced the efficiency of sea transportation, so that the warm water trade routes highlighted on the Mercator projection maps are far from losing their significance. When trying to determine the basic economic patterns which will affect trade relationships, it may thus turn out that Finland is closer to Japan than to Switzerland, at the least so that one should not be surprised at seeing Japanese automobiles on the streets of Helsinki. Something as simple as a tunnel under the English Channel can enormously alter the comparative gains and costs of various kinds of trade. At earlier points, this tunnel was analyzed, and vetoed, in terms of its more straightforward military power implications; would it not make it easier for some foreign power to invade Britain, or to hold the island under its control if it had once conquered Britain by other means of invasion? Would the Germans in 1914 not have aimed for Boulogne rather than Paris, if the tunnel were already in existence? More contemporaneously, such considerations seem obsolete, but the impact on trade flows and Britain's competitive position within the Common Market may still be of great significance.

Discussions of political geography in the end force some effort at redefining "regionalism." At earlier times, a "regional" analysis presumably was addressed to any group of nations which formed a contiguous cluster, which were therefore characterized by enough military, political, economic, or cultural interaction to require political analysis at higher than the national level. Perhaps it was shared access to a single river basin system that accounted for such closeness, or similar topographical features. More recently, some "regional" analyses have assembled groups of nations with no geographical proximity at all, simply because of a similarity in economic pattern, or cultural life, or political style. While the term "region" normally still suggests a geographical closeness, such analyses suggest some uncertainty on the relevance of physical closeness as the explanation of international similarity.

A resolution of this might be to adhere still to a basically geographical standard that any "region" must be characterized by high degrees of interaction in trade and personnel movement, interaction which may no longer require, however, direct contiguity. Whenever sea transportation claims or reclaims a significant cost advantage over land movement, the "regional" analysis may thus have to lump together such units as Spain, Mexico, and the Philippines at one stage, France and Indo-China at a second, Europe, North America, and Japan at a third.

FURTHER READINGS

Mackinder, Halford J. *Democratic Ideals and Reality*. New York: Henry Holt and
Company, 1919.
Mahan, Aldred Thayer. *The Influence of Seapower Upon History*. New York: Hill and
Wang, 1957.

The Limits of Theories

It must be clear by now that this author has not found any of the cited
theories convincing as a predominant explanation of international anarchy
and war, or as a source of solutions to the peace-maintenance problem. The
student must judge for himself whether any particular strand of theory has
been unfairly treated, whether its potential has been missed.

Yet each sort of theory and explanation has had something to contribute
to our understanding of international politics, and may have more in the
future. If a proponent of a particular economic or psychological approach
has invested his energies in the hope that all other approaches would
become unnecessary and redundant, he probably will have reason to feel
disappointed. Yet avenues for further research have nonetheless been
opened, research which does not just satisfy our curiosity about past wars
and past mistakes, but also may help us to avoid mistakes and wars in the
future.

International politics may thus be interesting not only because it is
played by different rules than domestic politics, but also because it serves
as a mirror of many of the tensions and processes of domestic society, be
they rational or irrational. The entire subject of "linkage politics" needs to
be probed further on the exact impact of domestic events on foreign policy
and the international arena, and then on the impacts in reverse. If we must
live on with the possibilities of diplomacy, arms races, and wars hanging
over us, how exactly do these phenomena affect the way we live on?

FURTHER READINGS

Alker, Hayward R., Jr. "The Long Road to International Relations Theory: Prob-
lems of Statistical Nonaddivity." *World Politics*. July, 1966.
Bull, Hedley. "International Theory: The Case for the Classical Approach." *World
Politics*. April, 1966.
Hoffmann, Stanley. "The Long Road to Theory." *World Politics*. April, 1959.

CHAPTER SIX

International Politics
In
The Future

The world of the 1970's thus has inherited a number of burdens from the past. Peace is by no means assured, even as war is certainly not inevitable. Is the world now to be more dependent on force than it used to be, or less? Are we conceptually better prepared to resolve conflicts than our grandfathers were, in part because of what we call social science? Or might it in the future be even more difficult to know and understand our international political environment? The most perverse conclusion might be that man never really understands any particular international system while it is in effect; by studying history, we can avoid repeating it, but what do we then get instead?

Nations will continue to try to reduce the risk of war, but at the same time they will also try to exploit the risk, as a means to winning political gains for themselves. If all such states succeed in walking this kind of tightrope carefully enough, disasters for all may be avoided. We can be surer that this game will be continued to be played, than that it will be played so well.

Despite some substantial uncertainties, therefore, we can close by discussing some possible tendencies that lie ahead in the international system and by very tentatively summarizing some conclusions here. We can thus come back to some classically important questions on the state of international affairs. Who has power today? Who has the greatest influence over human affairs? How does one measure such power or quantify it?

Some traditional indices looked to sources of power, comparing manpower, industrial production, or strategic geographic position. Perhaps an assessment of these imputs would allow us to predict accurately which countries and leaders get to call the tune from one political decision to another. Other objective indices might try to answer the same question by looking at the decision outputs themselves. How secure are American citizens abroad in their lives and property, as compared with citizens of country X? How much political deference is given to American diplomats or citizens, in terms of the superficial as well as real political trappings of various state political processes.

One can even look at the votes cast in international bodies such as the United Nations General Assembly, using sophisticated voting indices to measure who is most often in the winning coalitions, who most often gets his way. Yet while other indices might have suggested great power for the United States and the Soviet Union, the score in General Assembly votes is going down; a certain statistical fallacy might also be noted, if the United States is often forced to vote against its own preferences in the General Assembly simply for fear of alienating the large bloc of "nonaligned" nations.

Similarly confusing conclusions can be obtained by referring to certain economic consumption indicators on who gets more of the world's good things in life. Does the United States simply get more than its share of the world's wealth and resources, or does it also pay more than its share? A Martian with some economic training might indeed find a lot of merit in the clasically cynical question "Who won World War II?" Was it the United States, which since then has taxed itself heavily to pay the costs of extended military defenses, or was it Japan and Germany, with their booming economies and law tax rates and military expenditures? Who indeed dominates the Communist bloc, the Soviet Union? Or is it East Germany and Czechoslovakia with their higher per capita GNP's?

By some reasonable standards, Sweden is richer on a per capita basis than the United States. Does it therefore have more real power? Burdens as well as advantages accrue to a nation after it has achieved great aggregate size and industrial power. Consider the case if the United States had dissolved into a number of smaller national units in 1861. These states in the sum would play less of an international role, and expend fewer resources on it, then the United States as a unit does today. Perhaps Europe would then have had to unite more meaningfully to fill the vaccuum, or perhaps Britain would have had to assert itself to become more of a redoubt of power. Knowing that the United States is there to defend the West, knowing that the U.S. and the Soviet Union to a great extent check each other, allows many other states to devote less effort to the demands of the international arena.

There has thus developed a debate about the existing world of five nuclear powers, on whether it has been basically "bipolar" or "multipolar." One semantic resolution of this argument has been to stipulate that the *source* of political power has indeed been bipolar, in that only the U.S. and Soviet industrial and military establishments really amount to anything substantial; when referring to which *preferences* get satisfied and which get frustrated, however, the conclusion might well be that the world is multipolar. In terms of freeing nations to do as they will, the second major nuclear weapon state may balance out and neutralize the first. Two nuclear powers have the same impact on the distribution of influence as would five or twenty, in this view; everyone benefits, but the first and the second were the only ones that causally mattered.

A close examination of the policies of France, Britain, and China might conclude that these states have indeed gained (or retained) a little prestige from being "nuclear powers," over what would have been available otherwise. In the case of Communist China, nuclear weapons may even have added some real strategic independence. Yet it is not easy to demonstrate that these states are substantially more able to ignore and frustrate the great powers than other "nonnuclear" states (for example, Japan), or that they would have lost much of their freedom of action had they not gone nuclear. Acquisition of nuclear weapons might not give the next 15 club members much political influence beyond what they already have.

What other trends in the international system are we to project? It has several times been conjectured that the polarization of the world's nations is changing, so that the major divisive issues will no longer be the "East-West" of those aligned with Washington and those with Moscow, but rather a "North-South" with the developed countries, including Washington and Moscow on one side, and the underdeveloped countries grouping together on the other. A number of votes within the United Nations General Assembly have clearly been of this nature. In voting at the conferences of UNCTAD the "North-South" alignment is so obvious that it is the norm from which exceptions now have to be measured or defined. Similarly, the decision-making of the IAEA (International Atomic Energy Agency) shows the United States and the USSR on one hand, with the less developed countries, particularly India, taking quite opposite positions; here, however, such "northern" countries as Japan, West Germany, and Italy also stand against the two great powers, so that issue is almost nuclear-weapons state versus nonweapons state, rather than developed (north) versus less developed.

Determining the drift of such polarization by counting roll-call votes can be misleading, however, for we would have to know how important any particular issue is in substance, and how serious any particular nation is in casting its vote along one axis of disagreement rather than another. Students and practitioners of international politics alike may grow tired of stale foreign alignments; the mere thought of a "diplomatic revolution" can be refreshing enough to provoke some sloganizing or generalization which really would be quite premature. If the United States and the USSR agree in opposing further spread of nuclear weapons, and the less developed countries agree that these super-powers should be freer with technical and monetary assistance, this does not yet prove that such questions have outweighed and overwhelmed the disputes which defined the Cold War at its outset.

How best to control the spread of nuclear weapons may thus be an issue pitting the U.S. and the USSR against an array of potential "nth" nuclear powers, powers seeking to retain at least the option of acquiring such weapons. As noted above, such weapons may or may not enhance the international standing of a Britain or a Japan, as commentators on the international scene find it hard to agree on the political impact of such nuclear proliferation. Yet many potential "nth" nuclear powers will join Washington and Moscow in being opposed to further proliferation, for reasons not directly related to the distribution of political power.

A continued spread of nuclear weapons can change international politics in two disquieting ways; it can make war more likely, and it will surely make wars more horrible. International politics in the next century may well have to deal with so many nuclear powers that the prevention of nuclear war approaches impossibility, so that millions instead of thousands lose their lives in wars such as the one between India and Pakistan. Worse than this, small dissident factions within countries may be able to lay their hands on deadly nuclear or chemical weapons, threatening to destroy entire cities if their demands are not satisfied. Preventing the spread of nuclear weapons may thus be essential to keeping international politics from becoming more violent, but proliferation may not be preventable.

Is international politics today more or less violent than it has been in the past? Again common sense impressions can easily enough mislead us. On the basis of the statistics available, we might reach the depressing conclusion that war is steadily increasing its homicidal impact, almost logarithmically, in fact. Yet any such conclusion would have to ignore the lack of good data on the pre-1900 period, especially data on the world outside of Europe. There is speculative evidence, for example, that enormous numbers of people lost their lives in wars within China and Africa in the mid-19th century, wars which would have led a Martian observer to conclude that Europe was not the real focus of the phenomenon called war.

The experience of the war in Vietnam has cautioned us against regarding numerical casualty figures as overly reliable. Earlier wars and battles, for example, the Battle of Britain, have shown how claims of planes or soldiers downed in action can be greatly inflated. What is more, the subjective impressions implanted by involvement in the news can greatly distort the comparisons one is making. Few Americans today have internalized the fact that many more innocent civilians were killed in the Korean War than in the war in Vietnam, albeit the former lasted two years while the latter has exceeded twelve. Few Americans indeed internalized the casualty figures of the Nigerian Civil War, if only because this war did not appear on their television news programs on as regular a basis as the Vietnam War.

Casualty figures take on a life of their own. The figure of 30,000 persons killed in the 1940 German bombing of Rotterdam was released immediately after the bombing by the Netherlands Embassy in Washington; this figure has been cited and quoted ever since. The accurate figure was indeed closer to 700.

Apart from whether international politics is becoming more violent or less, is it more demanding of a nation's attention than it has been in the past? We can remember with a certain fond nostalgia the days in 1931 when President Hoover could settle his defense problems for the year with a single question put to the Secretaries of Navy and War: "Can you defend the United States against any imminent threat of invasion?" By contrast with this, we would all conclude that today's international arena is continually demanding of our attention, on economic, political, and military questions and perhaps that this proves some fundamental change in the nature of international politics.

Yet the United States might be a poor and misleading test case here, for it has moved from the role of isolationist bystander to major power and "policeman of the world." If we were to contrast the allocation of attention between domestic and foreign policy in some other countries from 1931 to 1971, we might find a very opposite trend. West Germans or Belgians today can hardly be called isolationist, but they share the frustrations as well as comforts of knowing that the primary determinants of war and peace now lie in other hands. It would be difficult to prove by any study of British or French press coverage that foreign policy has become vastly more engrossing since 1930. Much of the fascination of international activity derives from power in such activity. As power has shifted, so the fascination has also shifted.

Yet is it not true that the speed and range of modern weapons has forced nations to pay much more attention to each other? Armies could have protected us in the past, but nothing can assuredly stop missiles or bombers from destroying our communities today, and some profound observers have suggested that this should begin to erode the sense of "independent sovereignty" which underlies the traditional forms of international politics.

One can express a few doubts on any such trend. To begin, earlier periods of history have also seen communities vulnerable to attack, to the Vikings, for example, or to the Huns and Mongols. The reaction was hardly a quick move to a worldliness overruling all particular interests. The penetrability of society today is often credited to the atomic bomb and the airplane carrying it, but destruction equivalent to nuclear attack was widely expected as early as World War I, and most assuredly was thought real between the wars. If English mothers in 1916 could hush their children with warnings of "Go to sleep or the Zeppelins will get you," this did not presage any early surrender of the prerogatives of British independence. In 1935 the national leaderships of all the major powers expected that air attack could produce most horrible civilian suffering, but the League of Nations was not really bolstered by the prospect.

Analysis has varied on what the impact of nuclear threats is likely to be. At earlier stages, it was thought that a general nervousness would set in by which all of us flinched at the first sudden flash of light. Neuroses would increase, as would alcoholism and juvenile delinquency. At later stages, it seemed that we would all invest in fallout shelters and become a "mole society." Yet moving into the 1970's, it seems almost that the threat of nuclear war is becoming progressively less real and less meaningful in the daily lives of Americans and others. The perceptions of the international arena may have been changed by a continual awareness of the risks and assurances of overkill, but the details of this change will be complicated and quite subtle.

Analyists who believe that national sovereignty is being eroded might look for supporting evidence in various movements toward economic and political integration. Yet as noted, such communities for the moment hardly demonstrate any irresistible momentum toward full surrender of sovereignty, or merger into a grander transnational unit. The European Communities of "The Six" are the only major success, but even here the political resistance of France has been sufficient to freeze integration at about the level it has attained to date. The addition of such new members as Denmark, Ireland, and Britain suggests further limits to how much political union can be hoped for, as more and more disparate traditions and systems are collected.

Other possibly interesting cases of international integration have appeared in Eastern Europe with Comecon, among the outer seven European states with EFTA, and with various preliminary experiments in Africa and Latin America. Comecon owed its unity mostly to brute force and pressure from Moscow, and has drifted toward greater national independence ever since the Soviet Union was forced to grant some autonomy in the wake of de-Stalinization. EFTA never showed signs of becoming more than the loosest form of customs union, and integration hopes in Latin America and Africa have largely faded.

Leaving aside the aborted drives toward integration, the world would in any event have seen a great increase in the number of independent political entities even if the Six had become one; this is of course due simply to the continuing process of decolonization, and inevitable consequence of the decline of European power relative to the peoples of Africa and Asia.

If one indeed were simply listing the number of independent states, all obvious indices would suggest that the number has more than doubled, whatever pressures there may be for erosions of sovereignty. Some attention might be directed at the size distribution of states; if we aligned states in order of population, would the upper one-tenth of the world's powers have more or less of its population than was the case in 1930? Is there any tendency for larger states to grow still larger, or conversely, to break down to the benefit of smaller? No clear trends emerge here. Most of the "new emerging nations" of the world are small, some so small that full membership in the United Nations will not be possible, but India and Indonesia are significant exceptions, as are, to a lesser extent, Nigeria and the Philippines. The net effect of these additions is thus to generate a relative distribution curve not very dissimilar from that which applied before decolonization. The evidence we have does not support tendencies either toward integration or disintegration.

If the threat of nuclear weapons has not thus driven nations to sacrifice their sovereignty by integrating into regional or worldwide governments, this hardly means in the end that the international system has not been enormously changed by such weapons. As noted, we are now compelled to work continuously within the rational processes of our adversary, motivating him to let us live, since we cannot *prevent* him from killing us. The world must give up "unconditional surrender" when those whose surrender was being compelled could wipe out city after city as the price.

Perhaps nuclear proliferation in the future will produce more and more of such inviolate national capitals; for the moment, we must rule out the possibility of conquering armies entering into Moscow or Paris or London or Washington or Peking. The "last hostage" will command a continuing respect, therefore, as whole countries may escape any warfare within their now sacred sanctuary borders. This logic already describes the way nuclear weapons have been managed since 1945, and the way conventional wars have been limited and political conflicts moderated, in the shadow of the nuclear arsenals. It has thus made possible blends of cooperation and conflict which might have been unthinkable in 1942 or 1842. There is nothing revolutionary or unique about the logic of bargaining and cooperative exchanges. What is revolutionary in the case of nuclear weapons is that such bargaining can never again be suspended or forgotten.

FURTHER READINGS

Kahn, Herman, and Wiener, Anthony J. *The Year 2000*. New York: Macmillan, 1967.

Rosecrance, Richard. "Bipolarity, Multipolarity, and the Future." *Journal of Conflict Resolution.* September, 1966.
Russett, Bruce. *Trends in World Politics.* New York: Macmillan, 1965.
Waltz, Kenneth. "The Stability of a Bipolar World." *Daedalus.* Summer, 1964.

Index